Government Regulation and Business

Government Regulation and Business

Allyn Douglas Strickland
George Washington University

Houghton Mifflin Company
Boston

Dallas
Geneva, Illinois
Hopewell, New Jersey
Palo Alto
London

Credits appear on page 399.

Printed in the U.S.A.

Library of Congress Catalog Card Number: 80-50981

ISBN: 0-395-30751-1

To my dear wife
Samira

Contents

Part six Conclusion

Preface

This book was written for undergraduate courses on government control of economic activity. It examines four different types of government intervention in the American economy: (1) antitrust enforcement, (2) economic regulation, (3) social regulation, and (4) direct participation. A microeconomic approach is adopted that analyzes the rationale for, and effectiveness of, government intervention policies. When appropriate, the microeconomic analysis—which rarely exceeds that taught in most introductory courses—is supplemented with legal, historical, and institutional perspectives on government intervention. The objective is to enable students to understand the development of current government policies as well as the proposals made for their reform.

This text does not cover *all* government policies that affect economic activity. There is, for example, little discussion of government stabilization and transfer programs, as well as government regulation of the financial sector of the economy. It simply did not seem feasible to discuss all of these government policies in a single text, especially since material was included on the fast-growing area of social regulation. In addition, these other policies are thoroughly addressed in more specialized courses on macroeconomics, money and banking, and public finance.

The text is divided into six parts. Part One introduces the student to the topic of government intervention and should be read first. It provides an overview of the government's role in the American economy and constructs a framework within which it can be subsequently analyzed. This core material is especially important because students generally do not have a strong background in law and economics. After Part One, Parts Two through Five can be presented in whatever order seems most appropriate to the instructor. Each part is *completely* self-contained. I do believe, however, that the book's order is logical—antitrust enforcement, economic regulation, social regulation, and direct participation—and is that frequently used by instructors in government and business courses. Finally, the book concludes in Part Six with an overall evaluation of the American experience with government intervention.

In order to facilitate the student's understanding of government regulation in general and specific policies in particular, Chapters 2, 4, and 11 provide essential economics background for the policy chapters that follow them. (While most of the economic discussion is of an elementary nature, more advanced material may be found in chapter appendices.) Each policy chapter then follows a standard format: it is divided into three sections of approximately equal length—introduction, policy, and evaluation. The introductory section establishes the necessary legal and economic background for the policy at issue. The economic material normally includes some single graphical analysis. Once this background is established, the major government policies are discussed. The number of policies addressed is carefully limited, so that they can be discussed in depth without confusing the student (as is so common with encyclopedic approaches). Finally, each policy chapter concludes with a detailed evaluation of the policies. The objective is to provide the student with a balanced assessment of current policies as well as proposals for their reform.

Many people have contributed to the development of this text, although they are obviously not responsible for any remaining errors. I owe a considerable debt to Leonard Weiss, my teacher and thesis adviser while I was a graduate student at the University of Wisconsin—Madison. I am also indebted to Catherine Hoffman, Giles Burgess, Erwin Blackstone, Robert Ekelund, and Walter Held, who read different parts of the manuscript and provided valuable criticisms. In addition, many of my graduate students at George Washington University kindly provided me with information about different government policies. I am also grateful to Ed Jaffe, who, as sponsoring editor, encouraged me to undertake this project. Finally, I now know why authors always acknowledge their spouses. It simply would have been impossible to complete this undertaking without the constant support and self-sacrifice of my wife.

ADS

Government Regulation and Business

Part One

Introduction

Part Three

Introduction

The Role of Government in a Market Economy

Chapter 1

Many of the great personal fortunes in the United States were acquired during the industrial revolution of the late 1800s. This era witnessed the formation of giant corporations by an aggressive new generation of entrepreneurs. Businessmen such as John D. Rockefeller of Standard Oil and James B. Duke of the American Tobacco Company employed shrewd, and sometimes ruthless, tactics to attain dominant positions in their industries. In one celebrated encounter, James Fisk tried to gain control of the Albany and Susquehanna Railroad by forcibly removing his rival—J. Pierpont Morgan—from the railroad tracks.[1] Fisk's effort failed when his train derailed after colliding head-on with Morgan's train. This episode colorfully shows the impunity with which these "captains of industry" waged industrial warfare in front of the American public. Their attitude was perhaps most eloquently summarized in a remark by William Vanderbilt: "The public be damned. I am working for my stockholders."[2]

American industry is still influenced by the events that occurred during this period. Many industries remain dominated by those original in-

1. Matthew Josephson, *The Robber Barons* (New York: Harcourt Brace & World, 1962), pp. 138-39.
2. Josephson, *The Robber Barons*, p. 187.

dustrial giants or their corporate descendants. The entrepreneurs of today, however, operate in an environment radically different from that of their nineteenth century counterparts. Nowhere is this more apparent than in the current relationship between government and business. Indeed, the distinguishing feature of this economic era may well be the pervasive role of government in the American economy.

Government Intervention in the American Economy

The United States Constitution delegates substantial economic power to the Congress. Congress is empowered, among other things, to collect taxes, coin money, raise and support armies, establish patents and copyrights, and regulate commerce among the states and with foreign nations. These delegated powers mandate a major role for the federal government in the nation's economy. State and local governments play a supporting, but by no means insignificant, role. Through its actions, the government sector—federal, state, and local governments combined—defines the environment within which private economic activity occurs. Government intervention occurs when government policies affect, directly or indirectly, the allocation of society's resources. An overview of the nature and magnitude of such government intervention in the American economy is given in this section.

The Government Sector: Government as Consumer

In a market economy, resources are allocated among alternative uses according to consumers' preferences as reflected by their expenditure decisions. The government, therefore, allocates resources *directly* whenever it purchases goods and services. In this respect, the government is the same as any other consumer, although obviously much larger. The government's direct control over resources can thus be determined by examining its purchases of goods and services. An alternative, though less inclusive, measure of the importance of the government sector is its direct employment of workers.

Table 1.1 shows the government's share of gross national product and employment in selected years since 1929.[3] In 1929, the government sec-

3. These figures are for government purchases only and do not include other government expenditures such as transfer programs. In 1978, the federal government spent more money on transfer programs ($185.4 billion) than on goods and services ($152.6 billion) (U.S. Bureau of Economic Analysis, *Survey of Current Business* [Washington, D.C.: Government Printing Office, January 1980], p. 16.). Transfer programs reallocate income across consumers, but consumption decisions are still made by private individuals and not government agencies.

Table 1.1 Government Expenditures and Employment, 1929–1978

Year	Government Expenditures as a Percentage of GNP			Government Employment as a Percentage of Total Employment		
	Federal	State and Local	Total	Federal	State and Local	Total
1929	1.4	7.2	8.6	1.7	5.4	7.1
1939	5.7	9.1	14.8	2.7	6.7	9.4
1949	7.9	7.0	14.9	5.9	6.7	12.6
1959	11.1	9.0	20.1	7.1	8.7	15.8
1969	10.4	11.8	22.2	7.6	11.6	19.2
1978	7.2	13.3	20.5	5.0	13.2	18.2

Sources: 1. U.S. Department of Commerce, *Historical Statistics of the United States, Colonial Times to 1970* (Washington, D.C.: Government Printing Office, 1975), Chapter Y.

2. U.S. Bureau of Labor Statistics, *Monthly Labor Review* (Washington, D.C.: Government Printing Office, February 1980), pp. 75, 81.

3. U.S. Bureau of Economic Analysis, *Survey of Current Business* (Washington, D.C.: Government Printing Office, January 1980), p. 12.

tor purchased 8.6 percent of the economy's output of goods and services (GNP) and accounted for 7.1 percent of total employment. By 1978, those figures had increased to 20.5 and 18.2 percent respectively, indicating that the government sector has grown substantially, although it declined from 1969 to 1978.

The factors behind the government's increased role in the economy can be ascertained by examining the purchases at each level of government. As Table 1.1 illustrates, the composition of the government sector has been changing. The federal government's share of gross national product and of total employment has been decreasing, while the share of state and local governments has generally been increasing. This difference has been due to the different types of services that each level of government provides.

The federal government's principal area of both expenditure and employment has historically been national defense. For example, in 1978, defense expenditures accounted for 64.9 percent of the federal government's purchases of goods and services.[4] The federal government's share of gross national product, therefore, fluctuates with changes in the level of defense expenditures, rising during wartime and declining during peacetime. The recent decline in the federal government's share has

4. *Survey of Current Business*, p. 16.

resulted from a smaller percentage of gross national product being allocated to national defense.

The major items of expenditure for state and local governments are education, health, highways, and police protection. Education alone accounted for 36.7 percent of all state and local government expenditures in 1976.[5] The increased size of the state and local government sector (13.3 percent of the gross national product in 1978) reflects fundamental changes that have occurred in American society. The post-World War II baby boom brought about massive expenditures for public education. Increased urbanization necessitated more police and fire protection, while the American love affair with the automobile led to an extensive network of inter- and intrastate highways. In short, as Americans have simultaneously become more numerous, more urbanized, and more affluent, they have demanded more and more of those services that state and local governments provide.

In summary, the government sector purchases a substantial portion of the nation's output of goods and services. Approximately 20 percent of the gross national product is thus determined by political decisions instead of by private market decisions. The future growth of this sector will depend on the American people's preference for private versus public consumption of their income.

The New Market Environment: Government as Rule Maker

Producers and consumers interact in a legal environment defined by the government. As in a professional sports league, the government establishes the "rules" of the economic game and provides a means for their subsequent modification, arbitration, and enforcement. The rules may also affect the allocation of society's resources. First, government rules may mandate a specific course of action that would not otherwise take place. For example, American industry has invested heavily in pollution control devices in order to comply with environmental regulations.[6] Second, government rules may prohibit specific economic activities. The Eighteenth Amendment to the Constitution prohibited the "manufacture, sale, or transportation of intoxicating liquors [as well as their import and export] within ... the United States for beverage purposes."

5. U.S. Department of Commerce, *Statistical Abstract of the United States, 1979* (Washington, D.C.: Government Printing Office, 1979), pp. 292-93.

6. It is estimated that the cost of complying with federal pollution control regulations was $84.8 billion from 1970 to 1977 (Environmental Protection Agency, *The Cost of Clean Air and Water—Report to Congress*, August 1979, p. xiii).

While the environmental regulation diverted resources into the pollution abatement industry, the Prohibition amendment diverted resources out of the alcoholic beverage industry.

Government regulation of private economic activity is neither new nor uniquely American. The Babylonians had usury laws that limited the interest that could be charged on loans. Queen Elizabeth I granted monopoly privileges to favored businessmen until her power to do so was voided by the courts and subsequently taken over by Parliament. What is new, however, is the recent expansion of government intervention in the American economy. Government intervention has expanded at a rate reminiscent of the depression-dominated 1930s. Of 53 major federal regulatory agencies, 20 were established in the 1970s and 6 in the 1960s.[7]

A Case Study: General Motors. The nature and extent of the federal government's intervention in the economic sphere are illustrated in the business operations of General Motors Corporation (GM). In 1978 GM was the second largest American corporation, with annual sales of $63.2 billion, net income of $3.5 billion, and annual employment of approximately 839,000 persons.[8] Although GM operates in many industries, sales of automobiles (Buick, Chevrolet, Cadillac, Oldsmobile, Pontiac) account for most of its profits and employment.[9] GM sells cars in a market environment defined by numerous direct and indirect contacts with the federal government. The government plays a role in the design, production, and distribution of GM automobiles.

General Motors, as well as other domestic and foreign automobile manufacturers, must design cars to meet a plethora of federally mandated performance standards. For example, cars must not exceed the pollution emission standards of the 1970 Clean Air Act, but they must simultaneously satisfy the gasoline mileage standards of the 1975 Energy Policy and Conservation Act. In addition, cars must comply with the safety standards established under the 1966 National Traffic and Motor Vehicle Safety Act. Because of these laws, the federal government has a major role in determining the types of cars that are offered to consumers in the marketplace.

7. Marcia B. Wallace and Ronald J. Penoyer, *Directory of Federal Regulatory Agencies* (St. Louis: Center for the Study of American Business, Working Paper no. 36, September 1978).

8. General Motors, *Annual Report 1978*, p. 1.

9. In 1978, 96 percent of GM's net income came from its automotive operations (*Annual Report 1978*).

General Motors' production of automobiles also comes under government supervision. At the production level, government involvement focuses on two broad areas: pollution and working conditions. The first issue involves the relationship between GM's production facilities and the surrounding environment. A factory's disposal of waste material must comply with standards set under the 1970 Clean Air Act and the 1972 Water Pollution Control Act. These standards can affect the operation of existing plants as well as the construction of new ones. The second issue is the health and safety of workers in GM plants. The goal of the Occupational Safety and Health Act of 1970 was to provide work environments that minimize occupational injuries. To meet this goal, existing production processes may have to be modified or replaced by new, safer production processes.

General Motors also interacts with the federal government when it distributes automobiles through its extensive dealer network. GM ships its cars using rail and truck transportation services, both of which are heavily regulated by the Interstate Commerce Commission (ICC). For example, the ICC approves trucking companies' rates, specifies the commodities they can haul, and determines the exact routes over which they can travel. When new cars arrive in a dealer's showroom, potential customers examine price labels required by the Automobile Disclosure Act of 1958. Finally, when customers drive their new cars up to the gasoline pump, they must purchase unleaded, and hence more expensive, gasoline.

Throughout this entire process, General Motors must compete against the other automobile companies without violating the federal antitrust laws. GM's dominant position in an industry so important to the American economy guarantees that its business tactics will constantly be scrutinized by federal antitrust authorities. Indeed, a proposal to restructure the domestic automobile industry by breaking up GM into several competing firms has become an annual event in Washington, D.C. GM has reportedly responded to this situation by "pulling its punches" and not exceeding its traditional 50 percent share of the domestic market.[10] (An interesting footnote to this story is the recent assertion by GM's rivals that federal regulations *favor* GM and will enable it to increase its share of the domestic automobile industry!)[11]

10. This is one of the standard stories in the field of industrial organization. See, for example, F. M. Scherer, *Industrial Market Structure and Economic Performance*, 2nd ed. (Chicago: Rand McNally, 1980), p. 540.

11. "GM's Juggernaut: Riding Over the Competition to Push Market Share Up and Up," *Business Week*, March 26, 1979, pp. 62-77.

The relationship between General Motors and the federal government is not unique, though it is undoubtedly more complex and more publicized than other situations because of the importance of the automobile. Nonetheless, it is illustrative of the government's pervasive role in creating a new market environment for American firms: an environment in which government regulations can substantially affect the allocation of society's resources. The government's control over resources is much more encompassing than expenditure or employment statistics alone can show.

Table 1.2 **Impact of Government Regulations on General Motors, 1978 (Calendar Year)**

	Expenditures ($millions)	Employment
Regulation of Vehicles		
Auto safety	466	11,100
Auto emission control	446	4,300
Vehicle noise control	23	400
Total	935	15,800
Regulation of Plant Facilities		
Plant pollution control		
Air	146	700
Water	95	800
Solid waste	75	600
Total	316	2,100
Occupational Safety and Health	103	1,400
Government Reports and Administrative Costs Related to Regulation		
Business statistics	4	100
Energy management	36	400
Environmental activities	48	1,000
Industrial relations	73	1,700
Legal activities	36	800
Marketing functions	15	300
Taxes	17	400
Other	37	800
Total	266	5,500
Grand Total	1,620	24,800

Source: General Motors, "Impact of Government Regulations on General Motors," June 25, 1979, Attachments A and B. In-house report.

This conclusion is dramatically supported by two studies of the cost of federal regulations. General Motors annually conducts a study to determine its costs in complying with federal regulations. Table 1.2 reproduces a table from GM's 1978 study that provides a breakdown of the annual cost of various federal regulations. GM's analysis indicates that in 1978 federal regulations necessitated the expenditure of $1.620 billion and the employment of 24,800 people.[12] To put these figures in perspective, GM's expenditure on federal regulations was 46 percent of its net income for that year and accounted for 3 percent of its employment.

A study by M. Weidenbaum and R. DeFina examined the cost of federal regulations to the entire economy in 1976.[13] They estimated both the administrative costs and the compliance costs of federal regulations. *Administrative costs* represent the federal government's expenditures on regulatory activities, while *compliance costs* are the costs incurred by the private sector to comply with those regulations. The results of the study are summarized in Table 1.3. In 1976, the federal government

Table 1.3   **Annual Cost of Federal Regulation, by Area, 1976**
(Millions of dollars)

Area	Administrative Cost	Compliance Cost	Total
Consumer safety and health	1,516	5,094	6,610
Job safety and working conditions	483	4,015	4,498
Energy and the environment	602	7,760	8,362
Financial regulation	104	1,118	1,222
Industry specific	484	19,919	20,403
Paperwork	—[a]	25,000	25,000
Total	3,189	62,906	66,095

[a]Included in other categories.

Source: Murray L. Weidenbaum and Robert DeFina, "The Cost of Federal Regulation of Economic Activity," American Enterprise Institute Reprint no. 88, May 1978, Table 1, p. 2.

12. These figures "do not include the cost of hardware added to GM products to meet government standards, nor do they include taxes or workers' compensation payments," according to General Motors ("Impact of Government Regulations on General Motors," June 25, 1979, p. 1. In-house report).

13. Murray L. Weidenbaum and Robert DeFina, "The Cost of Federal Regulation of Economic Activity," American Enterprise Institute Reprint no. 88 (Washington, D.C.: May 1978).

spent $3.189 billion regulating private economic activity; these regulations led to an additional expenditure of $62.906 billion by the private sector. Every dollar spent by the federal government thus required an expenditure of $19.73 by the private sector, a multiplication factor of almost 20!

Even though these studies provide only broad estimates of the costs of federal regulations, they do indicate that regulations can have an enormous impact on the allocation of society's resources.

Economic Analysis of Government Intervention

The preceding section points out the important role played by the government sector in the American economy. The government allocates resources *directly* through its expenditure decisions and *indirectly* through its regulatory decisions. The overall magnitude of government intervention may seem paradoxical in a market economy that has traditionally emphasized the benefits of private enterprise. The purpose of this book is to analyze the rationale for, and the effectiveness of, government intervention in the American economy. This section introduces the analytical approach that will be used throughout the book. This approach emphasizes three basic issues. First, what is the rationale for government intervention in a market economy? Second, if government intervention is warranted, what policy options does the government have? Third, what is the impact of those policies that are finally adopted by the government? Answers to these three questions are essential for understanding and evaluating government intervention in the American economy.

The Rationale for Government Intervention

Every society must make three basic economic decisions. First, *what goods should be produced?* Society faces an almost unlimited menu of goods from which it can choose to consume. Which of these goods should be produced and in what quantities? Second, *how should these goods be produced?* Each good can generally be produced by a variety of production techniques. Which techniques should society use? Third, *who should receive the goods that society produces?* Once goods have been produced, they must be allocated among the members of society. How should this be done?

The distinguishing feature of a market economy is its reliance on a decentralized network of markets to answer these important economic questions. There is no central authority guiding the economy, only the impersonal forces of the marketplace. Each member of society independently pursues his or her self-interest through private market transactions. When aggregated across all of society, these market transactions resolve the economy's problems of allocation, production, and distribution. First, consumers purchase those goods that maximize their welfare. Consumer preferences thus determine how resources will be allocated across markets. Second, firms manufacture goods using production techniques that minimize their costs and so enable them to maximize their profits when their goods are sold. Third, goods are distributed among consumers through market transactions, according to consumers' preferences and incomes.

Since a market economy makes these economic decisions automatically, the government's role is necessarily minimal. It is only to establish an environment that facilitates market transactions. The government must determine the "rules of the game" and provide for their modification, arbitration, and enforcement. This responsibility mandates three major roles for government: (1) preserving law and order; (2) enforcing contracts; and (3) defining property rights. Each of these roles will be examined in more detail.

A basic premise in a market economy is that market transactions are voluntary and therefore beneficial to both parties. If one party is coerced by the other party, however, this premise is no longer valid and the exchange process is undermined. An extreme example is a business owner who agrees to sell a company for one dollar while the new "owner" holds a pistol to his head. This agreement is made under duress and is not beneficial to both parties. If it were, there would be no need for the pistol. The government's police function is to ensure that market transactions are truly voluntary and not the result of coercion.

Many exchanges of goods and services do not occur at the moment when the transaction is agreed upon, but over time or at some point in the future. In such situations, both parties sign a contract specifying their mutual obligations over the time period in question. For example, a professional athlete may sign a long-term contract with a sports team. If this contract is not binding on both parties, one party may be damaged by the other party's nonfulfillment of the contract. A superstar may jump to another team, thereby damaging the owner and the season ticket holders of the old team. If markets are to allocate resources over time, the government must guarantee that contracts will be enforced.

The government's final role in a market economy is to define property rights. If markets are to allocate resources into their most valued uses, property rights to those resources must be well defined. For example, farmers are entitled to the crops they grow on their land. If they did not have this property right, they would not grow crops, for anyone could harvest them. As a result, the land would lie fallow, to the mutual disadvantage of both the farmers and society. The government must provide a means for defining property rights as well as arbitrating disputes over them.

These three responsibilities constitute the government's *minimum* role in a market economy. This limited role of government has historically been called a *laissez faire* economic policy. *Laissez faire* has been variously translated as "let things proceed without interference" and "let the market alone." This policy dictates that government intervention in the economy should be minimal. The underlying philosophy is that economic decisions should be made by private individuals in the marketplace and not by bureaucrats in the government. Once the ground rules have been established, society's welfare will be promoted best by each person's unbridled pursuit of her or his self-interest.

This economic philosophy is innately appealing and has been supported on both political and economic grounds. On political grounds, it is consistent with democracy and the preservation of individual freedoms.[14] It minimizes the role of government while maximizing the role of the individual. On economic grounds, this philosophy is consistent with the maximization of society's economic welfare. As will be discussed in Chapter 2, a market economy can lead to the *optimal* allocation of society's resources. Firms will produce those goods most desired by consumers and will use the minimum resources necessary to do so. In such a situation, it is impossible to reallocate resources and increase consumers' welfare.

There may be situations, however, in which a *laissez faire* economic philosophy does not maximize society's welfare. These situations are known as *market failures*, since market forces fail to bring about an optimal allocation of society's resources. The individual's self-interest conflicts with the interests of society, and government intervention becomes necessary. This book examines government responses to three types of market failures: (1) monopoly, (2) externalities, and (3) imperfect information. A brief introduction to each type follows.[15]

14. See Milton Friedman, *Capitalism and Freedom* (Chicago: Phoenix Books, 1963) and Friedrich A. von Hayek, *The Road to Serfdom* (Chicago: University of Chicago Press, 1945).

15. Each type of market failure is examined in more detail in Chapter 2.

Monopoly.   It was argued previously that a market economy will lead to an optimal allocation of society's resources. This assumes, however, that each market is *competitive*; there are so many buyers and sellers that no individual can control the market price. This assumption is violated when there is a *monopoly*, a single or dominant seller of a good. A monopolist can restrict production artificially and increase the market price. Consumer welfare is reduced as the higher price forces consumers to reduce their consumption of this good and switch to less attractive substitutes. By exploiting its unique position, the monopolist maximizes its profits, but not society's welfare.

A recent example is the case of the Organization of Petroleum Exporting Countries (OPEC). Though OPEC is not the single seller, its member countries dominate the worldwide production of crude oil and set the price at which it is sold. From 1973 to 1974, OPEC exploited its market position and raised the price of a barrel of oil from approximately $2 to $10, an increase of 400 percent! This dramatic price increase forced consumers to reduce their consumption of petroleum products and switch to more expensive, alternative sources of energy.

Externalities.   In a market economy, individuals pursue their self-interests through voluntary market transactions. It is assumed implicitly that each transaction does not affect people outside that transaction. This is not always the case, however. One individual's action may impose costs or bestow benefits on other individuals. Such effects are called *externalities*, and they arise whenever the benefits and costs of a transaction do not fall completely on the parties to that transaction. Since in theory, individuals pursue only their own self-interests, they ignore any externalities associated with their transactions. As a result, the market process will lead to a misallocation of society's resources.

One very visible externality is the pollution caused by both consumers and producers. An infamous example of industrial pollution was Allied Chemical's production of kepone. The company manufactured kepone, a powerful pesticide, in Hopewell, Virginia, a small town on the James River. The chemical, which can cause nervous disorders in humans, was discharged into the James River and subsequently absorbed into the bodies of fish. Parts of the James River had to be closed to commercial and pleasure fishermen. At one point it was even feared that the kepone would contaminate Chesapeake Bay, one of the richest seafood beds in the United States.

Imperfect Information.   The basic principle underlying a market economy is consumer sovereignty; that is, consumers determine the composition of the economy's production of goods and services. This principle is based on a very strong assumption: perfect knowledge. Each consumer is assumed to know the prices and characteristics of each good available in the marketplace. This assumption is frequently unjustified in the real world, however, where consumers make decisions based on incomplete information. It is highly unlikely that consumers in this case will make the same decisions as they would if they had perfect information. Consumers still determine the composition of society's output, but that composition will not necessarily maximize their welfare.

The consumption of cigarettes provides an excellent example of the role of information in the consumer's decision-making process. Cigarette smoking was not very common prior to World War I. During the war, it gained acceptance among men and has subsequently spread to women and teenagers. Throughout the 1950s and 1960s, however, medical research indicated that smoking is not a harmless activity, but substantially increases the risk of lung cancer and heart disease. This new information has had a marked impact on consumers' behavior in the marketplace. Some consumers have quit smoking altogether, while others have switched to brands containing low tar and nicotine.

In summary, the market process does not always guarantee an optimal allocation of society's resources. Market failures may occur, causing overproduction or underproduction of some goods. These market failures reduce society's welfare and argue for a more substantive government role than a *laissez faire* economic philosophy dictates. Market failures mandate government intervention in order to improve market performance and society's welfare.

The Types of Government Intervention

Before the government intervenes in response to a market failure, it must determine what policy is appropriate. All market failures are not the same, and the government's response should take differences into account. From an economic perspective, the government should adopt the policy that will achieve the desired improvement in market performance with the minimum expenditure of society's resources. This criterion recognizes the economic reality of scarce resources and the political reality of a limited budget. Two qualifications should be added to this economic criterion, however. First, there may be a substantial difference between the theoretical and the actual effectiveness of a given policy. The government should not ignore the lessons learned from past experiences when it formulates its intervention policies. Second, the government, as the representative of the people, does not operate in a political vacuum. Its final decisions are a composite of political, social, and economic opinions. Political and social factors may dominate economic factors and lead to government policies that would not be selected on economic grounds alone.[16]

When determining the optimal response to a specific market failure, the government must first decide a broad policy issue: should it work within the existing market environment or replace it with an alternative economic organization? If it decides to work within the market framework, it can modify firm behavior indirectly by changing the rules of the game. The goal is to improve market performance by making the market process work better. This indirect approach minimizes government interference and maximizes business independence. Antitrust enforcement and social regulation are two types of indirect government intervention.

The other broad policy option is for the government to assume a more direct role by replacing the market with an alternative economic organization. This direct approach is appropriate when a market solution is not feasible. The government tries to improve market performance by participating in economic decision-making. Basic economic decisions on price, investment, and entry may no longer be made by private individuals, but by the government. This direct approach obviously requires a more substantial government role and greater commitment of resources. Examples of direct government intervention are economic regulation and direct participation.

These government policies—antitrust enforcement, economic and social regulation, and direct participation—constitute the bulk of government intervention in the American economy and will be examined in detail throughout this book. They are introduced briefly here.

Antitrust Enforcement.   Antitrust enforcement is one possible response to the monopoly problem. Through legal suits initiated under the antitrust laws, the government tries to eliminate corporate practices

16. For example, a particular industry may be regulated by the government even though regulation is not justified from an economic perspective. This issue is addressed in Part III of this book: Economic Regulation.

and structures that restrain the natural competitive forces of the market. A classic illustration of the government's role is its antitrust suit against the Standard Oil Company of New Jersey in the early 1900s. Standard Oil had used some highly questionable business practices to attain a near-monopoly position in the domestic petroleum industry. In 1911, it was convicted of violating the Sherman Antitrust Act and, in an effort to restore competition to this industry, was dissolved into 33 separate companies. Such industrial giants as Exxon, Mobil, Standard Oil of California, Standard Oil of Indiana, Standard Oil of Ohio, Continental, Marathon, and Atlantic Richfield are corporate descendants of the original Standard Oil Company. (Chapters 4 through 10 explore the many dimensions of antitrust enforcement.)

Economic Regulation. Another possible response to the monopoly problem, economic regulation, is appropriate whenever it is not feasible or desirable to increase market competition. For example, a single firm may be able to produce a good more cheaply than several smaller firms. Society would like to benefit from this firm's efficiency without being subjected to such monopolistic abuses as restricted output and high prices. The government permits the firm to be a monopolist, but it regulates the firm's prices. Economic regulation, then, is a response to market failure in a *specific* market. The classic examples of economic regulation are the traditional public utilities: electric power, telephone, and water companies. This is one area in which state and local governments play a major role, because most public utilities operate in local markets. (Economic regulation is analyzed in Chapters 11 through 15.)

Social Regulation. The newest and fastest growing type of government intervention is social regulation. Here the concern is with market failures such as imperfect information and externalities that occur simultaneously across many markets. The goal is to improve market performance by establishing specific standards that all firms must meet. The standards are designed to modify behavior so as to eliminate the underlying causes of the market failures. For example, highway litter has been a problem since the construction of the first highway. States have unsuccessfully attempted to reduce this visual pollution by fining litterbugs. A more promising approach is to place a deposit on beverage containers (a major source of roadside litter), which creates an incentive for people to recycle containers. (Chapters 16 and 17 discuss social regulations in the areas of environmental, consumer, and worker protection.)

Direct Participation.   The first three types of government intervention involve varying degrees of government control of private firms. The fourth option—one of generally last resort in a market economy—is for government to participate directly in the market as a consumer and/or producer of goods and services. Instead of using antitrust enforcement or economic regulation against a monopolist, the government can be the monopolist. This is rare in the United States. Even though the U.S. government is a substantial consumer, it is not a large producer. The federal government operates the post office and intercity passenger railroad service, while some local governments own their own public utilities. (Chapter 18 provides a more comprehensive examination of the government's small but growing role as a producer and consumer.)

In summary, the government can exercise several options when it responds to specific market failures. When deciding on the appropriate response, the government should compare the advantages and disadvantages of each type of intervention. In the United States, this has generally meant government control of private firms instead of government production of goods and services. Frequently the result has been that firms are simultaneously subjected to more than one type of government intervention. For example, an electric power company could be subject to economic regulation by a state public service commission, social regulation by the Environmental Protection Agency, antitrust enforcement by the Antitrust Division of the Justice Department, and competition from the Tennessee Valley Authority, a public enterprise!

The Impact of Government Intervention

Government intervention will benefit society if it promotes the public interest. From an economic perspective, government intervention promotes the public interest if it is consistent with three performance criteria: (1) efficiency; (2) equity; and (3) stability.[17] These three economic concepts are introduced here and discussed in detail in Chapter 2.

Efficiency.   The word *efficiency* has a general connotation of productivity. Efficient workers consistently perform their tasks without any wasted effort. The economic concept of efficiency is similar, though

17. Another criterion frequently mentioned is growth. Growth is partially included under efficiency, since dynamic efficiency is concerned with the rate of technological progress and, as indicated later, technical change is a major determinant of growth. At the same time, growth is affected by government stabilization policies, a topic that is addressed only peripherally in this text.

more precise. Economic efficiency has two dimensions: static and dynamic. *Static efficiency* examines the utilization of society's resources at a given time, while *dynamic efficiency* examines their utilization over time.

There are two requirements for static efficiency. First, each firm must manufacture its products using the minimum resources necessary. Society thus can obtain the maximum output from its limited resources. Second, resources must be allocated optimally throughout the economy. When resources are allocated across markets in response to consumer demand, each resource is employed in its most valued use. It is impossible to reallocate resources and increase consumer welfare. A common argument against economic regulation is that it does not force firms to minimize costs and thereby wastes some of society's scarce resources.[18]

In contrast to static efficiency, dynamic efficiency is concerned with maximizing society's welfare over time. This requires technological progress, the invention of new goods and production processes. New products enlarge society's consumption possibilities by providing options that were not previously available. New production processes enable firms to produce their products using fewer resources than before. Dynamic efficiency enables society's standard of living to increase over time. In his pioneering study, R. M. Solow estimated that in the period from 1909 to 1949, technical change accounted for 87½ percent of the increase in output per worker-hour in the non-farm sector of the economy.[19]

Equity. This performance standard cannot be defined as rigorously as efficiency because it is based primarily on value judgments, not objective standards. *Equity* generally implies some notion of fairness or reasonableness. Economists use this concept in two different contexts. In one usage, equity refers to the distribution of a society's income and wealth among its members. The focus is not on the existing distribution of income and wealth, but on how government intervention may affect that distribution. Do government policies systematically benefit one group of society at the expense of another group? Second, equity encompasses the concept of economic opportunity. Do individuals have equal access to markets, or are there artificial constraints that limit their ability to compete? The two aspects of equity are illustrated in the cur-

18. For a detailed discussion of this problem, see Alfred E. Kahn, *The Economics of Regulation: Principles and Institutions*, vol. 2 (New York: Wiley, 1971), Chapter 2.

19. Robert M. Solow, "Technical Change and the Aggregate Production Function," *Review of Economics and Statistics* 41 (August 1957): 312–20.

rent debate over deregulation of the trucking industry. Deregulation will probably lower the income of existing trucking companies while making it easier for firms to enter the industry.[20] There is thus a conflict between the interests of existing and potential trucking firms.

Stability. The attainment of full employment with minimal inflation—*macroeconomic stability*—is a major economic goal of the government. It tries to achieve this goal through a combination of monetary and fiscal policies. The government's stabilization policy raises different issues than do government intervention policies, for it is not concerned with market failures per se. Nonetheless, there is some overlap between policies of stabilization and intervention. Government intervention may adversely affect the government's ability to achieve macroeconomic stability. For example, the Environmental Protection Agency establishes emissions standards that require firms to purchase pollution control equipment. To cover these costs, firms raise their prices, thereby increasing the rate of inflation in the economy.[21]

We can, then, evaluate the impact of government intervention with respect to three economic performance criteria: efficiency, equity, and stability. The primary rationale for government intervention is to minimize static inefficiencies arising from market failures. Government intervention policies to improve static efficiency should, however, also be consistent with dynamic efficiency, equity, and stability. In practice, there are likely to be conflicts among these different criteria, and trade-offs will have to be made. For example, a monopolist may reduce static efficiency but increase dynamic efficiency. The government will have to decide which trade-offs are in the best interest of society.

Summary

The distinguishing feature of today's American economy may well be the pervasive role of government. The government plays a major role, both directly and indirectly, in allocating resources in the economy. The economic rationale for government intervention is the correction of market failures that lead to a misallocation of society's resources. The government uses four policies to counter these market failures: antitrust enforcement, economic regulation, social regulation, and direct partici-

20. Thomas Gale Moore, "The Beneficiaries of Trucking Regulation," *Journal of Law and Economics* 21 (October 1978): 327-43.

21. It has been estimated that environmental regulations will increase consumer prices by .2 to .3 percent each year from 1970 to 1986 (Environmental Protection Agency, *The Cost of Clean Air and Water*, p. xvii).

pation. These government policies are consistent with the public interest if they promote three criteria for economic performance: efficiency, equity, and stability.

Suggested Readings

Bator, Francis M. "The Anatomy of Market Failure," *The Quarterly Journal of Economics* 48 (August 1958): 351-79.

Friedman, Milton. *Capitalism and Freedom* (Chicago: Phoenix Books, 1963).

Nutter, G. Warren. *Growth of Government in the West* (Washington, D.C.: American Enterprise Institute, 1978).

Schultze, Charles L. *The Public Use of Private Interest* (Washington, D.C.: The Brookings Institution, 1977).

Stigler, George J. "The Goals of Economic Policy," *Journal of Law and Economics* 18 (October 1975): 238-92.

The Economic Framework

Chapter 2

Economics offers a unique framework in which to analyze government intervention in the American economy. Simple microeconomic theory can provide a clear, concise analysis of the rationale for, and effectiveness of, government intervention policies. It is thus necessary to have some knowledge of the market process, in particular, what factors determine whether an unregulated market will perform well or badly. This chapter presents the basic model of perfect competition and then discusses situations that will lead to market failures. The economist's tool of benefit-cost analysis is also introduced, along with some empirical evidence on market performance in the American economy.

The Model of Perfect Competition

In a market economy, the basic economic decisions of *what, how,* and *for whom* are made by market prices. Market prices determine which goods will be produced, how they will be produced, and for whom they will be produced. Economic models of markets explain how consumers and producers of goods interact to determine the market prices of those goods.

The model of perfect competition is defined by four basic assumptions.[1] First, there are so many buyers and sellers that no single buyer or

1. For more background discussion on the model of perfect competition, see any of the numerous introductory economics texts.

seller can control the market price of a good. Each one is so small compared with the total market that his or her individual actions cannot affect the market price. Second, all the sellers produce an identical, or
homogeneous, good. Consumers view the goods as perfect substitutes
and do not have any preferences among sellers. Third, sellers have easy
entry into and exit from this market. No barriers, either economic or legal, impede the flow of resources into or out of a market. Fourth, both
consumers and producers possess perfect information. Consumers know
the price and quality of each good in the market, while producers know
market prices as well as the production techniques for producing their
goods.

Given these assumptions, market price is determined by the joint interaction of market supply and demand. This is illustrated in part (a) of
Figure 2.1. The market demand curve, D, indicates that consumers will
purchase more as price decreases, while the market supply curve, S,
indicates that firms will supply more as price increases. The intersection of the supply and demand curves determines the market price, P_o.
At this price, the quantity demanded by consumers equals the quantity
supplied by producers, Q_o. The market is in short-run equilibrium.

Figure 2.1 Short-Run Equilibrium in a Perfectly Competitive Market

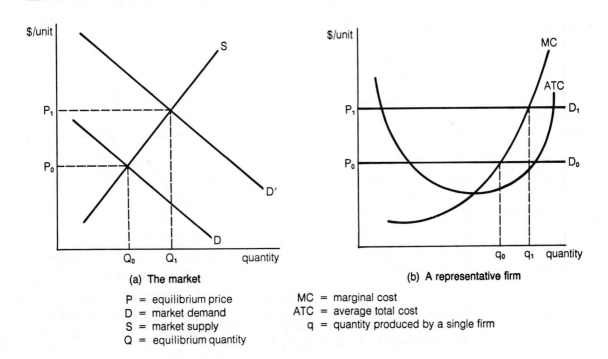

(a) The market

P = equilibrium price
D = market demand
S = market supply
Q = equilibrium quantity

(b) A representative firm

MC = marginal cost
ATC = average total cost
q = quantity produced by a single firm

The position of a "representative" firm in this market is depicted in part (b) of Figure 2.1. The firm faces a horizontal demand curve at the market price of P_0 and maximizes its profits by producing q_0 units, where price equals marginal cost. Several things should be noted about this firm's situation. First, its output level depends on market price. If market demand shifts to the right and increases market price to P_1, the firm will expand output to q_1. The higher price makes it profitable for the firm to increase its level of production. Second, the market supply at any price is simply the sum of the output of each firm in the market. For example, at the price P_1 the market supply is Q_1, and each firm produces q_1 units. Third, this firm is earning economic profits, because the market price is greater than its average total cost.[2] Its resources are earning more in this market than if they were employed in their best alternative use.

The situation depicted in Figure 2.1 will not persist in the long run, however. The profits being earned in this market will invite entry by new firms. (And it is assumed that there are *no* barriers to their entry.) The long-run equilibrium for a perfectly competitive market is illustrated in Figure 2.2. There are three things to note about this long-run situ-

Figure 2.2   Long-Run Equilibrium in a Perfectly Competitive Market

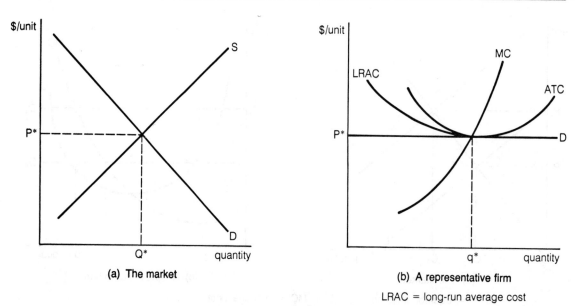

(a) The market

(b) A representative firm

LRAC = long-run average cost

2. Economists define a firm's total cost to include a normal rate of return on the firm's investment. Economic profits occur when a firm's total revenue exceeds all of its costs, indicating that it is earning more than a normal return on its investment.

ation. First, economic profits are equal to zero; the firm just covers the opportunity costs of its inputs. It will remain in this market, though, since it could not do better anywhere else in the economy. Second, the firm must minimize its production costs or it will lose money. It must build a plant that is on the minimum point of the long-run average cost curve, and then operate that plant efficiently.[3] Third, there is the optimal amount of resources in this market. Market price equals the marginal cost of the last unit produced by each firm in the market. The value placed by consumers on these units—market price—is thus exactly equal to the cost incurred by society to produce them—marginal cost.

In sum, the perfect competition model has desirable economic properties.[4] It guarantees that the two requirements for static efficiency are met. Each firm minimizes its production costs and each market has the optimal amount of resources. Resources are allocated in response to consumer demand, and it is impossible to increase society's welfare by reallocating those resources. Because there are no barriers to entry, there are no restrictions on individuals' opportunities to compete in this market. This is a desirable equity property of the perfect competition model.

Before examining other economic models, it will be worthwhile to define an economic market. What does an economist mean by the word *market?* One common definition is the area over which a group of sellers supplies a product to a group of buyers. Another definition is simply the area within which the price of a good is determined. Regardless of its specific definition, an economic market has two dimensions: the product market and the geographic market. The product market includes those products that are reasonable substitutes for one another; the geographic market includes the area within which competition occurs among those products.

The economic definition of a market can be illustrated by examining the housing market for college students. The product market includes

---

3. The long-run average cost curve initially decreases and then becomes horizontal, indicating that a firm can select many different plant sizes and still minimize its average costs of production. The smallest plant that attains minimum costs is called *minimum optimal scale.* To minimize its use of society's scarce resources, each firm should have a plant that is at least as large as minimum optimal scale. For an example of how economists estimate long-run average cost curves, see L. R. Christensen and W. H. Greene, "Economies of Scale in U.S. Electric Power Generation," *Journal of Political Economy* 84 (August 1976): 655–76.

4. A more rigorous examination of these properties is provided in F. M. Bator, "The Simple Analytics of Welfare Maximization," *American Economic Review* 47 (March 1957): 22-59.

dormitories, fraternity and sorority houses, cooperatives, rooming houses, apartment buildings, condominiums, and houses. The degree of substitutability among these alternatives depends on their prices as well as the students' tastes and incomes. The geographic market depends on the transportation services available to students. The number of housing units available depends on the commuting distance via walking, bicycling, driving, and using mass transit. In general, the empirical determination of an economic market is not a simple task, but it plays a major role in the design and implementation of government policies.

Market Failures

The model of perfect competition, though desirable, is based on a set of very restrictive assumptions that are unlikely to be fulfilled in many markets. Whenever these assumptions are violated, market performance will be worse than the competitive ideal. These situations are known as *market failures,* because market forces fail to lead to the optimal allocation of society's resources. This section briefly examines three different types of market failures: (1) monopoly; (2) externalities; and (3) imperfect information.[5]

Monopoly and Oligopoly

The perfect competition model assumes that there are many sellers, none of which is large enough to influence the market price. This assumption is violated whenever a single seller *can* affect the market price. At the extreme, this occurs when there is a *monopolist* or single seller of a good. More realistically, there may be several sellers who can influence the market price. These firms are known as *oligopolists.* The competitive assumption about easy entry also can be violated; there can be barriers that prohibit or limit the ability of new firms to enter a market. This section examines how variations in the number of sellers and in entry conditions can affect market performance by giving firms some degree of control over price.

Monopoly. A monopoly market differs from a competitive market in two respects. First, there is only one producer. There are no other firms in the market, and there are no close substitutes for the monopolist's product. Second, entry into this market is blockaded. There are economic or legal barriers that make it impossible to enter this market. For ex-

5. For more detail, see F. M. Bator, "The Anatomy of Market Failure," *Quarterly Journal of Economics* 72 (August 1958): 351-79.

ample, a potential entrant may not be able to obtain the necessary production technology or government operating certificate.[6]

Because the monopolist is the only firm in the market, its demand curve is also the market demand curve.[7] This is illustrated in Figure 2.3. The monopolist maximizes its profits by applying the same decision-making rule as all firms: produce where marginal revenue equals marginal cost. It therefore produces Q_m units and sells them at a price of P_m. As price is greater than average total cost, the monopolist earns profits. These profits can persist in the long run because entry is blockaded. New firms cannot enter this market and compete the profits away.

The monopoly solution differs substantially from that in a competitive market. First, profits can persist in the long run. This is not possible in

Figure 2.3 **Monopoly**

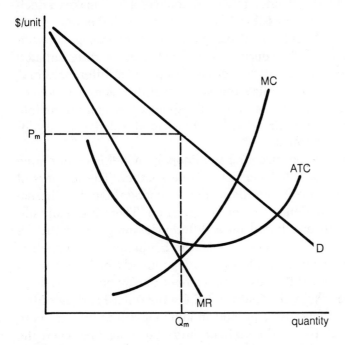

MR = marginal revenue

6. For example, an airline company must obtain a certificate of public convenience and necessity before it can fly interstate routes.

7. Marginal revenue is less than price for a monopolist because it has a downward-sloping demand curve. To sell another unit, it must lower its price and move along its demand curve. The change in total revenue—marginal revenue—equals the gain from selling one more unit minus the loss from selling the other units at the new, lower market price.

perfect competition, because entry can occur. Second, the monopolist is not forced to minimize costs. It will do so if it wants to maximize profits, but it is not forced to do so by competition. Its unit costs may therefore be greater than indicated by its ATC curve. Third, monopoly leads to a misallocation of resources across markets. The monopolist's price exceeds its marginal cost, indicating that consumers value the last unit more than it costs society to produce it. Resources should be added to this market until price equals marginal cost, but this is not possible because entry is blockaded. In sum, monopoly is not consistent with static efficiency.[8]

Oligopoly. An oligopoly differs from a perfectly competitive market in three respects. First, by definition, there are only a "few" sellers in the market. More specifically, there are so few firms that a "recognized interdependence" is created among them. Whenever a firm makes a decision, it must take the possible reactions of its competitors into consideration. Second, oligopolists can produce either homogeneous or differentiated products. As consumers do not perceive differentiated products as perfect substitutes, real or fancied product differences may create brand loyalty and reduce the substitutability across products. Third, no single assumption can be made about entry conditions into the market. Entry by new firms may be blockaded, relatively easy, or between these two extremes.

The main problem in constructing an oligopoly model is determining how the oligopolists will behave toward one another. The fewness of sellers creates a recognized interdependence among them, but the nature of that interdependence cannot be specified. There are many oligopoly models, each one based on a different assumption about the oligopolists' behavior.[9] The main issue is whether or not the oligopolists pursue cooperative strategies. Do they independently or jointly try to maximize their profits? If they can limit competition among themselves, they can set a price that will yield profits. On the other hand, interfirm rivalry may lead to competitive pricing and no long-run profits. In short, the oligopoly solution is indeterminate and may range between the competitive (P_cQ_c) and monopolistic extremes (P_mQ_m), as illustrated in part (a) of Figure 2.4.

8. A more detailed argument against monopoly is provided in Appendix B to this chapter.

9. A good discussion of oligopoly models is provided in F. M. Scherer, *Industrial Market Structure and Economic Performance*, 2nd ed. (Chicago: Rand McNally, 1980), Chapters 5–8.

Figure 2.4   **Oligopoly**

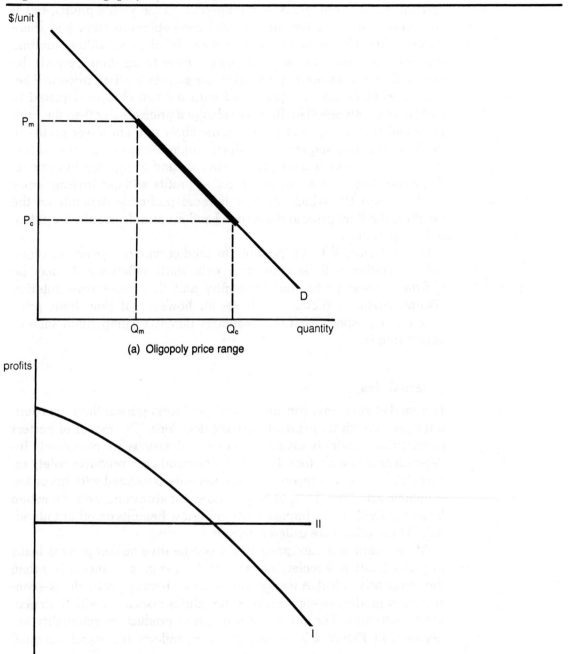

(a) Oligopoly price range

(b) Alternative profit streams

If the oligopolists can limit competition, they must determine their optimal pricing strategy. A noncompetitive price yields profits, but it also creates an incentive for potential competitors to enter and share those profits. The maximum price that can be charged without inviting this entry is known as the *limit price*. Other things being equal, the more difficult it is to enter the market, the greater the limit price will be. The oligopolists are thus presented with the two choices depicted in part (b) of Figure 2.4. The first is to charge a price greater than the limit price and earn substantial profits in the short run, but lower profits in the long run. This sequence is reflected by profit stream I. Alternatively, they can pursue a limit pricing strategy and charge the limit price. They can then earn a constant level of profits without inviting entry (profit stream II). Which strategy is more profitable depends on the height of the limit price and the speed and magnitude of entry by potential competitors.

In conclusion, it is not possible to predict whether or not an oligopolistic market will be consistent with static efficiency. It may be if firms pursue profits independently and the competitive solution obtains. Static inefficiency will result, however, if they limit price competition, especially if this increases nonprice competition such as advertising.[10]

Externalities

In a market economy, consumers and producers pursue their own self-interests through their private market decisions. The model of perfect competition implicitly assumes that these decisions are completely independent of one another. Each consumer and each producer solely incurs all the costs and receives all the benefits associated with his or her economic activities. This, of course, does not always happen. An action by one individual can impose costs or bestow benefits on other individuals. These effects are called *externalities*.

When externalities are present, the competitive market process leads to a misallocation of society's resources. Market performance is less than the competitive ideal. A market failure arises because individuals—consumers or producers—ignore any externalities associated with their economic activities. The results of a negative production externality are depicted in Figure 2.5. Supply curve S_1 reflects the social marginal

10. This was the case in the cigarette industry until the government controlled advertising by preventing the cigarette companies from advertising on television. This issue is discussed in Chapter 17.

Figure 2.5   Negative Externalities and Market Equilibrium

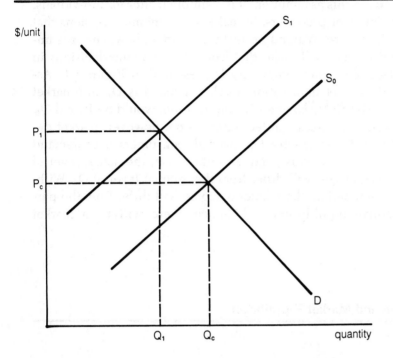

costs, including the externality, that are incurred in the production of this good. The intersection of this supply curve with the market demand curve would yield an equilibrium price of P_1 and quantity of Q_1. But this will not be the market equilibrium, because producers will not voluntarily take the externality into account. They will focus instead purely on their own production costs, which are captured by market supply curve S_0. As a result, the competitive equilibrium is a price of P_c and a quantity of Q_c. From the point of view of society, this good will be overproduced.[11] That is, the presence of the negative externality causes a market failure.

Imperfect Information

An important, though frequently overlooked, assumption in the perfect competition model is perfect information.[12] Both consumers and pro-

11. In a similar vein, there would be an underproduction of this good if there were a positive production externality.

12. Many economists use the term *pure competition* to refer to markets in which all the assumptions for perfect competition are fulfilled except that of perfect information.

ducers are assumed to have complete information about all their market alternatives. Given this assumption, it is a simple matter for individuals, whether consumers or producers, to make the economic decisions that maximize their welfare. Without perfect information, however, it is unlikely that individuals will make the "correct" economic decisions in the marketplace. One such possibility is presented in Figure 2.6. Assume that with perfect information, market demand is D_0 and market supply is S. The perfectly competitive equilibrium would be P_0 and Q_0. If consumers do not possess perfect information, however, market demand is unlikely to be exactly D_0. Instead, consumers may demand more (D_1) or less (D_2) of this good. In either case, the actual level of consumption—Q_1 or Q_2—will differ from the optimal level of Q_0. Without complete information, the market outcome will differ from the perfectly competitive equilibrium and, hence, there will be a market failure.

Figure 2.6   Imperfect Information and Market Equilibrium

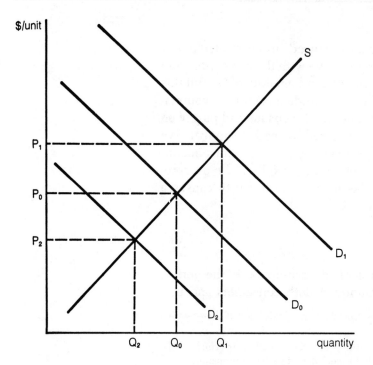

The previous section described how market failures can result when some of the underlying assumptions—implicit or explicit—of the perfect competition model are violated. This suggests that actual performance should vary across markets in response to these market failures. Numerous studies have been made of the impact of monopoly power on market performance. This section examines this issue in more detail.

Empirical Evidence on Markets

The Structure-Conduct-Performance Model

The three major economic models of markets—perfect competition, monopoly, and oligopoly—predict that the degree of static efficiency will vary with the type of market. This suggests that there may be causal relationships between market structure and market performance. This basic premise underlies the structure-conduct-performance model of industrial organization economics.[13] Market structure is hypothesized to determine market conduct, which in turn is hypothesized to determine market performance. This model is outlined in Table 2.1.

Table 2.1 The Structure-Conduct-Performance Model

Market Structure	$\rightleftarrows$	Market Conduct	$\rightarrow$	Market Performance
Number and size distribution of buyers and sellers		Pricing behavior		Efficiency
		Product design		Static
Product differentiation		Advertising		Dynamic
Barriers to entry		Research and		Equity
Capital requirements		development		Stability
Economies of scale				
Product differentiation				
Firm structure				
Diversification				
Integration				

Market structure comprises those economic factors that define the market environment within which firms operate. The most important elements of market structure are the number of sellers and the entry conditions into the market. The number of sellers affects their ability to limit competition; the entry conditions affect the ability of potential

13. An excellent treatment of the industrial organization literature is provided in Scherer, *Industrial Market Structure.*

competitors to enter the market in the future. Market conduct encompasses all the policies that firms adopt in an effort to maximize their profits. Attention has focused on the pricing and advertising strategies employed to market existing products and on the research and development effort to develop new products. The end result of these policies is market performance. Economists evaluate market performance with respect to the three economic performance criteria of efficiency, equity, and stability.

The structure-conduct-performance model has important policy implications. The government can modify market performance by altering market structure or conduct or both. Government policies, however, must take possible "feedback" effects into consideration. Market conduct may affect market structure as well as market performance. For example, if the government tries to improve market performance by regulating market conduct, an unintended side effect may be a decrease in the number of firms in the market. Feedback effects add an interesting, but complicating, dimension to the structure-conduct-performance model.

Market Concentration

As noted earlier, one of the most important elements of market structure is the number and size distribution of sellers. Economists frequently use seller concentration as a measure of this element of market structure.[14] The most common specific measure is probably the four-firm sales *concentration ratio*—the percentage of industry sales accounted for by the four largest firms in that industry. Table 2.2 lists concentration ratios for some selected industries in 1972. The average concentration ratio for all of manufacturing was 34 percent, so this sample is obviously not representative of the manufacturing sector of the economy. This table does, however, indicate the extreme variation that can occur in concentration ratios across industries.

Concentration ratios frequently are used as the measure of the degree of competition within a particular market. The structure-conduct-performance model, for example, suggests that seller concentration is an important, if not the most important, determinant of market competition. As an industry becomes more concentrated, it becomes easier for firms successfully to limit competition among themselves. Based on these

14. M. Adelman, "The Measurement of Industrial Concentration," *Review of Economics and Statistics* 33 (November 1951): 269–96.

Table 2.2 **Concentration Ratios for Selected Manufacturing Industries, 1972**

Industry	Four-Firm Concentration Ratio
Ready-mixed concrete	6
Newspapers	17
Meat-packing	22
Petroleum refining	31
Blast furnaces and steel mills	45
Elevators and moving stairways	55
Aircraft	66
Cigarettes	84
Cereal breakfast foods	90
Passenger cars	99

Source: U.S. Bureau of the Census, *Census of Manufactures, 1972*, Special Report Series: "Concentration Ratios in Manufacturing" (Washington, D.C.: Government Printing Office, 1975), pp. 6-49.

concentration ratios, one would thus predict that the meat-packing industry is more competitive than the automobile industry.

Concentration ratios, though convenient and intuitively appealing, should be used with caution because they can be misleading. First, there are other elements of market structure—especially barriers to entry—that can affect market competition. Although seller concentration is important, it is not by itself determinative of market competition. Second, the four-firm concentration ratio conceals any variations in the sizes of the four leading firms. For example, a concentration ratio of 80 would result whether four firms have market shares of 20 or if a single firm has 77 percent and three competitors have one percent each. It is doubtful that the degree of market competition would be the same in these two markets. Third, most concentration ratios cover only domestic sales and so overstate concentration by ignoring imports. The concentration ratio for passenger cars does not include the considerable import competition provided by Toyota, Datsun, and Volkswagen. Fourth, concentration ratios commonly refer to national sales and so understate concentration if the relevant economic markets are regional or local. For example, the four-firm concentration ratio for newspapers is 17, implying that the market is very competitive. In fact, the newspaper market is local, and most cities have only one daily newspaper. All these qualifications must be kept in mind when using concentration ratios as proxies for the degree of market competition.

Empirical Studies of Market Performance

The structure-conduct-performance model hypothesizes that there are causal relationships between market structure, conduct, and performance. Unfortunately, it is not possible to test empirically all these hypothesized relationships. Real world data rarely correspond to the theoretical variables used in economic models. This data constraint has forced economists to search for simple, direct relationships between market structure and performance. This section discusses the general conclusions that seem justified by numerous empirical studies in the United States and in other industrialized economies.

Efficiency.   There are static and dynamic dimensions to economic efficiency. Empirical studies have focused on the relationships between elements of market structure (primarily seller concentration) and various proxies for static and dynamic efficiency.[15] The main proxy for static inefficiency is market profitability. Market profits should increase as the market diverges from the competitive solution and approaches the monopoly solution. Dynamic efficiency is necessarily more complicated than static efficiency, as there is no absolute standard to which actual performance can be compared. Economists have used measures of both inventive inputs (research and development expenditures) and outputs (patents) as proxies for dynamic efficiency.

Economic theory predicts that prices will be greater in concentrated markets where barriers to entry are substantial. Profits also should be larger unless they are reduced by increased costs. This prediction is supported by a large number of empirical studies that have found a positive relationship between seller concentration and market profitability. The current controversy is not the existence of this relationship, but its interpretation. Do oligopolists earn higher profits because they are colluding or because they are efficient?[16] The general belief is that their profits result from collusion and probably even understate the true degree of their static inefficiency.[17] Oligopolists may not be minimizing

15. For an excellent discussion of these relationships, see Harvey J. Goldschmid, H. Michael Mann, and J. Fred Weston, eds., *Industrial Concentration: The New Learning* (Boston: Little, Brown, 1974).

16. For different views, see Sam Peltzman, "The Gains and Losses from Industrial Concentration," *Journal of Law and Economics* 20 (October 1977): 229-63; and F. M. Scherer, "The Causes and Consequences of Rising Industrial Concentration: A Comment," *Journal of Law and Economics* 22 (April 1979): 191-208.

17. W. S. Comanor and H. Leibenstein, "Allocative Efficiency, X-Efficiency, and the Measurement of Welfare Loss," *Economica* 36, new series (August 1969): 304-9.

their production costs and may be engaging in cost-increasing forms of nonprice competition such as advertising. A more competitive market would increase static efficiency by reducing production costs as well as profit margins.

Given that seller concentration leads to static inefficiency, is it also incompatible with dynamic efficiency or technological progress? The empirical evidence is not conclusive, but it does suggest that a moderately concentrated market—a four-firm concentration ratio of from 40 to 60—may be the ideal environment for maximizing dynamic efficiency.[18] Technological progress is commonly divided into the two stages of *invention* and *innovation*. Invention is the creation of a new product or production process, while innovation is the first commercial application of that invention. A substantial number of important inventions have come from small firms and individual inventors.[19] Two musicians in Rochester, New York, invented color film; a patent attorney, Chester Carlson, invented the basic xerography process underlying Xerox's dominant position in the copying machine industry. The most powerful computers are not designed by IBM, but by Seymour Cray, the president of Cray Research, Inc.[20] Large firms appear to have an advantage at the innovation stage of technological progress, however. They have the necessary financial resources and experience to develop an invention into a commercially successful product. For example, Carlson's basic xerography patent was initially improved by the Batelle Institute and subsequently by the Haloid Corporation, who reportedly spent $100 million before producing the first Xerox copier. In short, the empirical evidence suggests that neither perfect competition nor monopoly is the ideal market structure for maximizing dynamic efficiency. A moderately concentrated market seems most promising, for it combines the creativity of small firms with the technological expertise and financial resources of large firms.

Equity. The primary equity issue concerns the possible relationship between market structure and the distribution of income and wealth in the United States. Market structure may affect these distributions, be-

18. See F. M. Scherer, *Industrial Structure*, Chapter 15; and M. I. Kamien and N. L. Schwartz, "Market Structure and Innovation: A Survey," *Journal of Economic Literature* 13 (March 1975): 1–37.

19. John Jewkes, David Sawers, and Richard Stillerman, *The Sources of Invention* (New York: St. Martin's, 1959).

20. "The Whiz—Seymour Cray Shows Computer World How to Build Big Machines," *Wall Street Journal*, April 12, 1979, p. 1.

cause firms in concentrated markets earn higher profits than firms in unconcentrated markets. Higher profits redistribute income from the consumers of these goods to their producers. The impact of this redistribution depends on who owns the corporations. Approximately 80 percent of the corporate stock in existence is owned by private households, and stock ownership by households is highly concentrated. In 1972, the top one percent of individuals owned 56.5 percent of all privately held stock![21] Highly concentrated markets thus worsen the inequalities of income and wealth in America by transferring income from the public to a select group of stockholders. This effect may be partially offset to the extent that firms in concentrated markets pay their employees higher wages and provide better fringe benefits than firms in less concentrated markets.

Stability.   The aggregate level of economic activity in a market economy—output and employment—fluctuates over time. Industrial organization economists have tried to determine the role that concentrated markets play in the business cycle. This analysis was inspired by the casual observation that prices do not fluctuate as much in concentrated markets as they do in unconcentrated or competitive markets.[22] Subsequent studies indicate that price changes in concentrated markets are out of step with the rest of the economy.[23] During the boom part of the business cycle, concentrated markets lag behind competitive markets in raising prices. This is not surprising, because competitive markets are more responsive to changes in demand and costs than are concentrated markets, where prices may be set through collusive agreements. During recessions, however, prices fall in competitive markets while they remain constant or increase in concentrated markets. Oligopolists appear to be catching up with the effects of inflation by restoring their traditional markups on their products. Because they have market power, they can perform the seemingly contradictory act of raising prices in the face of declining demand.

This analysis has two implications for government stabilization poli-

21. U.S. Department of Commerce, *Statistical Abstract of the United States, 1979* (Washington, D.C.: Government Printing Office, 1979), p. 470.

22. Gardiner C. Means, *Industrial Prices and Their Relative Inflexibility* (U.S. Senate Document 13, 74th Congress, 1st Session, Washington, D.C., 1935).

23. See, for example, Leonard W. Weiss, "Business Pricing Policies and Inflation Reconsidered," *Journal of Political Economy* 74 (April 1966): 177-87.

cies.[24] First, concentrated markets help prolong the boom period of the business cycle by slowing the overall rate of inflation. The boom can thus continue for a longer time before the government institutes recessionary policies. Second, concentrated markets may also prolong the recessionary phase, maintaining inflation while output and employment are decreasing. The recession will last longer and delay the implementation of policies to stimulate the economy. In sum, concentrated markets present government authorities with a classic economic trade-off: longer booms versus longer recessions.

Benefit-Cost Analysis

Consumers and producers both try to maximize their welfare through voluntary market transactions. Consumers must decide how to spend their take-home pay, while firms must decide how to reinvest their profits. The optimal strategy for both consumers and producers is the same: to allocate their dollars where the benefit per dollar is the greatest. This requires that consumers and producers evaluate all their options and rank them according to the benefit per dollar spent. Transactions are then consummated, in decreasing order of benefit per dollar, until all of the dollars are spent. This strategy allocates consumers' and producers' dollars into those uses that yield the greatest benefit to them.

The formal economic technique underlying this decision-making process is *benefit-cost analysis*. It is doubtful whether consumers commonly use formal benefit-cost techniques, although they may make rough calculations for major purchases such as automobiles and houses. Corporations and governments, however, frequently use formal benefit-cost analyses to allocate their finite resources into their most valued uses. The Army Corps of Engineers, for example, is well known for its use of benefit-cost analysis in evaluating proposals for new dams and inland waterways.

For all of the expected benefits and costs of a project to be compared, they must be measured in the same units. The standard practice is to place a dollar value on all items. This introduces two major measurement problems, which can be illustrated by examining certain benefits and costs of airport security programs. These programs have been very successful in reducing airplane hijackings. The first problem is how to

---

24. Market concentration does not seem to have any discernible impact on investment and employment throughout the business cycle. See F. M. Scherer, "Market Structure and the Stability of Investment," *American Economic Review* 59 (May 1969): 72-79; and *Industrial Market Structure*, pp. 365-67.

value benefits that do not have a market value. One major benefit is the saving of human lives, but what is the value of a human life? This is a very controversial issue, and there is no clear-cut solution.[25] Economists normally use a person's income as a minimal approximation of that person's value to society. (If an infinite value were placed on a human life, then society should spend an infinite amount of money to protect every individual's life!) The second problem arises when benefits or costs must be summed over time. Metal detectors installed this year, for example, will provide benefits for more than a single year. It is not appropriate, however, to simply sum these benefits over time. A dollar today is worth more than a dollar one year from today. For example, $1.00 invested in a 5 percent savings account would yield $1.05 one year later. The solution to this problem is to compute the present value of the benefit stream.[26] The present value discounts future dollars and converts them into their equivalent number of current dollars, facilitating the direct comparison of the total benefits and costs of a project.

Table 2.3   Hypothetical Benefit-Cost Data

	Project			
	I	II	III	IV
Benefits	80	120	120	200
Costs	100	100	100	100
Benefit-cost ratio	.80	1.20	1.20	2.00

The role of benefit-cost analysis in allocating resources can be demonstrated simply by Table 2.3, which shows benefit and cost data for four hypothetical projects. The analysis is simplified by assuming that each project costs $100. The benefits, however, vary. If funds are unlimited, which projects should be approved? All except for project I. It is the only project with a benefit-cost ratio less than one: each dollar spent on project I yields only eighty cents in benefits. Society would be

25. M. J. Bailey, *Reducing Risks to Life—Measurement of the Benefits* (Washington, D.C.: American Enterprise Institute, 1980).

26. The present value of a stream of benefits can be calculated with the following formula:

$$PV = \sum_{t=1}^{T} \frac{B_t}{(1+r)^t}$$

where B_t is the benefit received in the tth year, T is the number of years over which benefits are received, and r is the discount rate.

better off if those resources were allocated to projects with benefit-cost ratios in excess of unity. On the other hand, if only one project can be implemented, it should be project IV, which offers the most benefits per dollar of expenditure. In both of these situations, the responses of government and business would be identical. The outcomes may differ, however, if equity considerations are important. For example, one project may benefit low-income people, while the other one benefits high-income people. A profit-maximizing firm would not take these differences into account, while the government may be influenced by the distributional impacts of different projects. The government may thus select projects that would not be chosen on a purely benefit-cost basis.

In reality, the choices are not as clear-cut as those in the figure. Both the benefits and the costs of projects can vary and may not be accurately measured by market values. When equity considerations are interjected along with political compromises, the situation becomes much more complicated. Nonetheless, benefit-cost analysis remains a powerful tool if its limitations are kept in mind.

Summary

Microeconomics provides a robust framework within which to analyze the rationale for, and effectiveness of, government intervention in the American economy. The cornerstone of microeconomics is the model of perfect competition. Under a stringent set of assumptions, market competition yields desirable economic performance. In particular, it guarantees static efficiency. These effects will not occur, however, if the necessary assumptions are violated. Market failures will result. Major attention has focused on the market failure associated with monopoly power. Microeconomic theory predicts, and empirical studies support, relationships between market structure, conduct, and performance. These relationships suggest that the government can counter market failures and improve market performance by modifying market structure and conduct. Finally, benefit-cost analysis can be used to evaluate current government policies and to formulate new ones.

Appendix A: Elasticity

A downward-sloping demand curve indicates that consumers demand more of a good as its price decreases; that is, quantity demanded is inversely related to price. The *price elasticity of demand* indicates exactly how responsive demand is to price changes. It is defined as the percentage change in quantity demanded divided by the percentage change in price: $\frac{\%\Delta Q_d}{\%\Delta P}$. The more responsive quantity demanded is to changes in price, the larger the price elasticity. For example, if the price elasticity is negative three, a 10 percent decrease in price will lead to a 30 percent increase in quantity demanded. If the price elasticity were negative one-half, the same decrease in price would increase quantity demanded by only 5 percent. For simplicity, economists frequently define the price elasticity of demand as a positive number (more technically, the absolute value of the original formula). Demand, then, is considered to be *elastic* if the price elasticity is greater than one and *inelastic* if it is less than one.

The main determinant of the price elasticity of demand for a given good is the availability of substitutes. Consumers' responses to a price change will be strongly influenced by the alternatives available to them in the marketplace. If a firm increases the price of its product and there are good substitutes available in the same price range, consumers can switch to other goods. Or, if the firm lowers its price, consumers can switch from the other goods to this firm's product. In both cases, the availability of substitutes makes the quantity demanded of this product very sensitive to price changes. If good substitutes are not available, however, consumers' choices are limited, and demand will be less sensitive to price changes. In that case, a firm will have more discretion in pricing its product. This is one reason why firms try to differentiate their products through advertising and product styling. If they can create brand loyalty, they can reduce the price elasticity of demand for their products.

The price elasticity of demand also tells the firm how its total revenue will change in response to price changes. If demand is inelastic, total revenue and price will change in the same direction; if demand is elastic, they will move in opposite directions. The relationship between price elasticity and total revenue is illustrated in Figure 2.7. Two demand curves, D and D', are drawn through the common point P_0, Q_0. Assume that price now increases to P_1. Two things can be noted. First, the demand curve D is less elastic than D'. The demand for its product is barely affected by the price increase, while the demand for the other product is substantially reduced. Second, total revenue for the inelastic good increases from area P_0Q_0 to area P_1Q_1, while total revenue for the elastic product decreases to area P_1Q_2. Consumers using the elastic good have easily switched to substitute goods, while this option was not as available to consumers of the inelastic good.

Three other elasticities should also be mentioned. The *cross-price elasticity of demand* captures the relationship between the quantity demanded of one good and the price of another good. It is defined as the

Figure 2.7   **Price Elasticity and Total Revenue**

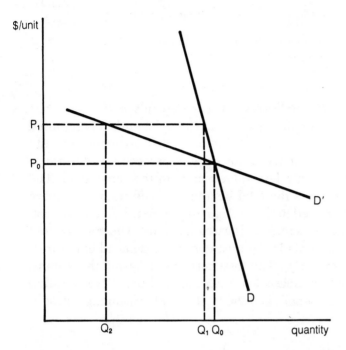

percentage change in quantity demanded of good A divided by the percentage change in price of good B: $\frac{\%\Delta Q_A}{\%\Delta P_B}$. The cross-price elasticity indicates how two goods are related and is helpful in defining the product dimension of a market. For example, if the cross-price elasticity is positive, the two goods are substitutes. For instance, an increase in the price of butter will lead to an increase in the quantity demanded of margarine. If the cross-price elasticity is negative, the two goods are complements; if it is zero, the two goods are unrelated. The *income elasticity of demand* is defined as the percentage change in quantity demanded divided by the percentage change in income: $\frac{\%\Delta Q_d}{\%\Delta Y}$. It captures the impact of changes in consumers' income on the quantity demanded of a good. If the income elasticity is positive, the good is called a *normal good:* an increase in income leads to an increase in quantity demanded. If the income elasticity is negative, the good is called an *inferior good.* Dining out and vacations are generally considered to be normal goods, while cheap cuts of meat and bus travel would normally be inferior goods. The *supply elasticity* reflects the responsiveness of quantity supplied to changes in market price. It is defined as the percentage change in quantity supplied divided by the percentage change in price: $\dfrac{\%\Delta Q_s}{\%\Delta P}$. Supply is classified as elastic or inelastic if the supply elasticity is greater than or less than one.

Appendix B: Consumer's Surplus and Welfare Loss

The price that a consumer will pay for a good depends on the benefit he or she expects from consuming that good. This relationship is captured by the consumer's demand curve. It indicates that price and quantity demanded are inversely related; a lower price is necessary to induce consumption of increasingly less valued units of the same good. The demand curve also reflects the total benefit received from consuming this good. This is illustrated in the diagram in Figure 2.8. At the competitive price of P_c, the consumer purchases Q_c units. The total benefit from consuming these units is the area under the demand curve from the origin to the quantity Q_c. The total cost of purchasing these units, however, is area P_cQ_c, which is less than the total benefit. The difference between the total benefit and the total cost of consuming a good is

Figure 2.8   The Welfare Loss of Monopoly

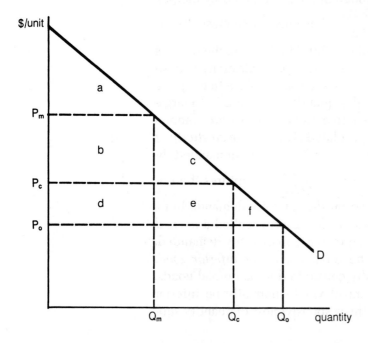

called *consumer's surplus*. It arises because consumers value each unit differently, though they pay the same price for each. In the diagram, consumer's surplus is the sum of areas a, b, and c.

The diagram indicates that the lower the market price, the greater the amount of consumer's surplus. A competitive market maximizes consumer's surplus because it offers a good at the lowest long-run price. A monopolist, then, will reduce consumer's surplus, because it produces fewer units (Q_m) and sells them at a higher price (P_m). What is the loss in consumer's surplus? Originally, consumer's surplus was the sum of *a*, *b*, and *c*; now it is just *a*. The total loss in consumer's surplus is not the sum of *b* and *c*, however; *b* is the monopolist's profits, representing a transfer of income from consumers to the monopolist. It is not possible to determine how this transfer affects society's welfare. So, economists arbitrarily assume that the loss to consumers is exactly offset by the gain to the monopolist. This leaves area *c* as a total loss in consumer's surplus. This area is known as the *deadweight* or *welfare loss* of monopoly and historically has been the economist's main argument against monopoly.

Several attempts have been made to measure the welfare loss to society of monopoly or, more accurately, of concentrated markets. The earliest and most famous of these studies was by Harberger.[27] He concluded that during the time period 1924–1928, the welfare loss was a maximum of one-tenth of one percent of gross national product. In 1978, this would amount to approximately ten dollars for each person in the United States. This is a rather small amount and pales in comparison to the costs to society of unemployment. The most plausible of many explanations is that the welfare loss is understated because firms are not minimizing costs.[28] If the true competitive price is P_0, then the true welfare loss is areas *c*, *e*, and *f*, while *d* represents the inflated costs of the monopolist. It is likely that these inflated costs are the main burden of monopoly and are substantially larger than the welfare loss.

Suggested Readings

Adams, Walter. *The Structure of American Industry,* 5th ed. (New York: Macmillan, 1977).

Goldschmid, Harvey J., Mann, H. Michael, and Weston, J. Fred, eds. *Industrial Concentration: The New Learning* (Boston: Little, Brown, 1974).

27. A. C. Harberger, "Monopoly and Resource Allocation," *American Economic Review* 44 (May 1954): 77–97.

28. W. S. Comanor and H. Leibenstein, "Allocative Efficiency, X-Efficiency and the Measurement of Welfare Loss," *Economica* 36, new series (August 1969): 304–9.

McGee, John S. *In Defense of Industrial Concentration* (New York: Praeger, 1971).

Scherer, F. M. *Industrial Market Structure and Economic Performance*, 2nd ed. (Chicago: Rand McNally, 1980).

Singer, Neil M. *Public Microeconomics*, 2nd ed. (Boston: Little, Brown, 1976).

Weiss, Leonard W. "Quantitative Studies of Industrial Organization," in *Frontiers in Quantitative Economics*, edited by M. D. Intriligator (Amsterdam: North-Holland, 1971), pp. 362-411.

The Legal Framework

Chapter 3

The United States is often termed "a nation of laws." This statement recognizes the important role of government in defining the environment within which society functions. A thorough understanding of government intervention in the economy requires some knowledge of judicial and administrative processes, since the impact of laws depends on their interpretation and enforcement by courts and regulatory agencies. This chapter provides a brief introduction to the operations of federal courts and regulatory agencies.[1]

The American judicial system is based on the premise that the adversary process is the best method for resolving disputes, and that truth will eventually emerge from a series of confrontations between the parties involved in a dispute. The resolution of disputes or administration of justice through a court system is known as the judicial process. Since government intervention commonly occurs at the federal level, this section provides a broad overview of the judicial process in the federal court system.

The Judicial Process

1. For a more detailed discussion, see H. H. Liebhafsky, *American Government and Business* (New York: Wiley, 1971).

The Federal Court System

Article VI, Section 2 of the United States Constitution declares that the "Constitution, and the Laws...; and all Treaties made... shall be the Supreme Law of the Land." Federal laws thus supersede conflicting state and local laws. Furthermore, state courts cannot resolve disputes arising from federal laws. Only federal courts have *jurisdiction*, that is, the authority to hear and resolve disputes, over federal laws. Federal courts also have sole jurisdiction over constitutional issues and disputes directly involving the federal government or one of its agencies. This means that federal courts must decide the constitutional and legal issues raised by federal intervention policies. The final resolution of these disputes depends on the specific laws and courts involved.

Types of Laws. A law is simply a rule that regulates the behavior of members of a society. Thus, the very essence of laws is to circumscribe human behavior, according to the rationale that some personal freedoms must be limited if other, more important, freedoms are to be preserved. One's right to own a pet lion, for example, must be balanced against one's neighbors' right to live in a reasonably safe neighborhood. This balancing of opposing interests is particularly apparent in laws that control private economic activity.[2]

It should be emphasized that not all laws originate with the legislative branch of a government. Islamic law, for example, is not based on government statutes, but on interpretations of the Moslem holy book, the Koran. Another example is the *common law*, a legal system that the United States inherited from Great Britain. Common law is made by the courts, not the legislatures. It was created when judges resolved disputes that were not specifically covered by existing statutes. In deciding such cases, the judges relied heavily on the general customs and beliefs of the time, and their decisions gained added weight through the legal principle of *stare decisis*. (Under this principle, a court's decision constitutes a *precedent* which should be followed by that court, as well as courts inferior to it, when resolving future disputes.) Common law provides a flexible and adaptive response to the changing needs of society. At the same time, common-law precedents lend both predictability and stability to the law.

A violation of a law is called a wrong. The American legal system differentiates between private wrongs and public wrongs; a private wrong affects specific individuals, and a public wrong affects society in gener-

2. Rent control laws, for example, transfer income from landlords to their tenants.

al. For example, giving trade secrets to a competitor is a private wrong, but giving government secrets to a foreign agent is a public wrong. Public wrongs are frequently classified as felonies or crimes, in which case they can be punished by the state. It should be stressed, however, that the concept of crime is not absolute. A crime is something that is defined by a society and can vary over time as well as across governments. The effects of changing attitudes are illustrated by the recent efforts to decriminalize the use of marijuana throughout the United States.

Types of Courts.   As in Great Britain, the source of our basic legal framework, there were originally several different types of courts in the United States. Each court specialized in a specific type of law. Criminal courts decided criminal cases; courts of law resolved only common-law issues. One of the most interesting, as well as powerful, courts was the court of equity. This court arose in response to the rigidity of English common law. Because of strict adherence to the principle of *stare decisis*, a common-law decision might not provide adequate relief for a private wrong. The wronged party could then appeal to the King's Chancellor for an equitable solution to the dispute. The Chancellor, and subsequently the courts of equity, could provide compensation that was not available under the common law. For example, an employee might leave a firm and take along trade secrets. Common-law precedents would enable the old employer to obtain damages from the new employer, but could not prevent future illegal use of the trade secrets. A court of equity could, however, prevent the employee from using the trade secrets in the future.[3]

Separate courts for each type of law no longer exist, as they have been consolidated into a single court. A federal court, for example, can decide a criminal case in the morning and employ its equity powers to resolve a private dispute in the afternoon. The main distinction now is between courts of *original jurisdiction* and those of *appellate jurisdiction*. A dispute is presented initially in a court of original jurisdiction. At the federal level, these are called district courts; there is at least one district court in every state as well as the District of Columbia and Puerto Rico. A decision of the district court can subsequently be contested before an appellate court. There are 10 circuit or appellate courts throughout the United States that review the district court decisions for errors. Their decisions can, in turn, be further appealed to the court of last resort—the Supreme Court. The Supreme Court's decision is final and can be over-

3. The court could issue an *injunction*—a flexible court order that can require an individual to perform, or to refrain from performing, a particular act.

turned only by new legislation or a constitutional amendment. Given the principle of *stare decisis*, the Supreme Court's decisions are binding on all the lower courts, while the decisions of the appellate courts similarly are binding on the district courts in their circuit.

Processing a Case

In the federal court system, a lawsuit begins when a complaint is filed with the clerk of a federal court.[4] The complaint specifies the offense that is alleged to have occurred. There are two types of legal actions: civil and criminal. A civil suit is designed to enforce private rights or to seek compensation for private wrongs; a criminal suit is used to punish a public wrong. Before a lawsuit is finally resolved, however, it will traverse the well-defined slopes of judicial "due process."[5] *Due process* refers to the legal rules that must be satisfied throughout the resolution of the lawsuit. These legal requirements are codified in the federal rules for civil and criminal procedure. The three main stages of litigation are pretrial, trial, and appellate.

Pretrial Stage. This stage of a lawsuit is concerned with clarifying the dispute between the party initiating the legal action—the plaintiff—and the party responding to the action—the defendant or respondent. The plaintiff files a written statement with the court that outlines the allegations. The defendant responds by contesting the plaintiff's allegations and, in many cases, filing a counterclaim. A common rationale for a counterclaim is that "the best defense is a good offense." The counterclaim also consolidates all of the relevant issues in a single case.

A major part of the pretrial stage is the discovery of evidence. In order to speed up trials, more and more of the evidence now is introduced prior to the actual trial. Written and oral information is exchanged between the plaintiff and the defendant, often in the form of *depositions,* or statements by witnesses questioned under oath in front of a notary public. Based on the pretrial discovery process, stipulations of uncontested facts may be submitted to the court. This saves time, because these facts cannot then be disputed during the trial.

---

4. The lawsuit must be filed before the statute of limitations for the alleged offense has expired. Otherwise, the action will not be timely and the claimant will have no legal recourse.

5. Under the Fifth (federal government) and the Fourteenth (state governments) Amendments to the Constitution, no person shall be deprived of "life, liberty, or property, without due process of law."

It is possible, in fact likely, that a lawsuit will never go to trial. This can happen for two main reasons. First, the judge may issue a *summary judgment* in favor of one of the parties. In this situation, there is no dispute about the facts of the case, only about their interpretation. The summary judgment thus decides the merits of the case as a matter of law. Second, the parties may reach an out-of-court settlement. Judges encourage such settlements as an efficient and equitable solution to legal disputes. A formal trial is the last step in the judicial resolution of a dispute. In civil cases, the judge holds a pretrial conference with the opposing parties' attorneys in an effort to find the common ground necessary for a settlement. In criminal cases, it is common for the defendant to *plea bargain* with the government; that is, to admit guilt to a lesser offense in return for the dropping of more serious charges.

Table 3.1 presents some data on the actual disposition of civil and criminal cases in federal courts for 1978. Of the 123,200 civil cases terminated in that year, more than one-third were settled without court

Table 3.1 **United States District Courts: Disposition of Civil and Criminal Cases, 1978**

Item	Number	Percentage of Total
Civil Cases Terminated		
No court action	45,300	36.8
Court action		
before pretrial	48,700	39.5
pretrial	19,700	16.0
trials	9,400	7.6
Total	77,800	63.1
Grand Total[a]	123,200	100.0
Criminal Cases Disposed of		
Not convicted		
dismissed	7,800	17.0
acquitted	1,600	3.5
Total	9,400	20.5
Convicted		
by guilty plea	31,100	67.8
by court or jury	5,400	11.8
Total	36,500	79.6
Grand Total[a]	45,900	100.1

[a]Totals may not add up to 100% because of rounding off.

Source: U.S. Department of Commerce, *Statistical Abstract of the United States, 1979* (Washington, D.C.: Government Printing Office, 1979), p. 192, Table 324.

action, and more than another one-third were settled before the case reached the pretrial stage. Only 7.6 percent were actually decided by a trial. In federal criminal cases, the conviction rate was almost 80 percent. Approximately six out of every seven convictions resulted from guilty pleas, not from court or jury decisions.[6]

Trial Stage.   If the lawsuit is not settled out of court, it will eventually go to trial. The trial formally resolves the dispute by determining the facts and applying the relevant law. The end result is a court decree outlining the final decision as well as the appropriate relief. This entire process occurs within well-defined constitutional guidelines. These constitutional due-process requirements are different for civil and criminal cases.

The first thing to note is that the trial does not always take place before a jury.[7] All criminal defendants have a constitutional right to a jury trial, but parties in a civil suit can demand a jury trial only if the amount in dispute exceeds 20 dollars.[8] The role of the jury is to determine the facts of the case based on the evidence presented to them. The judge decides the legal issues raised by the case and advises the jury of the applicable law. The judge, along with the lawyers, also questions prospective jurors during jury selection to determine their objectivity. If there is no jury, the judge also decides the facts of the case.

Throughout the trial, both sides present evidence in an effort to determine the truth and resolve the dispute. The constitutional due-process requirements guarantee defendants the right to present evidence, confront their accusers, cross-examine witnesses, and, if desirable, testify in their own behalf. After the evidence has been presented, the judge or jury must reach a decision. Judicial standards differ for criminal and civil cases. In a criminal case, the defendant is innocent until proven guilty. The government must prove "beyond a reasonable doubt" that the defendant is indeed guilty. This standard is more rigorous than that employed in civil cases, where the issue is a dispute between two parties. The court bases its decisions in civil cases on a "preponderance of

6. For an economic analysis of the decision between a pretrial settlement and a trial, see William M. Landes, "An Economic Analysis of the Courts," *Journal of Law and Economics* 14 (1971): 61-107.

7. In 1978, 27.7 percent of civil and 54.4 percent of criminal trials occurred before a jury. (U.S. Department of Commerce, *Statistical Abstract of the United States, 1979* [Washington, D.C.: Government Printing Office, 1979], p. 193, Table 326.)

8. The constitutional rights to a jury trial are discussed in the Sixth (criminal cases) and the Seventh (civil cases) Amendments to the Constitution.

evidence." The issue is not whether a party is guilty of a crime, but rather which party is judged to be entitled to relief.

Once the court has resolved the legal issues and reached its decision, it must determine the appropriate legal remedy. The remedy may be designed to enforce rights or to redress wrongs. Federal courts can impose civil as well as criminal sanctions. In a criminal case, the court can use whatever criminal sanctions are available under the law, ranging from monetary fines and imprisonment to capital punishment. Civil sanctions include fines, damage awards, and equitable relief. As noted earlier, equitable relief historically was awarded by courts of equity when ordinary relief did not seem adequate. Good examples are *injunctions*, court orders that mandate a specific course of action. They may require a party to perform an act or, alternatively, to refrain from some action.

Appellate Stage. Once the district court has announced its final decision, the plaintiff and the defendant can either accept the court's decision or petition an appeals court for review.[9] The defendant *always* has the right to appeal an adverse decision, while the plaintiff can appeal only in civil cases. This distinction arises from the constitutional prohibition against *double jeopardy*—being tried twice for the same criminal offense.[10] An appeal of a decision in a criminal case is viewed as the second prosecution of the defendant for the same offense. As a result, only the defendant can appeal the district court's decision in a criminal case.

A party must petition the appeals court for a review of the case. The standard practice is that cases can be appealed only on legal, not factual, issues. The district court is responsible for determining the facts, while the appellate court ensures that the district court's decision is consistent with the relevant law and legal precedents. In practice, however, the appeals court can rationalize any decision to review a district court's ruling and can also examine the factual issues of a case. When the appeals court has reviewed a case, it takes one of three possible actions. First, it can affirm the district court's decision if it agrees with it. (The appeals court may reach the same decision as the district court, but for different reasons.) Second, the appeals court can reverse the district court's decision if it disagrees with it and may send the case back to the

9. The party initiating the appeal is called the appellant, while the party responding to the appeal is called the appellee.

10. According to the Fifth Amendment to the Constitution, "nor shall any person be subject for the same offence to be twice put in jeopardy of life or limb. . . ."

district court for a rehearing on some or all of the original issues. Third, the appeals court may affirm part of the decision and reverse another part. Such a modification of the district court's decision is likely to lead to a rehearing of those issues reversed on appeal.

The appellate court's decision can be appealed subsequently to the Supreme Court. This is the final step in the review process. The Supreme Court can affirm, reverse, or modify the appellate court's decision. Since it is the "highest court in the land," its decision becomes a controlling legal precedent for district and appellate courts throughout the United States. Given the legal principle of *stare decisis*, those courts will then adjudicate disputes within the guidelines established by the Court's decision. If the Court declines to review a case, the appellate court's decision is controlling. In this situation, the Supreme Court is establishing a precedent indirectly by its implicit agreement with the appellate court's decision. This precedent, however, is not so strong as that set by a Supreme Court decision, since the Court does not indicate its reasoning.

The Administrative Process

The United States Constitution established a division of powers among the executive, legislative, and judicial branches of the government. A system of checks and balances was created that dispersed powers so as to prevent the dominance of government by a single branch. The legislature passes the laws that are enforced by the president and interpreted by the courts. There is no clear-cut niche in this classification scheme for federal agencies, which can have legislative, executive, *and* judicial powers. The term "administrative process" refers to the procedures adopted by agencies in exercising these different powers.

The Federal Agency System

The first federal agency created to regulate private economic activity was the Interstate Commerce Commission, established in 1887 to regulate the interstate operations of the nation's railroads. The substantial increase in government intervention since the turn of the century has led to a plethora of federal regulatory agencies. There are currently 55 different federal regulatory agencies, each responsible for some type of economic activity.[11] Some of the major federal regulatory agencies are

11. For a current listing of these agencies, see Marcia B. Wallace and Ronald J. Penoyer, *Directory of Federal Regulatory Agencies* (St. Louis: Center for the Study of American Business, Working Paper No. 36, September 1978).

listed in Table 3.2 along with their primary area of responsibility. Even though these agencies have different jurisdictions, they have certain common characteristics.

Table 3.2   **Major Federal Regulatory Agencies**

Agency	Primary Responsibility
Interstate Commerce Commission (1887)	interstate surface transportation
Antitrust Division (1903)	antitrust
Federal Trade Commission (1914)	antitrust and consumer protection
Food and Drug Administration (1931)	food, drugs, and cosmetics
Federal Communications Commission (1934)	interstate communications
Civil Aeronautics Board (1938)	civil aviation
Federal Railroad Administration (1966)	railroad safety
Federal Aviation Administration (1967)	airline safety
Consumer Product Safety Commission (1970)	consumer products
Environmental Protection Agency (1970)	physical environment
National Highway Traffic Safety Administration (1970)	auto safety, fuel economy, and emissions
Occupational Safety and Health Administration (1970)	worker safety and health
Nuclear Regulatory Commission (1975)	civilian nuclear reactors
Federal Energy Regulatory Commission (1977)	oil and natural gas and wholesale electric power

The Reason for Agencies.   Agencies are commonly viewed as congressional response to the shortcomings inherent in both Congress and the courts. These two branches of government are not capable of maintaining constant, informed supervision of economic activities. As a result, Congress created *agencies,* government bodies that have administrative, quasi-legislative, and quasi-judicial powers.[12] Some of these agencies are completely independent (for example, the Interstate Commerce Commission), while others are associated with particular executive departments. The Food and Drug Administration, for example, is part of the Department of Health, Education, and Welfare.[13]

Agencies are considered to have two advantages over Congress and the courts in regulating economic activity. First, agencies can acquire

12. These agencies are normally headed by a group of commissioners who are appointed by the president. These commissioners are served by a staff of lawyers, economists, and other relevant professionals.

13. A regulatory agency that is located within an executive department is obviously subject to more political pressure since the secretary of that department is appointed by the president and serves in the cabinet.

specialized knowledge of the economic activities under their supervision. It is unlikely that Congress or the courts could obtain the same expertise that is so essential for competent regulation. Second, agencies can provide more flexible regulation; they can respond more quickly and devise more adaptive responses to changes than can the courts or Congress (neither of which is renowned for its speed). In sum, agencies are more suited to the difficult task of regulating private economic activity in a complex and dynamic world.

Agencies' Powers. It has already been pointed out that agencies possess powers traditionally associated with all three branches of the government. First, agencies exercise quasi-legislative power when they formulate specific rules or regulations. Congress cannot technically transfer its lawmaking powers to an agency, but it is not unconstitutional to grant an agency rule-making authority. This authority enables the regulatory agency to translate its broad legislative mandate into practical guidelines. Second, an agency utilizes executive power when it enforces its rules. Regulations do not achieve their purpose if they are ignored. Enforcement is aided by the agency's ability to obtain information from the firms subject to its regulations. Finally, agencies act in a quasi-judicial capacity when they adjudicate disputes over their rules. An agency may initiate a suit if it believes that someone is not in compliance with its rules. The agency not only initiates a suit, but also determines the facts and reaches a decision. If there has been a violation, it can issue an order preventing future violations. In this situation, an agency is in the novel position of being prosecutor, judge, and jury. In sum, a federal regulatory agency is probably unique among government institutions: it writes, enforces, and adjudicates its own rules.

Degree of Independence. Even though federal regulatory agencies are generally considered to be the fourth branch of government, they are not completely independent. All three branches of the government— executive, judicial, and legislative—exercise various degrees of indirect control over the agencies. The president can influence an agency's policies through the power to fill vacancies among its commissioners. A few appointments may be sufficient to change the agency's majority and hence alter its policies.[14] Policies are, in turn, subject to review and

14. The appointment of Alfred Kahn, a noted regulatory economist, to the Civil Aeronautics Board was generally considered to be instrumental in the subsequent deregulation of the airline industry.

modification by the courts. An agency's actions must be consistent with the Constitution as well as its legislative mandate.

The most important relationship is undoubtedly that between an agency and Congress. Indeed, federal regulatory agencies are often viewed as agents of Congress, for congressional authority is extended through them. Congress creates agencies, defines their powers, and establishes their broad mandates. Once an agency is created, Congress maintains its control through the budget process. It can increase appropriations for agency activities that it deems desirable and decrease appropriations for those activities it considers inappropriate. Congress periodically reviews the agency's performance to determine whether new legislation is necessary. All in all, Congress clearly exerts greater control over federal regulatory agencies than do the president or the courts.

Agency Proceedings

Federal regulatory agencies conduct two main types of proceedings: adjudicatory and rule making.[15] An adjudicatory proceeding addresses a specific issue raised by a specific case: for example, is a firm subject to the agency's regulations? Adjudicatory proceedings, which are judicial in nature, can be contrasted with the legislative character of rule-making proceedings. These are a response to a perceived regulatory problem and seek to devise rules that will solve that problem. Both types of proceedings create new agency policies, either through the establishment of a new rule or the expansion of existing case law.[16] Regardless of the type of proceeding, the agency must hold hearings and conform with the due-process requirements codified in the Administrative Procedures Act of 1946. These hearings are analagous to court proceedings and can also be analyzed in three distinct stages: prehearing, hearing, and appellate.

Prehearing Stage. At this stage, the primary concern is gathering the information essential for the adjudication of a complaint or the establishment of a new rule. An agency's ability to obtain information depends on the powers it was granted by Congress and on the cooperation

15. For an excellent summary of the administrative law process, see William A. Rutter, *Administrative Law*, 5th ed. (Gardena, CA: Gilbert Law Summaries, 1976).

16. For example, the Federal Trade Commission could establish its policy toward deceptive practices in an industry through a series of different cases or by a single rule-making proceeding.

of the firms it regulates. Although most information is obtained voluntarily, an agency can compel firms to provide information through its use of subpoenas, required reports, and physical inspections. When the agency uses these techniques, it must make sure that its requests are consistent with basic constitutional freedoms. For example, corporations cannot invoke the Fifth Amendment right against self-incrimination, but physical searches can violate the Fourth Amendment prohibition of "unreasonable searches and seizures."[17] In any event, the cooperation of the regulated firms is essential if the information is to be obtained with minimal delay.[18]

Hearing Stage.   One of an agency's most important functions is to conduct hearings. These serve several different purposes: they determine facts, provide a forum in which interested parties can express their opinions, and serve as a record for judicial review. Two things should be noted about agency hearings, however. First, formal hearings are required for adjudication, but not for rule making (unless required by law). The due-process requirements for rule-making hearings are thus less demanding than those for adjudicatory hearings. Second, the legal standards for hearings are generally less rigorous than those required by courts of law. For example, hearsay evidence (statements made outside the hearing) is admissible in agency hearings, while every Perry Mason fan knows that it is generally not admissible in a court of law and the constitutional protection against self-incrimination does not apply at agency hearings.

The general due-process requirements for an adjudication hearing are as follows. First, the hearing must be well publicized so that defendants have sufficient opportunity to prepare their defense. Second, defendants must be able to present their defense adequately before the *administrative law judge* presiding over the case.[19] Defendants have the

17. In *Marshall v. Barlow's Inc.*, 436 U.S. 307 (1978), the Supreme Court ruled that employers did not have to permit inspectors from the Occupational Health and Safety Administration to enter their premises unless they had search warrants.

18. In 1976, the Federal Trade Commission filed an 1,800-page subpoena with eight major oil companies. The oil companies challenged the subpoena in court and it was subsequently reduced to 58 pages. This smaller, though still substantial, subpoena is currently being contested by the companies.

19. Administrative law judges are quasi-judicial officers who resolve disputes in administrative agencies. There are more administrative law judges than federal trial judges, and federal regulatory agencies process more cases than the federal court system! (*Administrative Law Process: Better Management is Needed*, Comptroller General's Report to the Congress, May 15, 1978.)

right to be confronted with the evidence against them, to cross-examine witnesses and rebut that evidence, and to be represented by legal counsel. Third, the administrative law judge must be impartial and base the final decision solely on the evidence presented at the hearing. For example, it would be improper for a case to be heard by an administrative law judge who had previously participated in that case in some capacity.

The due-process requirements for a rule-making hearing are substantially less demanding, as this is a legislative, not a judicial, hearing. The hearing must be well publicized so that interested parties may have a chance to participate. A party's right to be heard may be satisfied through the submission of written material, although agencies are coming to allow more and more oral arguments. Finally, the agency must provide a concise statement of the reason for any proposed rule.

Two interesting issues that commonly arise in both adjudicatory and rule-making hearings are jurisdiction and standing. The issue of *jurisdiction* concerns an agency's right to hold hearings about a specific issue. Does a proposed action fall within the agency's area of expertise, or is the agency exceeding its legislative mandate?[20] This issue is normally resolved by the courts, though Congress may legislate a solution. The issue of *standing* concerns the right of individual parties to participate in agency proceedings. In general, a party must show that its interests would be affected adversely if it were not allowed to appear at the hearing. It is necessary to place some limitation on the number of participants attending such proceedings, or they may become so large as to effectively delay any proposed policy. On the other hand, good decision-making requires knowledge of all aspects of a policy. The agency must thus strike a balance between the costs and benefits of increased participation by outside parties. [21]

Appellate Stage.   Once the hearing has been concluded, the agency's final decision can usually be appealed to a federal appeals court.[22] The general presumption is that, unless it is explicitly prohibited by legislation, agency decisions are subject to *judicial review*. Review begins in

20. This issue arose with the Federal Communications Commission's regulation of cable television companies (see *United States* v. *Southwestern Cable Co.*, 392 U.S. 157 [1968]).

21. The Federal Trade Commission distributed approximately $750,000 to different public groups in 1979 in order to increase the diversity of viewpoints that it hears at its proceedings ("Paying to Hear Divergent Views," *Business Week*, January 15, 1979, p. 110).

22. In adjudicatory hearings, the administrative law judge's decision can be appealed initially within the agency to the commissioners, who may adopt, reject, or modify the decision. Their decision can, in turn, be appealed to a federal appeals court and ultimately to the Supreme Court.

an appeals court, thus bypassing the federal district court, and concludes in the Supreme Court. To obtain judicial review of an agency's decision, appellants must show that they will be adversely affected by this decision. This requirement is easy to fulfill if the appellants have been ordered by the agency to pursue some course of action. If the potential damage is irreparable, appellants may be able to obtain a stay of the agency's order pending judicial review.

With respect to the scope of judicial review, the courts focus on questions of law, not findings of fact. Given the agency's unique expertise, it is presumed that the findings of fact are correct. If the agency has followed due-process requirements, its decisions are usually supported. The courts are reluctant to reverse an agency decision unless it is clear that the agency has abused its powers and exceeded its legislative mandate.

Summary

Laws define the environment within which private economic activity occurs. As a result, they can affect, both directly and indirectly, the allocation of society's finite resources. The exact impact of government laws depends on their interpretation and enforcement by federal courts and regulatory agencies. These institutions, in turn, must operate in an environment defined by the United States Constitution and the Congress. This chapter has provided a brief glimpse of the judicial and administrative processes that can determine both the extent and nature of government intervention in the American economy.

Suggested Readings

Coughlin, George G. *Your Introduction to Law.* 2nd ed. New York: Barnes & Noble, 1975.

Harron, Thomas J. *Law for Business Managers.* Boston: Holbrook Press, 1977.

Landes, William M. "An Economic Analysis of Courts." *Journal of Law and Economics* 14 (1971): 61-107.

Liebhafsky, H. H. *American Government and Business.* New York: Wiley, 1971.

Posner, Richard A. *Economic Analysis of Law.* Boston: Little, Brown, 1972.

Part Two

Antitrust Enforcement

The Antitrust Environment

Chapter
4

Antitrust enforcement is a uniquely American response to the monopoly problem. Its primary objective is to improve market performance by preserving *and* enhancing the natural competitive forces of the marketplace. A good understanding of antitrust enforcement requires knowledge of both the individual antitrust statutes and the federal agencies that enforce them—the Justice Department and the Federal Trade Commission. It also requires knowledge of the American economy. This chapter establishes the background necessary for the more detailed discussions of antitrust policy in Chapters 5 through 10.

It is not easy to generalize about any economy, much less one as large and dynamic as the American economy. Nonetheless, it is possible to describe the major sectors of the economy and to estimate the degree of competition within them. This broad overview is followed by a more detailed discussion of the manufacturing sector and the firms that dominate it.

The Structure of the American Economy

Overview

The American economy can be divided into 12 sectors, each corresponding to a different type of economic activity. The relative importance of each sector is indicated in Table 4.1, which lists the share of national income that originated in each sector for the years 1958 and 1978.[1] These figures can be interpreted from both static and dynamic perspectives. From a static perspective, manufacturing is the dominant sector in the economy, accounting for approximately one-fourth of all economic activity. The trade and government sectors are next in size, with approximately one-sixth of national income. From a dynamic perspective, the relative importance of each sector can change over time. During this 20-year period, for example, the manufacturing sector has declined in relative importance, while the service and government sectors have increased.

Table 4.1 also includes information on the competitive structure of

Table 4.1   The Structure of the American Economy

Sector	Percentage of National Income		Breakdown of National Income by Market Structure, 1958		
	1958	1978	Workably Competitive	Effectively Monopolistic	Government-Controlled
Agriculture, forestry & fisheries	5.0	3.1	4.3		.7
Mining	1.5	1.5	1.2	.2	
Construction	5.4	5.0	5.4		
Manufacturing	28.2	26.0	17.6	10.7	
Transportation	4.5	3.9			4.5
Communication	1.9	2.3		.2	1.6
Public utilities	2.0	2.0			2.0
Wholesale and retail trade	16.6	14.8	14.8	1.8	
Finance, insurance & real estate	10.2	11.9	7.3	3.0	
Services	11.4	13.9	11.4		
Government and government enterprises	12.7	14.5			12.7
Rest of world	.6	1.2			
Total	100.0[a]	100.0[a]	62.0	15.9	21.5

[a] Total may not add up to 100% because of rounding off.

Sources: 1. Henry A. Einhorn, "Competition in American Industry, 1939-58," *Journal of Political Economy* 74 (October 1966): 507, Table 1.
2. U.S. Department of Commerce, *Survey of Current Business*, July 1979, Table 6.3, p.53.

1. National income is the income earned by the factors of production in the economy. Gross national product is equal to national income plus indirect business taxes and depreciation.

the American economy in 1958. These data are from a study by Einhorn, who grouped domestic industries into three categories: workably competitive, effectively monopolistic, and government-controlled.[2] An industry was considered to be "workably competitive" if the four largest firms produced less than 50 percent of industry output, and "effectively monopolistic" if they produced 50 percent or more. The "government" category includes government production and regulation of goods and services.[3] Einhorn's data indicate that 62.0 percent of national income originated in workably competitive industries, while 15.9 percent originated in effectively monopolistic industries. The government sector accounted for the remaining 21.5 percent of national income.

Even though Einhorn's results are necessarily based on subjective evaluations, they are consistent with previous studies in two important respects.[4] First, it would be incorrect to characterize the American economy as "monopoly" capitalism. The majority of economic activity occurs in markets that are workably competitive, although there is a substantial monopoly element in the economy. As a general rule of thumb, one-half of the economy could be considered competitive, one-fourth monopolistic, and one-fourth government-controlled. Second, there is no pronounced trend toward increased monopoly in the economy. Some industries become more competitive, while others become less so. All in all, it is very unlikely that there will be a significant expansion or contraction of the monopoly sector in the near future.

The Manufacturing Sector

Einhorn's analysis emphasizes the crucial role played by the manufacturing sector in determining the overall competitive structure of the American economy. In 1958, this sector accounted for approximately one-fourth of national income, but two-thirds of the nation's "monopoly problem." Not surprisingly, there is considerable diversity within this important sector. Table 4.2 documents the diversity in seller concentration among manufacturing industries in 1972. The majority of industries are relatively unconcentrated, with four-firm concentration ratios of less than 40; 17 percent of them, on the other hand, are relatively concen-

2. Henry A. Einhorn, "Competition in American Industry, 1939–58," *Journal of Political Economy* 74 (October 1966): 506–11.

3. These topics are covered later in Chapters 11–15 and 18.

4. M. A. Adelman, "The Measurement of Industrial Concentration," *Review of Economics and Statistics* 33 (November 1951): 269–96; G. Warren Nutter, *The Extent of Enterprise Monopoly in the United States: 1899–1939* (Chicago: University of Chicago Press, 1951).

Table 4.2   Distribution of Manufacturing Industries by Four-firm Sales Concentration Ratios, 1972

Four-firm Concentration Ratio Range	Number of Industries	Percentage of All Industries[a]
0-19	87	19.3
20-39	168	37.3
40-59	118	26.2
60-79	55	12.2
80-100	22	4.9

[a] Total may not add up to 100% because of rounding off.

Source: F.M. Scherer, *Industrial Market Structure and Economic Performance*, 2nd ed. (Chicago: Rand McNally, 1980), Table 3.6, p. 68.

trated, with ratios of at least 60. This leaves approximately one-fourth of the industries in the middle, with concentration ratios between 40 and 59.[5]

Because of the importance of the manufacturing sector, considerable attention has been focused on possible competitive or monopolistic trends. A recent study by Mueller and Hamm, for example, suggests that manufacturing may have become more monopolistic from 1947 to 1970.[6] This conclusion is questionable, however, since the study ignored the increasingly important role played by imports in the American economy. From 1963 to 1975, for example, the percentage of imports in automobile sales increased from 2.6 to 21.7 percent.[7] Unless the government restricts imports through tariffs or quotas, imports can reduce the monopoly power possessed by many American industries.

Aggregate Concentration

One final, and very controversial, dimension of the economy's structure is *aggregate concentration*. Whereas the concept of market concentration focuses on how a few firms may dominate a particular economic

5. A four-firm concentration ratio of 50 is frequently considered to be the minimum necessary for collusion. Industries with concentration levels around this figure are considered to be in a "gray zone" between the concentration levels necessary for workable competition and for effective monopoly.

6. Willard F. Mueller and Larry G. Hamm, "Trends in Industrial Market Concentration, 1947 to 1970," *Review of Economics and Statistics* 56 (November 1974): 511-20.

7. Frank Kottke, *The Promotion of Price Competition Where Sellers Are Few* (Lexington, Mass.: Lexington Books, 1978), p. 104.

Table 4.3 **Share of Corporate Manufacturing Assets Held by the 200 Largest Corporations, 1929.-1978**

Year	Share Held by 100 Largest	Share Held by 200 Largest
1929	39.7	47.7
1931	43.4	50.9
1935	42.3	49.6
1941	39.6	46.7
1947	39.3	47.2
1950	39.8	47.7
1954	43.3	52.1
1958	47.1	56.6
1963	46.5	56.3
1968	49.3	60.9
1971	48.9	61.0
1978	45.5	58.3

Sources: 1. U.S. Federal Trade Commission, *Economic Report on Corporate Mergers* (Washington, D.C.: Government Printing Office, 1969), p. 173.
2. U.S. Department of Commerce, *Statistical Abstract of the United States, 1979* (Washington, D.C.: Government Printing Office, 1979), Table 952, p. 573.

activity, aggregate concentration examines how a group of firms may dominate overall economic activity. Table 4.3 presents the shares of manufacturing assets held by the top 100 and 200 firms for selected years from 1929 to 1978. Two things about these aggregate concentration ratios should be emphasized. First, the top 200 corporations constitute a very small percentage of all manufacturing corporations. In 1976, for example, there were approximately 214,000 active corporations in the manufacturing sector.[8] This means that less than one percent of the corporations (the top 200) controlled approximately one-half the assets! Second, aggregate concentration has been increasing, but at an uneven pace. In 1929, the top 100 corporations held 39.7 percent of all corporate manufacturing assets, while the top 200 controlled 47.7 percent. By 1971, these figures had increased to 48.9 percent for the top 100 and 61.0 percent for the top 200. Aggregate concentration did, however, decline after 1971.

Although these figures are striking, their implications for the American economy are not clear. First, no direct relationship has been estab-

8. U.S. Department of Commerce, *Statistical Abstract of the United States, 1979* (Washington, D.C.: Government Printing Office, 1979), p. 553.

lished between aggregate concentration and market competition. If aggregate concentration is to affect market performance, it must operate through market structure or conduct. There has been much conjecture about such relationships, but little empirical support.[9] Second, aggregate concentration figures refer to control over all manufacturing assets, foreign as well as domestic. It is not known whether control over domestic assets has increased during this time period. It is likely that aggregate concentration has increased because the ownership of foreign assets is highly concentrated among the top 200 corporations. Third, dominant firms may lessen competition by manipulating the political process. Possibly, new legislation benefits these firms at the expense of their smaller, less politically powerful, competitors. As will be shown throughout the book, however, the best manipulators of the political process may very well be small, independent businesses. In sum, there is little concrete information on the economic impact of aggregate concentration. Most attention, at both the domestic and the foreign level, has focused on the potential for abusing the political process.

The Antitrust Laws

Three laws, with their numerous amendments, constitute the statutory foundation of American antitrust policy. These laws are the Sherman Act (1890), the Clayton Act (1914), and the Federal Trade Commission Act (1914).[10] All three laws define antitrust violations, while the Federal Trade Commission Act also established the Federal Trade Commission (FTC) as an enforcer of antitrust and consumer protection legislation.[11] This section examines the history and goals of these antitrust laws and then analyzes some of their major provisions.[12]

Historical Background

It is not surprising that the first antitrust law, the Sherman Act, was passed during the late 1800s. This period witnessed a dramatic alteration of the American industrial landscape. The industrial revolution in-

9. Some of these issues are addressed in the Chapter 7 discussion of the competitive aspects of conglomerate mergers.

10. Excerpts from these three laws are presented in the appendix to this chapter.

11. The Federal Trade Commission's consumer protection activities are discussed in Chapter 17.

12. For a more detailed discussion of the background of America's antitrust program, see Hans B. Thorelli, *The Federal Antitrust Policy* (Stockholm: Stockholms Högskola, 1954).

troduced new production processes and new forms of business organization that substantially increased the size of firms. At the same time, larger markets were created as a result of the post-Civil War expansion of the nation's railroad system. The end result was the demise of small local firms and the creation of large national firms.

The stage was thus set for intense competition among these industrial giants. But the expected competition was frequently eliminated through the creation of a *trust*, a legal device by which property is controlled by one group for the benefit of another group. This device was inaugurated in 1879 by Samuel Dodd, a lawyer employed by John D. Rockefeller.[13] In an *industrial trust*, two or more companies transfer control over their stock to the directors of the trust. The directors can then control these separate companies without violating any prohibitions against one corporation's owning stock in another corporation. In this way, a trust can control all the firms in a market, thereby eliminating competition among ostensibly independent firms.

Rockefeller subsequently used the trust device successfully to dominate the refining of petroleum products in the United States. His oil trust was not alone, however, for trusts quickly came to control the sugar, tobacco, and gunpowder industries. The rise of these industrial trusts led to a decrease in market competition and an increase in anticompetitive practices. Trusts were accused of eliminating small competitors by means of localized price wars and preferential treatment from the railroads. Small businesses and farmers found themselves paying higher prices for railroad services and goods that the trusts produced. These abuses by the trusts, along with the notoriety created by their wealthy owners, nicknamed the "Robber Barons," led to public demand for action by the federal government.[14]

The federal government responded to this populist uprising by passing the Interstate Commerce Act (1887) and the Sherman Act (1890). The Interstate Commerce Act established the Interstate Commerce Commission and initiated government regulation of the railroads. The Sherman Act was the first federal antitrust law and, among other provisions, made it illegal for a trust to monopolize a market. It should be stressed that federal antitrust action was necessary since state actions had been ineffective; a firm could always leave one state for one with less restrictive laws. This was convincingly illustrated by the intense

13. For a discussion of this and other types of business associations, see H. H. Liebhafsky, *American Government and Business* (New York: Wiley, 1971), Chapter 9.

14. For anecdotal stories about this exciting time period, see Matthew Josephson, *The Robber Barons* (New York: Harcourt, Brace & World, 1962).

competition that developed between New Jersey and Delaware in trying to offer the most lenient corporate charters.[15]A federal antitrust law eliminated this problem by establishing a nationwide rule against anticompetitive agreements.

Interestingly enough, the trust device became obsolete even before the Sherman Act was passed! When New Jersey legalized intercorporate stock ownership, *holding companies* became a more efficient technique for controlling two or more corporations. Nonetheless, the term "antitrust" is still used to describe laws that promote competition, and federal enforcers of the antitrust laws are still referred to as "trustbusters."

The Sherman Act was supplemented in 1914 by the Clayton and the Federal Trade Commission acts. These laws were enacted in the belief that the Sherman Act could attack existing trusts, but not prevent the creation of new ones.[16] The House and the Senate disagreed over the appropriate solution, however. The House wanted to prohibit specific practices that were believed to create monopoly power, thereby preventing the formation of monopolies. The Senate, on the other hand, thought that absolute prohibitions could always be evaded by creative business owners, and that an expert agency was the only solution. The congressional compromise was the passage of both the Clayton and the Federal Trade Commission acts. The former prohibited specific practices whose effect "may be substantially to lessen competition," while the latter empowered the FTC to outlaw "unfair methods of competition."

These three laws have been amended repeatedly in response to real or perceived threats to competition in the American economy. Two of the more famous amendments are the Robinson-Patman Act (1936, price discrimination) and the Celler-Kefauver Act (1950, mergers). Both these amendments were heavily influenced by Federal Trade Commission reports on the anticompetitive nature of chain stores and mergers.[17] Through such amendments, it is possible to adapt the antitrust laws to the changing needs of the American economy.

15. In 1974, Delaware was the "corporate home" for 448 of Fortune's 1,000 largest corporations. Corporation franchise taxes are a major source of state income, enabling Delaware to remain one of the few states without a sales tax. (Ralph Nader, Mark Green, and Joel Seligman, *Taming the Giant Corporation* [New York: Norton, 1976], p. 57.)

16. A. D. Neale, *The Antitrust Laws of the U.S.A.*, 2nd ed. (London: Cambridge University Press, 1970), pp. 178-80.

17. Federal Trade Commission, *Chain Stores: Final Report on the Chain Store Investigation* (Washington, D.C.: U.S. Government Printing Office, 1935) and *Report on the Concentration of Productive Facilities, 1947* (Washington, D.C.: Government Printing Office, 1949).

Goals

The primary goal of the antitrust laws is to promote competition. As stated by Justice Hugo Black in a 1958 Supreme Court decision, there are many advantages to competition.

> The Sherman Act was designed to be a comprehensive charter of economic liberty aimed at preserving free and unfettered competition as the rule of trade. It rests on the premise that the unrestrained interaction of competitive forces will yield the best allocation of our economic resources, the lowest prices, the highest quality and the greatest material progress, while at the same time providing an environment conducive to the preservation of our democratic political and social institutions.[18]

Justice Black thus recognized the role of competition in achieving both static and dynamic efficiency. Competition leads to the optimal allocation of society's resources across markets and the minimization of costs within each market. It also maximizes dynamic efficiency—the rate of technological progress. At the same time, competition promotes equity, eliminating the income inequality generated by monopoly profits and minimizing artificial restraints that limit economic opportunity.

Competition can also be consistent with the attainment of other social goals such as democracy. The dispersion of economic power makes it more difficult for any group to abuse the political process. On the other hand, social goals may conflict with the economic goal of competition. The Supreme Court reached the following conclusion in evaluating the Celler-Kefauver Amendment to the Clayton Act.

> It is competition, not competitors, which the Act protects. But we cannot fail to recognize Congress' desire to promote competition through the protection of viable, small, locally owned businesses. Congress appreciated that occasional higher costs and prices might result from the maintenance of fragmented industries and markets. It resolved these competing considerations in favor of decentralization. We must give effect to that decision.[19]

This populist theme was again evident in a recent bill before Congress entitled the "Small and Independent Business Protection Act."[20] In short, the primary antitrust goal of promoting competition may sometimes be modified in order to attain other goals important to society.

18. *Northern Pacific Railway Company v. United States*, 356 U.S. 1, 4 (1958).

19. *Brown Shoe Co. v. United States*, 370 U.S. 294, 344 (1962).

20. Kenneth W. Dam, "Kennedy's 'Big Is Bad' Bill," *Wall Street Journal*, May 22, 1979, p. 26.

Major Provisions

The antitrust laws represent America's commitment to competition in the marketplace. The impact of these laws depends heavily on three related legal issues: jurisdiction, standing, and remedy. Jurisdiction refers to the applicability of the federal antitrust laws to various types of economic activity. Assuming that the laws apply, an individual's right to sue under these laws is called *standing*, and the relief that may be obtained is known as the *remedy*.

Jurisdiction.   The antitrust laws are based on the federal government's constitutional authority to regulate commerce among the states and with foreign countries. As a result, they can apply only to activities involving interstate or foreign commerce. The Supreme Court has played a very important role in defining this "commerce" requirement. In its first antitrust case, the Court ruled that manufacturing by itself was not commerce and so could not be attacked under the Sherman Act![21] The Supreme Court subsequently modified this position, and "commerce" now includes most forms of economic activity. In general, the antitrust laws apply whenever an action has a direct or indirect effect on interstate commerce. This broad construction of the interstate commerce requirement means that even purely intrastate activities can be attacked under the federal antitrust laws.[22]

An area of rapidly increasing importance, but of unknown dimensions, is the application of American antitrust laws to foreign commerce. The antitrust laws apply to actions taken outside the United States that substantially affect domestic commerce, such as agreements among foreign firms to limit imports to the United States.[23] On the other hand, actions that are compelled by foreign laws or are performed by foreign governments in their sovereign capacity are not subject to the American antitrust laws.[24] This defense is very important, as much of the world does not share the American enthusiasm for increasing market competition. Britain, Canada, Australia, and West Germany, in fact, have passed

21. *United States* v. *E.C. Knight Co.*, 156 U.S. 1 (1895).

22. In *McLain* v. *Real Estate Board Inc.*, 62 L. Ed. 2d 27 (1980), the Supreme Court ruled that the activities of local real estate brokers affect interstate commerce and therefore are subject to the federal antitrust laws.

23. *United States* v. *Aluminum Company of America*, 148 F.2d 416 (1945).

24. See the Foreign Sovereign Immunities Act of 1976, PL 94-583, October 21, 1976.

laws prohibiting their citizens from cooperating with American antitrust investigations![25]

Standing. One unique aspect of the Sherman and Clayton acts is the provision for private antitrust suits. Under Section 4 of the Clayton Act, a private individual or corporation who has been "injured in his business or property by reason of anything forbidden in the antitrust laws" can initiate a civil suit under the Sherman and Clayton acts.[26] Standing has also been extended to state, local, and foreign governments. These suits can supplement the federal government's efforts, thereby increasing the enforcement of the antitrust laws.

Private suits related to a government action are encouraged by a provision that final judgments won by the federal government constitute *prima facie evidence* of an antitrust violation. Prima facie evidence is a fact from which some legal conclusion can be drawn. In this case, a government victory, indicating a violation of the antitrust laws, creates a presumption in the related private case that the defendant has violated the antitrust laws. This shifts the burden of proof to the defendant and encourages invididuals to initiate private suits. A dramatic illustration of this side effect occurred after the government's 1962 victory in a price-fixing suit against manufacturers of electrical equipment. The manufacturers became defendants in more than 2,000 private antitrust actions![27]

These antitrust suits must be "timely,"or initiated before the statute of limitations has expired. (A *statute of limitations* establishes a time period within which a suit must be initiated or the plaintiff will lose the right to bring an action.) For private civil suits, the time limit is four years; for criminal suits it is five years; but there is *no* statute of limitations for government civil suits. Moreover, the private statute of limitations is suspended whenever the government initiates a suit charging violations of the antitrust laws. The suspension period lasts for one year past the date when the final decision is entered in the case. This covers the entire time from the filing of the suit through the exhaustion of all appeals. The purpose of this suspension of the statute of limitations is to encourage private suits.

25. "Multinational Antitrust Violators Told by Bell They'll Be Pursued Outside U.S.," *Wall Street Journal,* August 9, 1977, p. 12.

26. The injury must have resulted from a violation of the antitrust laws and not simply any business practice. See *Brunswick Corp.* v. *Pueblo Bowl-O-Mat, Inc.,* 429 U.S. 477 (1977).

27. Richard A. Posner, "A Statistical Study of Antitrust Enforcement," *Journal of Law and Economics* 13 (October 1970): 371.

Table 4.4   Plaintiffs in Antitrust Cases, 1890–1969

Time Period	Department of Justice	Federal Trade Commission[a]	Private[b]
1890–1899	16	—	16
1900–1909	45	—	74
1910–1919	134	206	109
1920–1929	125	237	80
1930–1939	87	177	144
1940–1949	380	150	669
1950–1959	354	149	2,146
1960–1969	410	145	6,490
Total	1,551	1,064	9,728

[a] Excludes Robinson-Patman cases that do not allege predatory pricing.
[b] Figures up to 1939 are estimates, and the total for 1940–1949 does not include cases initiated in 1940.
Source: Richard A. Posner, "A Statistical Study of Antitrust Enforcement," *Journal of Law and Economics* 13 (October 1970): 366, 369, 371.

The importance of private antitrust suits is indicated in Table 4.4, which lists the number of private and government cases initiated since the passage of the Sherman Act in 1890. Since the period 1945–1949, private suits have increasingly outnumbered government suits. The explosion in private antitrust activity is illustrated by the legal experiences of International Business Machines (IBM), the leading manufacturer of computers. Nineteen antitrust suits, including a major one by the Justice Department, have been filed against IBM.[28] There is even a firm that publishes a newsletter informing subscribers of the most recent antitrust developments involving IBM!

Remedy.   Violations of the Sherman Act can be criminal as well as civil offenses, while violations of the Clayton Act are civil offenses only. The relief obtainable thus depends on the plaintiff initiating the suit and on the statute(s) involved in the suit. Only the Justice Department, acting in its capacity to protect the public, can prosecute criminal cases under the Sherman Act. The rationale behind criminal penalties is that the offender should be punished for wrongs committed against society. In civil suits, the remedies are not designed to punish, but to redress a private wrong that has been committed. In practice, this is an arbitrary distinction, and it is difficult to apply because the government can also initiate

28. "An Antitrust Breakthrough for IBM," *Business Week*, August 28, 1978, p. 31.

civil suits. Indeed, a given violation of the Sherman Act may constitute both a civil and a criminal offense.

Two types of criminal penalities are available under the Sherman Act: fines and imprisonment. Violations of the Sherman Act are felonies, and private individuals can be fined a maximum of $100,000 and incarcerated a maximum of three years. The specific corporations involved in the crimes can be fined up to $1 million per violation.

Two types of remedies also are available to both the government and private plaintiffs in civil suits: equitable relief and damages. Equitable relief consists of court orders (injunctions) that affect the defendant's future behavior. Injunctions can prohibit or command specific actions by the defendant. Injunctive relief is very inclusive and can even require the defendant to divide into two or more independent corporations.[29] This type of relief is called *dissolution* and can be obtained only by the Justice Department acting on behalf of the public.

Monetary damages are designed to compensate the plaintiff for the illegal actions of the defendant. Private plaintiffs as well as foreign governments are entitled to treble damages (three times the damages that resulted from the antitrust violation) plus reasonable attorney's fees and court costs. The federal government, however, is limited by statute to recovering only single damages in its civil antitrust suits. Treble damage awards provide a substantial financial incentive for private enforcement of the antitrust laws and are generally credited with increasing the number of private suits throughout the 1960s and 1970s. A good example is Telex's private antitrust suit against IBM.[30] Telex initially was awarded total damages of $352.5 million, which were subsequently reduced to $259.5 million. Unfortunately for Telex, the district court's decision was overturned by the appellate court, but IBM's counterclaim for $18.5 million was upheld. IBM and Telex then settled out of court before the Supreme Court announced whether it would hear Telex's appeal of the appellate court's decision. An interesting footnote to this case is that Telex's side was handled by a Texas lawyer, Floyd Walker, on a contingency fee basis.[31] If the suit were successful, Walker was to receive a percentage of the damage award; otherwise he would receive nothing. After the district court's decision, his share was $50 million, but that quickly disappeared with the out-of-court settlement with IBM.

---

29. As will be noted in Chapter 5, however, this type of relief is very rare.

30. *Telex Corp.* v. *International Business Machines*, 510 F.2d 894 (1975).

31. "When Lawyer Loses His $50 Million Fee, What Does He Do?," *Wall Street Journal*, October 26, 1976, p. 1.

Walker promptly turned around and sued his former employer, Telex, for $1.5 million!

The Enforcement Agencies

The major differences between the two federal enforcement agencies—the Federal Trade Commission (FTC) and the Justice Department—are organizational structure and jurisdiction. The Justice Department is part of the executive branch of the government; the FTC is an independent agency. The Antitrust Division of the Justice Department thus initiates antitrust suits in the federal court system, whereas the FTC initiates in-house proceedings. With respect to jurisdiction, Justice can initiate suits under both the Sherman and the Clayton acts. The FTC, on the other hand, is technically limited to enforcing the Clayton and the FTC acts, although Supreme Court decisions suggest that the FTC can also attack Sherman Act offenses as "unfair methods of competition."

The Justice Department

The Justice Department's antitrust activities are performed by its Antitrust Division. This specialized division was established in 1903, reflecting the importance placed on antitrust policy. The Antitrust Division is run by an assistant attorney general who reports to the attorney general, who is in turn responsible to the president of the United States. The president can thus influence antitrust enforcement policy through the selection of an attorney general.

Antitrust enforcement by the Justice Department begins with investigations of possible antitrust violations. An investigation of a firm or a group of firms may be started for a variety of reasons. First, the Antitrust Division may receive a complaint from the public that an antitrust violation has occurred. (The division encourages public tips of possible antitrust violations and has even used an antitrust hot line with a toll-free number for informants![32]) Second, firms are encouraged to disclose possible antitrust violations voluntarily in exchange for a more lenient treatment from the division. Finally, the division's staff conducts research that may lead to investigations.

The investigative techniques employed by the division depend on whether the expected antitrust violation is civil or criminal. In criminal investigations, the division can gather information by calling a grand

32. "Antitrust Hotline Started in New England by U.S.," *Wall Street Journal*, June 7, 1978, p. 6.

jury to investigate the potential violations.[33] It can then utilize the grand jury's extensive powers to compel witnesses to testify and produce relevant documents. It is not so easy to obtain information in civil investigations where grand juries cannot be used. As a result, Congress has empowered the division to issue civil investigative demands (CIDs). CIDs can compel firms suspected of violations, along with their competitors and customers, to submit documents related to those violations. Although a firm might voluntarily permit a division lawyer or an FBI agent to examine its business files, it is highly unlikely in most instances, for the constitutional protection against self-incrimination does not apply to corporations.

If the Antitrust Division believes that a violation has occurred, it files a complaint with the federal district court where the case will be tried. This initiates legal proceedings and enables the government to obtain evidence through the normal channels of criminal and civil procedure. The defendant in a criminal suit has a constitutional right to a jury trial, while both parties in private suits can request a jury trial. The big issue in a jury trial always is determining which issues will be submitted to the jury for resolution. As discussed in Chapter 3, the district court establishes the basic facts and reaches a decision by applying the relevant legal precedents.

The district court's decision can be appealed to an appeals court or, in some cases, directly to the Supreme Court. An expedited appeal is possible if the district court trial judge determines that the case is of "sufficient importance."[34] In criminal cases, the government cannot appeal adverse decisions; only the defendant can. If the government loses at any stage of the case, the suit is over. This is not true in civil suits, where both parties have the right to appeal a lower court's decision. This difference in the right to appeal is one reason why the division may file concurrent civil and criminal suits in a Sherman Act case. The civil part of the case guarantees that the government can appeal an adverse district court decision. This is especially important if the case is novel and will expand current case law, for the district court can be expected to strictly adhere to Supreme Court decisions. Given the legal principle of *stare decisis*, the division generally expects to lose at the district court level, and to win—if at all—on appeal to the Supreme Court.

33. A grand jury has broad powers to investigate possible crimes and, if the evidence warrants it, issue indictments that accuse people of committing those crimes. Those people will then be bound over for trial.

34. Antitrust Procedures and Penalties Act of 1974, PL 93-528, December 24, 1974.

When a case is appealed to the Supreme Court, that judgment is final. If the Court supports the government's contention that an antitrust violation has occurred, it remands the case to the district court for a determination of the appropriate remedy. The district court hears opposing arguments from the government and the defendant before fashioning the appropriate relief. Its relief decree, like the original trial decision, can also be appealed as high as the Supreme Court.

It should be apparent that litigation of antitrust cases can be a very lengthy process. Antitrust suits can, however, be settled out of court. This is common at the pre-trial stage, where a negotiated settlement eliminates the need for a trial. Nonlitigated settlements in civil cases are called *consent decrees*. The criminal counterpart is a plea of *nolo contendere*. Neither type of decree constitutes an admission of a violation of the antitrust laws and consequently cannot be used as prima facie evidence in related private suits. The *nolo* plea is, however, generally considered to be a tacit admission of guilt because the defendant does not contest the charges and submits to the "mercy of the court." Consent decrees must be accepted by the court in which the suit was initiated, while *nolo* pleas must be accepted by the Justice Department. Once a decree is accepted, it cannot subsequently be modified without the approval of both parties to the decree. Judges view decrees as contracts and are reluctant to approve unilateral requests for changes. If the defendant violates the provisions of the decree, the Justice Department can initiate criminal contempt proceedings that will force compliance.

The Justice Department relies heavily on nonlitigated settlements to dispose of antitrust cases. From 1965 to 1969, consent decrees accounted for 90 percent of the civil antitrust judgments, while *nolo contendere* pleas accounted for 87 percent of the criminal convictions.[35] By reducing the time it takes to dispose of a case, nonlitigated settlements enable the Antitrust Division to process a larger case load with its limited resources. There is a trade-off involved, however, as it is extremely unlikely that a consent decree will provide the same remedy that could be obtained through litigation. The decree's provisions depend on the evidence available, the type of case, and, perhaps most important, the bargaining prowess of the Antitrust Division vis-à-vis the defendant.

Another method of reducing litigation is the division's business review procedure. A firm can ask the Antitrust Division about the legality of a proposed course of action. The division can guarantee the firm that it will not initiate *criminal* proceedings in the future. This is known as a

35. Posner, "A Statistical Study," pp. 375, 390.

"railroad release" and limits the firm's future legal liability to civil actions. The problem is that a firm will ask for advice only when the law is unclear, and this is where the division is the most reluctant to commit itself. A firm could probably obtain the identical advice from its in-house legal staff without alerting the antitrust authorities to possible future violations.

The Federal Trade Commission

The Federal Trade Commission (FTC) was established in 1914 by the Federal Trade Commission Act. Its five commissioners oversee the commission's diverse responsibilities in antitrust enforcement and consumer protection. Its ability to fulfill its legislative mandates is aided by its powers to gather information. The FTC can conduct industry investigations and require firms to submit specialized data. It has recently instituted a "line of business" program that requires major firms to report detailed sales and profit data. This investigative authority substantially exceeds that of the Justice Department and can be used to formulate commission policy and uncover possible antitrust violations.[36]

The FTC can initiate antitrust investigations on its own volition or on the basis of private complaints. Private complaints historically have played a major role in allocating the commission's antitrust resources. If the evidence warrants it, the FTC staff files a formal complaint. The case is adjudicated before an administrative law judge who determines the facts, analyzes the law, and issues a final decision. If the decision is that the antitrust laws have been violated, the judge issues a cease and desist order. This order is analogous to an injunction and prohibits the defendant from continuing the illegal practices in the future. The commission cannot impose the criminal penalties of fines or imprisonment and cannot provide structural relief such as dissolution.[37] It can, however, impose a maximum fine of $10,000 per day for each violation of a cease and desist order.[38] It should be noted that cease and desist orders do not constitute prima facie evidence of an antitrust violation for related private suits. This presents the interesting possibility that a firm

36. The FTC can also investigate possible relief decrees for Justice Department cases if they are requested to do so.

37. As discussed in Chapter 6, however, the FTC is seeking the divestiture of refining and pipeline assets in its current proceeding against the oil companies.

38. In addition, the FTC can ask the court to issue an injunction requiring a firm to comply with its order. If a firm continues to violate the order, it can then be held in contempt of court and subject to criminal penalties.

might prefer to be sued by the FTC rather than the Justice Department, where a conviction would constitute prima facie evidence.

The administrative law judge's decision can be appealed to the full commission by both the defendant and the FTC's staff attorneys. The commissioners can affirm, reverse, or modify the administrative law judge's decision. Once the internal appeals process is exhausted, the FTC's final decision can be appealed to an appellate court and finally to the Supreme Court itself. The same standards for judicial review apply. It is assumed that the findings of fact are correct unless there were violations of the due-process requirements. The primary judicial focus is on the commission's application of the relevant law in pursuit of its legislative mandate.

The FTC also has procedures for settling antitrust complaints that do not require a formal adjudicatory hearing. An investigation can be terminated if the firm being investigated submits an "assurance of voluntary compliance" to the FTC. The firm states that it will discontinue the practices under investigation, thereby eliminating the need for further investigation and possible adjudication. Once an investigation is concluded, the complaint may be settled through a *consent order*—the FTC's version of a consent decree. A firm has 10 days from the filing of a formal complaint to decide whether it will contest the action or seek a consent order. If the firm negotiates a consent order with the FTC, the consent order has the same legal standing as a cease and desist order, and the firm can be fined for violating its conditions. Finally, the FTC has a preventive program similar to the Justice Department's business review procedure. The commission will give a firm an advisory opinion that protects the firm from litigation unless it is rescinded. This program is also not very useful, however, because the immunity is limited and most firms are reluctant to draw attention to their activities.

The FTC's most important antitrust weapon, however, may be the issuance of trade regulation rules, not the adjudication of individual cases.[39] These rules are specific to a given industry and prohibit practices that the FTC believes to be clear violations of the antitrust laws. A firm that violates one of these rules can be fined a maximum of $10,000 a day. Through trade regulation rules, the commission can establish policy in a single step and avoid the inherent delays in case-by-case litigation. This approach has been used extensively in the consumer

---

39. The FTC's authority to issue trade regulation rules may be substantially modified by the Congress. For a discussion of the relevant issues, see Chapter 19.

protection area and has only recently been used by the FTC to enforce the antitrust laws.[40]

As noted earlier, the federal antitrust laws apply to actions that directly or indirectly affect interstate commerce. This jurisdictional requirement is sufficiently broad to encompass most economic activities, and federal jurisdiction rarely is contested in antitrust proceedings. Some economic activities, however, are exempt from federal antitrust laws. These activities have received immunity through special legislation or, less frequently, through judicial interpretation. This section presents some of the more important and famous antitrust exemptions.[41]

Antitrust Exemptions

Agriculture

In an effort to help farmers receive "fair" prices for their products, Congress has exempted two main types of economic activity: agricultural cooperatives and federal marketing orders. The exemption for cooperatives enables farmers to perform collectively such business activities as processing and marketing their products. It was hoped that this would minimize farmers' reliance on intermediate processors or distributors who might take advantage of them. Federal marketing orders secure higher prices for farmers by directly restricting their production or, as in the case of milk, directly setting a product price. (In the case of milk, the government establishes the minimum prices both for fluid milk sold for drinking and for milk used in producing powdered milk and cheese.)

Export Trade Associations

The Webb-Pomerene Act of 1918 permits firms to combine in order to sell their products abroad. The rationale is that these associations could increase exports by using joint selling agencies in foreign countries. Export associations are legal as long as they do not restrain trade within the United States or adversely affect competitors that are not members. In practice, export associations are not very common and do not play a ma-

40. The FTC is, for example, establishing rules for different professions rather than attacking the alleged anticompetitive practices by initiating suits against each state professional association.

41. For a more detailed discussion of these and other exemptions, see U.S. Department of Justice, *Report of the Task Group on Antitrust Immunities* (Washington, D.C.: Government Printing Office, January 1977).

jor role in the export of American goods and services to foreign countries.

Government Enterprises

The government can participate directly in the marketplace as a buyer and seller of goods and services. The question raised by government enterprise is whether or not the government itself is subject to the antitrust laws. It presumably is legal for a government agency to lessen competition, as the government has the right to regulate private economic activity. An alternative approach, frequently used in the international arena, is to differentiate between government activities that are clearly political and those that are clearly commercial. Commercial activities would be subject to the antitrust laws, but political activities would be exempt. This is a new and complex issue that will have to be resolved by the courts and legislatures in the United States and foreign countries.

Labor Unions

By their very nature, labor unions restrain trade. A union restricts competition among its members in the areas of wages and fringe benefits. The objective is to obtain better compensation by offsetting the bargaining power of the employer. At the same time, unions may lessen competition in product markets. For instance, they may serve as a vehicle through which firms reach restrictive agreements. Or the unions themselves may restrict competition by boycotting labor-saving products such as prefabricated houses. In general, the antitrust exemption will apply only to those activities that the courts view as legitimate union functions.

Professional Sports Organizations

With the exception of baseball, professional sports teams have not been exempt from the federal antitrust laws. Baseball's unique position follows from the Supreme Court's rigid adherence to the principle of *stare decisis*. In 1922 the Court exempted baseball on the grounds that it was not commerce and was not interstate in character! This special exemption for baseball was supported in two subsequent cases, although it was not applied generally to other professional sports. Other sports organizations had to petition Congress for legislative exemptions so that they could merge (in the case of the American and National Basketball Associations) or could jointly offer broadcasting rights to the television networks (the National Football League).

Truck Transportation

Part of the nation's trucking industry has been regulated since 1935 by the Interstate Commerce Commission (ICC). This federal regulatory agency controls the entry of new firms into regulated trucking markets and approves the rates that may be charged for trucking services. Economic regulation of an industry may conflict with the goals of antitrust enforcement. This conflict can be resolved through a determination of *primary jurisdiction*: which agency has the primary responsibility for the economic activity in question? In the trucking industry, for example, mergers among trucking companies are subject to approval by the ICC but not by the Justice Department or the Federal Trade Commission. The exact resolution of conflicts among the different types of government intervention must by made by Congress or the Supreme Court.

Summary

The antitrust laws represent America's commitment to a competitive economy in which resources are allocated in response to market, not political, forces. The primary goal of antitrust enforcement is to promote competition by preserving and enhancing the natural competitive forces of the marketplace. The main responsibility for antitrust enforcement rests with the Justice Department and the Federal Trade Commission, though private treble damage suits are becoming more and more important. Antitrust suits can promote market competition by modifying market conduct and altering market structure. The antitrust laws do not apply, however, to economic activities exempted by special legislation or judicial interpretation.

Appendix A: Major Provisions of the Antitrust Laws

Sherman Act (1890)

1. Every contract, combination in the form of trust or otherwise, or conspiracy, in restraint of trade or commerce among the several States, or with foreign nations, is declared to be illegal. Every person who shall make any contract or engage in any combination or conspiracy hereby declared to be illegal shall be deemed guilty of a felony, and on conviction thereof, shall be punished by fine not exceeding one million dollars if a corporation, or, if any other person, one hundred thousand dollars,

or by imprisonment not exceeding three years, or by both said punishments, in the discretion of the court.

2. Every person who shall monopolize, or attempt to monopolize, or combine or conspire with any other person or persons, to monopolize any part of the trade or commerce among the several States, or with foreign nations, shall be deemed guilty of a felony, and, on conviction thereof, shall be punished by fine not exceeding one million dollars if a corporation, or, if any other person, one hundred thousand dollars, or by imprisonment not exceeding three years, or by both said punishments, in the discretion of the court.

4. The several district courts of the United States are hereby invested with jurisdiction to prevent and restrain violations of Sections 1 to 7 of this title; and it shall be the duty of the several United States attorneys, in their respective districts, under the direction of the Attorney General, to institute proceedings in equity to prevent and restrain such violations. . . .

8. The word "person", or "persons", wherever used in this . . . title shall be deemed to include corporations and associations. . . .

Clayton Act (1914)

2. (a) It shall be unlawful for any person engaged in commerce, in the course of such commerce, either directly or indirectly, to discriminate in price between different purchasers of commodities of like grade and quality, where either or any of the purchases involved in such discrimination are in commerce, . . . where the effect of such discrimination may be substantially to lessen competition or tend to create a monoply in any line of commerce, or to injure, destroy, or prevent competition with any person who either grants or knowingly receives the benefit of such discrimination, or with customers of either of them: *Provided,* That nothing herein contained shall prevent differentials which make only due allowance for differences in the cost of manufacture, sale, or delivery. . . . *And provided further,* That nothing herein contained shall prevent price changes from time to time where in response to changing conditions . . . such as but not limited to actual or imminent deterioration of perishable goods, obsolescence of seasonal goods, distress sales under court process, or sales in good faith in discontinuance of business in the goods . . . concerned.

(b) . . . nothing herein contained shall prevent a seller [from] showing that his lower price . . . was made in good faith to meet an equally low price of a competitor. . . .

3. It shall be unlawful for any person engaged in commerce, in the course of such commerce, to lease or make a sale or contract for sale of goods ... or other commodities ... on the condition, agreement, or understanding that the lessee or purchaser thereof shall not use or deal in the goods ... or other commodities of a competitor or competitors of the lessor or seller, where the effect of such lease, sale, or contract ... may be to substantially lessen competition or tend to create a monopoly in any line of commerce.

4. Any person who shall be injured in his business or property by reason of anything forbidden in the antitrust laws may sue ... without respect to the amount in controversy, and shall recover threefold the damages by him sustained, and the cost of suit, including a reasonable attorney's fee.

7. No corporation engaged in commerce shall acquire, directly or indirectly, the whole or any part of the stock or ... the whole or any part of the assets of another corporation engaged also in commerce, where in any line of commerce in any section of the country, the effect of such acquisition may be substantially to lessen competition, or to tend to create a monopoly.

Federal Trade Commission Act (1914)

5 (a) (1) Unfair methods of competition in or affecting commerce, and unfair or deceptive acts or practices in or affecting commerce, are declared unlawful.

Suggested Readings

Areeda, Phillip, and Turner, Donald F. *Antitrust Law* (Boston: Little, Brown, 1978).

Neale, A. D. *The Antitrust Laws of the U.S.A.*, 2nd ed. (London: Cambridge University Press, 1970).

Posner, Richard A. *Antitrust Law: An Economic Perspective* (Chicago: University of Chicago Press, 1976).

Thorelli, Hans B. *The Federal Antitrust Policy* (Stockholm: Stockholms Högskola, 1954).

Weaver, Suzanne. *Decision to Prosecute: Organization and Public Policy in the Antitrust Division* (Cambridge, Mass.: MIT Press, 1977).

Monopoly

Chapter
5

The monopoly problem is the raison d'être of the American antitrust program. The Sherman Act was passed in 1890 in response to the monopoly power of the industrial trusts, and public concern over monopolies continues to this day. Indeed, a suit against monopoly has become the classic antitrust case, in which the evils of monopoly are contrasted with the virtues of competition. It is also the most dramatic of all antitrust cases. The defendant commonly is a well-known corporation, which hires a prestigious law firm to defend its dominant market position. The end result is a lengthy and complex antitrust duel whose outcome can affect society in general and the defendant in particular.

The Setting

A *pure monopolist* is the only seller of a good for which there are no close substitutes. No other firms compete directly with a monopolist. In practice, this condition is rarely satisfied outside the regulated sector, where the government frequently limits entry.[1] Newspapers in smaller cities and towns probably come close to being monopolists, though even they face competition from metropolitan newspapers, national

1. See Chapter 12 for a discussion of the rationale behind government controls over entry into the trucking and airline industries.

magazines, and local radio stations.[2] There are, however, perhaps a dozen firms that clearly dominate their industries. Some examples would be Campbell Soup (canned soup), Boeing (commercial aircraft), International Business Machines (computers), and Xerox (copying machines). The "monopoly" problem in America consists of these dominant firms, not pure monopolists.

Legal Issues

The monopoly problem is addressed by Section 2 of the Sherman Act, which reads in part:

> Every person who shall monopolize, or attempt to monopolize, or
> combine or conspire with any other person or persons, to monopolize any
> part of the trade or commerce among the several States, or with foreign
> nations, shall be deemed guilty of a felony. . . .[3]

This section of the Sherman Act raises several legal issues that must be addressed by the courts. First, what is the relevant market? The act specifies "any part of the trade or commerce" but does not define these terms. This issue is important because a defendant's alleged market dominance depends on how its market is defined. Second, the act prohibits three different criminal offenses: successful monopolization, attempts to monopolize, and conspiracies to monopolize. The courts must establish the legal standards for each offense. Finally, the act does not prohibit monopolies per se, but rather the *act* of monopolizing. This implies that the possession of monopoly power is necessary, but not sufficient, for a monopolization conviction. Congress's refusal to outlaw monopolies explicitly reflected the public's general ambivalence toward them. Monopolies may abuse their market positions, but those positions resulted from their superior efficiency. As a result, the courts must determine what additional evidence is necessary to convict a monopolist of monopolizing its market.

In sum, Section 2 of the Sherman Act is very broad and requires substantial interpretation by the courts. This broad construction is similar to that used in constitutional amendments and is typical of antitrust laws. The courts are forced to create a "common law" of antitrust through their cumulative decisions.

2. In 1978, there was competition between separately owned newspapers in only 35 of the 1,536 cities with daily newspapers ("Newspaper Monopoly Assailed," *Washington Post*, December 16, 1978, p. C9).

3. The Sherman Act, 15 U.S.C. Sec. 2 (1976).

Assuming that a firm has violated Section 2 of the Sherman Act, the court also must fashion an appropriate remedy. The remedies available depend on the nature of the suit—civil or criminal or both. Because violations of the Sherman Act are felonies, criminal sanctions (fines and imprisonment) may be imposed if the Justice Department brought a criminal suit. In civil cases, the court can use its substantial equity powers to provide injunctive relief. The relief granted by the court should help deter future violations, while undoing the damage caused by the defendant's violation.

Economic Issues

Section 2 of the Sherman Act makes it illegal for a firm to monopolize a market. This prohibition raises two important economic questions. First, what is the rationale underlying this restriction on a firm's conduct? Second, what remedies are appropriate in monopolization cases? The answers to these two questions are essential for understanding and evaluating this crucial dimension of American antitrust enforcement.

Economic Performance of Monopolies.   The standard economic analysis of a monopoly is illustrated in Figure 5.1, which compares the monopoly and competitive solutions. A monopolist produces less output (Q_m) and charges a higher price (P_m) than if the industry were competitive (Q_c, P_c). As a result, the monopolist does not achieve static efficiency. It artificially restricts output and devotes too few resources to this market. It may not even minimize costs, for there is no competitive pressure to do so.[4] In this case, its average total costs are LRAC' and it will sell Q'_m units at a price of P'_m. At the same time, the monopolist earns profits that redistribute income from consumers to the monopolist's stockholders. This tranfer may worsen the inequalities in the distribution of income and wealth.[5]

As noted earlier, however, a more common situation in the real world is the existence of a *dominant firm* surrounded by a fringe of many small producers. This situation is illustrated in Figure 5.2. The fringe firms act like perfect competitors, and their market responses are cap-

4. All profit-maximizing firms, monopolists as well as perfect competitors, will minimize costs if they want to maximize profits. A monopolist, however, is not forced by competition to minimize costs and will not do so if it conflicts with other objectives. (See H. Leibenstein, "Allocative Efficiency vs. X-Efficiency," *American Economic Review* 56 [June 1966]: 392-415.)

5. William S. Comanor and Robert H. Smiley, "Monopoly and the Distribution of Wealth," *Quarterly Journal of Economics* 89 (May 1975): 177-94.

Figure 5.1   Monopoly

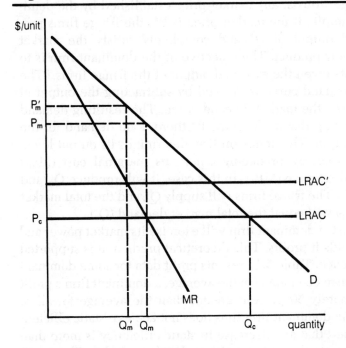

Figure 5.2   Dominant Firm

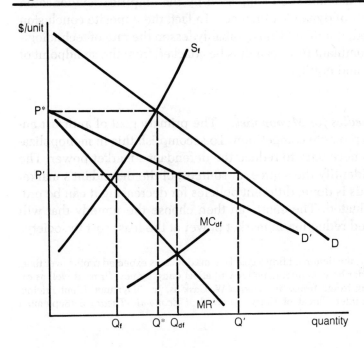

tured by the supply curve S_f. This supply curve indicates the combined output of the fringe firms at any market price established by the dominant firm. For example, if the market price is P*, the fringe firms produce a combined output of Q* and completely satisfy the market demand (D) for their product. The objective of the dominant firm is to maximize its profits given the expected output of the fringe firms.[6] The dominant firm's demand curve is derived by subtracting the output of the fringe firms from the market demand curve. The resulting demand curve is D', indicating that at the price P* there is no demand for the dominant firm's output. The dominant firm determines its output level, and the market price, by producing where its marginal cost (Mc_{df}) equals its marginal revenue (MR'). In this case, it will produce Q_{df} and charge a price of P'. The fringe firms will supply Q_f, and the total market supply (Q_f plus Q_{df}) will equal the total market demand (Q').

Like a monopolist, a dominant firm will exercise its market power and set a price that yields it profits. This theoretical prediction is supported by empirical evidence. Table 5.1 presents profit data for some dominant firms in the American economy. On the average, a dominant firm's profit rate was approximately 50 percent greater than the average for all of manufacturing. The dominant firm thus does not achieve static efficiency. It may be argued that any decrease in static efficiency is more than offset by an increase in dynamic efficiency, but (as noted in Chapter 2) this proposition has not been supported by the empirical evidence on the determinants of dynamic efficiency. In fact, the opposite conclusion seems warranted; dominant firms probably lessen the rate of technological progress. Dominant firms can thus be attacked from the standpoint of both efficiency and equity.

Economic Remedies for Monopolies.   The primary goal of antitrust enforcement is to promote competition. To accomplish this in monopolization cases, it is necessary to reduce the defendant's market power. The first step is to identify the source, or sources, of the defendant's market power. Once this is done, different policies for decreasing it can be proposed and evaluated. The court can then choose the remedy that will yield the desired reduction in market power at the least cost to society.

---

6. More technically, the dominant firm's goal is to maximize its expected profits over time. It must thus consider how its pricing policy will affect entry by new firms as well as expansion by existing fringe firms. See Darius W. Gaskins, Jr., "Dynamic Limit Pricing: Optimal Pricing Under Threat of Entry," *Journal of Economic Theory* 3 (September 1971): 306-22.

Table 5.1 Average Profit Rates of Dominant Firms, 1960–1970

Firm	Profits after Tax (Percentage of Sales)	Profits after Tax (Percentage of Equity)
IBM	13.0	17.6
Western Electric	4.7	10.7
Eastman Kodak	14.7	19.9
Caterpillar Tractor	8.1	17.2
Boeing	2.0	10.6
Xerox	13.3	22.5
Campbell Soup	6.9	12.5
Gillette	2.4	32.4
Ethyl	7.1	18.3
Los Angeles *Times-Mirror*	6.2	13.2
Timken	9.8	13.4
Joy Manufacturing	4.2	9.3
Knight Newspapers	6.6	13.0
William Wrigley, Jr.	10.0	14.0
Average	7.8	16.0
Average All Manufacturing	4.8	11.0

Source: Leonard W. Weiss, "The Concentration-Profits Relationship and Antitrust" in *Industrial Concentration: The New Learning* , ed. H. Goldschmid, H. Mann, and J. Weston (Boston: Little, Brown, 1974), Table 10, p. 187.

There are many avenues to market dominance, although in the United States, four sources of market power have been prominent: (1) efficiency; (2) scarce inputs; (3) business combination; and (4) government grants.[7] If a firm is more efficient than its competitors, it will have lower unit costs. It will then be able to underprice its rivals and expand its market share at their expense. A similar advantage may result if a firm has preferential access to a scarce input that is essential for the manufacture of its product. Through its control of this input, the firm can arbitrarily fix the market shares, if any, of its rivals. A more common approach is to dominate a market by combining small independent firms into a single larger firm. Indeed, the creation of industrial trusts in this way led to the passage of the Sherman Act. Finally, a firm may obtain market dominance through a grant by the government. The government may establish a prohibitive tariff and so eliminate foreign

7. A firm also may become a monopolist because of chance. It may simply have made the right decisions at the right times, while its rivals did not and went out of business. See Oliver E. Williamson, *Markets and Hierarchies: Analysis and Antitrust Implications* (New York: Free Press, 1975), Chap. 11.

competition, or grant an exclusive franchise and eliminate domestic competition.

These different sources of market power indicate that no single remedy is appropriate for all dominant firms. In some cases, competition may not be practical for economic or political reasons. Efficiency considerations may dictate that an entire market be served by a single seller.[8] Political considerations may mandate the curtailment of market competition.[9] Where competition is feasible, however, the solution is to increase the number of actual and potential competitors. This can be accomplished by modifying the dominant firm's structure or conduct or both. The number of actual competitors can be increased directly by simply dissolving the defendant into two or more independent firms. Or the number of actual and potential competitors can be increased indirectly by reducing any barriers to entry into the market. The defendant may be forced to stop anticompetitive practices and even to provide technical assistance (such as its patents) to new firms. The optimal combination of structural and conduct relief will vary with each market, and the court must tailor its remedy to fit the defendant's unique circumstances.

The Case Law

As noted earlier, Section 2 of the Sherman Act covers monopolizations as well as attempts and conspiracies to monopolize. Primary attention has been given to monopolization cases, especially those involving large corporations. This section thus emphasizes the development of monopolization case law and its application in recent cases; the legal standards applicable in cases alleging attempts or conspiracies to monopolize are discussed briefly.

Early Cases

The Supreme Court decided its first Section 2 case, *United States* v. *E. C. Knight,* in 1895.[10] E. C. Knight was one of four Philadelphia sugar refineries acquired by the American Sugar Refining Company, a New Jersey corporation. All sugar refineries acquired were located in the state of Pennsylvania. As a result, the Court concluded that even though the acquisitions gave American a practical monopoly in sugar refining

8. This is called a natural monopoly and is discussed in Chapter 11.

9. This is probably the case with the U.S. Postal Service, which has been granted a monopoly over the delivery of first class mail. See Chapter 18.

10. *United States* v. *E. C. Knight Co.,* 156 U.S. 1 (1895).

(98 percent of national sales), there was no direct effect on interstate commerce. Hence, there was no violation of the Sherman Act. This case illustrates how judicial interpretation can determine the effectiveness of the antitrust laws. The interstate commerce requirement was substantially loosened in subsequent rulings, however, and no longer hinders antitrust enforcement.

The first government victory under Section 2 came in 1904 in the case of *Northern Securities* v. *U.S.*[11] This case involved the creation of a holding company, Northern Securities, that had a controlling interest in the Great Northern and the Northern Pacific railroads. Through the holding company, competition was eliminated between the two railroads, effectively giving them a monopoly over rail traffic between the Great Lakes and the Pacific coast. The Court ruled that Northern Securities was monopolizing this market and must be dissolved.[12] In the Court's view, combining the two railroads showed the positive drive necessary to justify a finding of monopolization.

Seven years later, the Supreme Court applied the Sherman Act to manufacturing firms in cases against the oil and tobacco trust.[13] As the Court's decisions were similar—both American Tobacco and Standard Oil monopolized their markets—only the Standard Oil case need be examined. The defendant, the Standard Oil Company of New Jersey, was a holding company founded in 1899 by John and William Rockefeller. Through an aggressive campaign of acquiring its competitors, it eventually controlled 90 percent of the domestic petroleum market and was able to set the price of both crude and refined petroleum.

The Supreme Court began its analysis by noting that there was no "direct prohibition against monopoly" in the Sherman Act. The offense of monopolizing, therefore, requires something more than the mere possession of monopoly power. The Court then examined the manner in which Standard Oil had obtained its dominant market position. It found that this position was not attributable to "normal business practices," but to highly questionable conduct. Standard Oil was accused of such practices as establishing dummy corporations to engage in local price wars, receiving preferential rates from the railroads, and coercing competitors' suppliers and customers. It was clear that Standard Oil not only

11. *Northern Securities* v. *United States*, 193 U.S 197 (1904).

12. The practical effect of this case was undone more than 60 years later when the Interstate Commerce Commission approved the merger, thereby creating the Burlington Northern System.

13. *Standard Oil Co.* v. *United States*, 221 U.S. 1 (1911); *United States* v. *American Tobacco Co.*, 221 U.S. 106 (1911).

had monopoly power, but also had used bad conduct to attain it and maintain it. This constituted monopolization, and the Court ruled that the Standard Oil Company must be dissolved.[14]

The Court's position on monopolization offenses was further elaborated in its acquittal of U.S. Steel in 1920.[15] U.S. Steel was created in 1901 by the famous "billion dollar merger" that combined seven steel companies into a single firm with a 65 percent share of the market. Its market share had declined to 50 percent by the time the government's monopolization suit reached the Supreme Court. The crucial issue for the Court was whether or not U.S. Steel possessed the monopoly power requisite for monopolization. The Court concluded that it did not, and therefore could not be monopolizing the steel industry.[16] Even though it was now moot, the Court examined U.S. Steel's behavior and decided that it was acceptable. It went on to state:

> The corporation is undoubtedly of impressive size, and it takes an effort of resolution not to be affected by it or to exaggerate its influence. But we must adhere to the law and the law does not make mere size an offense or the existence of unexerted power an offense. It, we repeat, requires overt acts, and trusts to its prohibition of them and its power to repress or punish them. It does not compel competition, nor require all that is possible.[17]

This ruling suggested that there was a simple dichotomy between "good" trusts and "bad" trusts. A monopolist would not be violating the Sherman Act if its behavior were within the bounds of accepted business ethics.

Alcoa

The U.S. Steel decision was followed by a lull in monopolization cases until the government filed a major suit against the Aluminum Company of America (Alcoa) in 1937. Alcoa was charged with monopolizing the

14. This was easy to do since it was a holding company for 33 geographically separate companies. Such major oil companies as Exxon, Mobil, Continental, Marathon, Atlantic Richfield, and the Standard Oil Companies of California, Indiana, and Ohio are all corporate descendants of the original Standard Oil Company.

15. *United States* v. *U.S. Steel Corp.*, 251 U.S. 417 (1920).

16. One reason the Court reached this conclusion was that U.S. Steel had tried unsuccessfully to collude on price with its competitors. This indicated that they did not have monopoly power in the steel industry and that the government should have simultaneously filed a price-fixing complaint under Section 1 of the Sherman Act.

17. *United States* v. *U.S. Steel Corp.*, 251 U.S. 417 (1920).

primary or "virgin" aluminum market. It was the only domestic producer of virgin aluminum ingots made from aluminum bauxite ore. It did,
however, face competition from imported primary aluminum and from
secondary aluminum made from aluminum scrap. Alcoa's dominant position initially resulted from its ownership of the Hall and Bradley patents for manufacturing virgin aluminum. After those patents expired,
Alcoa protected its dominant position by aggressively acquiring aluminum bauxite reserves and the hydroelectric sites most suitable for aluminum production. It was estimated that Alcoa controlled as much as 90
percent of the world's known reserves of aluminum bauxite ore!

The final decision in this case was issued by a circuit court of appeals
because the Supreme Court could not achieve a quorum of six justices.[18]
Four justices had disqualified themselves because of prior involvement
in the case. The appeal was presided over by Judge Learned Hand, who
addressed the two basic issues in a monopolization case: First, did Alcoa possess monopoly power in the aluminum market? Second, did Alcoa actively seek its dominant position in the aluminum market?

The issue of monopoly power, as always in Section 2 cases, requires a
determination of the relevant market. In this case, the degree of Alcoa's
control over the aluminum market depended on the role of secondary
aluminum. Did it compete with virgin aluminum? The analysis focused
on four different components of the aluminum industry:

A = virgin aluminum that Alcoa sold to others

B = virgin aluminum that Alcoa used internally

C = secondary aluminum made from aluminum scrap

D = imports of virgin aluminum

Given these components, Judge Hand examined three different market
definitions and hence three different market shares for Alcoa:

$$\frac{A}{A+B+C+D} = 33\% \quad (1)$$

$$\frac{A+B}{A+B+C+D} = 64\% \quad (2)$$

$$\frac{A+B}{A+B+D} = 90\% \quad (3)$$

The district court judge chose definition (1), concluded that Alcoa did
not have monopoly power, and acquitted Alcoa of the monopolization

18. *United States* v. *Aluminum Company of America*, 148 F.2d 416 (1945).

charge. Judge Hand disagreed, opting for definition (3) instead. The importance of the market definition and its implications for the case were stated by Hand: "That percentage (90) is enough to constitute a monopoly; it is doubtful whether 60 or 64 percent would be enough; and certainly 33 percent is not."

Alcoa thus fulfilled the first requirement for a successful monopolization suit: the possession of monopoly power. Judge Hand then turned to the issue of conduct: did Alcoa intend to monopolize the aluminum market? And here Judge Hand made an important departure from past decisions by emphasizing general intent instead of specific intent. Previous decisions had required a showing of specific intent; that is, a conscious intent or motive as indicated by some illegal action. (This resulted in the differentiation between "good" trusts and "bad" trusts that followed the U.S. Steel decision.) Judge Hand argued that a showing of general intent was sufficient; a firm should be held responsible for the logical end results of its actions. A normal business practice, though ostensibly legal, may result in monopolization. For example, Judge Hand believed that Alcoa excluded potential entrants by always maintaining excess capacity. A potential entrant would be less inclined to enter a market in which a dominant firm already had sufficient capacity to meet expected increases in demand.[19] This "normal business practice" was thus instrumental in helping Alcoa maintain its monopoly position in the production of virgin aluminum. Judge Hand's reasoning thus shifted the focus from the means chosen to the end result obtained.

There are, however, defenses available to a firm charged with monopolization. More specifically:

> A firm may not have achieved monopoly; monopoly may have been thrust upon it. . . . A single producer may be the survivor out of a group of active competitors, merely by virtue of his superior skill, foresight and industry. . . . The successful competitor, having been urged to compete, must not be turned upon when he wins.[20]

Courts must thus examine very carefully the factors that have enabled a monopolist to attain and maintain its dominant market position. Society would not benefit, for example, from the dissolution of a natural monopolist that can supply the market more efficiently than two or more firms.

19. For a more detailed discussion of this argument, see A. Michael Spence, "Entry, Capacity, Investment and Oligopolistic Pricing," *Bell Journal of Economics* 8 (Autumn 1977): 534-44.

20. *United States* v. *Aluminum Company of America* at 429-30.

After a careful examination of the history of Alcoa, however, Judge Hand decided that none of these defenses was applicable.

Given that Alcoa had in fact monopolized the aluminum market, Judge Hand had to determine the appropriate relief. The obvious remedy of dissolution was not necessary; as the government was beginning to dispose of aluminum plants that it had built during World War II, an opportunity existed to create competitors for Alcoa. The court simply prevented Alcoa from acquiring any aluminum plants disposed of under the Surplus Property Act of 1944. This left Alcoa with 50 percent of the market, while Reynolds had 30 percent and Kaiser 20 percent. The net effect of the case was the replacement of a monopoly with a three-firm oligopoly.[21]

Post-Alcoa Cases

Judge Hand's reasoning in the Alcoa case was subsequently endorsed by the Supreme Court in 1946.[22] It thereby was established as the controlling precedent for Section 2 monopolization cases. Recent cases have refined the issues raised in monopolization cases, but have not changed the substantive doctrine. United Shoe Machinery (1953), for example, monopolized the market for shoe-making machinery partly through its leasing arrangements, a normal business practice.[23] The DuPont (1956) and Grinnell (1966) cases emphasize the extreme importance of how the market is defined in Section 2 cases.[24] A broad market definition understates the defendant's monopoly power (DuPont), while a narrow one overstates it (Grinnell). A monopolization case may thus be won or lost depending on how the relevant market has been defined.

The Justice Department initiated major monopolization suits against American Telephone and Telegraph (AT&T) in 1974 and International Business Machines (IBM) in 1969.[25] The AT&T case focused on the

21. For a history of the aluminum industry, see Robert Lanzillotti, "The Aluminum Industry," in *The Structure of American Industry*, ed. W. Adams, 3rd ed. (New York: Macmillan, 1967), pp. 185-233.

22. *American Tobacco v. United States*, 328 U.S. 781 (1946).

23. *United States v. United Shoe Machinery Corp.*, 347 U.S. 521 (1954).

24. *United States v. E.I. DuPont de Nemours*, 351 U.S. 377 (1956), *United States v. Grinnell Corp.*, 384 U.S. 536 (1966).

25. *United States v. International Business Machines Corp.*, U.S. District Court for the Southern District of New York, civil action no. 69 CIV. 200 (1969); *United States v. American Telephone and Telegraph Co.*, U.S. District Court for the District of Columbia, civil action no. 74-1698 (1974).

competitive impact of AT&T's control of Western Electric (communications equipment), its Long Lines Department (long-distance service), and its operating companies (local exchange service). Because AT&T is regulated by the Federal Communications Commission as well as by state public service commissions, the issues raised by this case are addressed in Chapter 13's broader discussion of the domestic communications industry.

IBM.   The IBM case has been characterized as the classic antitrust confrontation between the government and a glamorous blue-chip company. IBM was charged with monopolizing the "general purpose digital computer market." To increase competition, the government sought to dissolve it into several independent corporations.[26] This civil suit was filed in January 1969, and trial began in May 1975. The government completed its presentation in 1978, and IBM began its lengthy defense. With all of the expected appeals, the case is not likely to be resolved until the mid-1980s at the earliest.[27]

As in all monopolization cases, the first issue concerns monopoly power. Does IBM possess the requisite monopoly power in the relevant market? As in other cases, this depends on how the general purpose digital computer market is defined. If the market is commercial computers, excluding military and mini-computers, IBM's market share is approximately 70 percent. If the market is broadened to include the peripheral equipment used with these computers, IBM's share declines to approximately 50 percent. By analogy with the Alcoa decision, 70 percent probably constitutes a monopoly while 50 percent does not.[28] Not surprisingly, the Justice Department endorses the narrow market definition while IBM supports the broad one. In any event, it seems difficult to argue that IBM does not have the power to control the market price of computers.

Assuming that IBM does have monopoly power, the court must address the conduct issue. Did IBM seek its dominant position or was it thrust upon it? The Justice Department has contended that IBM

26. "Divestiture of IBM Into Full-Line Firms is Seen Being Pressed by Justice Agency," *Wall Street Journal*, September 17, 1979, p. 4.

27. This assumes, of course, that there will not be an out-of-court settlement in the case. Although IBM and the Justice Department have held talks on a possible settlement, it seems unlikely that they will reach an agreement as long as the government wants to break up IBM ("IBM, Justice Agency Close to Reaching Framework to Guide Talks on Settlement," *Wall Street Journal*, March 12, 1980, p. 6).

28. United Shoe Machinery's market share was estimated to be between 75 and 85 percent, which was considered sufficient to constitute monopoly power.

purposely adopted policies to limit competition. It cites, for example, IBM's introduction of two new computer systems as evidence of anticompetitive conduct.[29] The IBM 914 "supercomputer" has been called a "fighting machine" designed to attack Control Data Corporation, while the company's "premature" announcement of its 360 series may have prevented customers from switching to competitors' systems.

IBM has countered that its business policies have been procompetitive and that its market position is due to its superior products, a defense that was recognized by Judge Hand in the Alcoa decision. A potentially important factor in this monopolization case is the changes that have occurred in the computer industry since the IBM case began in 1969. Several domestic firms and one Japanese firm have entered the general purpose computer market.[30] As a result, it would not be surprising if the district court were to decide that IBM had violated the antitrust laws, but that drastic relief (such as dissolution) was not necessary because the industry has become more competitive.

The Federal Trade Commission has pursued a parallel path to the Justice Department even though it cannot technically initiate monopolization suits under the Sherman Act. The FTC can attack monopolizing behavior, however, as an unfair method of competition in violation of Section 5 of the FTC Act.[31] In its most famous monopolization effort to date, the FTC reached a consent order with Xerox whereby Xerox agreed to license its copying machine patents.[32]

Attempts and Conspiracies to Monopolize

Two requirements must be met before a firm can be convicted of attempting to monopolize a market.[33] First, the defendant must have had a *specific* intent to monopolize the relevant market. This is a more stringent criterion than the *general* intent necessary in a monopolization case, and generally involves some unfair conduct by the defendant. Second, there must be a "dangerous probability" that the defendant will actually succeed and monopolize the market. It must be shown that

29. Two other conduct charges against IBM concern its pricing policies (specifically *bundling*, or charging a single price for computer hardware and software) and its policy of granting discounts to educational institutions.

30. "The New Wave of Change Challenging IBM," *Business Week*, May 29, 1978, pp. 92-99.

31. *Grand Caillou Packing Co.*, 65 F.T.C. 799 (1964).

32. *Federal Trade Commission, in the Matter of Xerox Corp.*, docket no. 8909, July 29, 1975.

33. *Times-Picayune* v. *United States*, 345 U.S. 594 (1952).

competitors will be adversely affected by the defendant's behavior. Finally, a conspiracy to monopolize is also a conspiracy in restraint of trade and thus overlaps with Section 1 of the Sherman Act. The requirements for bringing a conspiracy charge are examined in Chapter 6.

Evaluation

Under the Sherman Act, it is illegal for a firm to "monopolize" a market. This prohibition constitutes the antitrust response to the monopoly problem or, more accurately, the dominant firm problem. An evaluation of this key element in the antitrust program requires an examination of current policy as well as proposals for its reform. Emphasis is placed on the incentives and disincentives created by government and private monopolization suits.

Appraisal of Current Policy

Current antitrust policy toward dominant firms has been widely criticized. Unfortunately, there is no consensus as to its shortcomings. Monopolization policy has been criticized for being both too lenient and too strict. The economic impact of any antitrust policy depends on three interrelated factors: (1) legal standards; (2) remedies; and (3) enforcement. In this case, factors (1) and (2) concern the courts' interpretation and application of Section 2 of the Sherman Act, while factor (3) deals with the actual litigation of monopolization suits.

Legal Standards. Controlling precedents for monopolization cases indicate that two requirements must be fulfilled for a suit to succeed. First, the defendant must have monopoly power, the "ability to control price or exclude competitors." The standard measure of monopoly power is the defendant's market share in the relevant market. A common generalization is that 50 percent is not sufficient and 80 percent is; the dividing line between the two is unknown. Second, the defendant must have committed some "purposeful act" to attain and/or maintain its dominant market position. The focus is on general, not specific, intent, and normal business practices may be sufficient to monopolize a market. Identical actions by a small firm would presumably be legal, since they would not have an adverse impact on competition. Finally, the defendant's market position will not be illegal if it resulted from a "superior product, business acumen, or historic accident." The burden of proof, however, rests with the defendant.

These legal standards have been criticized for being too unpredictable and for encouraging inefficient behavior. The monopoly power requirement places substantial importance on the defendant's market share, but it is only as reliable as the market definition accepted by the court. And, the courts are not known for their economic expertise, although their command of economic principles is indeed improving.[34] This standard can also lead to inefficient behavior if it encourages dominant firms to "pull their punches." For instance, a dominant firm may artificially limit its market share in an effort to avoid a monopolization suit. The competitive fringe is thus larger than it would be if the dominant firm were competitive. Protecting the smaller competitors is efficient only if they eventually become viable competitors. (Anecdotal evidence suggests that because General Motors historically has restricted its market share to a "safe" 50 percent, this has helped preserve the fourth, and smallest, domestic producer, American Motors.)

Similar criticisms have been voiced about the conduct standard. Businesspeople claim that the Alcoa standard is so broad that it is impossible to know when they are violating it. Such uncertainty can encourage firms to adopt nonaggressive behavior in the marketplace. They also contend that it is unfair to convict a firm for using "normal business practices," arguing that this is tantamount to making monopoly illegal per se. On the other hand, broad standards give the courts the discretion necessary in a world of changing business practices and industrial climates. It would be too easy for businesses to evade specific standards. Finally, it is frequently argued that monopoly should be illegal per se. The goal of antitrust policy should be the elimination of monopoly power, regardless of the dominant firm's conduct.

Remedies. The standard complaint in monopolization cases is that "the government wins the case, but loses the decree." Defendants who lose their cases are rarely broken up into two or more competing entities. From 1890 to 1974, the Justice Department obtained substantial divestiture of the defendant's assets in only 23 percent of its single-firm monopolization cases.[35] The dissolution in 1911 of Standard Oil into 33 separate companies is not representative of the relief granted by the courts.[36] Three reasons are frequently cited to explain the lack of struc-

34. It is widely believed that the courts frequently choose the market definition that is consistent with their final decision and not necessarily the definition that would be favored on economic grounds alone.

35. Richard A. Posner, *Antitrust Law* (Chicago: University of Chicago Press, 1976), p. 82.

36. It was also not very effective for two reasons. First, the companies were located in different parts of the country and hence were generally not direct competitors. Second, John D. Rockefeller still retained stock control over the companies.

tural relief in monopolization cases. First, government lawyers tend to lose interest in a case once it has been decided in their favor.[37] Lawyers gain personal satisfaction and professional recognition from litigating the case, not from fashioning the appropriate remedy. This attitude reduces the government's effectiveness during the relief stage of the case. Second, dissolution may not be necessary to increase competition in the dominant firm's market. There may be alternative ways of creating new competitors (as in the Alcoa case), or market competition may have increased since the suit was initiated (as with IBM). Finally, courts are generally reluctant to dissolve a successful, ongoing concern, especially if it has a good reputation. As the Supreme Court stated in its U.S. Steel decision:

> In conclusion we are unable to see that the public interest will be served by yielding to the contention of the Government respecting the dissolution of the Company or the separation from it of some of its subsidiaries; and we do see in a contrary conclusion a risk of injury to the public interest, including a material disturbance of, and, it may be serious detriment to, the foreign trade. And in submission to the policy of law and its fortifying prohibitions the public interest is of paramount regard.[38]

The Court's concern that dissolution may not promote the public interest requires an examination of the pros and cons of dissolution.

The argument in favor of dissolution is straightforward. It is the quickest, most effective policy for increasing competition in a market dominated by a single firm. Structural relief directly increases the number of competitors while simultaneously decreasing the dominant firm's monopoly power. This approach is desirable for two reasons. First, monopoly power is persistent and only gradually eroded by natural market forces. Table 5.2 indicates that the market shares of a group of dominant firms changed little in a recent 25-year period. Second, conduct relief cannot guarantee that the dominant firm's monopoly power will be eliminated. It may reduce barriers to entry and make entry more likely, but this is an indirect route that may or may not be successful.[39] In sum, structural relief attacks the heart of the monopoly problem and provides a quick solution.

Courts tend to emphasize both efficiency and equity arguments in their objections to structural relief. The equity issue concerns the possi-

37. Posner, *Antitrust Law*, p. 88.

38. *United States* v. *U.S. Steel* at 457.

39. W. Baldwin, "The Feedback Effect of Business Conduct on Industry Structure," *Journal of Law and Economics* 12 (April 1969): 123–53.

Table 5.2   **Estimated Market Shares of Dominant Firms**

Firm	1948	1973
General Motors	60	55
Western Electric	100	98
Kellogg	50	45
Eastman Kodak	80	80
IBM	90	70
Campbell Soup	85	85
Caterpillar Tractor	50	50
Gillette	70	70
Hershey	75	70
Coca-Cola	60	50

Source: William G. Shepherd, *The Treatment of Market Power* (New York: Columbia University Press, 1975), Table B.2, p. 309.

ble effects of dissolution on employment and wealth. There is a fear that dissolution will reduce employment, although it is not clear why this would happen. More than likely, it would increase employment by reducing market price and hence increasing the quantity demanded. The effect on wealth results from the possible impact of dissolution on the stockholders of the dominant firm. Dissolution may reduce the firm's profits, thereby decreasing the value of its stocks and the wealth of its stockholders.[40] The courts may thus view dissolution as confiscatory, especially since many of the stockholders are not the original owners who benefited from the monopoly in the first place. It should be noted, however, that any court action that reduces the defendant's profits will necessarily lower stock prices and injure stockholders. This holds for injunctions prohibiting specific conduct as well as for actual dissolution.

The efficiency issue questions the proposed economic benefits of dissolution. Will the dismantling of a firm with a proven "track record" necessarily improve market performance? If there is any improvement, will it outweigh the transitional costs associated with dissolution? Even though economists believe that the benefit-cost ratio of dissolution is substantially in excess of one, courts are reluctant to trade the tangible costs of dissolution for its potential benefits.

A possible compromise remedy is "contingent dissolution." In this situation, the court initially imposes conduct relief but retains the op-

40. This hypothesis was not supported by an empirical analysis of three dissolution cases in 1911. See Malcolm R. Burns, "The Competitive Effects of Trust-Busting: A Portfolio Analysis," *Journal of Political Economy* 85 (August 1977): 717–39.

tion of imposing structural relief in the future.[41] If competition is not restored within a given time, the court will then break up the company. This approach provides the court with flexibility, while encouraging the defendant to cooperate and possibly even to divest itself of some assets voluntarily. This type of remedy has drawbacks, however. The defendant may spin off subsidiaries that in the long run will not become viable competitors. Or, more importantly, the defendant may reduce its market share simply by charging higher prices. The immediate outcome of the monopolization suit would thus be higher prices, although increased competition might eventually reduce them.

Enforcement   The Justice Department initiates a major monopolization suit about once every decade. There are two reasons for this low rate of enforcement of Section 2 of the Sherman Act. First, as noted earlier, there are not that many dominant firms in the American economy. Within this sample, the department must select cases that are both winnable and economically important. Second, monopolization cases require a substantial commitment of the Justice Department's limited resources. These cases proceed very slowly because the defendant has a strong financial incentive to delay the case—every day of delay yields additional monopoly profits. At the same time, the government contributes to the delay because of turnover in its legal staff and its limited amount of resources. These problems have been amply illustrated by the government's suit against IBM. The case entered its second decade in 1980, and has set every longevity record imaginable.[42] The government has used three different teams of lawyers, 8,000 exhibits, 90,000 pages of transcript, and 473 days in court to present its case. IBM appears to have contributed to the normal delay whenever possible. For example, as part of its out-of-court settlement in a private suit involving Control Data Corporation, IBM had CDC destroy a document index for 27 million documents that the government had wanted to use for its own case!

Monopolization cases do not have to take this long to adjudicate, however. Berkey Photo's private monopolization suit against Eastman Kodak lasted only six months. Although parts of Berkey Photo's victory

41. This was the case in the government's monopolization suit against United Shoe Machinery. The case was decided with a conduct decree in 1953 specifying that the shoe machinery industry was to be reexamined in ten years. It was subsequently decided that "workable" competition had not been achieved, and in 1969 United Shoe was ordered to reduce its market share from 60 percent to less than 50 percent.

42. IBM Chairman Frank Cary has stated, that, "Day by day, it's becoming the lawsuit of the century—the 21st century" ("Cary Blasts Antitrust Efforts," *Washington Post*, May 1, 1979, p. D7).

were overturned on appeal and remanded for a new trial, this case does hold out the promise of shorter and more manageable Section 2 cases.[43] It also emphasizes the increasingly important role of private litigation in enforcing the Sherman Act. Indeed, as noted earlier in Chapter 4, IBM has had 19 different private suits filed against it in addition to the government's suit!

In sum, there are many problems with monopolization cases. Suits are initiated infrequently and become very protracted. The government may win the suit, but lose the relief decree. As a result, monopolization cases probably have little deterrent effect, although private treble-damage suits might be changing this. Ironically, any deterrent effect of government and especially of private suits may be to worsen, not improve, market performance. Dominant firms might choose to "pull their punches" and thereby preserve inefficient competitors. Potential defendants also might needlessly centralize or integrate their operations in order to make dissolution more difficult.[44]

New Directions for Antitrust Enforcement

The considerable controversy surrounding monopolization cases has led to many suggestions for reform. Not surprisingly, there is no consensus among economists and lawyers as to the "correct" approach. There are as many reform proposals as there are diverse views. This section examines some of those frequently discussed.

Legal Standards. Two major proposals for legislative changes have been made. One would make monopoly illegal per se; the other would repeal Section 2 of the Sherman Act. The first proposal, called "no-fault" monopoly, would eliminate the conduct requirement in monopolization cases. The persistent possession of monopoly power, probably 60 percent of the market, would create a rebuttable presumption that the defendant had violated the law. The defendant would then have to justify its market dominance in terms of economies of scale or patents. This approach would presumably streamline litigation since approximately one-third to one-half of trial time focuses on the firm's conduct.[45]

43. "Most of Kodak Case Judgment Overturned," *Washington Post*, June 26, 1979, p. D7.

44. GM has reportedly proceeded along this path. See "FTC Staff Weighs Antitrust Study of GM, But It Has Made No Recommendations," *Wall Street Journal*, November 10, 1975, p. 7.

45. National Commission for the Review of Antitrust Laws and Procedures, *Report to the President and the Attorney General* (Washington, D.C.: Government Printing Office, January 22, 1979), p. 152.

The saving in time might be offset, however, by expanded discussion of market definition and the defendant's justification of its market dominance.

The repeal of Section 2 is advocated by those who question the traditional economic analysis of dissolution. They believe that the costs of dissolution exceed the benefits. The threat of dissolution may encourage dominant firms to be less efficient, while actual dissolution may destroy economies of scale. The repeal of Section 2 still leaves Section 1 to attack restraints of trade. This approach is considered more equitable to business, as normal business practices would not violate the antitrust laws.

Remedies.   Primary attention has focused on increasing the probability of obtaining structural relief in monopolization cases. A common proposal is to require dissolution, thereby eliminating judicial discretion. The judge would be forced to impose structural relief and could not substitute conduct relief. It would be necessary to specify in great detail what constituted acceptable relief, so that the judge could not evade the law's intent. Another possibility is to make structural relief available in private monopolization cases. Currently, the courts are reluctant to grant structural relief except to the government, which is acting in the public interest. This change would take advantage of the tremendous increase in private monopolization suits.

Enforcement.   A major goal of enforcement is to speed up the litigation of complex antitrust cases in general and monopolization suits in particular. A recent evaluation of antitrust enforcement by the National Commission for the Review of Antitrust Laws and Procedures resulted in several recommendations.[46] First, and perhaps most important, the legal issues should be defined and narrowed early in the case. This would reduce the common complaint that the government is on a "fishing expedition." It would also reduce the defendant's ability to overwhelm the government with useless documents. The importance of this factor was illustrated recently when an FTC monopolization case was tried before an administrative law judge in only 14 days![47]

Second, precise time limits should be established for both the discov-

46. National Commission for the Review of Antitrust Laws and Procedures, *Report to the President and the Attorney General.*

47. DuPont was charged by the FTC with monopolizing the titanium dioxide industry. The administrative law judge disagreed ("FTC Judge Throws Out DuPont Antitrust Case," *Washington Post,* September 18, 1979, p. F1).

ery and the trial stages of the case. To force adherence to the time schedule, disincentives for dilatory behavior may be needed. For instance, the plaintiff might be awarded interest on the damages claimed beginning with the date of filing of the complaint, instead of the date of the judgment. This would reduce the defendant's financial incentive to delay. Both these approaches, however, would require much more involvement of the trial judge in the case. Indeed, judges are frequently criticized for losing control of these major cases.

Summary

Monopolization suits constitute the antitrust response to the monopoly problem in America. Under current interpretations of the Sherman Act, a firm monopolizes a market when it possesses monopoly power and when that power was consciously acquired and/or maintained. About once a decade, the government initiates a major monopolization suit against one of the country's handful of dominant firms. The government generally wins the case, and the defendant generally wins the relief decree. The result is a massive expenditure of resources by both sides, but little structural change in the defendant's market. Two possible changes are to eliminate the conduct requirement in monopolization cases and to require dissolution of the defendant. These policy changes will be consistent with the public interest only if the benefits of dissolution exceed its costs. This is a complex empirical issue that cannot be decided conclusively one way or the other. As a result, the debate over the optimal monopoly policy (if one exists) is likely to continue.

Suggested Readings

Baldwin, W. "The Feedback Effect of Business Conduct on Industry Structure," *Journal of Law and Economics* 12 (April 1969): 123–53.

Burns, Malcolm R. "The Competitive Effects of Trust-Busting: A Portfolio Analysis," *Journal of Political Economy* 85 (August 1977): 717–39.

National Commission for the Review of Antitrust Laws and Procedures. *Report to the President and the Attorney General* (Washington, D.C.: Government Printing Office, January 22, 1979).

Posner, Richard A. *Antitrust Law* (Chicago: University of Chicago Press, 1976), Chapters 2, 5.

Shepherd, William G. *The Treatment of Market Power* (New York: Columbia University Press, 1975).

Agreements among Competitors

Chapter 6

A firm does not manufacture and distribute its products in isolation from other firms. It interacts continuously with its suppliers and customers, and even its competitors. These interactions can result in agreements that directly or indirectly lessen competition. Of particular importance to antitrust authorities are agreements among competitors.[1] As Adam Smith noted perceptively more than 200 years ago: "People of the same trade seldom meet together, even for merriment and diversion, but the conversation ends in a conspiracy against the public or in some contrivance to raise prices."[2] Interfirm agreements can eliminate the independent action essential for competition and enable the participants jointly to act like a monopolist.

The Setting

"Agreement" is a broad term that covers a variety of different situations. In general, an agreement is a consensus among two or more individuals on some course of action. Two firms may agree, for example, not to sell their products in each other's territories. This agreement can be explicit or implicit depending on whether the course of action is expressly stat-

1. Interfirm agreements that affect the distribution of products are covered in Chapter 8.

2. Adam Smith, *The Wealth of Nations* (New York: Random House, The Modern Library, 1937), p. 128.

ed. For example, the firms may formally allocate sales territories *(explic-it agreement)*, or each firm may simply restrict sales to its own territory in the expectation that the other firm will reciprocate *(implicit agree-ment)*. The end result can be the same, although the type of the agreement is quite different. The question for antitrust authorities is whether or not the private agreement chosen, whether explicit or implicit, is consistent with the public interest.

Legal Issues

Agreements among competitors can violate Section 1 of the Sherman Act, which reads in part:

> Every contract, combination in the form of trust or otherwise, or conspiracy, in restraint of trade or commerce among the several States, or with foreign nations, is hereby declared to be illegal.[3]

They can also violate Section 5 of the Federal Trade Commission Act, which prohibits "unfair methods of competition" and "unfair and deceptive acts or practices."[4]

Section 1 of the Sherman Act raises two issues that must be resolved by the courts. First, what constitutes an agreement among competitors? The act specifically addresses contracts, combinations, and conspiracies, but it does not establish standards of evidence for each. This may be a simple exercise in such explicit agreements as contracts and business combinations, but not in conspiracies, where there is little, if any, direct evidence. Can the courts infer the existence of a tacit agreement from purely circumstantial evidence? Second, given that an agreement exists, does it restrain trade? This is an extremely broad prohibition, as even the simplest sales contract restrains trade by excluding other buyers and sellers from the transaction in question. The courts must determine which restraints are sufficiently onerous to warrant prohibition.

At the time the Sherman Act was passed (1890), the common law had dealt with the restraint of trade issue by adopting a *"rule of reason"* approach. In this approach, the legality of a specific practice is determined by examining the particular circumstances surrounding its use. The same business practice can be legal in one environment, but illegal in another. This is illustrated by the distinction between ancillary and nonancillary restraints of trade. An *ancillary restraint* is incidental to a

3. Sherman Act, 15 U.S.C. Sec. 1 (1976).
4. Federal Trade Commission Act, 15 U.S.C. Sec. 45 (1976).

legitimate business function, while the sole purpose of a *nonancillary* restraint is to limit competition. For example, it is very common for a person selling a business to agree not to compete with the new owner. Although this sales condition does restrict the future opportunities of the seller, it is incidental to a legitimate business function—the sale of the business. Without such a restriction, the seller could always reenter the market, compete with the buyer, and thereby reduce the value of the business purchased. Ancillary restraints have generally been legal under the common law as long as they are not unduly restrictive or injurious to the public.[5]

A rule of reason approach gives the courts substantial discretion in applying the law. This is not the case with a *per se approach*, which makes a given practice illegal in and of itself. No justification is possible, and so the court does not examine the reasonableness of the practice. If the practice occurred, the law has been violated. The per se approach thus focuses on the existence of the practice rather than on the rationale behind it. In general, courts examine three factors when determining whether a per se or rule of reason approach is most appropriate for a given practice. First, what are the expected costs and benefits? If the practice provides little benefit but can impose large costs, then it should be illegal per se. Otherwise, a rule of reason approach is necessary to balance the expected benefits and costs. Second, can the courts monitor the practice over time? If not, the harmless practice of today may become the harmful practice of tomorrow. Finally, can the objective sought be attained by a less restrictive practice? If so, the more restrictive practice should be illegal per se. The courts must weigh all these factors when interpreting the law and deciding which legal approach is most beneficial to society—rule of reason or per se.

Economic Issues

Interfirm agreements that restrain market competition, whether explicitly or implicitly, are referred to as *collusion*. Collusive activity raises two important economic questions. First, how does it affect a market's economic performance? Second, what factors determine whether or not firms in a given market will be able to collude successfully? The answer to the first question establishes the economic argument against collusion; the answer to the second suggests where it will be most prevalent.

5. For example, the restraint must be limited in time, scope, and locality. In the case of the sale of a firm, the restraint must be limited to a certain number of years, to the specified occupation, and to the relevant economic market.

Collusion and Economic Performance.   The goal of a collusive agreement is to restrict competition, thereby increasing the profits of the parties to the agreement. This can be accomplished by eliminating competition among existing firms and preventing the entry of new firms. If successful, collusion can increase a firm's profits, as shown in part (a) of Figure 6.1. This diagram contrasts the financial situation of a representative firm before and after a collusive agreement. Before the agreement, the market price is P° and each firm sells Q° units. No profits are earned, however, since price equals average total cost (ATC). The firms in the market subsequently reach a collusive agreement that sets P' as the market price. Each firm reduces its output to Q' units but still earns a profit because the collusive price exceeds the average total cost. Through the collusive agreement, the firms artificially raise price, as would a profit-maximizing monopolist.

The long-run profitability of the collusive pricing scheme depends on two factors: nonprice competition and entry. The first factor involves competition from existing firms; the second factor concerns competition from new firms. Because the collusive agreement limits competitive pricing, firms may direct their competitive energies into nonprice forms of competition, such as advertising and product styling. These nonprice activities will increase each firm's costs (as indicated in part [b] of Figure 6.1), shifting the average total cost curve from ATC° to ATC'.

Figure 6.1   Economic Impact of Collusion

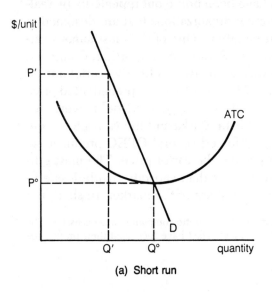

(a) Short run

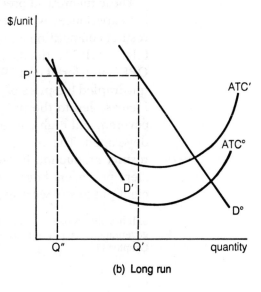

(b) Long run

Given the collusive price of P', the cost increase will necessarily lower the firm's profits. Unless the firms can also collude on nonprice forms of competition, their profits will be reduced and possibly even eliminated.[6]

The problem of entry arises because the profits created by the collusive price are an incentive for new firms to enter this market. Whether new firms do enter the market depends on the height of the collusive price. If it does not exceed the limit price for this market, new firms will not enter and erode the profits. But if the collusive price exceeds the limit price, entry will occur in the long run. As new firms enter, existing firms will sell less and less at the collusive price P'. Each firm's demand curve will continue shifting left until the collusive price equals the firm's new unit production costs. Each firm will now sell Q'' units and not earn any profits. The industry will have too many firms, each operating at less than capacity. Of course, as new firms enter, the collusive agreement might collapse, and price would return to the competitive level.

This analysis indicates that collusive agreements can worsen economic performance, leading to higher prices and reduced consumption. This classic effect of monopoly power is not the only cost to society of collusion. Through various forms of nonprice competition, firms may use more resources than necessary to produce and distribute their products. At the same time, new firms may enter the market and create excess capacity. The end result is too many firms charging too high a price and using too many resources.

These theoretical predictions have been borne out repeatedly by real-life experiences with *cartels*—formal organizations that are designed to restrict competition among their members. One of the most famous cartels is OPEC, the Organization of Petroleum Exporting Countries. OPEC was formed in 1960, but was not really an effective cartel until it quadrupled the price of oil from 1973 to 1974. This unprecedented price increase led to the predictable result—entry. New oil fields were discovered, and high-cost existing fields in Alaska and the North Sea were developed. The increase in supply forced several OPEC producers to restrict production in order to preserve the cartel price. The most efficient producers began to operate at less than capacity, while less efficient producers were expanding their share of the market. In short, the

---

6. It has always been claimed that advertising by cigarette companies was excessive. The government's ban on television advertising may in fact have increased their profits; see Chapter 17.

high price of oil attracted additional resources and encouraged production that would not have been profitable at a competitive price.

Determinants of Successful Collusion.   Two problems must be overcome if firms are to successfully replace a market-determined price with a collusive one. First, the firms must be able to reach a collusive agreement. Second, once the agreement is reached, the firms must be able to preserve it over time. Several factors affect the ability of firms to attain and maintain a collusive agreement.[7]

Reaching agreement on a collusive price is not an easy matter. For example, each firm can have different cost conditions and different expectations about future demand, making it difficult to reach a true consensus on the appropriate price. In general, the more concentrated the industry, the more homogeneous the product, and the greater the camaraderie among industry executives, the easier it should be to collude.[8] The first factor, seller concentration, is undoubtedly the most important determinant of collusion. As industry sales become more and more concentrated in the hands of a few firms, oligopolistic interdependence is increased, and it becomes easier to reach a consensus on the appropriate pricing policy. It is also less likely that any firm will be a "maverick" and not participate in the collusive agreement. The type of product is important also, because it determines the complexity of the collusive agreement. If the good is homogeneous, the firms only have to agree on a single price. When the good varies, however, it is necessary to set a whole array of prices to reflect quality differences among the firms' products. The camaraderie factor is related to the industry's social structure. Do the industry's executives know and trust one another? If so, it is more likely that they will adopt a common perspective on the industry's problems and the appropriate collusive solutions.

Assuming that the firms can attain a collusive agreement, how long will it be maintained? One year or one day? Price-fixing agreements automatically sow the seeds of their own destruction by creating an incentive for firms to cheat on the agreement. If a firm undercuts the collusive price, it can expand its sales and profits at the expense of competitors who abide by the collusive agreement. If this cheating is

7. This assumes that the firms do not use the government to restrict competition among themselves; see Chapters 11–15.

8. For a more detailed discussion of these and additional factors, see F. M. Scherer, *Industrial Market Structure and Economic Performance*, 2nd ed. (Chicago: Rand McNally, 1980), Chapters 5–7.

discovered by competitors, however, a price war may begin that destroys the collusive agreement. The durability of a collusive agreement thus depends on how difficult it is to cheat on the agreement without being detected by competitors. Stigler has shown that the probability of detection increases with a decrease in the number of sellers and an increase in the number of buyers.[9] That is, cheating is less likely, and collusion more effective, in markets where a few sellers face many buyers.

This discussion suggests several possible relationships between collusive activity and elements of market structure, especially the number and size distribution of sellers. Empirical evidence supports the primary hypothesis that collusion, both explicit and implicit, is more likely in markets dominated by a handful of sellers. Numerous empirical studies have found a significant positive relationship between seller concentration and market profitability. This relationship has generally been cited as proof that implicit or tacit collusion is feasible, and indeed commonplace, in highly concentrated markets. The fewness of sellers creates an oligopolistic interdependence that eliminates the need for explicit agreements.

Recent studies of explicit agreements among competitors support the general relationship between collusive activity and seller concentration, but question the belief that tacit collusion is common.[10] Based on their analysis of price-fixing conspiracies prosecuted by the Justice Department, Hay and Kelley concluded that explicit collusion "is most likely to occur and endure when numbers are small, concentration is high, and the product is homogeneous."[11] Their conclusion is supported by Posner, who found that most explicit agreements among competitors involve a small number of firms.[12] Table 6.1 reproduces Posner's data on the number of firms that participated in conspiracy cases tried by the Justice Department from 1890 to 1969. The data indicate that approximately two out of every three conspiracies involved ten or fewer firms, and one-third of the conspiracies involved five or fewer. These are very interesting statistics, because it is widely believed that explicit agreements are unnecessary when the number of firms is small. As Posner

9. G. Stigler, "A Theory of Oligopoly," *Journal of Political Economy*, 72 (February 1964): 44–61.

10. R. Posner, "A Statistical Study of Antitrust Enforcement," *Journal of Law and Economics* 13 (October 1970): 365–419; G. Hay and D. Kelley, "An Empirical Survey of Price Fixing Conspiracies," *Journal of Law and Economics* 17: (April 1974), 13–38.

11. Hay and Kelley, " An Empirical Survey," p. 27.

12. Posner, "A Statistical Study."

Table 6.1   Frequency Distribution of Number of Conspirators in Horizontal Conspiracy Cases, Department of Justice

Period in which Case Was Instituted	0-5	6-10	11-20	21-50	51-100	Over 100	Number of Observations
1890–1894							
1895–1899			1				1
1900–1904				1			1
1905–1909		1			1		2
1910–1914				4			4
1915–1919		1	1				2
1920–1924		1		1		1	3
1925–1929			1		1	2	4
1930–1934			2	1		1	4
1935–1939	1	5	2	2			10
1940–1944	20	9	10	3	4	1	47
1945–1949	19	10	10	4	4	1	48
1950–1954	21	18	13	2	2	2	58
1955–1959	29	18	19	5	1	1	73
1960–1964	28	23	10		1	3	65
1965–1969	12	16	7	6	1	1	43
Total	130	102	76	29	15	13	365

Source: Table reproduced from Richard A. Posner, "A Statistical Study of Antitrust Enforcement," *Journal of Law and Economics* 13 (October 1970): Table 26, p. 402.

commented: "The prevalence of small-number express-collusion cases casts some doubt on the practical importance of tacit collusion."[13]

The Case Law

Firms continually enter into agreements with their competitors. The purposes of these agreements vary, making it difficult to classify them as competitive or anticompetitive. Antitrust enforcement focuses on those agreements that may, directly or indirectly, lessen market competition. This section examines the case law that has determined the legality of both explicit and implicit agreements among competitors.

Explicit Agreements

By definition, an explicit agreement expressly states the course of action expected of the parties to it. The dispute is not about the existence of the agreement, but its legality. Does the agreement restrain trade, there-

13. Posner, "A Statistical Study," pp. 399, 402.

by violating the antitrust laws? As noted in the previous section, the common law adopted a rule of reason approach that distinguished between ancillary and nonancillary restraints of trade. This classification scheme is convenient for examining the current state of the law on explicit agreements among competitors.

Nonancillary Restraints. The Supreme Court first addressed the issue of nonancillary restraints in 1899, nine years after the passage of the Sherman Act.[14] Six manufacturers of iron pipe in the western United States were charged with violating Section 1 of the Sherman Act by fixing prices and dividing the market into separate geographic monopolies. The defendants admitted that they fixed prices, but argued that their prices were "reasonable." Judge Taft, the appellate court judge, ruled that the agreement violated the Sherman Act because price fixing was illegal per se. The Supreme Court affirmed Judge Taft's decision, but did not explicitly endorse his per se approach toward price fixing. The Court instead emphasized that "the effect of the agreement was to enhance prices beyond a sum which was reasonable."

It was not until the Standard Oil monopolization case in 1911 that the Supreme Court issued a detailed interpretation of the Sherman Act.[15] In this case the government had contended that there was no room for judgment under Section 1 of the Sherman Act, which prohibits every contract, combination, or conspiracy in restraint of trade, and so demanded a per se approach. The Supreme Court disagreed, however. Justice White noted that this approach would make all contracts illegal, for the very nature of a contract is to restrain trade. For example, a union contract may prohibit a firm from hiring someone who does not belong to the union or who will not agree to join it after becoming employed. The Court went on to conclude that a rule of reason approach was most appropriate when applying Section 1 of the Sherman Act.

Even though the Court adopted a rule of reason approach toward restraints in general, specific restraints may still be illegal per se. The Court established this principle in 1940, when it declared price-fixing agreements to be illegal per se in its Socony-Vacuum decision.[16] This

14. *Addyston Pipe and Steel Company v. United States*, 175 U.S. 211 (1899).

15. *Standard Oil Company of New Jersey v. United States*, 221 U.S.1 (1911).

16. *United States v. Socony-Vacuum Oil Co.*, 310 U.S. 150 (1940). Price fixing was technically declared illegal per se by the Supreme Court in 1927 *(United States v. Trenton Potteries*, 273 U.S. 392). The authority of this decision was cast in doubt just six years later, when the Court approved an exclusive selling agency for some coal companies *(Appalachian Coals, Inc. v. United States*, 288 U.S. 344). The Socony-Vacuum decision reaffirmed the per se illegality of price fixing and is considered to be the controlling precedent.

case dealt with an arrangement whereby major midwestern oil refiners purchased gasoline from independent refiners. The ostensible purpose of the agreement was to prevent the independent refiners from dumping their gasoline on the market, thereby lowering the already depressed market price of gasoline. Justice Douglas delivered the Court's opinion and declared in no uncertain terms that the agreement violated Section 1.

> ... Any combination which tampers with price structures is engaged in an unlawful activity.... Under the Sherman Act a combination formed for the purpose and with the effect of raising, depressing, fixing, pegging, or stabilizing the price of a commodity in interstate or foreign commerce is illegal per se.[17]

This opinion constituted a strong condemnation of nonancillary restraints of trade. In short, price-fixing agreements are illegal per se; no justifications are possible.

It should be noted that Justice Douglas's opinion includes restraints on foreign commerce as well as domestic commerce. Restrictive agreements among foreign firms can violate Section 1 if they affect domestic commerce.[18] International agreements require more complex litigation, however, as they raise jurisdictional issues not present in domestic agreements. First, does the agreement actually affect the American market? Second, are the firms exempt under the "sovereign immunity" defense? Actions that are compelled by foreign laws or are performed by foreign governments in their *sovereign* capacity cannot be prosecuted under American antitrust laws.

These issues were recently raised in the litigation surrounding the international uranium cartel.[19] From about 1972 to 1975, at the apparent instigation of the Canadian government, the major producers of uranium met secretly to set the world price of uranium. Even though the American market was specifically exempted from the agreement, the price of uranium increased from $6 a pound to $40 a pound while the agreement was in effect. The major American participant, Gulf Oil, claimed that it did not violate the antitrust laws because the agreement exempted the American market and Gulf's participation was compelled by the Canadian government. The Justice Department disagreed and filed suit. Gulf subsequently entered a plea of *nolo contendere* and was fined $40,000.

17. *United States* v. *Socony-Vacuum Oil Co.*, at 223.

18. *United States* v. *Aluminum Company of America*, 148 F.2d 416 (2d Cir. 1945).

19. "Issues on Trial in the Westinghouse Lawsuits," *Business Week*, September 26, 1977, pp. 125–31.

The legal issues are still unresolved, however, awaiting the outcome of a private antitrust suit initiated by Westinghouse against Gulf. Westinghouse was severely damaged by the price increase, since it had guaranteed its nuclear reactor customers a lower price for uranium.

Ancillary Restraints.   Since the Socony-Vacuum decision (1940), non-ancillary restraints of trade have been illegal per se. This prohibition has focused attention on ancillary restraints, which ostensibly are necessary for the furtherance of legitimate business activities. This section examines three such activities that raise antitrust issues: (1) information agreements; (2) trade associations; and (3) professional associations.

Information agreements involve the exchange of information among competitors. The antitrust problems raised by these agreements are illustrated in the case of *United States* v. *Container Corporation of America.*[20] Container Corporation was one of eighteen defendants that manufactured corrugated containers in the southeastern United States. The six largest firms had 60 percent of the market, although entry was relatively easy and market prices had declined throughout the 1950s and early 1960s. During this period, the defendants instituted an information agreement whereby they exchanged price data among themselves. At a competitor's request, a firm would divulge the prices that it had recently charged or quoted to specified customers. It was understood that the competitor would reciprocate and provide the same information in the future. The government claimed that the agreement lessened competition by stabilizing prices, while the defendants argued that it provided the information necessary for effective market competition. Believing that the agreement was ultimately anticompetitive, the Supreme Court ruled in favor of the government. Justice Douglas stated the majority opinion: "Price is too critical, too sensitive a control to allow it to be used even in an informal manner to restrain competition." The Supreme Court's strict position was vindicated when the defendants were subsequently indicted for price fixing by grand juries in Chicago and Houston.[21]

Trade associations present similar problems to antitrust authorities because they commonly collect and disseminate information about their members. Firms can benefit, for example, from aggregated data on trends in industry demand and production costs. Trade associations are not just formal information agreements, however. They frequently rep-

20. *United States* v. *Container Corporation of America,* 393 U.S. 333 (1969).

21. "Price-Fixing Charges Rise in Paper Industry Despite Convictions," *The Wall Street Journal,* May 4, 1978, p. 1

resent their industry before Congress and the various regulatory agencies. This lobbying function may be especially important to the smaller members of the trade association. On the negative side, trade associations are excellent breeding grounds for collusive agreements. The constant contact among representatives of competing firms can easily lead to anticompetitive behavior, such as price fixing or market sharing.

These conflicting considerations have been reflected in the legal tightrope that the Supreme Court has walked on trade association cases.[22] Based on the case law in this area, the following conclusions seem justified. First, trade associations should not discuss current or future prices. If they collect and disseminate data on *past* transactions, they should be aggregated so that the identity of individual buyers and sellers cannot be determined. In addition, the information should be freely available to both buyers and sellers. Second, the courts are considerably more lenient toward trade association activities that do not involve pricing practices. For example, an association may recommend that its members adopt standardized accounting procedures. It must be careful, however, not to provide average cost and markup figures that could easily be summed to obtain "suggested" prices. This would increase the risk that the accounting procedures could be used as a vehicle for price collusion.

Most of the case law on trade associations was established during the 1920s and 1930s. Since then, attention has shifted to professional associations like the American Bar Association, American Dental Association, and American Medical Association. These associations of the "learned" professions (law, dentistry, medicine) are unique in their degree of self-regulation. In an effort to increase the quality of practitioners, these associations were empowered to control entry into their professions. Through their accreditation powers, they determine the number of schools and hence the future supply of practitioners; through their licensing powers, they control the current supply. Once licensed, a practitioner is expected to follow the association's code of professional conduct that, among other things, generally restricts "commercial" practices such as advertising and price competition. Violators of the codes can be expelled from the association, thereby jeopardizing their right to practice their profession.

Professional associations have historically been immune from antitrust prosecution under the "learned profession" exemption. Some an-

---

22. See *American Column and Lumber Co.* v. *United States,* 257 U.S. 377 (1921); *Maple Flooring Manufacturers Association* v. *United States,* 268 U.S. 563 (1925); and *Cement Manufacturers Protective Association* v. *United States,* 268 U.S. 588 (1925).

cillary restraints are acceptable in order to establish minimum standards and preserve ethical conduct in the professions. This exemption was rejected, however, in the 1970s, when the Supreme Court ruled that minimum fee schedules violate Section 1 of the Sherman Act,[23] and prohibitions on advertising violate the First Amendment's guarantee of freedom of speech.[24] Restraints on professional activity imposed through state laws, instead of professional associations, might not be illegal. State actions are generally exempt from the antitrust laws, though this exemption is being threatened by the Federal Trade Commission. The FTC has enacted a trade rule that prohibits states and professional associations from banning advertising of eyeglasses, contact lenses, and eye examinations.[25] If upheld by the courts, its rule would preempt state laws.

Implicit Agreements

Explicit agreements to restrain trade, whether ancillary or nonancillary, can be attacked in a straightforward manner under the Sherman Act. This is not true for implicit agreements, even though they may achieve the same anticompetitive result as explicit agreements. The difference arises because the existence of an agreement is not admitted by the defendants and must be proved by the plaintiff. Antitrust authorities have adopted two different legal approaches for dealing with implicit agreements among competitors: (1) conspiracy; and (2) shared monopoly.

Conspiracy.   Section 1 of the Sherman Act prohibits contracts, combinations, and conspiracies in restraint of trade. A *conspiracy* exists when there is a "meeting of the minds" on some illegal course of action. The important legal issue in conspiracy cases is the evidence necessary to show that there has been a "meeting of the minds" among the defendants. Is "hard" evidence of an agreement necessary, or can it be inferred from circumstantial evidence? The evidentiary requirements demanded by the courts determine the extent to which implicit agreements can be attacked as conspiracies in restraint of trade.

The Supreme Court addressed this issue in the case of Interstate Circuit, a movie theater chain.[26] The chain sent a letter to eight film distributors demanding (1) a minimum price for subsequent runs of first

---

23. *Goldfarb* v. *Virginia State Bar Association,* 421 U.S. 773 (1975).

24. *Bates* v. *State Bar of Arizona,* 433 U.S. 350 (1977).

25. "The FTC's Move to Dump State Regulations," *Business Week,* July 10, 1978, p. 74.

26. *Interstate Circuit, Inc.* v. *United States,* 306 U.S. 208 (1939).

releases and (2) no double features containing those films. These actions would make subsequent showings by other theaters less attractive, thereby increasing the attractiveness and, hence, the profitability of the first releases shown by Interstate Circuit. All eight distributors complied with the two requests, though there was no explicit agreement among them to do so. The Court ruled that there was a conspiracy and that the meeting of the minds occurred in the common letter that Interstate Circuit had sent to all the distributors. The Court stated: "It was enough that, knowing that concerted action was contemplated and invited, the distributors gave their adherence to the scheme and participated in it." In short, a conspiracy could be inferred from circumstantial evidence—the common letter.

After the Interstate Circuit decision, attention focused on the minimum circumstantial evidence necessary to infer a conspiracy. The Supreme Court refined its position when it issued the Theatre Enterprises decision in 1954.[27] This case also involved the distribution of films. Theatre Enterprises, a suburban Baltimore theater, claimed that there was a conspiracy among film distributors not to supply it with first-run releases. There was, however, no evidence of any agreement among the distributors. They responded that it was simply more profitable to lease first-run movies to downtown theaters than to suburban ones. The Supreme Court decided that there was no conspiracy and hence no violation of the Sherman Act. The defendants' behavior, though parallel, could be explained by independent business judgment. As the Court concluded:

> . . . this Court has never held that proof of parallel business behavior conclusively establishes agreement or, phrased differently, that such behavior itself constitutes a Sherman Act offense. Circumstantial evidence of consciously parallel behavior may have made heavy inroads into the traditional judicial attitude toward conspiracy; but "conscious parallelism" has not yet read conspiracy out of the Sherman Act entirely.[28]

Some evidence of an agreement must be shown, such as the letter in the Interstate Circuit case. Otherwise, to infer an implicit agreement—and conspiracy—is appropriate only when the parallel behavior at issue is so complex that independent behavior seems unlikely.

Shared Monopoly. Because of the evidence needed in conspiracy cases, it has been difficult to attack tacit collusion under traditional in-

27. *Theatre Enterprises, Inc.* v. *Paramount Film Distributing Corp.*, 346 U.S. 537 (1954).
28. *Theatre Enterprises, Inc.* v. *Paramount Film Distributing Corp.*, at 1541.

terpretations of the antitrust laws. The Justice Department and the Federal Trade Commission have therefore developed a new legal approach toward oligopolies—the *shared monopoly*. The basic premise is that when a market is dominated by a few firms, they tacitly coordinate their policies and behave like a monopolist; explicit agreements to limit competition are not necessary. The principle of the new approach is that oligopolists should be held to a stricter standard of conduct than firms in less concentrated markets. Behavior that facilitates tacit collusion will be held to restrain trade (in violation of Section 1 of the Sherman Act) and to constitute an unfair method of competition (in violation of Section 5 of the FTC Act).

The shared monopoly concept has been most fully developed in the FTC's pioneering case against the three leading cereal manufacturers, Kellogg, General Foods, and General Mills.[29] This case was initiated in 1972, and trial began before an administrative law judge in 1976. With the obligatory appeal to the Supreme Court, a final decision is unlikely before the mid-1980s. The FTC alleges that these three companies have maintained a shared monopoly through marketing practices that exclude new competitors. For example, the cereal companies have introduced approximately 150 new cereal brands over a 20-year period. This proliferation of brands makes it more difficult for a new firm to successfully carve out a niche against the Big Three or even to obtain access to retailers' shelf space. The marketing policies that increase product variety for consumers increase barriers to entry for new cereal producers.

Evaluation

Firms participate in agreements with their competitors if these promote their private interests. Such agreements, however, can restrain trade and lessen market competition. The goal of antitrust enforcement is to ensure that any interfirm agreements are consistent with the public interest. This requires a balancing of the benefits and costs of these agreements. Antitrust policy should not prevent agreements that benefit society, but should prohibit those that prove harmful.

Appraisal of Current Policy

It is widely accepted that competitors will engage in restrictive agreements if it is profitable to do so. Consequently, there is little debate over the need to prohibit explicit trade restraints, though there are criticisms

29. In the Matter of Kellogg Co. et al., Docket No. 8883, Complaint, April 26, 1972.

of the remedies that have been found. The most controversial issue concerns the optimal antitrust response to tacit collusion. In particular, what are the pros and cons of the shared monopoly suit, government's current response to concentrated markets?

Legal Standards.   The courts and the FTC have both adopted a rule of reason approach toward restraints of trade. In the case of explicit agreements, nonancillary restraints are illegal per se, while ancillary restraints are evaluated on a case-by-case basis. This is clearly the correct approach. As the very purpose of nonancillary restraints such as price fixing or market division is to limit competition, society loses nothing if they are prohibited. The per se illegality of nonancillary restraints has prevented American industry from forming the inefficient cartels so common in foreign countries.[30] This is no small accomplishment, as Posner noted in his evaluation of antitrust enforcement: "The elimination of the formal cartel ... is an impressive, and remains the major, achievement of American antitrust law."[31]

On the other hand, the rule of reason approach toward ancillary restraints enables antitrust authorities to permit beneficial agreements and to prohibit harmful ones. This is illustrated by the government's control over the activities of trade and professional associations. A strict stance toward these associations is necessary because there is considerable empirical evidence that they tend to exceed their legitimate functions and impose trade restraints. For one example, Hay and Kelley found that trade associations were involved in seven of eight price-fixing conspiracies covering more than 15 competitors.[32] For another, dental fees and eyeglass prices are higher in states that have more restrictive licensing.[33]

A rule of reason approach is also necessary if the government is to adapt its policies to the constantly changing industrial climate in America. This was illustrated by the Justice Department's approval of a

30. American industry did have a quick experiment with cartels during the Great Depression. In 1933, Congress passed the National Industrial Recovery Act, which permitted competitors to establish codes of fair business conduct. The Supreme Court ruled the NIRA unconstitutional in 1935, however, and the United States was spared the widespread cartelization so common in many West European countries.

31. Richard Posner, *Antitrust Law: An Economic Perspective* (Chicago: University of Chicago Press, 1976), p. 39.

32. Hay and Kelley, "An Empirical Survey," p. 21.

33. Lawrence Shepard, "Licensing Restrictions and the Cost of Dental Care," *Journal of Law and Economics* 21 (April 1978): 187–201; Lee Benham, "The Effect of Advertising on the Price of Eyeglasses," *Journal of Law and Economics* 15 (October 1972): 337–52.

technology-sharing agreement between General Motors and Chrysler. Under the terms of the agreement, Chrysler was entitled to purchase information from GM on environmental and safety technology. In 1969 the Justice Department had opposed a similar agreement among the automakers on antipollution research and had obtained a consent decree prohibiting it. It was feared then that such an agreement would lessen competition and reduce the rate of product innovation. The change in position evidently reflected changes that occurred in the auto industry after 1969. Volkswagen began to produce cars in the United States, Honda planned to do the same, and both Datsun and Toyota were considering the idea. At the same time, Chrysler was in financial trouble, and probably could not have met government environmental and safety regulations without the technology-sharing agreement. The illegal agreement of 1969 thus became the legal agreement of 1979.

As has been mentioned, most of the controversy surrounding restraints of trade has focused on implicit or tacit agreements. Antitrust law has traditionally been ineffective against tacit collusion, even though it may have the same results as an explicit agreement. Critics contend that if antitrust law is to be consistent, price fixing should be illegal regardless of the means chosen. This dissatisfaction led to the development of the shared monopoly concept. If upheld by the courts, it will enable antitrust authorities to attack the tacit collusion associated with concentrated markets.

Two serious objections have been raised against shared monopoly suits, however. First, there is a debate about the interpretation of the positive relationship between market concentration and market profitability.[34] Some critics claim that this relationship is due primarily to economic efficiency, not tacit collusion. Large firms are more profitable because they are more efficient than smaller firms in their industry. This assertion questions both the prevalence of tacit collusion and the necessity for shared monopoly suits. Second, shared monopoly suits raise equity arguments. Many economists and lawyers consider shared monopoly to simply be another name for oligopoly, and shared monopoly suits to be a means of circumventing the legislative and judicial processes. Antitrust authorities are viewed as attacking industries unfairly for violating an antitrust policy that the courts and the Congress have not sanctioned.

34. Sam Peltzman, "The Gains and Losses from Industrial Concentration," *Journal of Law and Economics* 20 (October 1977): 229–63; and F. M. Scherer, "The Causes and Consequences of Rising Industrial Concentration: A Comment," *Journal of Law and Economics* 22 (April 1979): 191–208.

Remedies.   Price fixing has been illegal per se since 1940. Despite the clarity of the law, however, firms continue to engage in blatant price-fixing agreements. One industry notable for this practice is the paper industry, even though the government has successfully prosecuted major manufacturers of paper bags and cardboard boxes. According to a Justice Department official: "It's amazing. They just never seem to learn their lesson."[35] Such examples of recidivism question the deterrent value of the criminal and civil sanctions available in price-fixing cases.

The Justice Department initiates criminal proceedings when there have been flagrant violations of the Sherman Act; the criminal sanctions of fines and imprisonment can then be imposed. On January 1, 1975, violations of Section 1 of the Sherman Act changed from misdemeanors to felonies, increasing the criminal penalties to three years in prison and a $100,000 fine for individuals, and a maximum fine of $1 million for corporations. These penalties are not as imposing as they might seem at first, however. Historically, judges have been reluctant to send corporate executives to jail for price fixing. Generally, they require these "pillars of their communities" to perform community services such as working for charities or giving speeches on the evils of price fixing. In an effort to change this attitude, the Justice Department has been encouraging judges, with some success, to imprison price fixers. The experience with fines in such cases is parallel. Judges have tended to impose less than the maximum possible fine, amounting to only a small percentage of the sales affected by the price-fixing agreement. Table 6.2 presents data on the average fines imposed in price-fixing cases from 1890 to 1969. (The maximum fine varied in this time span, from $5,000 per violation in 1890 to $50,000 in 1955.) In general, fines have been small in both absolute and relative (compared with sales) terms.

Perhaps the most imposing penalty of all is the treble damage award available under the Sherman Act. There is no statutory limit to the compensation available in private treble damage suits.[36] In the great electrical conspiracy cases of the 1960s, for instance, more than $400 million in damages was awarded. Award settlements of this order of magnitude

35. "Price-Fixing Charges Rise," *Wall Street Journal*, May 4, 1978, p. 1.

36. One possible offset is that private damage payments, unlike fines, can be deducted from corporate income tax as an "ordinary and necessary expense." This deduction was modified in 1969 so that only one-third of the payments are tax deductible if the corporation was found guilty or submitted a *nolo* plea in a prior criminal action by the government (M. Green, et al., *The Closed Enterprise System* [New York: Grossman Publishers, 1972], p. 172).

Table 6.2   Fines in Price-fixing Cases, 1890–1969

Period in which Case Was Instituted	Average Fine per Case[a]	Average Fine as Percentage of Sales Involved in Conspiracy
1890–1899	$ 0 (0)[b]	
1900–1909	20,000 (11)	
1910–1919	20,000 (24)	
1920–1929	98,000 (15)	
1930–1939	61,000 (18)	
1940–1949	52,000 (149)	
1950–1959	40,000 (121)	0.08%
1960–1969	131,000 (103)	0.21%

[a]Rounded to nearest thousand.

[b]Number in parentheses is number of convictions during the period.

Source: Reproduced from Richard A. Posner, *Antitrust Law: An Economic Perspective* (Chicago: University of Chicago Press, 1976), Table 2, p. 32.

can provide a substantial financial incentive for firms to comply with the antitrust laws.

Enforcement.   As with all the antitrust laws, the primary responsibility for enforcement rests with the government. Most price-fixing schemes are attacked first by the Justice Department rather than by private parties or other governmental bodies.[37] The major role that private parties play in enforcement is the initiation of companion suits that seek treble damage awards, which may be the strongest deterrent to price fixing. The private role has been hindered, however, by restrictions on standing and by nonlitigated settlements in government suits. A recent Supreme Court decision denied standing to indirect purchasers from price-fixing agreements,[38] thereby limiting the scope of private suits. Consumers, for example, can only attack price fixing at the retail level, since they do not purchase directly from manufacturers. Nonlitigated settlements are a problem since they cannot be used as prima facie evidence of an antitrust violation in companion private suits. The acceptance of *nolo contendere* pleas and consent decrees makes it more difficult for private litigants to obtain the evidence necessary for a successful suit.

37. State attorneys general as well as foreign governments can initiate actions under the antitrust laws.

38. *Illinois Brick Company* v. *Illinois*, 431 U.S. 720 (1977).

In sum, current policy toward restraints of trade has its pluses and minuses. Formal cartels are nonexistent in the United States, although implicit agreements are relatively immune from antitrust attack. Criminal penalties seem low (even by "white-collar crime" standards), while civil penalties—treble damage awards—can be quite large. The overall deterrent effect of antitrust policy is difficult to determine, since it is impossible to know the amount of covert price-fixing activity throughout the economy.

New Directions for Antitrust

Most reform proposals have focused on the "oligopoly problem"—tacit collusion. The general objective is to make all price-fixing agreements, both explicit and implicit, actionable under the antitrust laws. This raises the related issue of the appropriate remedies for tacit collusion.

Legal Standards. The most controversial reform proposal would make oligopoly illegal per se. That is, it would apply to oligopolies a version of the no-fault monopoly proposal discussed in Chapter 5. This approach would outlaw the persistent possession of monopoly power by two or more firms. For example, there would be a rebuttable presumption of monopoly power if the four-firm concentration ratio exceeded 50 for five of the preceding seven years. The oligopolists could, of course, defend their market positions as the natural result of economies of scale or patents. The advantage of a structural approach is that it eliminates any analysis of the oligopolists' conduct and directly attacks the condition that is most conducive to tacit collusion—high seller concentration. On the other hand, this approach would create perverse incentives for oligopolists to manipulate their market shares in an effort to evade the market share guidelines. This problem is common to all structural proposals. A more damaging objection is that such a proposal would immediately outlaw approximately one-fourth of the economy, including most of the major manufacturing industries. There is little political support for such a massive disruption of the economy, especially given the uncertainty already created by inflation, unemployment, and foreign competition. Even a more modest proposal requiring a four-firm concentration ratio of at least 70 seems unlikely in the near future.

Posner advocates a less dramatic alternative: "an economic approach to detection and proof of collusion."[39] His solution to the oligopoly problem is straightforward: look for collusion in those markets where it

39. Posner, *Antitrust Law*, Chapter 4.

is most likely to occur and attack it only if it has been successful. This can be done by economic analysis of market structure and performance. For example, successful collusion would be inferred from circumstantial economic evidence such as supra-competitive prices and stable market shares for the leading firms. Emphasis would be on the consequences of collusion, instead of the method. Posner states:

> What is being proposed here is not so much the alteration of substantive contours of the law as a change in evidentiary requirements to permit illegal price fixing to be found in circumstances where, although explicit collusion cannot be proved, an actual meeting of the minds on a noncompetitive price can be inferred.[40]

This change, if adopted, would increase the economic rationality of antitrust enforcement, but would also increase the complexity of antitrust litigation. And this potential impact on litigation may make Posner's proposal impractical.

Remedies.   The most frequently recommended new remedy is mandatory dissolution, which would have the effect of restructuring the defendants, and hence the market. Dissolution is advocated for two reasons. First, it is necessary for effective relief, especially when the defendants' market is highly concentrated. Restrictions on future conduct do not eliminate the oligopolistic interdependence so conducive to the formation of collusive agreements. Only dissolution can directly increase the number of competitors and reduce the concentration of sellers. Second, dissolution constitutes a greater deterrent to price fixing than do the current remedies of fines, imprisonment, and even treble damages. It threatens the very corporate existence of each defendant. This stronger action is deemed necessary to combat the apparent corporate recidivism (as exemplified by the paper industry).

Given the perceived need for a stronger, more effective, remedy, is dissolution feasible? The dissolution of oligopolists raises all the issues associated with the dissolution of a monopolist, though with a different twist. First, the benefits of dissolving several firms simultaneously are less certain than in the dissolution of a monopolist. It is unlikely that their collusion will yield the monopoly price and so the potential reduction in market price is less. Dissolution in this case is also less likely to lead to a greater increase, if any, in dynamic efficiency. Second, the costs of dissolution may be greater than with a monopolist. The dissolu-

---

40. Posner, *Antitrust Law*, p. 75.

tion of a dominant firm is not likely to create firms that are too small to realize all economies of scale. This possibility is also remote for most oligopolists, though not inconsequential. Most empirical studies suggest that industrial deconcentration will not jeopardize production efficiency, although this conclusion is being questioned.[41] A major complication, however, is the uncertain impact of government regulations on the size of firm that is necessary to exhaust all economies of scale. Are larger and larger firms necessary to comply with government regulations?[42] Until these issues are resolved, dissolution does not appear to be a practical alternative to the existing remedies, which were substantially increased in 1975.

Enforcement.   As discussed earlier, private treble damage actions may be a greater deterrent than the criminal penalites of fines and imprisonment. Their effect could be increased by increasing the threat of private actions, and two proposals to accomplish this have been made. The first would expand consumers' right to sue by overturning the Supreme Court's Illinois Brick decision, which restricted standing to direct purchasers from price-fixing firms.[43] Consumers anywhere in the distribution chain could then attack collusive arrangements. The second, and more important, change would allow nonlitigated settlements to be used as prima facie evidence of an antitrust violation. This would reduce the burden placed on private litigants when the government accepts a *nolo contendere* plea or consent decree. There is a precedent for this in a case involving the price fixing of asphalt in which a clause was inserted in the consent decree making it a litigated decree for treble damage actions.[44] These so-called "asphalt" clauses would, however, undoubtedly reduce the willingness of defendants to reach out-of-court settlements with the government. The proper role of nonlitigated settlements in antitrust enforcement must also be evaluated; Chapter 10 discusses this issue in the context of an overall evaluation of antitrust enforcement.

41. H. Goldschmid, M. Mann, and J. Weston, eds., *Industrial Concentration: The New Learning* (Boston: Little, Brown, 1974), Chapter 2.

42. "GM's Juggernaut, Riding over the Competition to Push Market Share Up and Up," *Business Week*, March 26, 1979, p. 64. According to a Chrysler official, "the root of General Motors' current strength is the government and regulation. The government is playing GM's game. GM has got the volume and they've got the cash, so they can play the regulation game better than anybody else."

43. *United States* v. *Illinois Brick.*

44. Green et al., *The Closed Enterprise System*, p. 205.

Summary

Competitors may restrain trade, either directly or indirectly, through various interfirm agreements. Antitrust authorities have adopted a rule of reason approach that clearly prohibits nonancillary restraints, but preserves beneficial ancillary restraints. Antitrust enforcement has been more effective against explicit agreements than against implicit agreements such as tacit collusion. A major problem historically has been the low penalties imposed by the courts on such white-collar criminals as price fixers, and the impact of the increased penalties that became effective January 1, 1975, has not been determined. A common proposal of critics of current antitrust policies is a massive deconcentration of American industry. Widespread dissolution seems particularly ill-timed and possibly not consistent with the public's interest. It would seem more appropriate to "fine-tune" the current system, possibly by adopting Posner's economic approach to collusion and by increasing the probability of private antitrust actions.

Suggested Readings

Asch, P., and Seneca, J. "Is Collusion Profitable?" *Review of Economics and Statistics* 58 (February 1976): 1–12.

Fuller, John G. *The Gentlemen Conspirators* (New York: Grove Press, 1962).

Kottke, Frank. *The Promotion of Price Competition Where Sellers Are Few* (Lexington, Mass.: Lexington Books, 1978).

Posner, Richard A. *Antitrust Law* (Chicago: University of Chicago Press, 1976), Chapter 4.

Scherer, F. M. *Industrial Market Structure and Economic Performance*, 2nd ed. (Chicago: Rand McNally, 1980), Chapters 5–9.

Shepard, Lawrence. "Licensing Restrictions and the Cost of Dental Care," *Journal of Law and Economics* 21 (April 1978): 187–201.

Mergers

Chapter 7

Mergers are a common occurrence in the business world. Practically every edition of the *Wall Street Journal* contains articles discussing recently consummated mergers and proposals for new ones. Many of these mergers involve the leading corporations in America and, increasingly, in western Europe and Japan. As mergers are voluntary business transactions, they presumably are beneficial to the owners of the firms involved. For antitrust authorities, the question is whether mergers are beneficial to society.

The Setting

A *merger* is the consolidation of two or more independent firms into a single firm. All mergers are not the same, however. Both the merger process and the structure of the resulting consolidation can vary. A firm can acquire another by purchasing its stock or assets, or by exchanging its stock for that of the acquired firm. The merger is termed "friendly" if it is supported by the acquired firm's management and "hostile" if it is not. A merger can create a completely new firm, in which case both the acquiring and the acquired firms cease to exist. More commonly, though, the acquired firm is absorbed by the acquiring firm or continues to operate under its previous corporate identity.

Although the form of a merger can vary, the substance does not. Previously independent firms are brought under common control; the number of independent decision centers is reduced from two to one. Even though the acquired firm may retain substantial autonomy, ultimate authority rests with the acquiring firm's management. This centralization of control can affect the structures of the markets in which both firms operate. It is this potential impact on market structure, and subsequently on market competition, that has received most attention from antitrust authorities.

Legal Issues

An antitrust action against a specific merger can be initiated under both the Sherman and the Clayton acts. Because a merger consolidates two or more firms, it creates a combination that may violate Section 1 of the Sherman Act. Whether or not a merger restrains trade and is thus illegal under the Sherman Act must be established by the courts. A merger, or a series of mergers, can at the same time monopolize a market or represent an attempt to do so. The legal standards for a Section 2 violation of the Sherman Act would then be relevant (as discussed in Chapter 5).

Section 7 of the Clayton Act specifically addresses the competitive problems that may be posed by mergers. As amended by the Celler-Kefauver Act of 1950, it reads in part:

> That no corporation engaged in commerce shall acquire, directly or indirectly, the whole or any part of the stock or other shared capital and no corporation subject to the jurisdiction of the Federal Trade Commission shall acquire the whole or any part of the assets of another corporation engaged also in commerce, where in any line of commerce in any section of the country, the effect of such acquisition may be substantially to lessen competition, or to tend to create a monopoly.[1]

The application of Section 7 to mergers depends on the courts' interpretations of three key phrases: "any line of commerce"; "any section of the country"; and "may be substantially to lessen competition, or to tend to create a monopoly." The first two phrases refer to the product and to the geographic dimensions of the relevant economic market(s). How the relevant market is defined will determine both the type of the merger and the applicable legal precedents. The third phrase concerns the merger's possible impact on competition. The use of the word "may" in the act indicates that its focus is on the potential, not the actual, impact of a merger on competition. The Clayton Act is designed to be

1. Clayton Act, Sec. 7, 15 U.S.C. Sec. 18 (1976).

preventive and to forestall any actions that could lead to monopoly. It thus complements the Sherman Act, which is concerned primarily with monopolization.[2] The exact scope of Section 7 depends on the standards required by the courts to establish the necessary potential impact on market competition.

Economic Issues

Economics has played an increasingly important role in merger antitrust cases, providing a convenient framework in which to classify mergers and evaluate their potential impact on market competition. At the same time, it is also important to understand the motives for mergers as well as their historical role in the American economy.

Types of Mergers.   Economists classify mergers according to the economic markets within which the acquiring and acquired firms operate. Based on the product and geographic dimensions of their markets, mergers are divided into three separate categories: (1) horizontal; (2) vertical; and (3) conglomerate.

A *horizontal merger* combines two firms that produce the same product in the same geographic market. The two firms are competitors, and so the merger reduces the number of firms in the market by one. A merger between Boeing and Lockheed, for example, would be a horizontal merger, because they both supply commercial aircraft to airlines throughout the world.

A *vertical* merger combines two firms that previously had a potential or actual customer-supplier relationship. A product of one firm is used as an input by the other firm. A vertical merger replaces a market transaction with a purely intrafirm transaction; an input is supplied within the firm instead of being purchased outside it. The acquisition of U.S. Steel by General Motors would be a vertical merger, because GM uses flat rolled steel in manufacturing its automobiles and buses.

Any merger that is neither horizontal nor vertical is automatically classified as *conglomerate*. There are three different types of conglomerate mergers: (1) market extension; (2) product extension; and (3) "pure" conglomerate. A market extension merger combines two firms that produce the same product in *different* geographic markets.[3] A good

2. The phrase "or to tend to create a monopoly" is extraneous, for any such effect would clearly represent a substantial lessening of competition and hence be covered by Section 7.

3. Note that the only difference between a horizontal merger and a market extension merger is the geographic definition of the relevant markets.

example would be a merger between the *Washington Post* and the *Los Angeles Times*, both newspaper publishers, but on opposite sides of the country.

A product extension merger is defined more subjectively; some complementary relationship exists in the production and/or distribution of the two firms' products. One firm may be able to produce the other firm's product on its assembly lines or market it through an existing distribution system. This relationship can be illustrated by a hypothetical merger between Chrysler, a car manufacturer, and Coachmen, a major manufacturer of recreational vehicles. Chrysler might be able to produce recreational vehicles by converting its auto assembly plants. It certainly could market them through its existing network of automobile dealers.

"Pure" conglomerate is a residual category, including all mergers in which there is no apparent relationship between the products of the acquired and acquiring firms. The acquiring firm is venturing beyond its traditional production and distribution experiences. An example of a "pure" conglomerate merger would be the acquisition by International Business Machines, the leading computer manufacturer, of the Washington Redskins, a professional football team.

This classification scheme facilitates the economic analysis of a merger's potential impact on market competition. Two qualifications should be noted, however. First, this scheme assumes that the firms' product and geographic markets have been defined correctly. If they have not, any economic analysis based on them will be incorrect. Second, a merger is likely to be multidimensional in nature. A single merger can have horizontal, vertical, and conglomerate dimensions. For example, assume that General Motors were to merge with Nissan, the Japanese manufacturer of Datsuns. At a minimum, this merger would be partly horizontal (both firms sell cars in the United States), partly vertical (both firms produce auto parts), and partly market extension (GM does not produce cars in Japan). Not surprisingly, the analysis of the impact of a multidimensional merger is more complex than that of a simple merger.

Motives for Mergers.   If a firm wants to grow, it can do so through internal expansion or external acquisition. Mergers seem to offer several advantages. First, a merger can be quicker. Considerable lead time is needed to construct a new plant and obtain the necessary production know-how. And environmental regulations regarding the siting of new plants can increase this lead time. Second, a merger can be cheaper. The market for firms is not perfect, and a firm's stock may sell below its book value, especially during inflationary periods.[4] It can be less expensive to purchase an existing plant than to construct a new one. Third, a merger may be the only way to enter a market. This can be the case in regulated markets where *de novo* (new) entry is virtually impossible. For example, the Civil Aeronautics Board and the Interstate Commerce Commission have historically been very reluctant to allow *de novo* entry into domestic airline and trucking markets (see Chapter 12).

The exact type of merger the acquiring firm chooses depends on more complex considerations. Horizontal mergers, for example, eliminate competitors and may therefore lessen market competition. At the extreme, a series of horizontal mergers could transform a competitive market into a monopoly.[5] A more common rationale is that horizontal mergers enable the acquiring firm to realize economies, though it is not clear why.[6] Most economies are made at the plant level, and the acquisition of existing plants would not change this. Operating several plants can produce economies, although these are generally slight. A merger could, however, enable a firm to serve its larger market share with a single, more efficient plant instead of several smaller plants. This would occur if the smaller plants were *less* than minimum optimal scale (that is, the smallest plant size that minimizes average total cost).

The dominant motive for vertical mergers appears to be security. The acquiring firm protects itself by merging with a firm that distributes goods through its outlets (downstream integration) or produces inputs (upstream integration). In this way it becomes less dependent on market forces in its input or output markets.[7] The integration of successive stages in the distribution or production processes also are supposed to yield economies. One of the few known examples is the production of

4. The merger route may also yield tax advantages not available through *de novo* entry, especially if the acquired firm has tax credits from losses in previous years.

5. During the 1890s, a series of mergers consolidated over 200 steel firms into 20. Twelve of these firms were subsequently combined in 1901 to form U.S. Steel. This billion-dollar merger created the largest industrial firm in the economy, gave U.S. Steel a 65 percent share of the market, and rewarded the promoter, J. P. Morgan, with a fee of $62.5 million!

6. Economists distinguish between real and pecuniary economies. Real economies result when a given process can be performed using fewer resources. This enables society to produce more goods given its limited amount of resources. Pecuniary economies, on the other hand, enable a firm to reduce its costs, but not to reduce its use of productive resources. A firm may obtain more favorable input prices from its suppliers, but there is no increase in society's production possibilities.

7. A firm does not have to become fully integrated to reduce uncertainty and increase its security. General Motors is frequently cited as an example of "tapered" integration, whereby a firm internally supplies part of its input requirements. "Tapered" integration reduces, but does not eliminate, a firm's dependence on independent suppliers or dealers.

steel from hot iron. If a steel firm is vertically integrated, the hot iron can go straight into steel production, whereas if the iron is purchased, it must be reheated after it is delivered. Integration of iron and steel production thus eliminates the need to reheat the iron. By definition, vertical integration eliminates a market transaction and the costs associated with that transaction.[8] The saving in transaction costs must be compared to any reduction in economies caused by managing the additional operations. For example, in the 1950s cement companies acquired ready-mix companies even though they expected to incur higher costs from running both operations.[9] They considered the mergers necessary, however, to guarantee their access to the ready-mix market.

The dominant motive behind conglomerate mergers is diversification. A firm's risk is reduced because its activities are spread across several markets instead of being confined to a single one. A change in any one of the markets will have less overall impact. The degree of diversification achieved varies with the type of conglomerate merger. Market and product extension mergers, which deal with the same or related products, provide less diversification than pure conglomerate mergers. In the late 1960s, for example, many defense contractors made pure conglomerate mergers to reduce their dependence on military contracts.

There also are many reasons why a firm may consent to being acquired through a merger. First, the firm may be in financial trouble, and a merger may be the only alternative to bankruptcy or the only way to obtain more funds to finance growth. Second, mergers are an appealing exit route for owners of small firms. If there are no heirs to a family business, the owner can perpetuate the business by letting another firm acquire it. There are also tax advantages to a stock exchange. The owner pays the lower capital gains tax instead of the higher personal income tax. Finally, the acquiring firm's offer may seem so profitable that it would be imprudent to refuse it.

Historical Trends in Merger Activity.   Although the exact time periods are disputed, economists agree that the American economy has experienced three major waves of mergers. The first wave lasted from approximately 1897 to 1904 and followed the rapid industrialization of the economy. This wave created giant firms that dominated their respective

8. For a detailed analysis of this aspect of vertical integration see Oliver Williamson, *Markets and Hierarchies: Analysis and Antitrust Implications* (New York: Free Press, 1975), Chapters 5–7.

9. Bruce T. Allen, "Vertical Integration and Market Foreclosure: The Case of Cement and Concrete," *Journal of Law and Economics* 14 (April 1971): 251–74.

industries. About 70 major industries were transformed to near monopolies through mergers. Such corporate giants as American Can (cans), DuPont (explosives), Exxon (oil), American Tobacco (tobacco), and U.S. Steel (steel) rose to dominance through these "mergers for monopoly."[10]

The first wave crested in 1904. The downturn in merger activity has been attributed to the combined effects of the recession of 1903–1904 and the government's successful prosecution of the Northern Securities case in 1904. Mergers continued, but at a drastically reduced rate. General Motors was created in 1909 through the consolidation of Buick, Oldsmobile, Cadillac, and later Chevrolet. GM tried to acquire Ford, but was unable to raise the necessary funds. Another significant merger occurred in 1911 when International Business Machines was formed.

The merger pace remained slack until the second wave began around 1916.[11] Mergers during this period of "mergers for oligopoly" frequently created significant rivals for many of the dominant firms created during the first wave. Bethlehem Steel challenged U.S. Steel; Continental Can gave chase to American Can. There was also considerable merger activity among public utilities. Through giant holding companies, public utilities from different parts of the country were brought under unified control. This wave ended with the infamous stock market crash on "Black Tuesday," October 29, 1929.

Merger activity remained low throughout the Great Depression and did not increase significantly until the end of World War II. The third, and largest, wave lasted until the recession of 1970 and was distinguished by a dramatic increase in conglomerate mergers. This corporate trend was accentuated by the meteoric rise of small, relatively unknown firms to the forefront of American industry. A good example is the phenomenal growth of Ling-Temco-Vought (L-T-V) under the leadership of Jimmy Ling.[12] In 1961, L-T-V was primarily a defense contractor, ranking 335 on the *Fortune* list of the 500 largest domestic industrial corporations. From 1961 to 1969, L-T-V acquired 33 companies, including Braniff (airlines), Jones and Laughlin (steel), Okonite (wire and carpeting), and Wilson (meat packing and sporting goods). These mergers in-

10. J. Markham, "Survey of the Evidence and Findings on Mergers," in National Bureau of Economic Research, *Business Concentration and Price Policy* (Princeton, N.J.: Princeton University Press, 1955), pp. 141–82.

11. Carl Eis, "The 1919–1930 Merger Movement in American Industry," *Journal of Law and Economics* 12 (October 1969): 267–96.

12. For a detailed discussion of L-T-V and other prominent conglomerates during this period, see U.S. Federal Trade Commission, *Economic Report on Corporate Mergers* (Washington, D.C.: Government Printing Office, 1969).

creased L-T-V's annual sales from $148 million to $3.8 billion—an average annual growth rate of 300 percent. By 1968, L-T-V was ranked 22 on the *Fortune* 500. Though L-T-V subsequently encountered financial and antitrust difficulties, it remains a symbol of the conglomerate merger fever that typified this most recent merger wave.

After the 1970 recession, merger activity continued at a brisk pace, though slower than during the 1960s. The number of major mergers (more than $10 million in assets) increased throughout the 1970s, but it is too soon to tell if a fourth major wave has begun.

Mergers and Market Competition. The three major merger waves have had an indelible impact on the structure of the American economy. The first wave substantially increased both market concentration and aggregate concentration. Some of the giants formed during this period are still the leading firms in their industries. The second wave also increased both market and aggregate concentration, although the increases were not so pronounced. Also, many of the public utility mergers of the period were subsequently dissolved by the Public Utility Reorganization Act of 1946. The third wave had a unique impact because of the trend to conglomerate mergers. Aggregate concentration increased, but market concentration, by definition, was unaffected.

The impact of a specific merger on competition depends on both the type of merger and the market(s) involved. The primary economic argument against horizontal mergers is monopoly. A merger, or series of mergers, that creates a monopoly is obviously anticompetitive. Is every horizontal merger anticompetitive, however? A merger between two perfect competitors would not affect competition, while one between two oligopolists probably would. Where is the dividing line between harmless and harmful mergers? The conventional wisdom states that collusion becomes feasible if the four-firm concentration ratio is at least 50. Mergers that increase concentration to this level could thus be anticompetitive. At the same time, some horizontal mergers can be procompetitive. A merger may enable two small firms to compete more effectively against their larger rivals. A recent study by Kwoka suggests that horizontal mergers that create a large "Number Three" firm can increase market competition.[13] These considerations indicate that the relationship between horizontal mergers and competition is not simple. Each horizontal merger must be evaluated on its own merits.

13. John E. Kwoka, Jr., "The Effect of Market Share Distribution on Industry Performance," *Review of Economics and Statistics* 61 (February 1979): 101–9.

Vertical mergers can affect competition by reducing actual and potential competition in either or both of the markets involved. Actual competition in one market can be lessened by market *foreclosure,* the exclusion of competitors from part of the market. This occurs when an acquired firm's market transactions become purely intrafirm transactions with the acquiring firm. For example, if Coca-Cola acquired McDonald's, it could supply them with soft drinks, thereby preventing other firms such as Pepsi, Seven-Up, and Dr Pepper from competing for McDonald's business. How does market foreclosure affect competition? This issue has been hotly debated and there is no clear-cut answer. The key issue is whether vertical mergers can create market power. As an extreme example, assume that there are two competitive markets, each with 100 equal-sized firms. Each firm in one market now acquires a firm in the other market. There are now 100 vertically integrated firms, but both markets are still competitive. Vertical mergers by themselves cannot create market power. Only when there is existing market power at one stage can competition be affected at the other stage.[14] For example, Alcoa used its monopoly position in the production of aluminum ingots to acquire a dominant position in the fabrication of aluminum products.

The most likely anticompetitive effect of a vertical merger is a lessening of potential competition. This can occur for two reasons. First, the merger can increase the barriers to entry that a potential entrant faces. If a new firm must be vertically integrated, it will need more capital and may have to enter at a larger scale than if it produced in only a single market. Second, a vertical merger can eliminate one of the likely potential entrants into that market. The most likely entrants into a market frequently are the customers of that market. For example, Campbell Soup and the major beer companies are probably the most likely potential entrants into the can industry. Their entry into this market via the merger would lessen potential competition only if there were very few potential entrants. If there were 100 potential entrants, the loss of a few would not affect the degree of potential competition. On the procompetitive side, a vertical merger can increase competition if it enables a smaller firm to compete more effectively against vertically integrated rivals.

The economic analysis of conglomerate mergers is more complex than that for horizontal and vertical mergers. Such mergers have four potentially anticompetitive aspects. First, a conglomerate firm may lessen

14. Douglas Needham, *Economic Analysis and Industrial Structure* (New York: Holt, Rinehart, 1969), Chapters 8–9.

competition if it uses its profits from one market (the "deep pocket") to subsidize aggressive behavior in another market. Such cross-subsidization is rational, however, only if the conglomerate can drive out rivals and prevent them from reentering in the future;[15] this is not very likely. Second, product and market extension mergers can lessen potential competition, because the acquiring firm is a potential competitor of the acquired firm. By definition, it is already producing the same product in a different geographic market or a related product in the same one. Potential competition is lessened if the acquiring firm is one of a limited number of potential entrants into the acquired firm's market. Third, a conglomerate merger may lead to market foreclosure through *reciprocity*, or reciprocal dealing. One firm agrees to buy a product from another firm if that firm will "reciprocate" and purchase a product from it. Reciprocity gives conglomerates an advantage, for their single-product competitors do not have the leverage with which to obtain sales in other markets.[16] Finally, conglomerate mergers can lessen competition through "mutual forbearance" behavior. A conglomerate may not compete aggressively in one market for fear that rival conglomerates will retaliate in other markets. As a result, each conglomerate tacitly holds back in the expectation that its rivals will reciprocate, thereby presenting antitrust authorities with a multimarket version of conscious parallelism.

To further complicate the situation, conglomerate mergers also have three potentially procompetitive aspects. First, they can promote competition if the acquiring firm merges with a small firm and builds it into a viable competitor. This is called a "toe-hold" acquisition, because the acquiring firm uses the acquired firm as a base from which to expand. Second, conglomerate mergers can prevent firms from becoming inefficient and not competing aggressively. Such firms become likely merger prospects, and the threat of a takeover by another firm may force their management to be more efficient. Finally, conglomerates may transfer capital across markets more efficiently than do the capital markets. A conglomerate's investments are normally controlled by top management, who allocate funds internally to the most productive uses. If conglomerates respond to profitable opportunities more quickly than

15. The economics of predatory behavior is discussed in more detail in Chapter 8.

16. It also may be used as an indirect form of price competition in oligopolistic industries. Instead of lowering price, the seller agrees to pay a higher price for one of its customer's products. For an empirical analysis of reciprocity, see Bruce T. Allen, "Industrial Reciprocity: A Statistical Analysis," *Journal of Law and Economics* 18 (October 1975): 507–20.

market forces do, they will improve the allocation of resources throughout the economy.

Overall, mergers are complex business transactions that can have varied impacts on market competition.[17] A merger between two small firms can be procompetitive, while a similar merger between two large firms might be anticompetitive. Although each merger should be evaluated in its own light, a few generalizations seem valid. First, horizontal mergers pose the greatest threat to competition and proffer the fewest benefits. Second, vertical mergers offer the potential for more economies, though they are undoubtedly of a small order of magnitude. Third, conglomerate mergers probably promote market competition more frequently than they hinder it.[18]

The crucial role of the judiciary in interpreting, and hence determining, the effectiveness of the antitrust laws is illustrated in the government's litigation of merger cases. The Sherman Act was at first ineffective against most mergers. The courts would not proscribe a merger unless the defendant was on the verge of monopolizing the market. This deficiency was supposed to be remedied by Section 7 of the Clayton Act, but this section also had its problems. First, Section 7 applied only to horizontal mergers. Second, it covered the acquisition of a firm's stock, but not of its assets. The government's jurisdiction over a merger thus depended on whether it involved stock or assets. Asset acquisitions could not be prohibited. Finally, the courts ruled that an illegal merger was legal if the acquiring firm assumed control before the government contested the merger!

Such was the demoralized state of antimerger law before the passage of the Celler-Kefauver Act in 1950. This amendment closed the loopholes in the original Section 7 of the Clayton Act. The government has since initiated many suits under the amended Section 7, establishing a considerable body of merger case law. This section examines the cur-

The Case Law

---

17. For a detailed analysis of mergers, see Peter O. Steiner, *Mergers: Motives, Effects, Policies* (Ann Arbor: University of Michigan Press, 1975).

18. There is a growing body of empirical studies suggesting that conglomerate mergers do not lessen market competition. See, for example: Lawrence G. Goldberg, "Conglomerate Mergers and Concentration Ratios," *Review of Economics and Statistics* 56 (August 1974): 303–9; Jesse W. Markham, *Conglomerate Enterprise and Public Policy* (Boston: Harvard University Press, 1973); and Allyn D. Strickland, *Firm Diversification, Mutual Forbearance Behavior and Price-Cost Margins* (New York: Garland Publishing, 1980).

rent state of antitrust law regarding all three types of mergers—vertical, horizontal, and conglomerate—as well as joint ventures.

Vertical Mergers

The controlling precedent for vertical mergers—*United States* v. *Brown Shoe*—also happened to be the Supreme Court's first comprehensive review of Section 7 of the Clayton Act, as amended by the Celler-Kefauver Act.[19] Both the defendant, *Brown Shoe,* and the acquired firm, *Kinney Shoe,* were producers and retailers of shoes. Brown was the fourth largest manufacturer (4 percent of national sales) and the third largest retailer (6 percent of national sales). Kinney was the eighth largest retailer (1.2 percent of national sales) and the twelfth largest manufacturer (.5 percent of national sales). Brown did not supply any shoes to Kinney prior to the merger, but did supply 7.9 percent of its requirements afterward. As both firms were producers as well as retailers of shoes, the merger raised both horizontal and vertical merger issues. The importance of the case, however, lies in the Supreme Court's analysis of the vertical aspects of the merger.[20]

The Court addressed three basic issues in its decision. First, what satisfies the statutory requirement for a "substantial lessening of competition?" Second, what are the specific standards for determining the legality of a vertical merger? Finally, could Brown employ any defenses to justify the merger?

The first issue required an analysis of congressional intent in passing the Celler-Kefauver Act. The Court noted:

> ... Congress used the words *"may be* substantially to lessen competition" to indicate that its concern was with probabilities, not certainties. Statutes existed for dealing with clear-cut menaces to competition; no statute was sought for dealing with ephemeral possibilities. Mergers with a probably anticompetitive effect were to be proscribed by this Act.[21]

The emphasis is on probabilities, not certainties. It is not necessary to show an actual lessening of competition, only a probability that it might be lessened. The Court's endorsement of the easier evidentiary requirement is consistent with the Clayton Act's professed goal of stopping harmful acts in an incipient stage.

19. *Brown Shoe Co., Inc.* v. *United States,* 370 U.S. 294 (1962).

20. The Court also ruled that some of the horizontal aspects of the merger violated Section 7. More specifically, the merger substantially increased market concentration in retailing, but not in the production of shoes.

21. *Brown Shoe Co., Inc.* v. *United States,* at 323.

The Court's next step was to establish the specific criteria for determining the legality of vertical mergers. The Court concentrated on the amount of the market that the merger would foreclose. If the amount of foreclosure were *de minimus* (that is, very small), the merger would be legal. Otherwise, further inquiry would be warranted. Establishing a very strong precedent, the Court ruled that Kinney's 1.2 percent share of the retail market was not *de minimus*. It then examined additional evidence about the shoe industry in order to determine the probable impact of the merger. The Court saw a trend among manufacturers, especially Brown, to acquire retailers. This trend toward increased concentration in the shoe industry seemed exactly what the Clayton Act was designed to forestall. The merger was therefore illegal.

The Court's ruling also briefly discussed two defenses that might be used in merger cases. First, a merger might be legal if the acquired firm were a "failing firm" and would go bankrupt if not acquired. Such an acquisition would not be anticompetitive, as the firm would otherwise leave the market. Second, a merger might be legal if it combined two small firms into a more effective competitor. Neither one of these defenses was applicable in Brown's acquisition of Kinney, so the merger was proscribed.

Horizontal Mergers

The Supreme Court addressed the specific issues raised by horizontal mergers in *United States* v. *Philadelphia National Bank*.[22] A merger between two banks gave them a combined market share of 30 percent and increased concentration in the Philadelphia banking market. The merger partners argued that the consolidation enabled them to compete more effectively against the large New York banks and, in fact, increased competition. The Court rejected this argument, emphasizing instead the resulting increase in concentration in the Philadelphia banking market.

> Specifically, we think that a merger which produces a firm controlling an undue percentage share of the relevant market, and results in a significant increase in the concentration of firms in that market, is so inherently likely to lessen competition substantially that it must be enjoined in the absence of evidence clearly showing that the merger is not likely to have such anti-competitive effects.[23]

The merger was thus illegal.

22. *United States* v. *Philadelphia National Bank*, 374 U.S. 321 (1963).
23. *United States* v. *Philadelphia National Bank*, at 363.

The Court's adoption of a structural approach for determining the competitive impact of a horizontal merger raised one major question: What is the minimum necessary for "an undue percentage share of the relevant market?" This question was quickly answered in *United States v. Von's Grocery*.[24] This case involved the merger between the third largest (Von's) and sixth largest (Shopping Bag) grocery chains in Los Angeles, which gave Von's a market share of 7.5 percent, second only to Safeway's 8 percent. As in the Brown Shoe case, the disputed merger occurred against a backdrop of increasing merger activity and declining competitors. Once again the Court viewed the merger as anticompetitive, even though the market share involved was very small. Despite Justice Potter Stewart's stinging dissent, the Von's decision constituted a strong precedent against horizontal mergers.

The rigidity of the Von's case was subsequently relaxed by the Court's decision in *United States v. General Dynamics*.[25] The contested merger combined two coal producers in a market where concentration was increasing. The merger directly increased the share of the top two firms from 33.1 to 37.9 percent. The merger undeniably increased concentration, but would it necessarily lessen competition? The Court looked behind the production data and determined that future competition depended on the concentration of coal reserves, not current coal production. There the merger's impact was dramatically different, for General Dynamics controlled only one percent of the market's total coal reserves. Based on this economic analysis, the Court concluded that the merger did not violate the Clayton Act.

General Dynamics apparently represents a much more sophisticated approach by the Court to horizontal mergers. This conclusion is somewhat tenuous, however, since the majority was based on different considerations. Nonetheless, the Court did appear to be considering other factors besides concentration in determining the legality of horizontal mergers. In short, horizontal mergers among viable competitors are not illegal per se, but the burden of proof does rest with the defendant.

Conglomerate Mergers

The first conglomerate merger to reach the Supreme Court concerned the practice of reciprocity.[26] Consolidated Foods, both a food processor

24. *United States v. Von's Grocery Co.*, 384 U.S. 270 (1966).
25. *United States v. General Dynamics Corp. et al.*, 415 U.S. 486 (1974).
26. *Federal Trade Commission v. Consolidated Foods Corp.*, 380 U.S. 592 (1965).

and a wholesale and retail distributor, acquired Gentry, a leading manufacturer of dehydrated onion and garlic. The potential for reciprocity lay in Consolidated's ability to use its position as a distributor to "encourage" its suppliers to use Gentry's products whenever possible. There was in fact evidence that Consolidated had engaged in reciprocity, although its impact on competition was inconclusive. The Court stated that an actual anticompetitive showing was not required, as the Clayton Act is concerned with probabilities, not certainties. It concluded that if the acquired firm has a substantial market share, a finding of a probability of reciprocity is supported. As a result, Consolidated's merger with Gentry violated Section 7 of the Clayton Act.

Procter and Gamble raised the potential competition issue when it acquired Clorox.[27] Procter and Gamble is a major manufacturer of detergent and other consumer products, while Clorox dominated the liquid bleach market. Clorox's market share was 49 percent, approximately three times that of Purex, its nearest competitor. The Supreme Court prohibited the merger, emphasizing two possible anticompetitive effects. First, the merger would lessen potential competition in the bleach industry because Procter and Gamble was "the most likely entrant." This product extension merger would remove Procter and Gamble as a competitive threat. Second, the merger would give Clorox an "unfair advantage" over its potential and actual competitors, because it could benefit from Procter and Gamble's "deep pocket." This could lessen competition, as both potential and actual competitors would be reluctant to take on a Clorox owned by the leading advertiser in the country. Moreover, Clorox itself already had a strong product differentiation advantage over other bleach companies. As the Court stressed, possible economies cannot justify an illegal merger.

> Possible economies cannot be used as a defense to illegality. Congress
> was aware that some mergers which lessen competition may also result in
> economies but it struck the balance in favor of protecting competition.[28]

The Supreme Court subsequently refined its position on potential competition in a series of decisions concerning bank mergers. Its current position is illustrated in the case of *United States* v. *Marine Bancorporation*.[29] The National Bank of Commerce, a subsidiary of Marine Bancorporation, acquired Washington Trust Bank. National Bank was

27. *Federal Trade Commission* v. *Procter and Gamble Co.*, 386 U.S. 568 (1967).
28. *Federal Trade Commission* v. *Procter and Gamble Co.*, at 580.
29. *United States* v. *Marine Bancorporation*, 418 U.S. 602 (1974).

the second largest bank in Seattle, while Washington Trust was the third largest bank in Spokane. They did not compete directly in any market in the state of Washington. The government contested the merger, arguing that it would lessen potential competition in the Spokane market. They contended that National Bank was a likely potential entrant and would enter the Spokane market *de novo* or through a toehold acquisition if it were prevented from acquiring Washington Trust.

The Supreme Court disagreed and approved the merger. It reasoned that because of the regulatory environment in banking, the merger would not lessen potential competition. State and federal regulations control entry into banking and thus determine how viable alternative entry methods are. The government had failed to show that National Bank of Commerce could surmount these regulations and enter the Spokane market without merging with the local bank. If National Bank was not a potential competitor, then the merger could not lessen potential competition. The Court concluded its analysis by establishing three conditions that must be met if the doctrine of potential competition is to apply. First, the target market (the market of the acquired firm) must be concentrated. Second, the acquiring firm must be a potential *de novo* entrant into that market. Finally, the potential competition by the acquiring firm must affect the behavior of firms in the target market.

The government has not been very successful against "pure" conglomerate mergers that can increase aggregate, but not market, concentration. It has tried both direct and indirect approaches in its efforts to prohibit such mergers. In one of its first conglomerate merger cases, the government tried the direct approach, contending that it was illegal for a merger to increase aggregate concentration. The District Court disagreed.

> The issue of concentration raises a special question, for the Government is here urging that given a trend to economic concentration, the consolidation of two of the country's one hundred largest corporations constitutes a violation of Section 7 without any specific demonstration of a substantial lessening of competition in any section of the country. We do not so read Section 7.[30]

This case was settled out of court, so the Supreme Court did not address the government's direct attack on this type of merger. The Court has responded, however, to indirect approaches that introduce the mutual forbearance argument. In the Marine Bancorporation case, for example, the government claimed that such mergers would create a situation in

30. *United States v. Northwest Industries*, 301 F. Supp. 1066, 1096 (1969).

which a handful of banks would dominate banking throughout the state of Washington. The potential mutual forbearance behavior would lessen competition in banking markets throughout the state. The Supreme Court, however, did not agree.

Joint Ventures

A *joint venture* is a business undertaking by two or more firms for some specific, limited purpose. For example, domestic firms may form a joint sales agency to market their products in foreign countries or a joint research laboratory to deal with a problem common to their industry. Although these ventures are not mergers in themselves, they do raise similar antitrust issues because they result in combined activities by two firms. Joint ventures are illegal if formed for an illegal purpose; otherwise, the courts apply a rule of reason approach toward them. This is illustrated by the Supreme Court's classic decision in *United States* v. *Penn-Olin Chemical*.[31] The controversy centered on a joint venture by Pennsalt Chemical Corporation and Olin Mathieson Company—two of the four domestic producers of sodium chlorate—to build a sodium chlorate plant in the southeastern United States. On one hand, the joint venture could promote competition by adding additional capacity in this market. On the other, it would be anticompetitive if both firms were likely to have entered the market independently—or if one entered while the other was a potential entrant. The Court weighed these opposing considerations and approved the joint venture, believing it unlikely that the firms would unilaterally have entered the market.

Mergers have played an important role in forming the structure of the American economy. The first two merger waves are credited with increasing both market and aggregate concentration, while the conglomerate wave increased aggregate concentration. This trend continues today. In 1978, there were 80 mergers involving more than $100 million in assets, and they accounted for 61 percent of the value of all publicly announced mergers.[32] The pivotal role of mergers requires that current antitrust policy be assessed and suggestions be made for its modification.

Evaluation

31. *United States* v. *Penn-Olin Chemical Co.*, 378 U.S. 158 (1964).

32. U.S. Federal Trade Commission, *Mergers Policy Session*, May 10, 1979 (Washington, D.C.), p. 6.

Appraisal of Current Policy

The Celler-Kefauver amendment to Section 7 of the Clayton Act was intended to increase the ability of antitrust authorities to prohibit anticompetitive mergers. Has the amendment achieved its desired goal? An answer to this question requires an examination of the legal standards for mergers, the remedies available, and their enforcement by antitrust authorities. Most of the controversy over current merger policy has centered on the strictness of the legal standards.

Legal Standards. The legality of a specific merger depends on the controlling precedents for that type of merger. Antitrust laws are very strict against horizontal and vertical mergers, but fairly lenient toward conglomerate mergers. Pure conglomerate mergers are virtually impossible to prohibit, because they have no direct impact on market competition. Product and market extension mergers are more likely to be approved since the Supreme Court's refinement of the potential competition doctrine in the Marine Bancorporation case. This decision made it substantially more difficult for the government to show that a given merger was likely to lessen competition.

Changing legal standards have been reflected in the types of mergers consummated. Table 7.1 presents data on the relative importance of dif-

Table 7.1   Types of Major Mergers, 1926–1977[a]
(Percentages of total number)

Type of Merger	Time Period 1926-1930	Time Period 1961-1965	Time Period 1977
Horizontal	67.6	16.4	26.3
Vertical	4.8	17.5	4.0
Conglomerate			
Market Extension	8.3	6.1	0.0
Product Extension	19.3[b]	60.0[b]	38.4
Pure Conglomerate			31.3

[a]To be classified as a "major" merger, a merger must involve an acquired firm that is engaged primarily in manufacturing or mining and that has at least $10 million in assets.

[b]For the years 1926-1930 and 1961-1965 no separate figures for *Product Extension* and *Pure Conglomerate* mergers were available, only combined totals for both were given.

Sources: 1. U.S. Federal Trade Commission, *Economic Report on Corporate Mergers* (Washington, D.C.: Government Printing Office, 1969), p. 63.

2. U.S. Federal Trade Commission, *Statistical Report on Mergers and Acquisitions* (Washington, D.C.: Government Printing Office, 1978), p. 121.

ferent types of mergers from 1926 to 1977. During the second merger wave (1926–1930), the horizontal merger was clearly dominant. This situation changed dramatically in the 1960s as the conglomerate merger wave accelerated. From 1961 to 1965, 66 percent of the mergers were conglomerate, with the remaining one-third divided almost equally between horizontal and vertical mergers. By 1977, the total conglomerate share had barely changed, but horizontal mergers had increased at the apparent expense of vertical and market extension mergers. Given the current legal precedents and corporate desires for diversification, conglomerate mergers seem likely to dominate merger activity for some time.

Most criticism of current merger law has been centered on two aspects of the legal standards: strictness and consistency. The issue of strictness addresses the basic economic question of whether or not the standards make good economic sense. It seems that they do. Because vertical and horizontal mergers have few potential benefits but many potential costs, a strict, almost per se, approach is warranted. The economy cannot afford a repetition of the "merger for monopoly" wave that occurred at the turn of the century. At the same time, the government retains substantial discretion in selecting mergers that it will contest. It can approve mergers, such as the combination of two small competitors, that it believes will increase market competition.[33] Conglomerate mergers and joint ventures are so complex that a rule of reason approach is mandated. Current precedents are thus appropriate, although decisions such as Marine Bancorporation may have shifted too much of the burden of proof onto the government.

In the Von's Grocery decision, a dissenting Justice Stewart complained: "The sole consistency that I can find is that in litigation under Section 7, the Government always wins."[34] The inconsistent application of antitrust law reduces respect for it and hinders voluntary compliance. One problem area is consistent judicial interpretation of the relevant market (what the Clayton Act calls "the line of commerce" and "the section of the country"). The determination of the relevant market is a very important decision, as it determines the type of merger and the relevant

---

33. A recent celebrated case involved the merger between two steel companies—Lykes and Jones and Laughlin—who argued that the merger would increase competition in the steel industry. The attorney general approved the merger over the opposition of his own staff. Although the failing firm defense was frequently cited, it seems likely that political considerations of effects on employment also played a major role in the decision.

34. *United States* v. *Von's Grocery Co.*, at 301.

legal precedents.[35] In the case of Philadelphia National Bank, the Supreme Court defined the market as the area where "the effect of the merger on competition will be direct and immediate."[36] The actual definition employed may be quite loose, however, as the Court indicated in *United States* v. *Pabst*.[37] This case involved a merger between two Wisconsin brewers, Pabst and Blatz. The Court held that the merger would substantially lessen competition in Wisconsin, the United States, and the three-state area of Wisconsin, Michigan, and Illinois. This conclusion is obviously incorrect; all three geographic areas cannot simultaneously be an economically meaningful market for the brewing industry.[38] If antitrust law is to promote competition, it must be consistently applied.[39]

Remedies. If a merger violates antitrust law, the obvious remedy is for the defendant to divest itself of the acquired firm. The acquired firm must then assume its previous position as an independent, viable entity. This rarely happens, however. In a study of 39 merger cases settled by the government, Elzinga found that the government obtained insufficient relief in 29 of them.[40] There are several reasons for the government's poor performance. First, it frequently is difficult to restore the assets of an acquired firm. It may no longer exist as a corporate entity, for its assets are "scrambled" with those of the acquiring firm. Second, the settlement may require only partial divestiture of the acquired firm's assets. When diversified firms merge, frequently only part of the merger violates the Clayton Act. If the "offending" assets are divested, the merger can proceed, although it is less likely that a viable firm will

35. It is interesting to note that the government's and the defendant's definition of the market can vary with the type of antitrust case. In a monopolization case, for example, the government will argue for a narrow market definition so as to increase the defendant's market share. In merger cases, it adopts a broader market definition so that more mergers will be considered horizontal, the type for which legal precedents are the strongest. Private defendants obviously adopt a strategy opposite to the government's.

36. *United States* v. *Philadelphia National Bank*, 374 U.S. 321 (1963).

37. *United States* v. *Pabst Brewing Co.*, 384 U.S. 546 (1966).

38. For a discussion of this case in particular, and the beer industry in general, see K. Elzinga, "The Beer Industry," *The Structure of American Industry*, ed. W. Adams, 5th ed. (New York: Macmillan, 1977), pp. 221–49.

39. For a detailed criticism of the government's position in the Brown Shoe case, see John L. Peterman, "The Brown Shoe Case," *Journal of Law and Economics* 18 (April 1975): 81–146.

40. Elzinga, K., "The Antimerger Law: Pyrrhic Victories?" *Journal of Law and Economics* 12 (April 1969): 43–78.

be created. Third, it may not be possible to find a better buyer to acquire the firm. Other buyers may be discouraged from purchasing the acquired firm, or there may simply be no firms available that offer a more competitive alternative. In sum, many factors reduce the probability that antitrust authorities will obtain effective relief in merger cases. Once a firm has been acquired by another firm, it is difficult to reestablish it as a viable and independent competitor.

Enforcement. Delay is a major problem in the enforcement of the merger laws, as it is in antitrust actions in general. In his study of merger settlements, Elzinga found the average lag between the consummation of a merger and the filing of a complaint to be long: by the Federal Trade Commission—19.0 months; by the Justice Department—10.6 months.[41] The lag between the initiation and resolution of a suit was even longer—more than five years for both antitrust enforcement agencies. These delays reduce the government's ability to litigate merger cases successfully and subsequently obtain effective relief.

As a partial response to these problems, Congress passed the Hart-Scott-Rodino Antitrust Improvements Act of 1976.[42] This act enabled the government to establish a *premerger notification* program, which applies to mergers in which one firm has at least $100 million in assets and the other at least $10 million. If the merger involves 15 percent of the stock, or $15 million of the stock or assets of one of the firms, it cannot be consummated until 30 days after notice has been given to the Justice Department and the Federal Trade Commission.[43] If the government asks for additional information, the merger must be delayed until 15 days after it is provided.

Premerger notification not only gives antitrust authorities an advance warning, but also provides information necessary for a possible complaint. It should improve the government's selection of cases and reduce the delay in filing a complaint. To increase the probability of obtaining effective relief in a case, the government can seek a preliminary injunction and/or a "hold-separate" order. A *preliminary injunction* can prevent a merger pending adjudication of the relevant antitrust issues. A *hold-separate order* permits the firms to merge but prohibits the acquiring firm from controlling the acquired firm; it must be main-

41. Elzinga, "The Antimerger Law," p. 52.

42. Hart-Scott-Rodino Antitrust Improvements Act of 1976, PL 94–435, September 30, 1976.

43. Notification requirements can also apply to incorporated joint ventures with at least $10 million in assets.

tained as a separate corporate entity. Although these two tools are promising, the courts are reluctant to impose them. A court order based on preliminary information might kill a merger that would be found legal in subsequent litigation. Court orders would in effect be replacing the legal standards that have evolved under Section 7 of the Clayton Act.

Current antitrust policy toward mergers, in one of the major accomplishments of antitrust enforcement, has effectively eliminated the merger route to monopoly. The evidence regarding success with vertical mergers, conglomerate mergers, and joint ventures is less clear-cut. Although the legal standards seem reasonable, there are serious problems with merger policy. Legal delays have limited the number of mergers that can be contested, while weakening the relief that might eventually be obtained. Premerger notification may improve this situation, although the courts are generally reluctant to use preliminary injunctions and hold-separate orders.

New Directions for Antitrust

An important goal for merger policy is to increase the effectiveness of relief and the efficiency of litigation. These nuts-and-bolts issues have been overshadowed, however, by more dramatic proposals to limit acquisition activities by the largest firms in the economy. A concern about the size of firms has dominated legislative proposals, and is a unique departure from traditional antitrust considerations. As such, it deserves close scrutiny.

Legal Standards.   It is currently difficult for antitrust authorities to prohibit conglomerate mergers, especially "pure" ones, which can increase aggregate concentration without violating the Clayton Act. One possible solution is to prohibit the largest firms in the economy from making such mergers. A legislative bill introduced by Senator Edward M. Kennedy ("The Small and Independent Business Protection Act of 1979") would severely limit merger activity by the 500 largest corporations in the American economy. For example, one of the top 100 could not acquire another firm unless it divested itself of an equal amount of assets. The bill's objective is to prevent these large firms from increasing their size through mergers. It might not have this result, however, since the growth rate of the assets acquired might exceed that of those divested. The proposal would surely reduce overall mergers by this group of companies, though not necessarily increase market competition. If anything, it might worsen economic performance by restricting the options of some of the most successful firms in the economy. Overall, this and similar proposals address the conglomerate merger issue from social and political, not economic, perspectives. Congress must ultimately resolve these competing considerations.

An alternative approach is advocated by Williamson, who would permit economies to be used as a defense in merger cases.[44] His basic argument is shown graphically in Figure 7.1. Assume that a firm is initially producing Q° units that are sold for P°. The firm engages in a merger that simultaneously lowers its costs and increases its market power. Society benefits from the reduction in unit costs from ATC° to ATC′, but loses from the reduction in output to Q′ and the increase in price to P′. The net effect of the merger depends on the relative magnitudes of the specific effects on cost and price. Williamson's approach would give the courts more discretion in accepting or rejecting mergers.

This expanded rule of reason approach, though theoretically correct, does not seem necessary in the real world. First of all, economists believe that mergers rarely yield substantial economies. Horizontal merg-

Figure 7.1   Possible Economic Trade-offs of a Merger

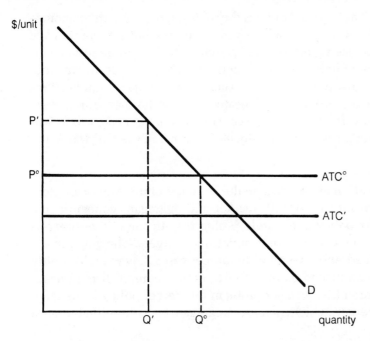

44. O. Williamson, "Economies as an Antitrust Defense: The Welfare Tradeoffs," *American Economic Review* 58 (March 1968): 18–36.

ers, for example, demand a strict approach that sacrifices few economies, but prohibits the likely increases in monopoly power. Second, Williamson's proposal does not seem workable. It would increase the delay in bringing and trying cases, but would bring few noticeable benefits except an increase in the demand for economic experts.

Remedies.   Remedies in merger cases generally have not restored the acquired firm as a viable and independent influence in its markets. The government should pursue policies that will strengthen the acquired firm, reducing the likelihood that it will go bankrupt if divested by the acquiring firm.[45] Two such policies suggest themselves. First, the government should seek full, not partial, divestiture of the acquired firm's assets. A firm is a complex organization that should not be fractured by the acquiring firm and then returned piecemeal to the marketplace. Second, the government should require the acquiring firm to provide technical and marketing assistance until the acquired firm has reestablished itself as a viable competitor. This assistance is especially important if the acquired firm has been under the other firm's control for an extended time.

Enforcement.   The government has the tools to improve enforcement—preliminary injunctions and hold-separate orders—but the courts have been reluctant to use them. New legislation may be warranted to facilitate the issuance of hold-separate orders. It might even be worthwhile to empower the government to issue such orders subject to judicial review. Hold-separate orders are advocated over preliminary injunctions because they allow the merger to be consummated, but make relief easier should the merger be found to violate Section 7 of the Clayton Act.

Summary

Mergers have had a major impact on the structure of the American economy. They have increased both market and aggregate concentration. Current antitrust policy adequately prohibits anticompetitive mergers and permits harmless or even procompetitive mergers. The government has rarely obtained effective relief in merger cases, however. Too little emphasis has been placed on reestablishing the acquired firm as a viable, independent entity. A major problem for merger policy is the large conglomerate merger, which increases aggregate concentration but does

45. The government has done this in isolated cases. See, for example, *Ford Motor Co. v. United States,* 405 U.S. 562 (1972).

not affect market competition. These mergers raise important political and social issues that cannot be resolved through economic analysis. Any merger policy designed to limit aggregate concentration should not ignore, however, the economic theory underlying the conduct of firms.

Suggested Readings

Allen, B. "Vertical Integration and Market Foreclosure: The Case of Cement and Concrete," *Journal of Law and Economics* 14 (April 1971): 251–74.

Elzinga, K. "The Antimerger Law: Pyrrhic Victories?" *Journal of Law and Economics* 12 (April 1969): 43–78.

Kilpatrick, M. W. and S. P. Mahinka. "The Supreme Court and the 'New Economic Realism' of Section 7 of the Clayton Act," *Southwestern Law Journal* 30 (Winter 1976): 821–37.

Markham, J. *Conglomerate Enterprise and Public Policy* (Boston: Harvard University Press, 1973).

Posner, R. *Antitrust Law* (Chicago: University of Chicago Press, 1976), Chapter 6.

U.S. Federal Trade Commission. *Conglomerate Merger Performance: An Empirical Analysis of Nine Corporations* (Washington, D.C.: Government Printing Office, 1972).

Marketing Practices   Chapter
8

The best product in the world cannot generate profits if it sits on a shelf in the factory's warehouse. *Marketing* is a broad term that encompasses the diverse strategies employed by firms in an effort to sell their products. These strategies can determine whether or not a new product will be successful in the marketplace. A firm's specific marketing strategy, though adopted unilaterally and independently, can adversely affect market competition. This chapter examines the antitrust issues that different marketing practices raise.

The Setting

Two important aspects of marketing are pricing and distributing the product.[1] A firm should devise a pricing strategy that will maximize profits over a product's expected lifetime. Resale price maintenance and price discrimination are two such strategies that historically have raised antitrust issues. *Resale price maintenance* is a pricing scheme in which the manufacturer, not the retailer, establishes the retail price of the product. For instance, General Motors might require its dealers to ob-

1. Advertising is obviously a very important dimension of marketing. The role of advertising, especially deceptive advertising, is discussed in Chapter 17.

serve its "suggested" list prices instead of negotiating with buyers. *Price discrimination* is more complex. It occurs when prices do not accurately reflect the cost conditions underlying separate transactions.[2] For example, a lawyer discriminates by charging different clients different fees for the same service (uncontested divorces). And the Post Office discriminates when it charges the same price for a letter sent across the street or across the country.

Of the various arrangements that firms make for the physical distribution of their products to customers, antitrust attention has focused on the use of exclusive distributors, "tying" agreements, and exclusive dealing contracts. An *exclusive distributor* has the sole right to distribute a firm's product in a specified geographic area. This has been customary for automobile dealerships. A *tying agreement* makes the sale of one product (the "tying" good) conditional on the purchase of another product (the "tied" good). Commonly, for example, a college student who wants to live in a dormitory must also purchase a food contract from the university's dining hall. An *exclusive dealing agreement* prohibits a distributor from carrying the products of a firm's competitors. For example, a Cadillac dealer may be prohibited from stocking automobile parts that are not manufactured by General Motors.

Legal Issues

Pricing practices can violate the Sherman Act ("monopolization") as well as Section 5 of the Federal Trade Commission Act ("unfair method of competition"). Price discrimination also is specifically addressed by Section 2 of the Clayton Act, as amended by the Robinson-Patman Act of 1936. Section 2 states that:

> It shall be unlawful . . . , either directly or indirectly, to discriminate in price between different purchasers of commodities of like grade and quality . . . where the effect of such discrimination may be substantially to lessen competition or tend to create a monopoly in any line of commerce, or to injure, destroy, or prevent competition with any person who either grants or knowingly receives the benefit of such discrimination, or with customers of either of them.[3]

2. More technically, price discrimination occurs whenever the ratio of price to marginal cost is different for two transactions: $\dfrac{P_1}{MC_1} \neq \dfrac{P_2}{MC_2}$.

3. Clayton Act, Sec. 2, 15 U.S.C. Sec. 13 (1976).

Several things about Section 2 should be emphasized. First, it applies only to commodities and therefore cannot cover discrimination in the providing of services. Such discrimination must be addressed under the Sherman or FTC acts. Second, the discriminatory purchases must involve similar goods, goods "of like grade and quality." Otherwise it is not possible to claim that discrimination has occurred. Third, Section 2 introduces a new standard for impact on competition. In addition to the Clayton Act standard of substantially lessening competition, Section 2 will be violated if there is an *injury* to competition. The courts must interpret this new standard. Several defenses that are available to defendants under Section 2 also require evaluation by the courts. For example, price discrimination is not illegal if it is made in good faith to meet a competitor's lower price.

Distribution practices can violate the Sherman and FTC acts as well as the Clayton Act. Section 3 of the Clayton Act states, in part:

> It shall be unlawful . . . to lease or make a sale . . . on the condition, agreement, or understanding that the lessee or purchaser thereof shall not use or deal in the goods, wares, . . . or other commodities of a competitor or competitors of the lessor or seller, where the effect . . . may be to substantially lessen competition or tend to create a monopoly in any line of commerce.[4]

There are several things to note about Section 3. First, a formal agreement is not necessary for a violation to occur. Any leverage by a seller or lessor can be sufficient. Second, Section 3 applies only to commodities. Any antitrust suits concerning services must be initiated under the Sherman or FTC acts. Third, Section 3 adopts the standard Clayton Act requirement for competitive impact: a probability that there will be a substantial lessening of competition.

Economic Issues

The economic impact of different pricing and distribution practices has been much discussed. The primary focus, as always, has been on how marketing practices can affect market competition. Because these practices often involve small retailers who have substantial political clout, the equity aspects of different marketing practices have also been emphasized.

4. Clayton Act, Sec. 3, 15 U.S.C. Sec. 14 (1976).

Pricing Practices. By definition, resale price maintenance transfers the control of pricing from the retailers of a product to the manufacturer. Any variation in retail price is eliminated, as all retailers adopt the manufacturer's price. The suppression of retail price competition can have several different effects on the market involved. First, prices are likely to be higher because there is no price competition among retailers. If the price increases profit margins significantly, it may invite entry that will dissipate the profits over time.[5] Second, nonprice competition may increase. Firms may offer customers more sales services because price competition is prohibited. Indeed, it is argued that resale price maintenance makes it profitable for retailers to provide these important services. The impact on sales, however, is indeterminate. Sales of the manufacturer's product may increase, decrease, or remain the same, because they depend on the response of the manufacturer's competitors. If the competitors do not follow suit in price maintenance, the manufacturer may lose sales to them. Overall, resale price maintenance is likely to worsen economic performance by raising prices and increasing costs.

The first thing to note about price discrimination is that it is not always possible for a firm to engage in it. Three conditions must be satisfied if a firm is successfully to discriminate among its customers. First, the firm must be able to control its price. Price discrimination is thus impossible in competitive markets. Second, the firm must be able to segment its customers according to their price elasticity of demand.[6] It can then adjust its prices in response to differences in customers' demand for the product, charging a higher price where demand is inelastic and a lower price where it is elastic. Third, it must not be possible for any buyers to practice *arbitrage*, the simultaneous purchase and sale of a good for profit. Arbitrage equalizes prices and makes discrimination impossible.

The mechanics of price discrimination is illustrated by a colorful episode in business history.[7] Two firms—Rohm & Haus and Du Pont—manufactured a chemical compound that was ideal for making dentures and also had some industrial uses. The firms charged denture manufacturers $22 a pound, while industrial users could purchase a similar compound for only $.85 a pound. This pricing scheme was rational and highly profitable, because there were no good substitutes for making

5. See the discussion of the economic model of a cartel with free entry in Chapter 6.

6. See the discussion of price elasticity in Appendix A of Chapter 2.

7. G. W. Stocking and M. W. Watkins, *Cartels in Action* (New York: Twentieth Century Fund, 1946), pp. 402–4.

dentures. Before long, however, some enterprising firms began buying the industrial compound, modifying it, and selling it to denture manufacturers at a substantial profit. In an effort to end this damaging arbitrage, Rohm & Haus planted rumors that the industrial compound contained arsenic and was obviously unfit for human dentures!

Assuming that price discrimination is feasible, a firm can earn greater profits than if it were constrained to charge a single price. Price discrimination is not a harmless practice, however. It can affect competition in both primary and secondary markets. The primary market contains the firm that initiates the price discrimination; the secondary market contains the customers of the firms in the primary market.

In the primary market, price discrimination can lessen competition by reducing the number of competitors. A firm that competes in several markets can sell below cost in one market until it is the only survivor. Its losses could be offset by the profits earned in its other markets, where it charges a remunerative price.[8] The Great Atlantic and Pacific Tea Company (better known as A&P) has been accused of using this pricing practice, which economists refer to as *predation*.[9] The predation process is depicted in Figure 8.1. The predator accepts short-run losses in anticipation of long-run profits. This is rational if the expected value of the future monopoly profits will exceed the short-run losses incurred to obtain the monopoly position. That, in turn, depends on the time it takes to drive out existing rivals and the ease with which firms can enter the market in the future when the price is raised. Of special concern is the ability of old firms to reenter the market and reestablish their operations. If future entry is difficult, the firm may have profit stream B, and predation might be rational. But if entry is not difficult, firms will enter and erode the predator's profits, resulting in profit stream A. In that case, predation would not be profitable. Overall, predation is a questionable pricing strategy and has rarely been adopted by American firms.[10]

Price discrimination poses more of a threat to competition in secondary markets. It can reduce competition by giving an artificial advantage

8. This could also hold for a firm that sells several products while its competitors sell only a single product in the same market.

9. *United States v. The New York Great Atlantic and Pacific Tea Company,* 173 F.2d 79 (1949). For an economic analysis of this case, see M. Adelman, *A&P: A Study in Price-Cost Behavior and Public Policy* (Cambridge, Mass.: Harvard University Press, 1959).

10. For an analysis of one of the most celebrated, but unproved, cases of predation, see J. S. McGee, "The Standard Oil (N.J.) Case," *Journal of Law and Economics* 1 (1958): 137–69.

Figure 8.1   **Potential Profit Streams from Predation**

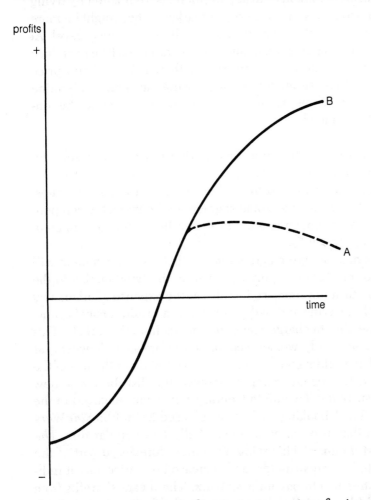

to the firm paying the lower discriminatory prices for inputs. The firm paying lower input prices can, other things being equal, underprice its rivals. Competition on merit is thus replaced by competition based on favoritism. Price discrimination in the input markets undermines the competitive process that has such desirable efficiency and equity properties.

The exact competitive impact of price discrimination in both primary and secondary markets depends on whether it is systematic or unsystematic. Price discrimination is systematic when it is persistent and consistent, and unsystematic when it is temporary and random. Unsystematic discrimination is less likely to be anticompetitive, because any impact is short lived; it may, in fact, be procompetitive. At the primary level, firms commonly engage in price discrimination by trying out new pricing strategies in selected test markets. They might be more reluctant to experiment if they could do so only on a national level. At the secondary level, large buyers such as Sears or A&P may induce price discrimination. These firms try to use their size to obtain price concessions from their suppliers. Such pressure can help undermine collusive pricing agreements among suppliers and should be encouraged, not discouraged.

Distribution Practices.   The three distribution practices at issue—tying, exclusive dealing, and exclusive distributors—all raise a common economic issue: market foreclosure. They place restrictions on sales, with the effect of "foreclosing" some segment of the market to competitors. This is the same economic issue raised earlier in the discussion of vertical mergers (Chapter 7).

A major concern about tying agreements is that this arrangement will enable a firm to transfer monopoly power from the tying market to the tied market. The firm can increase its sales at the expense of others that cannot offer both the tying and tied products. As a result, it may become dominant and be able to charge monopoly prices in both markets. This result will not necessarily worsen economic performance, however, as the firm could have achieved the same end result without the use of the tying agreement.[11] A recent example involved the distribution of new films. A film distributor, Twentieth Century-Fox Films, engaged in the practice called "block booking," whereby it leased its hit film *Star Wars* only to theaters that also leased a substantially less popular film, *The Other Side of Midnight.*[12] This tying agreement foreclosed part of the theater market to other distributors and increased the price, albeit indirectly, that theaters had to pay for *Star Wars*. The theaters' profits from *Star Wars* would be partially offset by the probable losses of showing the other movie. This arrangement indicates that the distributor could have charged a higher price for *Star Wars* by itself. There was a maximum price that theaters were willing to pay for *Star Wars;* the tying agreement simply allocated that revenue between the two films.

11. See R. Posner, *Antitrust Law: An Economic Perspective* (Chicago: University of Chicago Press, 1976), Chapter 8.

12. "Fox Film is Fined $25,000 on a Charge of Forcing Block-Booking on Theaters" (*Wall Street Journal,* September 13, 1978, p. 8). For an economic analysis of block booking, see G. Stigler, *The Organization of Industry* (Homewood, Ill.: Richard D. Irwin, 1968), Chapter 15.

Aside from the monopoly power issue, there are several other reasons why a firm might use a tying agreement. First, such agreements enable a firm to engage in price discrimination, if a customer's price elasticity of demand for the tying product is related to its use of the product. For example, Xerox could charge a flat fee for leasing its copying machines and a separate fee for each piece of paper used. This pricing scheme would differentiate between low volume (elastic demand) and high volume (inelastic demand) users. Second, a tying agreement can circumvent price controls on the tying product if the tied product is exempt from regulations. The firm can increase its profits by increasing the price of the (unregulated) tied product. Third, tying agreements can preserve the manufacturer's goodwill by requiring that only specific inputs be used with the manufacturer's machine. This can reduce the likelihood of machine breakdowns and any subsequent loss of customer goodwill. The same objective can generally be achieved, however, by simply specifying the quality of the inputs and letting the user choose among the alternatives available.

A major concern about exclusive dealing agreements is that they can increase barriers to entry into a market. By foreclosing a firm from the existing distribution network, such agreements force a new entrant to establish its own distribution network, substantially increasing the cost and time the firm must spend to successfully enter a market. The market penetration of foreign automobiles, for example, was initially limited by the need to establish a network of dealers that could sell and service the imports. On the other hand, exclusive dealing agreements can be procompetitive. They may facilitate entry by tying the success of an individual dealer to the success of the product. The dealer has a greater incentive to push the new product than if it were merely one more product in a large line. In sum, it is not possible to generalize about the competitive impact of an exclusive dealing agreement.

A closely related issue is the restraints that manufacturers sometimes place on their exclusive distributors. Besides tying and exclusive dealing agreements that limit interbrand competition, a manufacturer may limit intrabrand competition among its own dealers. Coca-Cola, for example, restricts its 566 bottlers to specific geographic territories.[13] The purpose of such restraints ostensibly is to encourage dealers to invest in facilities and sales promotion. Without these restraints, other firms could come in and benefit from a dealer's promotion. The prospect of

13. This practice has recently been attacked by the government ("FTC Orders an End to Territorial Limits Placed by Coca-Cola, PepsiCo on Bottlers," *Wall Street Journal*, April 24, 1978, p. 2).

"free riders" would weaken a firm's incentive to promote its product,[14] but dealer restrictions guarantee the firm that it alone will receive the benefits of its efforts. The end result is an increase in interbrand competition, but a decrease in intrabrand competition.

With the exception of tying agreements, it is not possible to generalize about distribution practices. Tying agreements can be beneficial to the firms that adopt them, but they rarely provide any benefits to society. If the tied product is superior to the substitutes available, consumers would choose it voluntarily, and coercion would not be necessary. Exclusive dealing and dealer restrictions are more complex; they may be procompetitive in one market environment, but anticompetitive in another. This probably is one area in which equity considerations may dominate the uncertain efficiency considerations.

The Case Law

The price discrimination case law that has evolved under the Robinson-Patman Act is probably the most esoteric of all antitrust case law. Because of this, it is possible to present only a brief illustrative introduction to it.[15] An increasingly important area for antitrust enforcement is the rights of dealers or franchisees. Changes in the distribution practices of franchises have the potential to affect the marketing of everything from McDonald's hamburgers to H. & R. Block's tax returns. Antitrust cases in this area can thus have a direct, discernible impact on consumers.

Pricing Practices

Manufacturers' efforts to establish retail prices for their products have been held illegal since the turn of the century.[16] The issue has periodically resurfaced, however, with the passage of laws designed to permit resale price maintenance ("fair trade" laws). The impetus for this movement did not come from manufacturers, but from retailers; the Miller-Tydings Act exempted resale price maintenance from prosecution under federal antitrust laws in 1937. This exemption was repealed by

14. This problem of "free riders" is also used to justify resale price maintenance. Without it, consumers could obtain information at higher priced stores that provide service, and then purchase the good in question at lower priced discount stores that do not provide any sales services.

15. For more detailed discussions, see R. Posner, *The Robinson-Patman Act* (Washington, D.C.: American Enterprise Institute, 1976) and C. Edwards, *The Price Discrimination Law* (Washington, D.C.: Brookings Institution, 1959).

16. *Dr. Miles Medical Co. v. John Park*, 220 U.S. 373 (1911).

the Consumer Goods Pricing Act of 1975, however, making resale price maintenance once again illegal per se.[17]

The great bulk of antitrust activity in this area has involved price discrimination, not resale price maintenance. Price discrimination became a separate antitrust offense under Section 2 of the Clayton Act. It was viewed as a possible tool for monopolizing a market. The original Section 2 was weakened by judicial interpretation and was ineffective until amended by the Robinson-Patman Act of 1936.[18] This amendment reflected public concern over the possible impact of price discrimination on competition in secondary, not primary, markets. The amendment also expanded coverage to include forms of indirect price discrimination. Two important issues under the Robinson-Patman Act are the competitive impact required for a violation and the defenses available to defendants in price discrimination cases.

Competitive Impact.   Price discrimination is illegal if it can substantially lessen or injure competition. The courts must thus establish the requirements for these standards in both primary and secondary markets. The Supreme Court established the legal standard for a primary line injury in a private antitrust case, *Utah Pie Company* v. *Continental Baking Company.*[19] Utah Pie was the local, but dominant, producer of frozen pies in the Utah market. Its dominance was threatened by three large national firms—Continental, Pet, and Carnation—that imported pies from their California plants. These firms, among other things, sold their pies for less in Utah than in San Francisco, which was closer to their plants. The controlling issue was not whether price discrimination existed, but whether it injured competition in the Utah market. Utah Pie's market share had declined, although it had remained profitable in an expanded market for frozen pies. The Court, obviously concerned over the fate of Utah Pie in a market of declining prices, concluded that competition had been injured.[20] In general, the courts find the requisite injury to competition if there has been a substantial and sustained drop in price by a large firm in the market.

17. Consumer Goods Pricing Act of 1975, PL 94-145 (1975), amending 15 U.S.C. 45(a).

18. The courts ruled that it was not possible to support a finding of price discrimination whenever the quantities in the contested transactions were not the same.

19. *Utah Pie Co.* v. *Continental Baking Co.*, 386 U.S. 685 (1967).

20. Utah Pie eventually went out of business in 1972, five years after the Supreme Court decision. Its demise was attributed to an incompetent second generation of family management rather than price discrimination. See K. Elzinga and T. Hogarty, "Utah Pie and the Consequences of Robinson-Patman," *Journal of Law and Economics* 21 (October 1978): 427–34.

The requirements for a secondary line injury were first established in a Federal Trade Commission suit against Morton Salt.[21] Morton Salt gave volume discounts for its salt that it could not justify by differences in the cost of supplying different-sized customers. Large retailers who received this discount could underprice smaller retailers who did not. As a result, the Court concluded that the requirement for an anticompetitive showing would be met if the price discrimination simply led to different retail prices for the good in question. This standard was subsequently modified by requiring that the resulting price difference must have a significant impact on a firm's sales and must not be temporary.

Defenses.   Three defenses are available to a firm accused of price discrimination under the Robinson-Patman Act: (1) cost differences; (2) changing conditions; and (3) meeting competition. The cost defense is an *absolute* defense. If the price differences can be justified by cost differences, there is no violation regardless of the competitive effect.[22] Judicial inquiry is at an end. In practice, it has been difficult to use this defense. It has proved to be very expensive to provide the necessary data, which can also benefit the defendant's competitors. The FTC has also insisted that the entire price differential, not 90 or 95 percent, must be justified by cost differences. A firm is therefore very unlikely to choose to use the cost defense.

The "changing conditions" defense is rarely used; it would apply if a firm has a "fire sale" or "going-out-of-business" sale. Of more economic interest is the "meeting competition," or "good faith" defense, which permits a firm to discriminate in response to competitors' lower prices. Although this seems simple enough, litigation over this defense has revealed some of the more bizarre aspects of the Robinson-Patman Act. In a celebrated case, Standard Oil Company of Indiana gave a lower price to prevent one of its wholesalers (jobbers) from switching to another supplier as three previous wholesalers had done. This incident raised two antitrust issues. The Federal Trade Commission initially argued that the good faith defense was not an absolute defense like the cost defense, and so could not justify price discrimination. The Supreme Court disagreed and remanded the case.[23] The FTC then claimed that Standard had not acted in good faith when it gave the discount to its

21. *Federal Trade Commission v. Morton Salt Co.*, 334 U.S. 37 (1948).

22. If the price differences are based on cost differences, however, there is no price discrimination!

23. *Standard Oil Company [of Indiana] v. Federal Trade Commission*, 340 U.S. 231 (1951).

wholesaler. Standard appealed the FTC's decision and was upheld by both the appellate and Supreme Courts.[24] All in all, it took Standard 17 years to justify a logical response to a common business situation: if you are losing your customers, lower your price.

Additional litigation has led to a substantial refinement of this defense. First, a firm can meet only a "lawful" lower price of a competitor. It is not clear, though, how a firm can ascertain this price without consulting with the competitor—a clear Sherman Act violation.[25] Second, a firm can meet, but not beat, the competitor's lower price. Third, a firm can lower its price to retain old customers, but not to attract new ones. Finally, a firm cannot give a discount to enable its customer to meet competition, but only in an effort to meet its own competition.

Indirect Price Discrimination. Indirect price discrimination occurs when firms pay the same prices for goods but receive different services from the seller. For example, customers may receive different allowances for advertising and displaying the seller's products. The end result is the same as with direct price discrimination: one firm pays a lower effective price than others. The Robinson-Patman Act addresses this issue with respect to brokerage fees and promotional services such as advertising allowances and display racks. Brokerage fees are payments that manufacturers make to firms (brokers) that procure business for them. It is illegal under the Robinson-Patman Act to pay brokerage fees if the broker is affiliated with a retailer. At the same time, all promotional services must be offered to retailers on proportionately equal terms. For example, each buyer is entitled to the same services for each dollar of sales, *regardless* of the buyer's overall volume of sales.

Distribution Practices

Because distribution practices can violate both Section 1 of the Sherman Act and Section 3 of the Clayton Act, cases are commonly brought simultaneously under both statutes. The standards for jurisdiction and legality vary, however.

Tying Agreements. The Supreme Court established a strong precedent

24. *Federal Trade Commission v. Standard Oil Company [of Indiana]*, 355 U.S. 396 (1958).

25. Four firms unsuccessfully used this to defend the exchange of price information among themselves ("Justices Allow 4 Gypsum-Board Firms New Trial," *Wall Street Journal*, June 30, 1978, p. 4).

against tying agreemments in *United States* v. *International Salt*.[26] International Salt leased its patented brine-making machinery to industrial users, but as a condition of the lease, required customers to purchase salt from them instead of other salt suppliers. International Salt claimed that this restraint was necessary to protect its goodwill; poor quality salt could damage its machinery and its reputation. The Supreme Court rejected this quality defense, sarcastically noting that International's machines were not "allergic" to salt from other companies. The court concluded that it was illegal per se to exclude competitors from a substantial amount of commerce, in this case $500,000. Even though this represented a small amount of the total salt market, it was deemed enough for antitrust litigation under Section 3 of the Clayton Act.

The controlling precedent for tying agreements under Section 1 of the Sherman Act was established by the Court in 1958.[27] In 1864 and 1870, the federal government had given the predecessor of the Northern Pacific Railway Company alternating stretches of land alongside its railroad tracks (20 miles wide in states and 40 miles wide in territories) as an inducement to expand railroad service. Northern Pacific subsequently sold or leased most of this land. In its contracts, it inserted a "preferential routing" clause that required the other party to use Northern Pacific if its rates were the same as those of other railroads. The antitrust action was initiated under the Sherman Act because the tied product, transportation, was a service, not a commodity as required for a suit under the Clayton Act.

The Supreme Court began its analysis with a cogent statement of the rationale behind per se prohibitions.

> There are certain agreements or practices which because of their pernicious effect on competition and lack of any redeeming virtue are conclusively presumed to be unreasonable and therefore illegal without elaborate inquiry as to the precise harm they have caused or the business excuse for their use. This principle of *per se* unreasonableness not only makes the type of restraints which are proscribed by the Sherman Act more certain to the benefit of everyone concerned, but it also avoids the necessity for an incredibly complicated and prolonged economic investigation . . . .[28]

The Court then established two criteria that would make a tying agreement illegal per se under the Sherman Act. First, the defendant must

26. *International Salt Co.* v. *United States*, 332 U.S. 392 (1947).
27. *Northern Pacific Railway* v. *United States*, 356 U.S. 1 (1958).
28. *Northern Pacific Railway* v. *United States*, at 5.

have "sufficient economic power with respect to the tying product to appreciably restrain free competition in the market for the tied product." Second, the tying agreement must affect a "not insubstantial" amount of commerce. In this case, the Court ruled that substantial commerce was involved and that the power of the railroad to impose a restraint showed that it had the necessary economic power. The tying agreements were therefore illegal.

The requirements under the Sherman Act, as usual, are more stringent than those necessary for a Clayton Act violation. The main difference is the additional requirement of "sufficient economic power" in Sherman Act cases. Courts have ruled that this requirement is fulfilled automatically if the tying good has a patent, trademark, or copyright, or is a franchise.[29] In practice, there is not much difference between litigating under the Sherman Act and the Clayton Act, and many commentators consider tying agreements to be illegal per se. Two defenses however, can be used to justify a tying agreement. The first is that the agreement is necessary to guarantee the quality of inputs used in conjunction with the tying good. Although this quality control defense has not been used successfully, the Supreme Court has hinted that it might be acceptable where the costs of establishing quality standards for the inputs are prohibitive. Second, a tying agreement may be necessary to protect a "new industry." This defense was successfully employed in *United States v. Jerrold Electronics Corporation*.[30] Jerrold, which manufactured and installed cable television systems (CATV), tied the servicing of the system to its installation, claiming that improper servicing could damage its system and prevent the CATV industry from maturing. The Supreme Court ruled that Jerrold's agreement was legal. It noted, however, that this "new industry" defense could not apply forever and must necessarily be limited in time.

Exclusive Dealing Agreements. The Supreme Court has treated exclusive dealing agreements similarly to tying agreements. In *Standard Oil v. United States,* the Court established a "quantitative substantiality" test for determining the legality of a particular exclusive dealing agreement.[31] The case involved Standard Oil of California's exclusive dealing contracts with 5,937 independent gasoline stations. These contracts

29. *Siegal v. Chicken Delight, Inc.*, 311 F. Supp. 847 (N.D. Cal. 1970).

30. *United States v. Jerrold Electronics Corp.*, 187 F. Supp. 545 (E.D. Pa. 1960), affirmed, 365 U.S. 567 (1961).

31. *Standard Oil Company of California (and Standard Stations, Inc.) v. United States*, 337 U.S. 293 (1949).

made Standard the exclusive supplier of petroleum products and some automobile accessories to these stations. The critical issue for the Court was to establish the proof necessary to show that an agreement might substantially lessen competition. As with tying agreements, the Court resolved the issue by adopting a quantitative standard: "The qualifying clause of Section 3 [of the Clayton Act] is satisfied by proof that competition has been foreclosed in a substantial share of the line of commerce affected." As a result, Standard's contracts, which foreclosed $58 million of sales from competitors, were held to violate the Clayton Act.

The standard of quantitative substantiality (or absolute dollar standard) was modified in a subsequent case involving an exclusive supply contract between a public electric utility (Tampa Electric) and a coal company (Nashville Coal Company).[32] Tampa Electric signed a 20-year contract whereby Nashville Coal would supply it with sufficient coal for a new generating plant. Nashville Coal backed out of the contract, claiming that it violated the antitrust laws. The contract was estimated to be worth $128 million, approximately twice the amount that was foreclosed in the Standard Oil case. The Supreme Court asserted, however, that it was not the absolute amount of commerce foreclosed by a contract that determined its legality under the antitrust laws, but the percentage of the market that was foreclosed. Using the broadest market definition possible, the Court concluded that less than one percent of the market was foreclosed by the agreement with Nashville Coal. This was clearly an insubstantial share, so the agreement did not violate Section 3 of the Clayton Act.

In sum, there are currently two evidentiary standards—absolute dollars and market share—that can be used to determine the legality of an exclusive dealing agreement. These two standards can be consistent with one another or inconsistent as in the Tampa Electric case. The end result is that some courts use one standard, while other courts use the other one. The legality of an agreement can thus depend on the particular court in which the case is litigated.

Exclusive Distributors. A manufacturer may desire to market its product through a network of exclusive distributors, each of which is given sole distribution rights for a specified geographic area. The legality of this distribution arrangement is subject to the rule of reason. The controlling precedent for a manufacturer's right to use exclusive distribu-

---

32. *Tampa Electric Co.* v. *Nashville Coal Co.*, 365 U.S. 320 (1961).

tors is *Packard Motor Car Company* v. *Webster Motor Car Company.*[33] This suit was precipitated when Packard did not renew the exclusive contracts of two dealers in Baltimore in an effort to solidify the position of its largest dealer there. Webster, one of the dealers whose contract was not renewed, sued Packard, charging that the termination violated the antitrust laws. The appeals court disagreed, holding that Packard's action constituted a reasonable restraint of trade. The court was obviously influenced by Packard's small share of the automobile market and its professed desire to retain its largest dealer in Baltimore.

The Packard decision established a manufacturer's general right to select its customers, but it did not resolve the related issue of "restraints upon alienation"—a manufacturer's restrictions on a distributor's resale of its product (for example, prohibiting a distributor from selling to specific customers or in specfic geographic areas). In 1969, the Supreme Court enunciated its "Schwinn Rule," making it illegal per se for a manufacturer to place any restraints on the resale of its product by an independent dealer.[34] The Court subsequently modified the policy in *Continental TV* v. *GTE Sylvania.*[35] GTE manufactured television sets and distributed them through a network of exclusive distributors, who were permitted to carry other television brands, but were limited to a specific geographic location. GTE canceled Continental's franchise when it opened an additional store at a new location without GTE's permission. The Supreme Court upheld GTE's territorial restriction as being necessary to increase brand promotion and, hence, interbrand competition. GTE's market share had in fact doubled (to approximately 5 percent of national sales) after the restraint was imposed on its distributors. The Court's substitution of a rule of reason approach for the per se illegality applied in the Schwinn case recognizes the delicate balance between intrabrand and interbrand competition.

Evaluation

Antitrust policy toward distribution practices has probably generated more controversy than any other area of antitrust enforcement. The major reason is the equity issues that are always raised by government policies affecting small businesses, in this case retailers and wholesalers.

33. *Packard Motor Car Co.* v. *Webster Motor Car Co.*, 243 F.2d 418 (D.C. Cir. 1957), *cert. denied*, 355 U.S. 822 (1957).

34. *United States* v. *Arnold, Schwinn & Co.*, 388 U.S. 365 (1969). (Such restraints are not illegal per se, however, when there is an agency relationship between the manufacturer and the dealer. In such a case, the manufacturer retains title to the product and the dealer merely acts as an agent.)

35. *Continental TV, Inc.* v. *GTE Sylvania, Inc.*, 433 U.S. 36 (1977).

The American preference for economic populism requires an assessment of the relative importance of the two economic performance standards of equity and efficiency.

Appraisal of Current Policy

The major criticism of government policies in this area is that they have deviated from the primary goal of promoting competition throughout the economy. Equity considerations have sometimes dominated efficiency considerations, especially in questions of pricing practices.

Legal Standards. It is currently illegal per se for a firm to engage in resale price maintenance. This seems correct, for resale price maintenance offers substantial benefits to retailers, but negligible benefits to consumers. The retailer's markup is guaranteed, thus guaranteeing its profits, unless they are eroded by new entry or cost increases.[36] Consumers pay the "fair trade" or guaranteed price instead of a lower competitive price. For instance, when the California Supreme Court declared the state's fair trade liquor law illegal in 1978, a dramatic 20 to 30 percent reduction in wine and liquor prices occurred as competition eliminated the "fair trade" markup.[37]

The complexity of the case law under the Robinson-Patman Act makes it difficult to generalize. Two broad conclusions seem justified, however. First, the act has tended to discourage price competition. A firm that cheats on a price-fixing agreement not only alienates its competitors, but may also violate the antitrust laws! This anticompetitive aspect of the Robinson-Patman Act can perhaps be minimized if the focus is on a price change's overall impact on market competition, rather than individual competitors. Antitrust authorities must also continue to differentiate between systematic and unsystematic price discrimination. Second, the act has tended to encourage discrimination, both direct and indirect, against large firms. FTC standards for the cost defense have made it difficult to use, thereby making it less likely that sellers will pass legitimate cost savings along to large buyers. Indirect discrimination occurs when large firms do not receive payments for brokerage services that they perform or when all firms receive the same promotional services though there is no cost justification for it. In sum, the Robinson-Patman Act is a unique antitrust act that tends to weaken, not strengthen, market competition.

36. See the discussion of the economic model of a cartel with free entry in Chapter 6.

37. "Liquor Consumers in California Discover Lower Prices in Wake of Court Decision," *Wall Street Journal,* June 14, 1978, p. 14.

The legal standards for distribution practices are not as controversial as those for pricing practices. Tying agreements are virtually illegal per se, while exclusive dealing agreements and distributor restraints are subject to the rule of reason. It is logical to prohibit tying agreements, for they rarely benefit society, though they can benefit the firm imposing them. An interesting issue concerns the exact definition of a tying agreement. General Motors was attacked by independent radio manufacturers for making radios a standard feature of its 1979 model compact cars.[38] Where is the line between selling a product that is a combination of parts and engaging in an illegal tying agreement? With respect to the legality of exclusive dealing agreements, the Supreme Court should clarify its sometimes inconsistent standards. If there is a conflict, which standard—quantitative substantiality or market share—should prevail? Overall, the legal standards for distribution practices are consistent with both economic efficiency and equity.

Remedies.   The standard civil sanctions—of treble damage awards and injunctive relief—are available to successful litigants under the Robinson-Patman and Clayton acts.[39] These remedies seem sufficient to compensate victims of past violations and to prohibit future violations. In a case study of the can industry, for example, McKie credited prohibitions against price discrimination and tying agreements as factors in increasing market competition.[40] One potential problem area is the replacement of formal agreements restraining trade by "informal agreements" between the manufacturer and a retailer. A retailer may be "encouraged" to adopt a specific marketing policy or risk losing the manufacturer's business.[41] These informal agreements are more difficult to attack and can undermine prohibitions against formal agreements.

Enforcement.   The primary problem with enforcement in this area of the antitrust laws is the incidence of price discrimination cases. Govern-

38. "GM Agrees It Won't Require that Buyers of Some Models Also Purchase Its Radio," *Wall Street Journal,* May 15, 1979, p. 10.

39. Some types of price discrimination may be considered crimes, though criminal sanctions available under the Robinson-Patman Act are rarely imposed.

40. James McKie, "The Decline of Monopoly in the Metal Container Industry," *American Economic Review* 45 (Papers and Proceedings of the American Economic Association, 1955): 499–508.

41. In a suit involving Dunkin Donuts, the appeals court held that a company can "encourage" its franchisees to buy products from it so long as it doesn't threaten to revoke the franchise ("Dunkin Donuts Inc. Antitrust Conviction Is Upset on Appeal," *Wall Street Journal,* March 9, 1976, p. 9).

ment antitrust suits under the Robinson-Patman Act have traditionally been initiated by the Federal Trade Commission, whose record is summarized in Table 8.1. This table indicates that since the enactment of the Robinson-Patman Act (1936), the FTC has initiated twice as many suits under this act as under the Clayton and FTC acts. A substantial amount of the FTC's antitrust effort is thus being diverted to cases that may in fact be anticompetitive! The apparent answer to this paradox is that the FTC has responded to political pressure brought by small businesses. During the 1970s, the FTC's enforcement of this act substantially diminished, though private antitrust cases may have taken up the slack. It is common in civil suits involving the distribution of goods and services to allege that the other party violated the Robinson-Patman Act. In sum, too many resources, both public and private, have been used to enforce this act.

Table 8.1   Antitrust Suits Initiated by the FTC

Time Period	FTC Restraint of Trade Cases	Robinson-Patman Cases[a]
1936–1939	110	75
1940–1944	103	106
1945–1949	47	94
1950–1954	57	66
1955–1959	92	227
1960–1964	69	545
1965–1969	76	102
Total	554	1,215

[a]Robinson-Patman cases alleging predatory pricing are classified as restraint of trade cases.

Source: R. Posner, "A Statistical Study of Antitrust Enforcement," *Journal of Law and Economics* 13 (October 1970): 369-70.

New Directions for Antitrust

Not surprisingly, the major recommendation for modifying antitrust policy toward marketing practices is to repeal the Robinson-Patman Act. This proposal has received broad, and thus unique, endorsement from a large number of economists. However, given the large number of private suits initiated under this act, its repeal seems less likely than that of the exemption for resale price maintenance in 1975.

Legal Standards.   The Robinson-Patman Act, like the fair trade laws, was ostensibly passed to protect small retailers ("Mom and Pop" stores) from the competition provided by large chain stores. Once known as the "anti-chain store act," it has not achieved its purpose. The decline of the small retailer has been due to the economies of mass distribution and to consumers' preference for one-stop shopping, not price discrimination. Independent grocers, in fact, have held their ground against the large national chains and tend to be more profitable.[42] If the Robinson-Patman Act were repealed, antitrust authorities could still attack predation under Section 2 of the Sherman Act and Section 5 of the FTC Act.

Remedies.   Again, even with the repeal of the Robinson-Patman Act, relief would be obtainable under the Sherman Act or FTC Act for subsequent price discrimination cases. As noted in the previous section, these remedies seem adequate for the pricing and distribution policies discussed in this chapter.

Enforcement.   Repeal seems the only sure way to end the government's prosecution of frivolous price discrimination cases. Although the FTC has admittedly tempered its zeal for these cases, government agencies are known to go through "life cycles" during which their competency varies.[43] Only repeal of the act can ensure that the FTC will not return to a daily diet of Robinson-Patman cases. Moreover, the FTC is required to investigate the complaints it receives, and these investigations are still subject to political pressure. This may have been the reason behind the FTC's unsuccessful 1979 price discrimination suit against A & P.[44] The FTC charged that A & P had violated the Robinson-Patman Act by inducing its milk supplier to give it sizable discounts for its private label milk. The Supreme Court disagreed with the FTC, upholding the legality of A & P's competitive action.

One final issue is the possible expansion of antitrust enforcement to cover marketing practices in nonproduct areas such as labor markets. For example, construction unions may prohibit contractors from using prefabricated products that require less labor and, hence, fewer workers. This practice affects sales of prefabricated products and could be viewed as an illegal tying agreement.

---

42. "Independent Grocers Outsell the Big Chains by Adapting to Markets," *Wall Street Journal,* November 28, 1978, p. 1.

43. This phenomenon is discussed in more detail in Chapter 19.

44. *Great Atlantic and Pacific Tea Company, Inc. v. Federal Trade Commission,* 440 U.S. 69 (1979).

Summary   Marketing practices, both pricing and distribution, can determine a firm's profitability and influence market competition. The antitrust laws should promote competition by ensuring that all firms are treated fairly throughout the marketing process. Each firm must be given an equal opportunity to compete on its merits in the marketplace. This objective is in conflict with resale price maintenance laws and with the Robinson-Patman Act, both of which were designed to protect small firms from the competition of large firms. These laws limit price competition and generally lead to higher prices. The political preference for economic populism is not supported by the American people in the marketplace. They patronize firms with the lowest prices, regardless of their size. One possible alternative is to preserve small businesses through direct government subsidies. This approach would not raise product prices and would provide voters with an estimate of the cost of preserving small businesses.

Suggested Readings

Ferguson, J. "Tying Agreements and Reciprocity: An Economic Analysis," *Law and Contemporary Problems* 30 (Summer 1965): 552-67.

McKie, J. "The Decline of Monopoly in the Metal Container Industry," *American Economic Review* 45 (Papers and Proceedings of the American Economic Association, 1955): 499-508.

Posner, R. *Antitrust Law* (Chicago: University of Chicago Press, 1976), Chapter 8.

Posner, R. *The Robinson-Patman Act* (Washington, D.C.: American Enterprise Institute, 1976).

Scherer, F.M. *Industrial Market Structure and Economic Performance*, 2nd ed. (Chicago: Rand McNally, 1980), Chapters 11 and 12.

Zelenitz, A. "Below-Cost Original Equipment Sales as a Promotional Means," *Review of Economics and Statistics* 59 (November 1977): 438-46.

Patents

Chapter 9

Article I, Section 8 of the United States Constitution declares, in part, that "Congress shall have the power ... to promote the Progress of Science and Useful Arts, by securing for limited times to authors and inventors the exclusive rights to their respective Writings and Discoveries." Inventors thus have the constitutional right to a monopoly of their inventions, for some limited period of time. This creation of monopoly power conflicts directly with the antitrust laws, whose goal is the elimination of monopoly power.

A patent is simply a legal device that grants an inventor the exclusive rights to his or her invention for 17 years. The inventor can use the patent or license someone else to use it. Alternatively, the inventor can sell (assign) the patent to someone else or not use the patent at all (suppress it). If someone uses the invention without the inventor's permission, the inventor can sue that person for infringing the patent grant, and can seek both injunctive relief to prevent future infringement and damages to compensate for past infringement. When the patent grant finally expires, the invention is dedicated to the public domain and can be used without restrictions by anyone.

The Setting

Table 9.1 Patent Applications Filed and Patents Issued 1901 to 1978

	Patent Applications Filed			Patents Issued						
				Inventions						
						Corporations		U.S.		Botanical
Year	Inventions	Designs	Botanical Plants[a]	Total	Individuals	U.S.	Foreign	Government[b]	Designs	Plants[a]
1901	43,973	2,361		25,546	20,896	4,370	280		1,729	
1911	67,370	1,534		32,856	24,756	7,580	520		1,004	
1921	87,467	5,596		37,798	27,098	9,860	840		3,265	
1931	79,740	4,190	37	51,756	26,618	23,149	1,961	28	2,935	5
1941	52,339	7,203	67	41,109	16,322	22,632	2,112	43	6,486	62
1951	60,438	4,279	71	44,326	19,192	22,305	2,163	659	4,163	58
1961	83,100	4,714	107	48,368	13,383	28,351	5,161	1,473	2,487	108
1971	104,566	6,211	155	78,316	17,299	43,022	16,048	1,947	3,156	71
1978	109,308	7,538	194	66,102	14,259	31,309	19,286	1,248	3,862	186

[a]Botanical plants became patentable in 1930.
[b]Data are not available prior to 1931.

Sources: 1. U.S. Department of Commerce, *Historical Statistics of the United States*, Part 2 (Washington, D.C.: Government Printing Office, 1975), p. 957.
2. U.S. Department of Commerce, *Statistical Abstract of the United States, 1979* (Washington, D.C.: Government Printing Office, 1979), p. 573 (1976 ed., p. 577).

Legal Issues

The initial decision on a patent is made by the United States Patent Office. A patent examiner reviews the patent application to determine if it meets the necessary requirements. If it does, a patent is granted.[1] If it does not, the applicant can appeal the decision within the Patent Office. If the application is still denied, he or she can appeal outside the Patent Office, to either the Court of Customs and Patent Appeals or the Federal District Court in Washington, D.C.

Table 9.1 presents data on the number of applications and patents issued for selected years since the turn of the century. In 1978, for example, applications were filed for 109,308 inventions, 7,538 designs, and 194 botanical plants. Of the 66,102 patents issued for inventions in that year, 14,259 (21.6 percent) were awarded to individuals, 31,309 (47.4 percent) to domestic corporations, 19,286 (29.2 percent) to foreign corporations, and 1,248 (1.9 percent) to the U.S. government. Since 1901, the role of individuals has obviously been declining, while domestic and, more recently, foreign corporations have been assuming an increasingly important role. This trend seems unlikely to change.

Two aspects of patent law have been the subject of considerable litigation before the courts: (1) patentability; and (2) patent exploitation. The issue of patentability concerns the criteria used by the Patent Office for granting patents. These criteria are enumerated in the Patent Act of 1952, which codified previous court decisions on this matter.[2] For example, a "composition of matter" can be patented by someone if it is "non-obvious" to a person with ordinary skill in the relevant art at that time.[3] It is up to the courts to determine what constitutes a "composition of matter" and when an invention is "non-obvious." These are important judicial decisions because they determine the number of patent monopolies there will be throughout the economy.

The issue of exploitation involves the right of the patent holder to maximize the profits that can be obtained from her or his invention. But does this mean that the patent holder has an unbridled right to pursue any activity that will increase the financial return from the patent? Or are these activities subject to the Sherman, Clayton, and FTC acts? For

1. A patent awarded by the Patent Office is not necessarily valid, because it is based primarily on the information furnished by the applicant. Subsequent analysis may indicate that the applicant withheld information, thereby making the patent invalid.

2. Patent Act of July 19, 1952 (Public Law 593, 82d Cong.).

3. Time requirements also must be fulfilled. For example, a patent will be denied if the invention was in public use for more than one year before the date of the patent application.

example, can a patent holder set the price of a patented good in a licensing agreement, or is that illegal resale price maintenance? And, can a patent holder engage in price discrimination by using a patented good in a tying agreement? The goal of patent law— to increase the inventor's profits—and the goal of antitrust law—to increase market competition— can thus conflict. The courts must resolve any such conflicts, determining whether the public interest requires a compromise of antitrust principles, patent principles, or both.

Economic Issues

Two fundamental economic issues are raised by a patent system. First, what is the economic rationale for having a patent system? Second, how can the exploitation of a patent grant affect competition in different markets? The answers to these two questions are important for understanding both current patent case law and the numerous proposals for reforming the American patent system.

The Economic Rationale for a Patent System.   The Constitution states that the purpose of a patent system, or patent protection, is to "promote the Progress of Science and Useful Arts." Patents are thus viewed as necessary to stimulate technological progress, the invention and innovation of new products and new production processes.[4] Patents can stimulate inventive activity by granting the inventor the exclusive rights to an invention and thereby preventing others from stealing it.[5] If someone could quickly and legally copy the invention, the inventor would receive less profits and would have little incentive to engage in research or disclose future inventions to the public. The aspect of a patent system that protects inventors and enables them to receive the profits generated by their inventions has been called the *reward theory* of patent protection. It assumes that the primary motivating factor in the inventive process is profits. Whether or not this is true, many actual and potential inventors are undoubtedly aware of the hundreds of millions of dollars earned by such famous inventors as Edwin Land (cameras) and Chester Carlson (xerography).

4. For a discussion of the process of technological progress, see Chapter 2.

5. This assumes, of course, that the patent is valid and that it can be successfully defended in court. The final outcome of any patent dispute can depend more on the litigants' legal resources than on the true legality of their positions. Independent inventors can thus be at a disadvantage compared to large corporations.

An alternative patent theory argues that patents are not necessary at the invention stage, but rather at the innovation stage of technological progress.[6] The argument is straightforward: Most research expenditures are incurred in developing an invention into a form that has the potential for commercial success. For example, Chester Carlson obtained his xerography patent while working full time as a patent attorney. But it took over a decade of research and an estimated $100 million before Xerox produced its first copying machine.[7] From this perspective, the function of a patent system is to assign the right to develop a particular invention. This is known as the *prospect function*. The patent protects a firm's (or inventor's) investment at the innovation stage and ensures the developer that it will receive the profits from any prospective applications of the invention.

Regardless of the exact incentive effects, society is clearly willing to grant temporary monopolies (17 years) in return for a potentially faster rate of technological progress. The short-run resource misallocation costs will presumably be outweighed by the long-run benefits of new products and new production processes. The trade-off society makes is illustrated in Figure 9.1 for a process invention.[8] It is assumed that this market is competitive and is initially in long-run equilibrium, selling $Q°$ units at a price of $P°$. A new production process is invented that lowers unit production costs from $ATC°$ to ATC'. The patent holder can license the invention to firms for slightly less than their unit cost savings ($C°$-C').[9] Firms will adopt the invention because it reduces their costs, although the drop in price will be small. Society saves the area A in resources, while the inventor receives approximately this amount in license royalties from producers. When the patent expires, the royalty payment goes to zero, and price will be reduced to P' in the long run.

Whether or not a patent system improves economic welfare depends on the relative magnitude of its costs (short-run monopoly) and benefits

6. E. Kitch, "The Nature and Function of the Patent System," *Journal of Law and Economics* 20 (October 1977): 265-90.

7. For a detailed discussion of Xerox's history, see Erwin Blackstone, "The Economics of the Copying Machine Industry" (Ph.D. dissertation, University of Michigan, 1968).

8. For a detailed exposition of this argument, see W. Nordhaus, *Invention, Growth, and Welfare* (Cambridge: M.I.T. Press, 1969), Chapter 5; and F.M. Scherer, "Nordhaus' Theory of Optimal Patent Life: A Geometric Reinterpretation," *American Economic Review* 62 (June 1972): 422-27.

9. The patent holder could also monopolize the market by producing itself and charging a price slightly below the current competitive price of $P°$.

Figure 9.1   Economic Analysis of a Process Invention

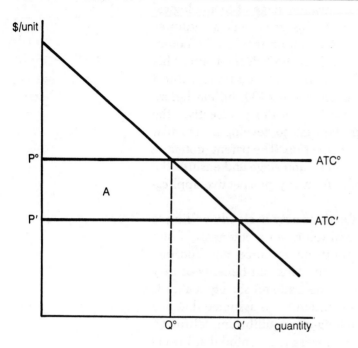

(long-run increase in technological progress).[10] Table 9.2 presents data on the time it takes for increased technological progress to offset the static inefficiency associated with monopoly. Static inefficiency reduces the country's output of goods and services (GNP); technological progress increases it. These hypothetical data indicate that the time in which technological progress offsets the static inefficiencies of monopoly ranges from less than a year to as many as 20 years. For the middle range, and more realistic, values of these variables, the offset period is .07 to 2.1 years, a relatively short time. This suggests that some type of patent protection can improve the economic welfare of society.

Exploitation of the Patent Grant.   As has been stated, a patent establishes an exclusive right to a specific invention, thereby creating a monopoly. The patent holder is entitled to receive the monopoly profits associated with the invention. This is not as simple as it sounds, however, and many court cases have arisen over the proper "scope" of the

10. J. Markham, "Concentration: A Stimulus or Retardant to Innovation," in *Industrial Concentration: The New Learning*, ed. H. Goldschmid, H. Mann, and J. Weston (Boston: Little, Brown, 1974), pp. 247–72.

Table 9.2   **Years Required for Technological Change to Offset Monopoly Costs**

Average Growth Rate in GNP from Technological Change	Annual Cost from Monopoly (expressed as percent of GNP)					
	.05	.10	1.0	2.5	5.0	10.0
0.50	0.100	0.20	2.0	5.0	10.0	20.0
0.75	0.067	0.13	1.3	3.3	6.7	13.3
1.00	0.050	0.10	1.0	2.5	5.0	10.0
1.20	0.040	0.08	0.8	2.1	4.2	8.0
1.50	0.033	0.07	0.7	1.7	3.3	6.7
2.00	0.025	0.05	0.5	1.3	2.5	5.0

Source: J.W. Markham, "Concentration: A Stimulus or Retardant to Innovation," in Goldschmid, H., Mann, H., and Weston, F., eds., *Industrial Concentration: The New Learning* (Boston: Little, Brown, 1974), Table 14, p. 253.

patent grant. Specifically, can profit-maximizing exploitation of the patent extend monopoly power from the patented market to other related markets? This issue can be illustrated in the case of a tying agreement involving a patented product. The patent holder sells the patented product only to customers who simultaneously purchase some tied product. In this manner, the patent holder can discriminate among customers, thereby increasing profits.[11] At the same time, the tying agreement forecloses part of the tied market to other firms. The patent holder's right to exploit the patent thus conflicts with other firms' right to compete for business. The courts must resolve this trade-off between the profit incentive necessary for technological progress and the market access necessary for effective market competition.

The discussion so far has focused on the rights of a single patent holder that *unilaterally* exploits its patent grant. *Multilateral* patent agreements that involve two or more firms present other problems. Two firms may enter into an agreement whereby they share, or pool, their patents. This type of agreement poses problems for antitrust authorities because it can improve or worsen economic performance in a market. For example, two firms may have competing patents for the same invention.[12] If the contested patent is valuable, the firms are likely to incur substantial

11. The use of tying agreements in price discrimination was discussed in more detail in Chapter 8.

12. A patent dispute is resolved by determining the priority of invention. This depends on when each firm conceived the invention, performed any further modifications, and applied for the patent. For a recent example involving the invention of the laser, see "A Laser Patent Upsets the Industry," *Business Week*, October 24, 1977, pp. 122–30.

litigation costs in determining which patent, if either, is valid. By pooling their patents, they can avoid these litigation costs and the associated time delays. A patent pool also reduces the uncertainty of a "winner-take-all" court case or the possibility of a decision that neither side has a valid patent. The pooling agreement provides each firm with some royalties, according to the usage of its patent.

Not suprisingly, multilateral patent agreements can also worsen economic performance. Like all interfirm agreements, these agreements may simply be a front for collusion. The participants in the patent pool may use it to exclude competitors from the patents or to divide the market among themselves. Each firm uses a single patent, thereby having a monopoly on that patented product. A patent pool can also mask invalid patents that would not be supported if challenged in court. The firms thus receive monopoly profits when none in fact are warranted. Determining the net effect of a multilateral agreement requires that the potential benefits and costs to society be weighed.

The Case Law

This section examines the current case law with respect to the two major issues of patentability and exploitation. Interest in the question of patentability has been renewed since the creation of new life forms, or organisms, in laboratories. Most attention, however, still is focused on the basic rights of patent holders to exploit their patent grants unilaterally or multilaterally. A major concern of the courts has been the potential conflicts between the rights of patent holders to maximize their profits and the rights of consumers to have a competitive marketplace.

Patentability

How effective the patent system is in promoting technological progress depends in part on the standards employed by the Patent Office in granting patents. A too lenient policy needlessly creates additional monopolies, but a too strict policy denies legitimate inventions the recognition and potential profits they deserve. The Patent Office must walk a fine line between these two extremes. The requirements for patentability are addressed in Section 103 of the Patent Act of 1952.

> A patent may not be obtained . . . if the differences between the subject matter sought to be patented and the prior art are such that the subject matter as a whole would have been obvious at the time the invention was made to a person having ordinary skill in the art to which said subject

matter pertains. Patentability should not be negatived by the manner in which the invention was made.[13]

The requirement that an invention not be "obvious" codified prior judicial decisions about the degree of novelty necessary for patentability. In *Hotchkiss* v. *Greenwood*, the Supreme denied a patent to an inventor who merely substituted ceramics for wood in his production of doorknobs.[14] More recently, the Supreme Court criticized the Patent Office for awarding patents for "routinizing" or merely modifying existing inventions.[15] A patent should only be granted if the applicant has made substantive, nonobvious improvements. Computer programs, for example, are considered by the Court to be like "laws of nature" and generally are not patentable.[16]

The emergence of recombinant DNA technology, which can create new life forms, raised new questions about patentability. A major issue, in light of the computer decision, is whether these organisms are works of nature and would eventually occur naturally, or whether they are works of science and hence truly novel. This issue was addressed directly in a patent application by General Electric for a new life form that it had created in its laboratories—a type of bacterium that digests oil more efficiently than existing bacteria and can be used in cleaning up oil spills. The Patent Office had denied a patent to General Electric, but was overruled by the U.S. Court of Customs and Patent Appeals on two separate occasions. The Supreme Court decided that GE could patent the bacterium, clearing the way for the Patent Office to rule on the patentability of hundreds of newly created organisms.[17]

A related issue is the validity of patents for old inventions. As noted above, the Patent Office cannot guarantee that a patent is valid. It makes its decisions based on the limited information and resources at its disposal. For example, a patent application may be approved even though the invention was in the public domain for one year and so should be denied a patent. It is desirable, however, to discover invalid patents and eliminate any false monopolies. In an effort to eliminate invalid patents,

13. Patent Act of July 19, 1952 (Public Law 593, 82d Cong.), Sec. 103.

14. *Hotchkiss* v. *Greenwood,* 13 L.Ed. 683 (1850).

15. *Graham* v. *John Deere Co.,* 383 U.S. 1 (1966).

16. "Computer Program Is Denied a Patent in High Court Case," *Wall Street Journal,* June 23, 1978.

17. *Sidney A. Diamond, Commissioner of Patents and Trademarks* v. *Ananda M. Chakrabarty,* 48 LW 4714 (June 16, 1980).

the Supreme Court has ruled that a licensee can sue a patent holder and charge that the patent under which it was licensed is invalid.[18] Prior to this decision, a licensee could not legally sue the patent holder because this violated contract law. Those individuals most likely to know the validity of a patent—the licensees—had been prevented from exposing invalid patents. The Court resolved this conflict between patent law and contract law so as to minimize patent abuse.

Unilateral Patent Rights

A patent holder's rights to exploit a patent are a very important issue, for those rights determine the profitability of the patent. The controlling precedent for unilateral patent rights is still *United States* v. *General Electric*, a 1926 case.[19] General Electric owned the patents on the basic tungsten filament necessary for the production of electric light bulbs, and so by 1921 had a 69 percent share of the market, compared with 16 percent for Westinghouse, its main licensee. General Electric's licensing agreement with Westinghouse stipulated, among other things, that Westinghouse would follow the prices and terms of sale initiated by GE. The government charged that this provision constituted a restraint of trade and therefore violated Section 1 of the Sherman Act. The Supreme Court disagreed, however, arguing that the restrictions were necessary to protect GE's profits from the patent. Otherwise Westinghouse could undercut GE's price, reducing GE's profits from its patented light bulbs. It is thus acceptable for a patent holder to set the price at which its licensees can sell a patented product. Although antitrust authorities believe that the "GE Doctrine" is outdated, the Court has divided four-to-four on two separate attempts to overturn it.[20]

In many subsequent cases, the Supreme Court has delineated the line between acceptable and unacceptable exploitation of a patent grant by a single patent holder. A patent holder may, for example, restrict licensees to specific geographic areas of the country, thereby establishing regional monopolies of the patented product. It can also engage in price discrimination by restricting licensees to different uses of the patent.[21] Both these practices permit a patent holder to increase the profits it can realize from any of its patents.

18. *Lear, Inc.* v. *Adkins*, 395 U.S. 653 (1969).

19. *United States* v. *General Electric Co.*, 272 U.S. 476 (1926).

20. *United States* v. *Line Material Co. et. al.*, 333 U.S. 287 (1948); and *United States* v. *Huck Manufacturing Co. et al.*, 382 U.S. 197 (1965).

21. *General Talking Pictures Corp.* v. *Western Electric*, 305 U.S. 124 (1938).

The Court also, however, prohibited certain practices that could increase a patent's profitability. It is illegal, for example, to control the price at which a patented good is resold.[22] Once a patented good is sold, the patent holder cannot place any restraints on its future disposition. It is also illegal to tie an unpatented product to the sale or lease of a patented product.[23] This prohibition eliminates a common method of discriminating among customers according to how much they use the tying product.

Finally, the Supreme Court has affirmed the right of patent holders to insert so-called "grant-back" clauses in licensing agreements.[24] A grant-back clause requires a licensee to assign any improvement patents it obtains to the original patent holder (the licensor). The purpose of this clause is to encourage patent holders to license other firms to use their inventions. This expanded use benefits society because more producers will make the patented product, and the market structure will be more competitive when the patent eventually expires. At the same time, it can benefit the original patent holder by increasing the speed with which it can penetrate the market. The patent holder is less likely to license a patent if the licensee can in turn secure an improvement patent that will reduce the demand for, and profitability of, the original patent. The insertion of the grant-back clause in the licensing agreement precludes this possibility.

Multilateral Patent Rights

The rights of a single patent holder to unilaterally exploit a patent may be modified when patent holders exploit their patents collectively. A major issue in cross-licensing or patent pooling agreements, as in all interfirm agreements, is whether or not they are ancillary to some legitimate business function.

The restrictions placed on the multilateral exploitation of patents are illustrated by a case that involved the leading manufacturers of automatic glassmaking machinery and glass products.[25] A patent pool was formed by the defendants—Hartford-Empire (the industry leader), Corning, Owens, Hazel, Thatcher, and Ball—who controlled 842 patents on glassmaking machinery. Through cross-licensing agreements,

22. *United States* v. *Univis Lens Co.,* 316 U.S. 241 (1942).
23. See the discussion of the International Salt case in Chapter 8.
24. *Transparent-Wrap Machine* v. *Stockes & Smith,* 329 U.S. 637 (1947).
25. *Hartford-Empire Co.* v. *United States* 323 U.S. 386 (1945).

the defendants excluded competitors and effectively controlled the manufacture of glassmaking machinery and, by extension, glass products. This gave them control over the prices of both the patented glassmaking machinery and the unpatented glass products. Not surprisingly, the Supreme Court ruled that the defendant's patent pool violated Sections 1 and 2 of the Sherman Act.

The Hartford-Empire case indicates that it is generally illegal for several firms to do things that are legal for a single firm to do. If this were not the case, cross-licensing agreements could easily be used to turn entire industries into cartels. Firms would simply enter into bogus agreements to allocate the industry's business among themselves. Legitimate patent pools can still be used, though only under certain conditions. The pool must be open to all firms in the industry and cannot assign exclusive territories or establish product prices.

The Hartford-Empire case also provides an example of the problem of fashioning appropriate relief in patent litigation. The government had advocated the dissolution of Hartford-Empire along with the royalty-free licensing of all the defendants' present and future patents. Given the judiciary's general reluctance to dissolve defendants in monopolization cases, it is not surprising that the Court disagreed. The more interesting aspect of the Court's decision was its disapproval of royalty-free licensing. Its decision was strongly influenced by two factors. First, the patents used in the cross-licensing agreements were valid. The defendants were not using the agreements to protect invalid patents. Second, royalty-free licensing would deprive the patent holders of their legitimate profits and would therefore be confiscatory. The Court did approve a milder relief decree, ordering the defendants to dissolve their trade association (a vehicle for collusive activity), abstain from any future associations for five years, and, most importantly, license all comers at a reasonable royalty rate.

Patent pools can be used to protect invalid patents, as illustrated in the development of the antibiotic tetracycline.[26] After receiving a patent for tetracycline in 1955, Charles Pfizer Company ended two patent suits with American Cyanamid and Bristol by licensing them to produce the drug. All three firms profited handsomely from the agreement. They sold tetracycline to wholesale druggists at $30.60 for a 100-tablet bottle that had cost from $1.60 to $3.80 to produce.[27] Even though the FTC

26. See W. Measday, "The Pharmaceutical Industry," in *The Structure of American Industry*, ed. W. Adams, 5th ed. (New York: Macmillan, 1977), p. 263.

27. F. M. Scherer, *Industrial Market Structure and Economic Performance* (Chicago: Rand McNally, 1970), p. 391.

claimed that the patent had been fraudulently obtained, it was just as effective as a valid patent until 1968, when the courts ordered mandatory licensing, four years before the patent was due to expire. Since 1968, these companies have reportedly paid more than $230 million in damages to compensate consumers for overcharges.

The current patent system has generated considerable controversy, especially in light of claims that the United States is losing its technological superiority. A major issue is the profitability of inventive activity. Does the patent system underreward or overreward patent holders? This issue must be addressed before discussing proposals for modifying the patent system and its unique relationship with antitrust law.

Evaluation

Appraisal of Current Policy

The United States Patent Office awards patents for inventions that meet, among other criteria, the non-obviousness requirement. The financial reward that the patent holder receives depends primarily on the length of the patent grant and the exploitation of that grant. The length of the grant was established at 17 years by the Patent Act of 1952; its exploitation is tempered by the antitrust laws.

Legal Standards.   The 17-year term of the patent grant is not based on any theory of optimal patent protection. It simply represents a congressional compromise between 14 years and 21 years.[28] From an economic perspective, the term of the grant reflects a compromise between the inventor's desire for exclusive use and society's desire for rapid diffusion of the invention. The length of the grant thus allocates the benefits of an invention between the inventor and society.[29] Except for very costly inventions that offer modest cost savings, a 17-year grant should allow firms to more than adequately cover their research and development expenses as well as some risk premium.[30] This conclusion is supported by data in Table 9.3 on the expected profitability of research and development programs. For all manufacturing, 55 percent of the firms expected to recoup their investment (the pay-out period) in three years or less.

28. Fourteen years represented twice the traditional apprenticeship period of 7 years, while 21 years corresponded to three times this period.

29. This was illustrated earlier in Figure 9.1.

30. F. M. Scherer, "The Economic Effects of Compulsory Patent Licensing," New York University Monograph Series in Finance and Economics, Monograph 1977-2, pp. 25–34.

Table 9.3   **Expected Average Pay-out Periods from R&D[a]
Expenditures, 1961**

Industry	3 years or less	4 to 5 years	6 years and over
	(percentage of companies answering)		
Iron and steel	38	50	12
Nonferrous metals	64	18	18
Machinery	51	39	10
Electrical machinery	61	32	7
Autos, trucks, and parts	54	40	6
Transportation equipment (aircraft, ships, railroad equipment)	43	44	13
Fabricated metals and instruments	77	14	9
Chemicals	33	41	26
Paper and pulp	50	32	18
Rubber	38	38	24
Stone, clay, and glass	38	46	16
Petroleum and coal products	17	33	50
Food and beverages	54	43	3
Textiles	76	24	0
Miscellaneous manufacturing	71	25	4
All manufacturing	55	34	11

[a]R&D: research and development.

Source: E. Mansfield, *The Economics of Technological Change* (New York: Norton, 1968), Table 3.7, p. 66.

Only 11 percent expected the pay-out period to last six years or longer. Although these data are very crude, they do suggest that a 17-year patent grant is unnecessary except for a small subset of inventions.

The argument against the 17-year patent grant is reenforced by the possibility of an inventor's receiving improvement patents. An improvement patent results from some patentable modification in the process or product covered by the original patent grant. Improvement patents may come from the patent holder's own research or through grant-back clauses inserted in its licensing agreements. The end result is the same. The patent holder's original monopoly grant can be preserved through a succession of improvement patents. For example, General Electric at first dominated the electric light bulb industry through its control of the original Edison patents that were issued in 1892. It maintained its dominance after those patents expired, however, through its improvement patents for different types of filaments and light bulb shapes![31]

31. See Arthur Bright, *The Electric Lamp Industry* (New York: Macmillan, 1949).

The antitrust laws have restricted the ability of patent holders to exploit their patents, and those restrictions can reduce the ultimate profitability of a legitimate patent.[32] These points are not disputed. For example, the prohibition of tying agreements eliminates one form of price discrimination that could increase profits. And the stricter standards for multilateral patent agreements make it more difficult for firms to collude successfully through patent pools. It seems, however, that the current rights of patent holders, combined with the 17-year patent grant, provide ample profits. It is not clear that any increase in the exploitability, and hence the profitability, of patents is justified.

Remedies.   The standard remedy in antitrust cases involving the illegal use of patents is compulsory licensing. *Compulsory licensing* requires the defendant to license all comers at some reasonable royalty rate. A district court decision in 1979 argued that this is the only relief that should be available in private antitrust cases.[33] Even though a jury ruled that Xerox had violated the Sherman Act with some of its licensing agreements, District Court Judge Jon Newman ruled that the plaintiff, SCM Corporation, was not entitled to any damages as a matter of law, as a firm should not be liable to damages for exercising its legal patent monopoly. The Supreme Court has yet to review this decision.

There have been several efforts to examine the actual impact of antitrust decrees that require compulsory licensing.[34] The empirical evidence available is not definitive, but it supports the following tentative conclusions. Compulsory licensing decrees did not appear to affect significantly the research intensity of the firms involved. The patenting activity of these firms, however, did decrease. The more severe the licensing decree, the more substantial this decrease. This result suggests that firms subject to compulsory licensing decrees rely more heavily on secrecy than on patents to protect their inventions. Secrecy can provide greater protection for process inventions than for product inventions in which the actual product (and the new idea) can easily be examined by competitors.

Enforcement.   Two problems have historically plagued the patenting process in the United States. First, as noted earlier, when the Patent

32. Antitrust enforcement unambiguously increases society's welfare if it uncovers invalid patents.

33. "A Victory for Xerox Jolts Private Plaintiffs," *Business Week*, January 15, 1979, pp. 37–38.

34. Scherer, "Compulsory Licensing," pp. 50–78.

Office issues a patent, there is no guarantee that it is valid. The applicant may withhold relevant information and receive a monopoly grant to which it is not legally entitled. Second, there is considerable delay in the patenting process. It currently takes approximately three years to receive a patent from the Patent Office. Since the applicant's invention is legally protected while the patent is pending, the length of the patent grant is effectively increased from 17 to 20 years! The patenting process itself thus extends a time span that is already criticized as being excessive for most inventions.

New Directions for Antitrust

There have been many proposals for modifying, and even eliminating, the current patent system.[35] The primary objective is to preserve the incentives for invention and innovation, but increase the rate of diffusion of new inventions throughout the economy. This requires a "fine tuning" of the rights of patent holders.

Legal Standards. The most radical solution is obviously the elimination of the patent system. Without patent protection, the profitability of a new invention would depend on the speed with which other firms could imitate it. A major factor is the time it takes competitors to acquire the necessary know-how to produce and market a competing good. This time lag is even longer for potential entrants who must enter the market and establish operations. In general, patent protection is most important when there are many potential imitators and when the invention requires a substantial commitment of research and development funds.

There is a limited amount of empirical evidence on the importance of patent protection in stimulating technological progress. Although most countries have had some type of patent system, Switzerland and the Netherlands did not have patent protection for inventions from the mid-1800s to the late 1800s.[36] The empirical evidence from these limited experiences presents a mixed picture, however. Some industries in these two countries were technological laggards, while others, notably chemicals, were very progressive. Additional information is provided by the European practice of allowing patents for the production processes of pharmaceuticals, but not for the drugs themselves. This provides less protection for a new chemical entity, for a given drug can frequently be

35. See Scherer, "Compulsory Licensing," and Ward S. Bowman, Jr., *Patents and Antitrust* (Chicago: University of Chicago Press, 1973).

36. Scherer, "Compulsory Licensing," pp. 35–40.

produced by several different production processes, allowing competitors to circumvent the original patent grant.[37] This less protective system has apparently not damaged the progressive European chemical industry, especially the German and Swiss firms. The American pharmaceutical experience suggests, in fact, that the rate of introduction of new drugs depends less on the patent policy than on the cost of complying with government testing regulations.[38]

Another, equally radical, possibility is to eliminate the market valuation and reward of inventions. A government agency would award a suitable amount to the inventor and then make the invention available to the public for general use. This arrangement would undoubtedly increase the rate of diffusion, though at the expense of the rate of inventive activity. The government has adopted this policy in the area of atomic energy, although the awards are very small compared to those for private patents. Overall, it makes more sense to let the market value inventions as it does a firm's productive inputs and outputs.

A more realistic proposal is to shorten the length of the patent grant. This would decrease the patent holder's profits while increasing the rate of diffusion. This would not be appropriate for all inventions, however. An attractive alternative is the German practice of differentiating between major and minor inventions. A major invention would be entitled to the full length of the patent grant, while a minor invention would receive some fraction thereof. One drawback is that this could be even more complex than the current system, which has a built-in delay of three years.

Other reform proposals concern the licensing practices of patent holders. One possibility is compulsory licensing. A patent holder would have to license all comers at the same "reasonable" royalty rate. This is now commonly the relief granted in patent antitrust cases. A variant of this approach—nonexclusive licensing—would require a firm to license all comers once it has licensed a single firm. The patent holder would still retain the option of not licensing any firms, however. Licensing agreements could also be modified to eliminate grant-back clauses. A more equitable procedure would be for *both* the patent holder and the licensee to share the improvement patent. This arrangement is common in government aerospace and defense projects, where the defense con-

37. This contrasts with the American practice which permits the patenting of specific chemical compounds and creates an incentive for competitors to produce related compounds that yield the same benefits.

38. The impact of government regulation on the pharmaceutical industry is discussed in more detail in Chapter 17.

tractor and the government share any patents financed by the government contract.

In fact, no *single* policy is ideal. F. M. Scherer has advocated a patent system that combines several of these reform proposals.[39] His system would create a presumption in favor of compulsory licensing five years from the date of the patent application. Patent holders would thus have a five-year period (which seems adequate for most patents) to exploit their patent exclusively and maximize their profits. After five years they would have to diffuse their invention among their competitors, but would receive royalties. Scherer's approach, however, would be sufficiently flexible to allow an extension of the patent grant if it seems necessary to compensate the patent holder.

Remedies.   If the district court decision in the Xerox-SCM case is upheld by the Supreme Court, it will be necessary to restore the right of plaintiffs to receive damage awards in private patent cases. If a firm is injured by a violation of the antitrust laws, it should be able to obtain compensation, regardless of the source of the injury. The prospect of a treble damage award is also necessary to encourage private policing of the antitrust laws. Private policing is very important, given the limited resources of the government and the Patent Office.

Enforcement.   It is not clear how the enforcement problems of the Patent Office can be resolved without a massive increase in its resources. There now exists an obvious trade-off between validity and delay. A more thorough analysis of patent applications requires more time, which lengthens the already considerable delay. On the other hand, to reduce delay would increase the number of invalid patents awarded. This trade-off will presumably worsen if the patent system is modified along the lines of the German system or Scherer's proposal.

Summary

The patent system is designed to increase the rate of technological progress in the American economy. Patent holders are granted the exclusive right to their invention in return for disclosing it and dedicating it to the public domain 17 years later. By creating a legal monopoly of the patented good, patent law inherently conflicts with the antitrust laws. As a result, the antitrust laws have tended to circumscribe the rights of patent holders and limit their ability to exploit their patents either unilater-

39. Scherer, "Compulsory Licensing," pp. 84–88.

ally or multilaterally. Concern over the monopoly power granted by patents has led to many proposals to reform the patent system. A major issue is the 17-year term of the patent, which is extended to approximately 20 years through delays at the Patent Office. Any contraction of this period seems unlikely, however, given recent fears of declining American technological superiority.[40] The current climate is not a favorable one for proposals to reduce the potential rewards of inventive activity in the United States.

Suggested Readings

Bowman, W. S., Jr. *Patents and Antitrust* (Chicago: University of Chicago Press, 1973).

Kamien, M. I., and Schwartz, N. L. "Market Structure and Innovation: A Survey," *Journal of Economic Literature* 13 (March 1975): 1–37.

Kitch, E. "The Nature and Function of the Patent System," *Journal of Law and Economics* 20 (October 1977): 265–90.

Priest, G. "Cartels and Patent License Arrangements," *Journal of Law and Economics* 20 (October 1977): 309–77.

Scherer, F. M. *Industrial Market Structure and Economic Performance*, 2nd ed. (Chicago: Rand McNally, 1980), Chapter 16.

U.S. Department of Commerce. *Patent Laws* (Washington, D.C.: Government Printing Office, August 1976).

40. "Vanishing Innovation," *Business Week*, July 3,1978, pp.46–54.

Evaluation of Antitrust Enforcement

Chapter 10

Previous chapters presented, and then evaluated, antitrust policy toward specific types of market conduct and structure. This chapter adopts a broader perspective, examining general policy issues in order to identify major weaknesses in antitrust enforcement and evaluate proposals for their reform.

Appraisal of Current Policy

The dramatic increase in private antitrust actions has put antitrust policy in the public spotlight. More and more firms are becoming involved directly in litigation under the antitrust laws. Not surprisingly, this upsurge in antitrust activity has revived old criticisms and introduced a few new ones. A major issue is the amount of resources, both public and private, devoted to enforcing the antitrust laws.[1] This expense depends in turn on the legal standards and remedies used in antitrust litigation.

Legal Standards

The primary purpose of the antitrust laws is to promote competition. A logical question is whether they have been successful: do the legal stan-

1. The interesting issue of the efficiency of antitrust enforcement compared with other types of government intervention is examined in Chapter 19

dards that have evolved under the antitrust laws actually promote competition? As has been discussed in Chapters 5 through 9, the picture is mixed. On the positive side, the per se prohibitions against such interfirm agreements as price fixing and market sharing undoubtedly have prevented the cartelization of much of American industry. The strict policy toward horizontal mergers has prevented a recurrence of the "merger for monopoly" wave that monopolized many major industries around the turn of the century. These are major, and unquestionably beneficial, accomplishments of the American antitrust program.

On the other hand, there have been disappointments. Antitrust policy has not been very successful in enhancing competition in markets dominated by a single firm or a handful of firms. It seems unlikely that this situation will be substantially affected by the initiation of shared monopoly suits by the Federal Trade Commission. In another area, price discrimination suits under the Robinson-Patman Act have generally been anticompetitive, not procompetitive. Overall, it is obvious that the antitrust laws are not perfect. They have not increased competition in all markets, although they have undoubtedly prevented its deterioration in many markets. And this is no small achievement.

Whatever their effect on competition, the antitrust laws have frequently been criticized as being too vague. For example, Olinkraft, a paper manufacturer indicted for fixing the prices of cardboard containers, complained that:

> ... federal antitrust statutes are very complex and leave room for doubt as
> to their exact meaning. They are difficult to understand and
> interpretations are changing constantly, resulting in many gray areas.[2]

Although this criticism does not seem true for price fixing, the argument has some merit. Antitrust laws are intentionally broad so that they can adapt to the ever-changing business environment. At the same time, such flexibility increases the uncertainty surrounding the legality of business practices. A firm may not know the legality of its actions until long after they have been taken. This uncertainty can reduce voluntary compliance with the antitrust laws by making it more difficult for a firm to police itself. It also creates the impression that antitrust law is arbitrary or random. It can even deter beneficial conduct, when firms mistakenly avoid business practices that are in fact legal. For example, uncertainty over the antitrust laws is frequently cited as one factor hin-

2. "Indictment Cites 14 Paper Makers for Price Fixing," *Wall Street Journal*, January 26, 1978, p. 3.

dering the export activities of American firms.[3] In this uncertain situation, firms must rely heavily on the legal advice of their antitrust attorneys and on possible consultations with the Justice Department and the Federal Trade Commission. Unfortunately, these consultations are least effective where the law is most uncertain. A definitive resolution of any major legal question must await judicial interpretation.

Remedies

The deterrent value of the antitrust laws depends strongly on the remedies available under those laws. Both civil and criminal sanctions can be imposed for violations of the Sherman Act, while only civil remedies are available under the Clayton Act. Table 10.1 presents data on the number of civil and criminal suits initiated by the Justice Department from 1890 to 1969. These figures document the important role played by civil suits, and hence civil remedies, in antitrust enforcement. For the latest period, 1965-1969, for example, 73 percent of the suits were civil, while 27 percent were criminal. And these figures even understate the importance of civil remedies, as they do not include cases in which the Justice Department concurrently filed a civil suit in a criminal proceeding.

A criminal violation of the Sherman Act can lead to the offender's being imprisoned, as well as fines being imposed on the offender and the company. In practice, these criminal sanctions have not been used consistently and forcefully by the courts. Offenders have rarely been imprisoned, and fines have been so low as to be almost nonexistent.[4] It is too soon to tell how the increase in maximum fines and the reclassification of violations from misdemeanors to felonies in 1974 will affect the courts' sentencing practices. It seems likely, however, that two problems will continue to limit the imposition of criminal sanctions. First, violations of the antitrust laws are "white collar" crimes. Courts have traditionally imposed lighter sentences for corporate crimes than for other crimes. Second, defendants often argue that it is unfair to impose criminal sanctions for violations of laws that are so ambiguous. The Justice Department can counter this argument by prosecuting only violations of well-established antitrust principles, such as the per se prohibition of price fixing. In fact, the Justice Department is encourag-

3. This was one reason behind the Justice Department's publication of *Antitrust Guide for International Operations* (Washington, D.C.: Government Printing Office, January 26, 1977).

4. The magnitude of fines imposed in price-fixing cases was examined in Chapter 6.

Table 10.1   Criminal and Civil Cases Brought by the
Department of Justice, 1890–1969

Period in Which Case Was Instituted	Total Number of Cases	Criminal	Civil	Percentage Criminal	Civil
1890–1894	9	4	5	44	56
1895–1899	7	1	6	14	86
1900–1904	6	1	5	17	83
1905–1909	39	26	13	67	33
1910–1914	91	37	54	41	59
1915–1919	43	25	18	58	42
1920–1924	66	25	41	38	62
1925–1929	59	16	43	27	73
1930–1934	30	11	19	37	63
1935–1939	57	27	30	47	53
1940–1944	223	163	60	73	27
1945–1949	157	58	99	37	63
1950–1954	159	73	86	46	54
1955–1959	195	97	98	50	50
1960–1964	215	78	137	36	64
1965–1969	195	52	143	27	73
Total	1,551	694	857		

Source: R. Posner, "A Statistical Study of Antitrust Enforcement," *Journal of Law and Economics* 13 (October 1970): Table 15, p. 385.

ing judges to imprison price fixers.[5] It is too early to tell, however, whether the Justice Department can successfully change judicial attitudes toward white collar crime in general and antitrust crimes in particular.

In contrast, civil sanctions are employed commonly and successfully against violators of the antitrust laws. Injunctions have proven to be a powerful tool for eliminating the effects of past actions and preventing their recurrence in the future.[6] They can also provide a deterrent effect, for firms are reluctant to have their future conduct regulated by court decrees, especially when the decrees have no time limit. One example is the experience of Swift and Company, whose merger activities have

5. "U.S. Announces New Policy to Encourage Voluntary Disclosure of Antitrust Acts," *Wall Street Journal*, October 5, 1978, p. 6.

6. W. Baldwin, "The Feedback Effect of Business Conduct on Industry Structure," *Journal of Law and Economics* 12 (April 1969): 123–53.

been constrained by an injunction issued in 1903![7] Swift's experience shows that it is difficult to alter the provisions of a consent decree unless the government agrees to the modifications.[8]

The treble damage provisions of the antitrust laws became very controversial with the explosion of private antitrust activity in the 1970s. The historical source of these awards is England's Statute of Monopolies, which in 1623 provided for treble damage awards. The objectives are to compensate firms damaged by antitrust violations and to deter firms from committing future violations. Most of the criticism concerns the magnitude, not the existence, of the damage awards. First, it is argued that the prospect of high awards has encouraged firms to file nuisance suits in the expectation of making a profitable out-of-court settlement. Indeed, of the approximately 7,500 private suits filed in federal courts from 1963 to 1972, more than 70 percent were settled out of court.[9] Second, the prospect of having to pay high awards may also encourage large firms to be less competitive and more protective of their smaller competitors, in hopes of avoiding such nuisance suits. This unintended aspect of antitrust enforcement is obviously not beneficial to society. Third, business owners view treble damage awards as unfair when the legality of the disputed practices is not known. That is, they feel that firms are penalized by the ambiguities in the antitrust laws. Finally, treble damage awards may threaten the financial health of the defendant. The Justice Department was evidently influenced by such a possibility when it decided against suing Westinghouse in 1976.[10] Instead, it sought to modify a 1962 consent decree and to maintain Westinghouse as the only domestic producer of turbine generators besides General Electric.

Enforcement

Two major enforcement issues are the manner in which the antitrust agencies initially select their cases and how they subsequently dispose of them.

7. *Swift and Company* v. *United States*, 196 U.S. 375 (1905).

8. *United States* v. *Swift and Company*, 189 F. Supp. 885 (N.D. Ill. 1960), affirmed, 367 U.S. 909 (1961).

9. W. Breit and K. Elzinga, "Antitrust Enforcement and Economic Efficiency: The Uneasy Case for Treble Damages," *Journal of Law and Economics* 17 (October 1974): 329–56.

10. "U.S. Won't File Suit Naming GE, Westinghouse," *Wall Street Journal*, December 13, 1976, p. 2.

Table 10.2 Method of Detection in 49 Price-Fixing Cases

Method	Number of Cases[a]
Grand jury investigation in another case	12
Complaint by a competitor	10
Complaint by a customer	7
Complaint by local, state, or federal agency	6
Complaint by current or former employees	3
Complaint by trade association official	2
Investigation of conduct or performance initiated by Antitrust Division	2
Newspaper account	2
Referred to the Antitrust Division by the Federal Trade Commission	2
Complaint by anonymous informant	1
Merger investigation	1
Private suit	1
Total	49

[a]The sample consists of criminal cases that were either won in the courtroom or settled out of court with a *nolo contendere* plea from 1963 to 1972.
Source: Reproduced from G. Hay and D. Kelley, "An Empirical Survey of Price-Fixing Conspiracies," *Journal of Law and Economics* 17 (April 1974): Table 1, p. 21.

The case selection process has been criticized for relying too much on private complaints instead of internal investigations by antitrust authorities. Table 10.2 lists the different methods by which 49 price-fixing conspiracies were discovered by the Antitrust Division of the Justice Department. The two most common methods were grand jury investigations and complaints received from competitors. Only *two* conspiracies were discovered by an Antitrust Division investigation. The government's reliance on outside complaints, especially from competitors, can lead to a poor selection of cases. This has been illustrated by the FTC's prolonged preoccupation with Robinson-Patman cases. Economics has not played a major role in the initiation of complaints or in the selection of cases to be processed.[11] The lack of an economic rationale for the government's selection of cases is not too surprising, given the limited

11. W. Long, R. Schramm, and R. Tollison, "The Economic Determinants of Antitrust Activity," *Journal of Law and Economics* 16 (October 1973): 351–64; J. Siegfried, "The Determinants of Antitrust Activity," *Journal of Law and Economics* 18 (October 1975): 559–74; and Peter Asch, "The Determinants and Effects of Antitrust Activity," *Journal of Law and Economics* 18 (October 1975): 575–81.

role of economists.[12] Although the influence of economists at the FTC and the Justice Department is increasing, it is too soon to tell whether antitrust resources will be allocated in a more efficient fashion.

Once a case is selected (for whatever reasons), the defendant can expect a lengthy and expensive litigation process. In a civil case there can be a delay of four or five years before a court decision is reached, even longer if the decision is subsequently appealed to the Supreme Court.[13] Administrative proceedings at the Federal Trade Commission have lasted equally long. There are several reasons for the substantial delays that have become characteristic of antitrust litigation. First, the defendants generally have a financial incentive to delay the case. Delay postpones the awarding of any damages, enables the defendant to continue the contested practice in the interim, and may even encourage the plaintiff to drop the suit or settle out of court. Second, antitrust cases tend to raise complex issues that require considerable economic analysis. In one of the numerous private suits brought against IBM, the trial judge, Samuel Conti, stated that "the magnitude and complexity of the case . . . render it as a whole beyond the competency of any jury to understand and decide rationally."[14] Third, the government staff is subject to high turnover, which impedes the continuity in case development and reduces the number of experienced trial attorneys. Lawyers generally serve a short apprenticeship with the FTC or Justice Department before leaving for the substantially higher salaries available in private practice.[15]

Finally, it should be noted that the overwhelming majority of government cases, both civil and criminal, are settled out of court. The Justice Department's historical experience with criminal suits is summarized in Table 10.3. *Nolo contendere* pleas have become the most common solution in criminal cases, accounting for 87 percent of the government's convictions from 1965 to 1969. The frequency of *nolo* pleas has caused concern, for these pleas do not constitute prima facie evidence of an antitrust violation for follow-up private suits. It thus becomes more diffi-

12. Ralph Nader's Study Group on Antitrust Enforcement noted that economists "are second class citizens: they have little or no say in the type of cases brought, the legal theories used, or the relief sought" (M. Green, B. Moore, Jr., and B. Wasserstein, *The Closed Enterprise System: Ralph Nader's Study Group Report on Antitrust Enforcement* [New York: Grossman, 1972], p. 128).

13. R. Posner, "A Statistical Study of Antitrust Enforcement," *Journal of Law and Economics* 13 (October 1970): Table 7, p. 377.

14. R. Shaffer, "Those Complex Antitrust Cases," *Wall Street Journal*, August 29, 1978, p. 16.

15. M. Green, et al., *The Closed Enterprise System*.

Table 10.3   **Criminal Convictions in Justice Department Cases**

Period in Which Case Was Instituted	Disposed of on *Nolo Contendere* Plea	Other Convictions	Total Convictions	Acquittals and Dismissals	*Percentage of Convictions*
1890–1894	0	0	0	4	0
1895–1899	0	0	0	1	0
1900–1904	0	1	1	0	100
1905–1909	0	11	11	14	44
1910–1914	9	12	21	16	57
1915–1919	5	8	13	10	57
1920–1924	1	14	15	10	60
1925–1929	4	10	14	2	88
1930–1934	2	6	8	3	73
1935–1939	13	6	19	8	70
1940–1944	110	13	123	40	75
1945–1949	41	9	50	8	86
1950–1954	55	10	65	8	89
1955–1959	65	21	86	11	89
1960–1964	47	17	64	14	82
1965–1969	40	6	46	1	98
Total	392	144	536	150	

Source: Reproduced from R. Posner, "A Statistical Study of Antitrust Enforcement," *Journal of Law and Economics* 13 (October 1970): Table 18, p. 390.

cult for firms injured by the alleged violations to obtain compensation through treble damage suits. On the other hand, *nolo* pleas save time and enable the Justice Department to attack a larger number of antitrust violations with their limited resources. As a result, these pleas present the Justice Department with a trade-off between more convictions of antitrust violators and more financial compensation for their victims.

Many proposals have been made for overhauling antitrust enforcement in the United States. Indeed, from 1968 to 1979 there were three major presidential commissions on antitrust policy.[16] As it is impossible to discuss all their recommendations in this section, some of the major, and more controversial, recommendations will be presented.[17]

New Directions For Antitrust

16. The three were the Task Force on Antitrust Policy (1968), the Task Force on Productivity and Competition (1969), and the National Commission for the Review of Antitrust Laws and Procedures (1979).

17. Possible changes in the powers of administrative agencies, such as the FTC, are discussed in Chapter 19.

204 Antitrust Enforcement

Legal Standards

In the absence of changes in judicial interpretations of existing laws, the proposals for new legal standards would require that new antitrust laws be enacted. These laws in general would make antitrust law more definite by making certain activities illegal per se. This is the case with the bills discussed in previous chapters, which would create no-fault oligopoly and prohibit mergers among large corporations. These laws reduce the current uncertainty inherent in a rule of reason approach, but at the expense of considerable corporate freedom. As noted earlier, it is not clear that the potential benefits of these laws outweigh their potential costs. An alternative approach is advocated by Posner, who would repeal all antitrust laws except Section 1 of the Sherman Act. This action would substantially decrease the scope of the antitrust laws, thereby increasing corporate freedom in the marketplace. As Congress has yet to heed the virtually unanimous plea of economists to repeal the Robinson-Patman Act, it is extremely unlikely that they would venture down this more radical avenue.

Remedies

Probably the least controversial recommendation is to limit the scope and duration of court decrees. Decrees should not needlessly constrain corporate activities that are unrelated to the antitrust violation, and they should expire after a given time period, perhaps 10 years. These changes are necessary because the courts are not well suited to monitor their own decrees. More controversial recommendations would increase maximum jail terms and require mandatory minimum sentences. These changes could backfire, however, if they increased the already substantial reluctance of society to treat white collar crime harshly. Juries might be even less likely to convict an executive of an antitrust violation if a prison sentence were mandatory. Also, imprisonment is a costly remedy.[18] Society incurs the cost of imprisoning the offender, whose productivity is also lost during the period of incarceration.

Some of the more interesting reform proposals involve the financial penalties for an antitrust violation—treble damage awards and fines. One possibility is to provide trial judges with discretion to award single, double, or triple damages to successful plaintiffs. A judge could then

18. In 1975, for example, society spent $11,500 for each juvenile held in a public correctional facility (U.S. Department of Commerce, *Statistical Abstract of the United States, 1979* [Washington, D.C.: Government Printing Office, 1979], p. 194).

tailor the award to the nature of the violation. For example, treble damages might still be awarded for clear-cut violations such as price fixing, but only single damages would be given for practices in the gray areas of antitrust. Variable damage awards would counter the argument that treble damage awards are frequently excessive and therefore unfair. A more extreme proposal is the complete elimination of damage awards.[19] This would remove the major incentive for private suits, especially nuisance suits, and place all enforcement responsibility with the Justice Department and the Federal Trade Commission. The primary financial penalty would then be fines, which could be varied in response to the nature of the violation and the size of the firm. Fines might be set at a fixed percentage of a firm's sales, for example, with the percentage increasing for successive antitrust violations by the same firm. (This is one possible solution to the problem of corporate recidivism in the antitrust area.) The reliance on fines would reduce litigation costs substantially, but it would also prevent firms from receiving compensation for injuries associated with antitrust violations. This does not seem equitable. An easier solution to the nuisance suit problem would be to require the losing party to pay all litigation costs.[20] As it stands now, the worst thing that can happen to the losing party is that it pays its own litigation costs, which are tax deductible anyway.

Enforcement

One old proposal that received renewed attention after Judge Conti's decision in the IBM-Memorex case is the establishment of a special Antitrust Court. Such a court would hear only cases arising under the antitrust laws, analogous to the United States Tax Court, which resolves disputes under the Internal Revenue Tax Code. Judges in the Antitrust Court could receive special training in the legal and economic issues that arise in antitrust litigation. Their special background, plus the expertise that would be acquired over time, might enable the Antitrust Court simultaneously to expedite antitrust cases and provide more consistent rulings. As with other special courts, the decisions of such an Antitrust Court could ultimately be appealed to the Supreme Court.

19. Breit and Elzinga, "The Uneasy Case."

20. And these costs can be substantial. In Berkey Photo's lawsuit against Kodak, Berkey's three law firms sought "$29 million for themselves at an average rate of $350 an hour" ("The Legal Bill Facing Kodak," *Business Week*, July 3, 1978, p. 94). Another possibility is to extend the legal principle of *res judicata* to private antitrust cases. For example, once IBM had been acquitted of monopolizing a market, it would not have to defend itself against the identical charges brought by other firms.

Another frequent proposal is to merge the Antitrust Division of the Justice Department with the Federal Trade Commission's Bureau of Competition. The primary objective of this merger would be to centralize the government's antitrust resources in a single agency, thereby eliminating any problems associated with the dual enforcement of the antitrust laws by the FTC and the Justice Department. For example, businesses complain that dual enforcement increases the uncertainty surrounding the antitrust laws, because the two agencies may give conflicting opinions. This possibility was illustrated in 1978 when Senator Edward Kennedy asked the FTC to examine the legality of the merger between Lykes and L-T-V after it had been approved by the Justice Department.[21] At the same time, a consolidation of the antitrust agencies would eliminate waste from dual investigations of the same potential violations. The standard counter-argument to this merger proposal is that dual enforcement is a good insurance policy. It makes it less likely that antitrust enforcement will become stagnant or politicized. If one agency becomes ineffective, the other can fill in. In the 1950s and 1960s, for instance, the FTC was known as one of the worst federal agencies in Washington, D.C. In any event, this merger is unlikely, as noted by a private antitrust attorney in Washington:

> Talking in this city about abolishing the FTC is almost as dangerous as talking in Southern California about abolishing the B1 bomber. The agency is a major business in this town.[22]

Whether there are one or two federal antitrust agencies, antitrust enforcement can be improved by emphasizing economic criteria in the case selection process. This conclusion was reached by Weiss, who examined the allocation of resources within the Justice Department from 1968 to 1970.[23] He estimated the expected gains to consumers from a successful case and then compared them with the expected cost (in lawyer-years) of litigating the case. His results are presented in Table 10.4. Even though these estimates are necessarily rough, several conclusions seem warranted. First, the expected gain per lawyer-year varies substantially by the type of case. The expected gain from a civil collusion case, for example, is approximately 10 times that for a pure conglomer-

21. "Antitrust End Run," *Wall Street Journal*, November 21, 1978, p.22.

22. "Merger of Antitrust Division, FTC Unit Is Ordered for Study by Attorney General," *Wall Street Journal*, April 11, 1977.

23. L. Weiss, "An Analysis of the Allocation of the Antitrust Division Resources," in *The Antitrust Dilemma*, ed. J. A. Dalton and S. L. Levin (Lexington, Mass.: Lexington Books, 1974), Chapter 3.

Table 10.4 **Expected Gains of Different Types of Cases, 1968–1970**
(Millions of dollars)

Type of Case	Mean Annual Sales	Expected Gains of a Successful Case	Expected Gains per Division Lawyer-year
Criminal collusion	19	4	0.9
Civil collusion	173	168	46.7
Horizontal merger	18[a]	58	17.6
Vertical merger	59[a]	95	28.9
Potential entry merger	90[a]	37	4.8
Pure conglomerate merger	665[a]	77	4.0
Structural monopoly	2,680[b]	392[b]	13.7[b]
Leverage	1,657[c]	512[c]	122.0[c]
Regulation—merger	215[a]	63	13.1
Regulation—practices	600	53	52.8

[a]Sales of acquired firms.
[b]Inflated by the IBM case.
[c]Inflated by five large steel reciprocity cases.
Source: L. Weiss, "An Analysis of the Allocation of Antitrust Division Resources," in *The Antitrust Dilemma*, ed. J. A. Dalton and S. L. Levin (Lexington, Mass.: Lexington Books, 1974), Table 3-4, p. 49.

ate merger case. These differences, then, could be used to allocate the Antitrust Division's resources across cases. This economic approach would emphasize civil collusion, horizontal and vertical mergers, and restrictive practices in regulated industries. Structural monopoly cases, on the other hand, would be deemphasized. They yield lower expected gains per lawyer-year, and they require a heavy commitment of antitrust resources throughout the lengthy litigation process.

Summary

Antitrust enforcement is not perfect. Most notably, the litigation of antitrust cases, both civil and criminal, is lengthy and costly. But, as long as antitrust enforcement is effective, it will remain controversial. Nonetheless, the following changes seem reasonable and should improve antitrust enforcement. First, the Robinson-Patman Act should be repealed. It discourages price competition and reduces the respect of the business community for the antitrust laws in general. Second, damage awards from antitrust violations should be variable, not fixed, and litigation costs should be borne by the losing party. These changes would eliminate some of the inequities associated with treble damage awards and would also discourage nuisance suits. Third, economic factors should receive greater emphasis in the selection of cases by both the Justice

Department and the Federal Trade Commission. This could reduce the role of politics and increase the effectiveness of the government's limited antitrust resources. Finally, Congress should establish an Antitrust Court that would specialize in hearing antitrust cases. This specialization should reduce delay while increasing the consistency and quality of judicial decisions.

Suggested Readings

Bork, R. H. *The Antitrust Paradox* (New York: Basic Books, 1978).

Demsetz, H. "Economics as a Guide to Antitrust Regulation," *Journal of Law and Economics* 19 (August 1976): 371–84.

Elzinga, K., and Breit, W. *The Antitrust Penalties: A Study in Law and Economics* (New Haven: Yale University Press, 1976).

Long, W., Schramm, R., and Tollison, R. "The Economic Determinants of Antitrust Activity," *Journal of Law and Economics* 16 (October 1973): 351–64.

Posner, R. "A Statistical Study of Antitrust Enforcement," *Journal of Law and Economics* 13 (October 1970): 365–420.

———. *Antitrust Law: An Economic Perspective* (Chicago: University of Chicago Press, 1976), Chapters 9–10.

Part Three

Economic Regulation

The Regulatory Environment

Chapter

11

In a market economy, the forces of supply and demand determine market price, firm profitability, and entry. Economic regulation occurs whenever one or more of these important economic variables is determined by an administrative process instead of the market process. Although most of the American economy is not subject to economic regulation, there traditionally has been a sizable sector in which economic decisions have been made by government agencies. This extensive regulation of private economic activity has raised both constitutional and economic issues that illustrate the advantages and disadvantages of this type of government intervention.

As with its antitrust law, America's initial experience with economic regulation followed the English common law tradition.[1] Common law precedents required certain businesses to serve all comers at reasonable rates. This was true, for example, for inns, toll roads, and ferries.

Economic Regulation in America

1. The following discussion on the origins of economic regulation in the United States is based primarily on William K. Jones, *Regulated Industries* (Brooklyn: Foundation Press, 1967), Chapter 1.

This obligation to serve the traveling public was thought necessary to prevent those businesses from exploiting any monopoly power that they possessed. Under the common law, a business could be sued for not providing service or for charging an unreasonable price. The burden of proof was on the plaintiff, however, who could rarely match the defendant's financial and legal resources. Even if the suit were successful, the plaintiff ran the risk of antagonizing the defendant and jeopardizing any future service that might be necessary.

Economic regulation was formally introduced through corporate charters and franchises. Before general incorporation laws were introduced in the late 1800s, state legislatures passed corporate charters. Commonly, these charters established the maximum rates that the corporation could charge; a charter that created a railroad, for example, would also set the rates for specific services. In urban areas, franchises were a common method of providing public services. A franchise granted the exclusive right to provide a specific service, but under conditions established by the city. A water company, for example, would have to provide water of a minimum quality without exceeding the allowable rates.

Charters and franchises suffered from common deficiencies that reduced their effectiveness as a means of economic regulation. First, fixed rates are inappropriate in a dynamic world. A firm may be able to reduce its costs and earn considerable profits without violating any rate ceiling. On the other hand, costs may increase and make it uneconomical for the firm to provide the service at the established rate.

Second, it is difficult for the political body granting the franchise or charter (city councils or state legislatures) effectively to monitor a firm's performance. They have neither the time nor the expertise to determine whether a franchisee is satisfying all the conditions in the charter or franchise grant. Third, the awards process is very conducive to corruption, with the result that charters and franchises may be awarded on the basis of bribes, not the technical qualifications of the applicants.

Many of these deficiencies were remedied by the creation of independent regulatory commissions. State regulatory commissions were first set up in response to the inability of cities to regulate the railroads effectively. Cities lacked jurisdiction over the railroads because their operations went beyond the city limits. In 1869, Massachusetts created an "advisory" commission that could make recommendations, but not enforce them. The commission's only weapon was the indirect one of public opinion. Two years later, Indiana established the first state commission with the power to set railroad rates. The jurisdiction problem

Table 11.1 **Employment and Income Originating in Regulated Industries, 1978**

Industry	Income ($ millions)	Percentage of National Income	Employees[a] (1,000s)	Percentage of Total Employment
Transportation	68.2	3.86	2,645	2.80
Railroad	14.2	.80	535	.57
Water	4.7	.27	188[b]	.20
Air	12.1	.68	396	.42
Motor freight and warehousing	28.5	1.61	1,267	1.34
Local and interurban passenger	3.8	.22	259	.27
Communications	40.5[c]	2.29	1,232[c]	1.31
Telephone	35.8	2.03	992	1.05
Broadcasting	4.7	.27	177	.19
Electric, gas, and sanitary services	34.9	1.98	776	.82
Total	143.6	8.13	4,653	4.93

[a] The totals include data for private employment only. Government employment is thus not included.
[b] This figure includes employment for transportation services other than water, such as natural gas pipelines.
[c] Some industries not shown separately.
Source: U.S. Department of Commerce, *Statistical Abstract of the United States, 1979* (Washington D.C.: Government Printing Office, 1979), pp. 412, 442.

was still present, however, since the state commission could regulate only the intrastate activities of the railroads. Interstate rates constituted interstate commerce and could be regulated only by the federal government. This paved the way for the creation in 1887 of the first federal regulatory agency—the Interstate Commerce Commission (ICC).

Since the creation of the Interstate Commerce Commission, federal regulation has expanded to include other types of transportation as well as interstate and foreign communications. The approximate size of the regulated sector (federal, state, and local) in the United States can be deduced from the income and employment data presented in Table 11.1. In 1978, the regulated sector accounted for 8.13 percent of national income and 4.93 percent of total employment. These figures are only approximations, however. First, they include some activities that are not subject to economic regulation, such as the transportation of agricultural products (which is exempt from ICC regulation). Second, the figures leave out some regulated activities. The prices of crude oil, natural gas, and some agricultural products are set by the federal government, though those industries do not appear in Table 11.1. A major problem is

Table 11.2 Regulation by State Commissions

Industry	Number of States Regulating Prices[a]	Number of States Regulating Entry
Electricity		
Private	49	35
Public	17	12
Cooperative	29	23
Natural gas retailing		
Private	49	36
Public	17	11
Telephone	50	38
Airline service	21	25
Trucking		
Common carriers	47	45
Contract carriers	42	43
Railroad transportation	44	26

[a] Sales to ultimate consumers. (All totals include the District of Columbia.)

Source: Paul W. MacAvoy, *The Regulated Industries and the Economy* (New York: Norton, 1979), Table A.2, p. 148.

that government regulation is dynamic, not static. Its nature and extent are always changing. The regulated industry of today may become the unregulated industry of tomorrow and vice versa. For example, government regulation of the airlines, natural gas, and crude oil is slated to expire in the 1980s, while Congress is currently debating proposals to initiate government regulation of the health care industry. Nonetheless, Table 11.1 does provide some idea of the orders of magnitude involved in government regulation.

It should be noted that economic regulation is one type of government intervention in which state governments are active. Table 11.2 lists some economic activities that are subject to price and entry regulation by different states. In general, states are heavily involved in economic regulation of the traditional public utilities—electricity, natural gas retailing, and telephones—as well as trucking, railroads, and, to a lesser extent, airlines.

Finally, some general characteristics of regulated industries should be noted. First, they commonly provide services, not products. A railroad can ship products to different destinations, while the local telephone company enables people to communicate with those places. This characteristic is important because services, unlike products, cannot be

Table 11.3   Capital-Output Ratios for Selected Industries, 1972–75

Industry	Ratio
Unregulated industries	
Motor vehicles and equipment	.58
Textile mill products	.63
Primary iron and steel	.98
Petroleum refining	1.27
All manufacturing	.76
Regulated Industries	
Class A and B electric utilities	3.89
Class A telephone carriers	3.27
Class I railroads	2.63
Natural gas pipelines	2.25
Trunk airlines[a]	1.34
Class I and II common carrier truckers[a]	.20

[a]Data is for 1973 only.

Source: U.S. Senate Committee on Governmental Affairs, *Study on Federal Regulation*, vol. 6, *Framework for Regulation* (Washington, D.C.: Government Printing Office, December 1978), p. 14.

stored in inventory. A regulated firm must thus maintain sufficient capacity to satisfy the public's demand for its product. Second, regulated industries tend to be very capital intensive. As Table 11.3 indicates, with the exception of common carrier trucking, they are substantially more capital intensive than the average for all manufacturing. Among the manufacturing industries listed, only petroleum refining has a capital-output ratio greater than one. The capital intensiveness of regulated industries frequently is due to the construction of distribution networks for their services. Railroads need tracks; local telephone companies need wires. The net effect of these two characteristics is to give regulated industries high fixed costs, low marginal costs, and frequently idle capacity. Third, the construction of these distribution networks requires access to the public domain. This provides one justification for government control over entry in these industries.

Constitutional Issues

Economic regulation has raised two major constitutional issues that ultimately had to be resolved by the Supreme Court. First, what businesses can be regulated by the government? Second, once a business becomes regulated, what compensation is it entitled to? Both of these issues require an interpretation of the Fifth Amendment to the Constitution, which states that no person shall "be deprived of life, liberty, or property without due process of law." Economic regulation can affect property—the value of a business.[2]

The constitutionality of economic regulation was first addressed by the Court in *Munn v. Illinois*.[3] The controversy was over the regulation of the rates charged by grain warehouses in Chicago. In 1871, the state assembly passed a law that, among other things, established maximum fees for the storage of grain. Prior to this law, fees had been determined jointly by the 14 grain warehouses and then published in the January editions of local newspapers.[4] The owners of one warehouse, Munn and Scott, sued the state, claiming that the law violated the Constitution—specifically, that it confiscated private property and therefore violated the due-process clause of the Fourteenth Amendment. The owners' argument was straightforward: by controlling price, the law restricted the firm's income, thereby reducing its market value.[5]

The Supreme Court disagreed with Munn and Scott, ruling that Illinois had the right to regulate the grain warehouses. The warehouses were viewed as being similar to toll roads, because they charged a common fee for each bushel of grain that went through Chicago, and it was not possible to ship grain from the West to the East without going through Chicago. Given this perspective and common law precedents, it is not surprising that the Court could justify regulation by the state. The Court also addressed the broader issue of the constitutional basis for regulation:

> ... Property does become clothed with a public interest when used in a manner to make it of public consequence, and affect the community at large. When, therefore, one devotes his property to a use in which the public has an interest, he, in effect, grants to the public an interest in that

2. The Fifth Amendment to the Constitution pertains to actions undertaken by the federal government, while state government actions are covered under the Fourteenth Amendment.

3. *Munn v. Illinois*, 94 U.S. 113 (1877).

4. Note that it was not illegal for these firms jointly to set prices, as the Sherman Act was not passed until 1890. See Chapter 6 for more discussion of the legality of price-fixing agreements.

5. This same issue is currently being raised by laws that restrict the right of apartment owners to convert their buildings to condominiums. For a typical example, see "Philadelphia's Ban on Condominiums Runs into Problems," *Wall Street Journal*, October 2, 1979, p. 21.

use, and must submit to be controlled by the public for the common good, to the extent of the interest he has thus created.[6]

In sum, it is constitutional for governments to regulate businesses that are "affected with a public interest." At first glance, the public interest standard seems very logical. Upon closer examination, however, it is an empty box. It can be used to justify any and all regulation because the public always has some interest in a business. Not surprisingly, the "public interest" standard led to inconsistent rulings by the Court. For example, it upheld regulation of insurance agents, attorneys, and stock-yards, but not of food retailing, ticket brokers, gasoline, and ice manufacturing.

It was not until 1934, 57 years after the Munn decision, that the Supreme Court finally established more definitive standards. The case, *Nebbia* v. *New York,* involved the constitutionality of a New York law that fixed the retail price of milk at nine cents per quart.[7] The ostensible purpose was to benefit the state's sizable dairy industry by eliminating the intense competition at the retail level. Nebbia, a Rochester grocer, violated the law by selling two quarts of milk and a five-cent loaf of bread for a total of 18 cents. The Court upheld the constitutionality of the New York law and, in so doing, established more definitive standards for determining the constitutionality of economic regulations:

> So far as the requirement of due process is concerned, and in the absence of other constitutional restriction, a state is free to adopt whatever economic policy may reasonably be deemed to promote public welfare, and to enforce that policy by legislation adapted to its purpose. The courts are without authority either to declare such policy, or, when it is declared by the legislature, to override it. If the laws passed are seen to have a reasonable relation to a proper legislative purpose, and are neither arbitrary nor discriminatory, the requirements of due process are satisfied, and judicial determination to that effect renders a court *functus officio.*[8]

The Court's Nebbia decision constitutes a strong precedent because the first requirement—that the means are reasonably related to some goal— is generally ignored. This was true in the Nebbia case, where it was never explained how controlling the retail price of milk would increase the wholesale price. If anything, this law would benefit the retailers, not the producers, of milk. In any event, so long as a law is not arbitrary or

6. *Munn* v. *Illinois,* at 126.

7. *Nebbia* v. *New York,* 291 U.S. 502 (1934).

8. *Nebbia* v. *New York,* at 537.

discriminatory, a state can regulate whatever private economic activity it wants to.

While the debate over the constitutionality of regulation was going on, the Court was also confronting a related issue: the constitutionality of the rate of return permitted for regulated businesses. As noted above, regulation can reduce the profitability of a business. Is there, however, some mimimum level of profits to which regulated firms are entitled? In other words, can regulation have such an adverse effect on a firm's profitability that it becomes confiscatory and violates the firm's due-process guarantees under the Constitution?

Historically, this issue reached the Supreme Court in 1898 with the case of *Smyth* v. *Ames*.[9] The suit arose over a Nebraska law that established maximum rates for intrastate railroad service. Stockholders of the Union Pacific Railroad contended that the rates were so low as to deprive them of compensation for the use of their property. The dispute centered on determining the value of the railroad's property and the return to which it was reasonably entitled. The Court concluded that:

> ... the basis of all calculations as to the reasonableness of rates to be charged ... must be the fair value of the property being used ... for the convenience of the public. And in order to ascertain that value, the original cost of construction, the amount expended in permanent improvements, the amount and market value of its bonds and stock, the present as compared with the original cost of construction ... are all matters for consideration, and are to be given such weight as may be just and right in each case.... What the company is entitled to ask is a fair return upon the value of that which it employs for the public convenience. On the other hand, what the public is entitled to demand is that no more be exacted from it ... than the services ... are reasonably worth.[10]

The Union Pacific was thus entitled to a "fair return on the fair value" of its resources. Unfortunately, this was not as definitive as it may at first seem. Fairness, like beauty, is in the eye of the beholder. The Court listed factors that must be considered in determining fair value, but it then concluded that each factor is "to be given such weight as may be just and right in each case." And the inclusion of stock value as a factor is clearly erroneous, for it depends on the rates set by the government regulatory agency. This is circular reasoning. In short, the "fair return

9. *Smyth* v. *Ames*, 169 U.S. 466 (1898).
10. *Smyth* v. *Ames*, at 546–47.

on fair value" standard is so vague as to invite constant judicial involvement in the regulatory arena.

Given the Court's decision in *Smyth* v. *Ames,* courts were active in rate-making cases for 46 years. No clear judicial standards emerged, however, as different courts employed different procedures for determining fair return and fair value. Finally, in *FPC* v. *Hope Natural Gas (1944),* the Supreme Court exited from the rate-making arena.[11] This case focused on the procedures employed by the Federal Power Commission in determining the allowable return for natural gas pipeline companies. Delivering the opinion of the Court, Justice Douglas noted:

> ... Under the statutory standard of "just and reasonable" it is the result reached not the method employed which is controlling. ... It is not theory but the impact of the rate order which counts. If the total effect of the rate order cannot be said to be unjust and unreasonable, judicial inquiry under the Act is at an end. The fact that the method employed to reach that result may contain infirmities is not then important.[12]

This decision effectively eliminated judicial involvement in the rate-making process. In effect, the Supreme Court recognized that specialized administrative agencies were better suited than the courts for the complex task of rate-making.

Economic Issues

The resolution of constitutional disputes has not eliminated the controversy surrounding government regulation of private economic activity. Constitutional issues have simply been replaced by economic issues. For example, given that regulation is constitutional, when is it economically justified? Of the various methods for determining rates, which ones are consistent with economic principles of pricing? The answers to these questions provide a framework within which to evaluate both current regulations and proposals for their reform.

Economic Rationales for Regulation

The traditional economic argument for economic regulation is the presence of a "natural" monopoly. A monopoly is considered to be "natural" when it is the inevitable end result of the market process. Competition eliminates all the firms in the market except one, the natural monopolist. For this situation to occur, however, costs must be decreasing: aver-

11. *Federal Power Commission* v. *Hope Natural Gas Co.,* 320 U.S. 591 (1944).
12. *Federal Power Commission* v. *Hope Natural Gas Co.,* at 602.

age cost declines with increases in production. This is illustrated in part (b) of Figure 11.1. Part (a) presents the standard long-run average cost (LRAC) curve, which declines at first and then becomes horizontal. The smallest plant size that minimizes average cost is Q^*; this is frequently called minimum optimal scale (MOS). The number of plants of efficient size that can exist in a market depends on the size of the market compared with Q^*. For example, if total market demand is 100 and Q^* is 10 units, there could be a maximum of 10 efficient firms, each with a single plant. In the case of natural monopoly, average cost decreases continuously, so it is most efficient to have a single producer instead of many producers.[13] This is indicated in part (b) of the figure, which provides cost data for two points on a hypothetical LRAC curve. Assuming that total market demand is 200 units, it could be supplied by two firms producing 100 units each or by one firm producing all 200 units. Total cost would be $400 with two firms, but only $200 with a single producer. Although society thus benefits from the single producer, economic regulation is necessary if the monopolist is to be prevented from exploiting its unique position.

Aside from the natural monopoly case, it is also frequently argued that economic regulation is necessary in industries subject to "ruinous" or "destructive" competition.[14] The general argument is that there can be cases where there is too much competition. As a result, market prices will be too low and firms' profits too rare. This will be especially true in industries with long-lived assets and declining or cyclical demand. According to this argument, it may be necessary to control entry and set prices in these industries.[15] Economists are always skeptical of arguments that competition is not in the public interest, and that holds true in this case. The purpose of profits and losses in a market economy is to provide signals for the allocation of society's scarce resources. Economic regulation whose sole purpose is to guarantee profits would conflict with this function. If the allocation process in a particular industry is unusually painful, the government could adopt policies that speed up

13. For a more rigorous examination of the cost conditions necessary for a natural monopoly, see W. Baumol, "On the Proper Cost Tests for Natural Monopoly in a Multi-Product Industry," *American Economic Review* 67 (December 1977): 809–22.

14. The destructive competition argument is analyzed in more detail in F. M. Scherer, *Industrial Market Structure and Economic Performance*, 2nd ed. (Chicago: Rand McNally, 1980), pp. 212–20.

15. It has also been argued that it may be necessary to control entry into markets where there are natural monopolists. See J. Panzar and R. Willig, "Free Entry and the Sustainability of Natural Monopoly," *Bell Journal of Economics* 8 (Spring 1977): 1–22.

Figure 11.1 Long-Run Average Cost Curves

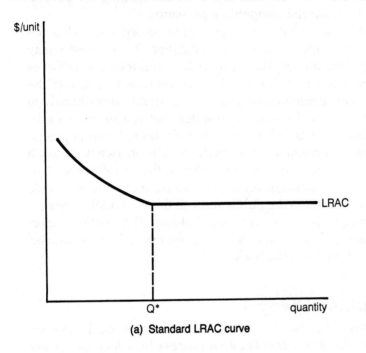

(a) Standard LRAC curve

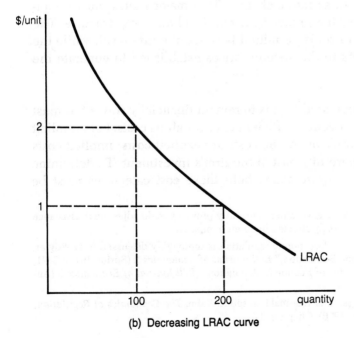

(b) Decreasing LRAC curve

the transfer of resources out of that industry.[16] More than likely, proponents of the "ruinous" competition argument are looking for government protection from normal competitive pressures.

This last point—that an industry may want to be regulated—has become known as the "capture" theory of regulation.[17] An industry may choose to be regulated if regulation furthers its self-interest. Whether or not an industry will pursue this route depends on its assessment of the benefits and costs of regulation. Regulation can enable firms legally to fix prices, deter entry, and control substitutes, but it also creates substantial administrative costs and subjects the industry to control by regulators and outside intervenors. As a result, regulation is not always a rational strategy, especially if firms can achieve their profit objectives through collusive agreements instead. The capture theory does provide an alternative explanation to the public interest theory, which views economic regulation as a response to market failures. The relative importance of each theory is an empirical issue, which will be examined throughout the remainder of the book.

Economic Principles of Rate-making

When an industry becomes regulated, market forces no longer set prices; regulators do. The administrative process by which prices are established is known as rate-making.[18] Two major issues must be addressed in a rate-making proceeding: rate level and rate structure. The total revenue that a firm is permitted is called the *rate level,* while the *rate structure* refers to the specific prices established to generate the rate level.

Rate Level.   If a regulated firm is to remain financially solvent, it must be able to generate revenue sufficient to cover all its costs, both implicit and explicit. The firm's operating costs are explicit costs; implicit costs result from the opportunity cost of the firm's investment. To determine the firm's revenue requirements, both these cost categories must be examined.

16. For example, the federal government currently provides trade adjustment assistance for industries that are adversely affected by foreign imports.

17. This alternative theory of economic regulation is thoroughly discussed in G. Stigler, "The Theory of Economic Regulation," *Bell Journal of Economics* 2 (Spring 1971): 3–21; and R. H. Posner, "Theories of Economic Regulation," *Bell Journal of Economics* 5 (Autumn 1974): 335–58.

18. For a detailed discussion of rate-making, see A. Kahn, *The Economics of Regulation,* vol. 1 (New York: Wiley, 1970), Chapters 3–7.

The major component of a firm's operating costs are the inputs it must purchase in order to provide its services to the public. This includes such things as material inputs, labor, and advertising. Because the firm's plant becomes worn out with use, depreciation is also considered to be an operating expense.[19] At the same time, the firm itself establishes some of its costs through its determination of management salaries and fringe benefits.

One inherent weakness of economic regulation is that it reduces (if it does not eliminate) a firm's incentive to minimize its costs. In a competitive market, a firm must minimize its costs or it will be driven out of business by more efficient competitors. This is rarely the case in regulated industries, where new entry may be prohibited and existing firms guaranteed that their costs will be covered. As a result, firms may not minimize their costs, secure in the knowledge that they will not be penalized by the market. Regulators may, however, try to determine if a firm is being operated efficiently. If it is not, they may penalize it by not providing sufficient revenue to cover all its costs. In practice, this is difficult to do, and regulators generally assume that the firm's costs are legitimate and the minimum necessary to provide its services.

A firm incurs implicit costs through its contribution of investment funds for its regulated activity. These funds are not free or costless, for they can obviously be allocated to alternative uses. A firm is thus entitled to a return on its investment. This must be determined administratively, however, since market forces are not operative. A two-step process is employed by regulators to determine the allowable return on a firm's investment. First, the exact value of that investment, called the firm's *rate base*, must be determined. Second, the exact *percentage return* to be allowed on the rate base must be computed.

As noted in the previous section, the evaluation of a firm's rate base has been a controversial issue. If regulators underestimate a firm's investment, they are, in effect, confiscating part of that firm's value. The rate base problem arises because of changes in prices over time due to deflation (down) and inflation (up). For example, as prices rise, the value of a firm's existing investment in plant and equipment also increases. The opposite situation holds during deflationary periods. These price effects tend to be very important for regulated firms, as they are capital intensive and their assets have long expected lives.

Several different methods have been used to evaluate a regulated

19. The exact amount of the depreciation depends on the particular accounting conventions adopted by the firm (e.g., straight-line or declining-balance) and is not necessarily related to the true economic depreciation of the firm's machinery and equipment.

firm's rate base. The most straightforward method is the "original cost" approach, which values an asset at its historical cost minus any accumulated depreciation. Although original cost valuations are convenient, they always understate a firm's value during inflationary periods. And inflation has been extremely persistent since the late 1960s.[20] An alternative approach is to value assets according to their "reproduction" cost—their current cost less accumulated depreciation. The current cost of an asset can be approximated using price indices of its main components. Reproduction cost tends to overstate a firm's value during inflationary periods, however, since no allowance is made for technological change. A firm would not build the same plant today that it did in the past. A compromise is offered by the "fair value" method, which computes a firm's value as a weighted average of its original and its reproduction cost values. Although this approach has some intuitive appeal, there is no guarantee that the weights chosen will yield accurate estimates of a particular firm's rate base.

The economically correct approach is to compute the "replacement" cost of a firm's assets: the current cost (adjusted for depreciation) of providing the same capacity, but incorporating the latest technology. Replacement cost makes allowances for technological progress that has occurred since the construction of the original plant. As a result, it provides the closest estimate of the true market value of a firm's existing plant. It is the maximum price that another firm could pay and still earn a normal return on its investment. Unfortunately, replacement cost is both subjective and expensive to compute.

In sum, no single approach is both inexpensive and accurate. Different regulators therefore have adopted different standards for the evaluation of rate bases. All federal commissions, as well as the majority of state regulatory commissions, use original cost estimates for rate-making proceedings. A declining number of states still use reproduction cost and fair value estimates. The popularity of original cost estimates is due to their low cost and speed. It is argued that the effects of inflation on the rate base can be offset by increasing the return allowed on the original cost estimate. Attention has thus shifted from the computation of the rate base to the rate of return on it.

The allowable rate of return for a firm should depend on the opportunity cost of the firm's investment. What return could the regulated firm obtain if it had allocated its investment to its best alternative use? In a

20. From 1968 to 1978, for example, the price index for industrial commodities more than doubled (U.S. Department of Commerce, *Statistical Abstract of the United States, 1979* [Washington, D.C.: Government Printing Office, 1979], p. 477).

competitive economy, this would be the normal rate of return earned by a firm in an industry that is in long-run equilibrium. This figure can be approximated by the average return available to the firm if it entered the manufacturing sector of the American economy. For example, from 1973 to 1978, the average after-tax return on stockholders' equity for manufacturing corporations was 13.75 percent.[21] The allowed return should, however, be adjusted for any differences in risk between the regulated industry and the manufacturing sector. Investors will generally accept a lower rate of return if there is less variability associated with it.[22]

More realistically, a firm's capital consists of both stocks and bonds. In this situation, a firm should be allowed a rate of return that enables it to obtain investment funds in the capital markets. Its cost of capital will be a weighted average of the cost of the two different sources of capital funds, stocks and bonds.[23] This is illustrated in Table 11.3 for a hypothetical firm. This firm's capital is equally divided between stocks and bonds, with $100 million of each. The interest rate of the bonds is five percent, requiring an interest payment of $5 million per year. This is straightforward, for the interest rate on the bonds is determined when the firm issues them. The regulator's job is to determine the rate of return that will be allowed on the firm's stocks. For simplicity, it is assumed that a 10 percent return is permitted, necessitating an additional $10 million in revenue. The total cost of the firm's capital is thus $15 million. Compared with the firm's capital stock of $200 million, this constitutes a 7.5 percent rate of return. If the regulators permit this amount,

Table 11.3 Cost of Capital for a Hypothetical Firm

Type of Capital	Amount ($ millions)	Rate of Return (percentage)	Revenue Required ($ millions)
Bonds	100	5	5
Stock	100	10	10
Total	200	7.5	15

21. U.S. Department of Commerce, *Statistical Abstract*, p. 569.

22. See, for example, John Lintner, "The Evaluation of Risk Assets and the Selection of Risky Investments in Stock Portfolios and Capital Budgets," *Review of Economics and Statistics* 47 (February 1964): 13–37.

23. And, it has been shown that a firm's cost of capital depends on its capital structure—its exact combination of stocks and bonds. See Franco Modigliani and Merton Miller, "The Cost of Capital, Corporation Finance and the Theory of Investment," *American Economic Review* 48 (June 1958): 261–97.

the firm will be able to meet exactly the price of its capital and maintain a good credit rating in the financial community.

Rate Structure. Once the rate base and rate level have been determined, there still remains the difficult problem of setting prices for the different services the regulated firm provides. In theory, there are an infinite number of rate structures that could yield the total revenue necessary to cover the firm's total costs and maintain its financial solvency. Aside from the obligatory statements that rates must be "just and reasonable" and not "unduly discriminatory," lawmakers provide little guidance for the regulators. The regulators therefore have substantial discretion in designing rate structures for the firms under their jurisdiction.

This is an area, however, where economic theory can provide invaluable assistance. The standard economic prescription is marginal cost pricing. That is, the price for a specific service should be set equal to the marginal cost of providing that service.[24] Equality between price and marginal cost is desirable because, at the margin, the marginal benefit received by the consumer is equal to the marginal cost incurred by the producer. The optimal amount of this service is being provided by this firm. If all markets are competitive, marginal cost pricing will lead to the optimal allocation of society's resources across those markets.

The position of an individual firm is illustrated in part (a) of Figure 11.2. At the market price of P^0, the firm will produce Q^0 units if it engages in marginal cost pricing. Several problems arise, however, with basing prices on a firm's short-run marginal costs.[25] First, prices will reflect the historical, not the future, costs of providing the service. As a result, they may not be giving the proper long-run signals to consumers, especially during inflationary periods. Second, it may not be possible to estimate the marginal costs of providing a specific service. When two services are provided jointly, it is not possible to determine each service's responsibility for the joint costs. Third, it may be too expensive to determine the marginal cost for each service. This simply reflects the fact that estimating marginal costs is not a costless process and, indeed, may be prohibitive for some multi-product firms. Fourth, these prices may be unstable and not as predictable as consumers would like. Because prices equal marginal costs, they will necessarily fluctuate as the firm's marginal costs vary with the level of output.

24. This will not be true when there are externalities associated with the provision of the firm's services. See Chapter 16.

25. The following discussion is based primarily on A. Kahn, *The Economics of Regulation,* vol. 1, Chapter 3.

Figure 11.2 Competitive Pricing in the Short and Long Runs

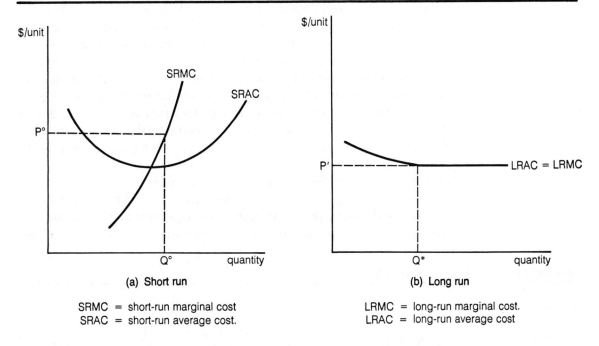

(a) Short run

(b) Long run

SRMC = short-run marginal cost
SRAC = short-run average cost.

LRMC = long-run marginal cost.
LRAC = long-run average cost

In an attempt to surmount some of these problems, economists have advocated the use of *long-run marginal cost (LRMC)* instead of its short-run variant. Long-run marginal cost indicates the additional cost of supplying an additional unit in the long run when all inputs are variable. There are two advantages to switching to a long-run cost concept. First, it will be more stable than short-run marginal cost. Rates will not fluctuate so much with variations in output. Second, the concept looks to the future, not to the past, by indicating the additional costs necessary to meet future demand. Consumers will receive the long-run signals so frequently necessary in purchasing decisions that involve durable goods. Graphically, the long-run pricing scheme is illustrated in part (b) of Figure 11.2. Price is equal to the minimum long-run average cost, which is constant beyond the output level Q*, indicating that LRAC equals LRMC. The shape of this cost curve is consistent with empirical studies that do not support the traditional U-shaped LRAC.[26] (Note that in long-run equilibrium in a competitive market, market price would equal both short-run and long-run marginal cost.)

26. For an interesting discussion of economies of scale, see F. M. Scherer, "Economies of Scale and Industrial Concentration," and John S. McGee, "Efficiency and Economies of Size," in *Industrial Concentration: The New Learning*, ed., H. Goldschmid, H. Mann, and J. Weston (Boston: Little, Brown, 1974), pp. 16–54 and 55–97.

Long-run marginal cost curves can be used to illustrate the economic rationale behind peak-load pricing schemes.[27] As noted earlier, regulated firms generally provide services, not products. And the demand for those services does not remain constant, but fluctuates over time. Given its obligation to meet the public's demand for its services, a regulated firm must have sufficient capacity to handle its peak (maximum) demand, and so will usually have idle capacity during off-peak time periods. The firm's cost of providing service for off-peak users is thus less than for peak users, because they can be served by the existing capacity. Peak users, on the other hand, determine a firm's capacity and thus impose higher costs on it. In Figure 11.3, this difference is reflected in a higher LRMC curve for peak users than for off-peak users.

In this situation, efficient pricing requires that a firm charge its customers two different prices: P_3 during peak periods and P_1 during off-peak periods. The price difference results from the assignment of the

Figure 11.3　Peak-Load Pricing

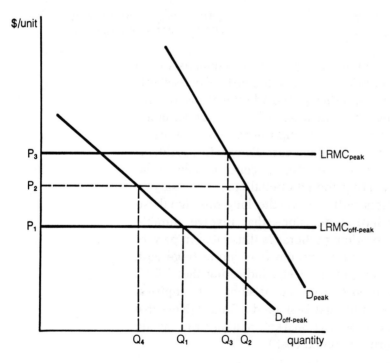

27. R. Turvey, "Peak Load Pricing," *Journal of Political Economy* 76 (February 1968): 101–13.

capacity costs to the peak users. It would be inefficient for the firm to ignore this cost difference and charge both peak and off-peak users the same price (P_2). This single price would lead to uneconomic expansion of the firm's capacity as well as a low utilization rate for it. In Figure 11.3, peak demand at price P_2 would require capacity to expand from Q_3 to Q_2. This larger capacity would be used less intensively, though, for off-peak use would decline from Q_1 to Q_4. In sum, peak-load pricing minimizes the firm's capacity while maximizing the use of that capacity.

There are strong objections to peak-load pricing schemes. First, the pricing structure may actually shift the peaks and so be impractical. This possibility is illustrated in Figure 11.4. Before the adoption of peak-load pricing, peak demand was Q_1 and off-peak demand Q_4 at the single price of P_2. With the peak-load prices of P_1 and P_3, however, off-peak demand (Q_2) now exceeds peak demand (Q_3). The price structure has shifted the peak demand from the peak to the off-peak period, thereby invalidating the new pricing scheme! Second, peak-load pricing may not seem fair. Since both peak and off-peak users benefit from the same capacity, they both should contribute toward the firm's overhead costs. The equity ar-

Figure 11.4   Peak-Load Pricing and Shifting Peak Demands

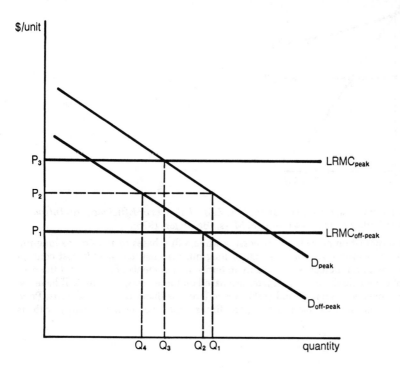

230 Economic Regulation

gument is a powerful one and has frequently prevented regulators from adopting the peak-load prices advocated purely on the grounds of efficiency. [28]

Finally, it may be necessary for a firm intentionally to depart from cost-based rates and engage in price discrimination. This situation arises when marginal cost pricing does not yield sufficient revenue to cover all the firm's costs. Efficient pricing thus conflicts with the firm's financial solvency. The classic example of a natural monopolist is presented in Figure 11.5.[29] At the efficient price of P_1, the firm produces the optimal output of Q_1, but cannot cover its costs. Price is less than

Figure 11.5 **Alternative Prices for a Natural Monopolist**

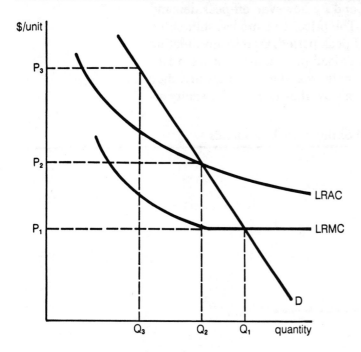

28. This trade-off is discussed in detail in E. E. Zajac, *Fairness or Efficiency: An Introduction to Public Utility Pricing* (Cambridge, Mass.: Ballinger, 1978).

29. Price discrimination may also be necessary when a firm bases its rates on its long-run incremental costs—the real world variant of long-run marginal costs. This cost concept recognizes that a firm increases its capacity in terms of increments of output, not the marginal unit of economic theory. When rates are based on these costs, the firm will have too much (little) revenue if incremental costs exceed (are less than) its historical costs. Price discrimination can then be used to bring the firm's total revenue into equality with its total costs.

average cost, so total revenue must be less than total cost. One possible solution is to charge the price P_2, which equals average cost at the output level Q_2. The firm can now cover all its costs, but it is not producing the efficient level of output.

The conflict between efficiency and financial solvency can be minimized if the firm is permitted to discriminate and charge several prices instead of a single price. For example, the firm might sell the first Q_3 units at a price of P_3, Q_3 through Q_2 units at P_2, and the final Q_2 through Q_1 units at the efficient price of P_1. The high profits on the initial units offset the losses incurred on the final units. In this manner, the firm is able to produce the efficient output level and still cover its costs.

Given that price discrimination may be necessary, the question arises: how should the firm discriminate in prices?[30] Which consumers will be discriminated against and which ones will benefit from that discrimination? An economic solution to this problem is offered by the "inverse elasticity rule."[31] This rule states that the degree of price discrimination should depend on a consumer's price elasticity of demand. More specifically, the deviation from marginal cost pricing should be inversely related to the price elasticity. In this case, the burden of generating more revenue for the natural monopolist will fall primarily on consumers who have inelastic demand. The logic underlying the inverse elasticity rule is illustrated in Figure 11.6. Two demand curves, one elastic and one inelastic, intersect at the efficient price of P_0 and quantity of Q_0. A given percentage increase in the firm's price from P_0 to P_1 will have a dramatically different impact on these two groups of consumers. Consumers with elastic demand sharply curtail their consumption, while those with inelastic demand are barely affected. The price increase will increase the expenditures of the inelastic users, while decreasing it for the elastic users. In short, by discriminating against the inelastic users, the firm can generate additional revenue with minimal impact on the quantity demanded.[32]

30. The reader should recognize that peak-load pricing is *not* price discrimination. The price difference between peak and off-peak rates simply reflects the cost differences of providing service during peak and off-peak time periods.

31. W. Baumol and D. Bradford, "Optimal Departures from Marginal Cost Pricing," *American Economic Review* 60 (June 1970): 265–83.

32. The opposite situation would hold when the firm has too much revenue (see footnote 29). In this case, the firm would lower its price more for consumers with inelastic demands than those with elastic demands.

Figure 11.6   Impact of a Price Increase on Quantity Demanded

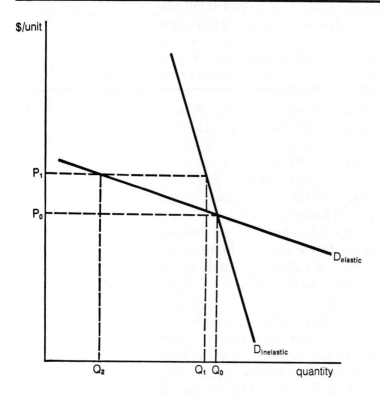

Summary

A significant amount of economic activity in the United States is subject to economic regulation. This type of government intervention has been applied to the agriculture and energy industries as well as the tradition- al public utilities. Although economic regulation has raised constitu- tional issues, these have been resolved in favor of the government's right to regulate. Economic theory argues that this right should be exer- cised only in markets where competition is not feasible—natural mo- nopolies. Once regulation is imposed, for whatever reasons, the government must engage in rate-making. A firm's rates should be effi- cient, but allow the firm to cover its total costs. The efficiency require- ment will be fulfilled if rates are based on long-run marginal costs, as illustrated in the case of peak-load pricing. If there is a conflict between an efficient rate structure and the firm's solvency, price discrimination will become necessary. The inverse elasticity rule provides guidance in determining the optimal adjustment in the firm's rate structure.

Baumol, W., and Bradford, D. "Optimal Departures from Marginal Cost Pricing," *American Economic Review* 60 (June 1970): 265–83.

Migue, J. "A Market Approach to Regulation," *Journal of Law and Economics* 20 (April 1977): 213–22.

Nelson, J., ed. *Marginal Cost Pricing in Practice* (Englewood Cliffs, N.J.: Prentice-Hall, 1964).

Stigler, George. "The Theory of Economic Regulation," *Bell Journal of Economics* 2 (Spring 1971): 3–21.

"Symposium on Peak Load Pricing," *Bell Journal of Economics* 7 (Spring 1976): 197–250.

Williamson, Oliver. "Peak Load Pricing and Optimal Capacity Under Indivisibility Constraints," *American Economic Review* 56 (September 1966): 810–27.

Suggested Readings

Transportation

Chapter 12

Transportation services, both passenger and freight, have long been subject to economic regulation. Federal regulation began, in fact, with the creation of the Interstate Commerce Commission and its mandate to control the nation's railroads. Transportation regulation has been very controversial, however. Proponents claim that it is essential for dependable service, while opponents argue that it is both unnecessary and inefficient. Economics has played a major role in this policy debate, focusing attention on the rationale for, and effectiveness of, economic regulation of transportation.

The Setting

Transportation services are provided by a variety of different modes or transport types. An oil company, for example, may ship its product by pipeline, barge, railroad, or truck. The major transportation modes in the American economy, along with their relative importance in the domestic freight and passenger markets, are presented in Tables 12.1 and 12.2 respectively. These figures indicate that the transportation sector of the economy has undergone substantial changes since the 1950s. In the freight market, the railroads' dominant position has steadily eroded, while the market shares of the other modes have increased, particularly those of motor vehicles (trucking) and oil pipelines. In the passenger

Table 12.1 **Intercity Freight Traffic, by Type of Transport**
(Selected Years)[a]

Year	Railroads	Motor Vehicles	Inland Waterways	Oil Pipelines	Airways
1950	57.44	15.80	14.93	11.81	.029
1955	50.43	17.20	16.68	15.66	.037
1960	44.73	21.46	16.56	17.19	.058
1965	43.67	21.76	15.89	18.56	.116
1970	39.83	21.28	16.46	22.26	.170
1975	36.74	21.97	16.55	24.54	.193
1977	36.10	24.08	15.97	23.69	.173

[a]Percentages of total ton-miles.
Source: U.S. Department of Commerce, *Statistical Abstract of the United States, 1979* (Washington, D.C.: Government Printing Office, 1979), Table 1075, p. 635.

Table 12.2 **Intercity Passenger Traffic, by Type of Transport**
(Selected Years)[a]

Year	Private Automobiles	Airways	Bus	Railroads	Inland Waterways
1950	86.20	1.98	5.20	6.39	.23
1955	89.01	3.18	3.56	4.01	.24
1960	90.10	4.33	2.47	2.75	.34
1965	88.86	6.31	2.58	1.91	.34
1970	86.60	10.01	2.14	.92	.34
1975	86.09	10.95	1.92	.74	.30
1977	85.10	12.14	1.79	.69	.28

[a] Percentages of total passenger-miles.
Source: U.S. Department of Commerce, *Statistical Abstract of the United States, 1979* (Washington, D.C.: Government Printing Office, 1979), Table 1075, p. 635.

market, the market shares of all modes have decreased, except for airways and waterways. Private automobiles continue to overwhelm the other modes, while the airlines have a stranglehold on the runner-up position. As will be discussed later, the specific trend in each transportation mode reflects the joint influence of government regulation and transportation economics.

The History of Transportation Regulation

As noted in Chapter 11, federal regulation of the railroads was a response to the constitutional limitations on state regulation. State regulatory commissions could control the intrastate, but not the interstate, activities of the railroads that operated in their states. The obvious solution was the establishment of the Interstate Commerce Commission in 1887.

The basic decision that regulation of the railroads was necessary has been attributed to two extremely different factors.[1] First, regulation was initiated during a time of strong populist sentiment and distrust of "big business" in general and railroads in particular. The railroads were accused of abusing their monopoly positions by engaging in frequent price discrimination. One such practice was to charge more for a short haul than a long haul, even though both hauls were made over the same railroad tracks. This discrimination was feasible because there was competition for the long haul business, but not for the short hauls. For example, two railroads might provide service between Chicago and New York, but only one would go through Cleveland. Second, the railroads may have wanted government regulation. There had been a tendency toward price wars on long haul routes, such as Chicago to New York, that were served by two or more railroads. Regulation offered the prospect of eliminating this highly unprofitable price competition. In sum, the initial regulation of the railroads was consistent with both the public interest and the capture theories of government regulation (discussed in Chapter 11).

Whatever the reasons behind the formation of the ICC, regulation of the railroads was at first ineffective. Under the Interstate Commerce Act, the ICC could declare a given rate illegal, but it could not set a maximum rate that could be charged for a specific service. As a result, the railroads could evade ICC regulation by continuously filing new rates that were only marginally different from the rates that had been found illegal. The new rates would be applicable till the ICC voided them. Given the inevitable delay in regulation, the railroads could always stay one step ahead of their regulators. This loophole was subsequently closed by the Hepburn Act of 1906, which empowered the ICC to set maximum rates. The Transportation Act of 1920 went even further by permitting the ICC to set minimum and exact rates as well as maximum rates.

The ICC's control over railroads was soon expanded to two competing transportation modes—interstate motor (1935) and water (1940) carri-

1. For a discussion of the early regulation of the railroads, see G. Kolko, *Railroads and Regulation, 1877-1916* (Princeton, N.J.: Princeton University Press, 1965).

ers.[2] The regulation of motor carriers (trucking) was particularly interesting. Beginning with World War I, trucking companies began to make significant inroads into the freight market. This trend accelerated during the Great Depression as unemployed workers became free-lance truck operators. As competition in the declining freight market increased, the railroads became more aware of the competitive threat posed by the trucking industry. It was not long before the railroads and the ICC both advocated the extension of federal regulation to the trucking industry. They were soon joined by some large trucking companies who thought that regulation was necessary to end the "ruinous" competition in their industry. The result was the Motor Carrier Act of 1935, which brought interstate trucking under the jurisdiction of the Interstate Commerce Commission.

At this time, the ICC was also involved in the regulation of domestic airlines. It shared this responsibility with the Post Office, which paid the air carriers for transporting air mail. In 1938, control of the airlines was transferred to a separate regulatory agency, the Civil Aeronautics Board (CAB).[3] The CAB was empowered to regulate domestic carriers as well as to represent American interests at the International Air Transport Association (IATA), an organization of foreign air carriers. A major reason offered for airline regulation was the "excessive" competition during the depression era, though the requirements of national defense and postal service were also mentioned. There was also concern that uncontrolled competition would reduce airline safety, as firms reduced costs by overworking pilots and deferring necessary maintenance.[4] Since 1958 airline safety has been under the jurisdiction of the Federal Aviation Administration (FAA). Among other things, the FAA establishes safety regulations for the construction, operation, and maintenance of aircraft (it also operates National and Dulles airports in the Washington, D.C. area).

The nature and extent of transportation regulation changed in the late 1970s. The Railroad Revitalization and Regulatory Reform Act of 1976

2. The Motor Carrier Act of 1935 and the Transportation Act of 1940.

3. The Civil Aeronautics Act of 1938. The history of airline regulation in America is discussed in R. Caves, *Air Transport and Its Regulators* (Cambridge, Mass.: Harvard University Press, 1962).

4. This safety argument was also central to government regulation of trucking in 1935. Safety regulation is now handled by the Federal Aviation Administration and is still a problem. See "FAA Seeks a $1.5 Million Fine on Braniff For Alleged Maintenance Rule Violations," *Wall Street Journal*, November 7, 1979, p. 8.

reduced ICC regulation of the railroads, while the Airline Deregulation Act of 1978 mandated the elimination of the CAB in early 1985.[5] Congress also lessened government control of the trucking industry with its passage of the Motor Carrier Act of 1980. It is too early to tell if these changes represent a permanent reduction in government control or merely a short-run aberration from the long history of economic regulation of the transportation sector.

The Economics of Transportation

The transportation sector, like all sectors of the economy, is subject to the basic economic laws of supply and demand. There is a demand for, and supply of, transportation services. Before analyzing transportation services, however, it should be noted that they are not homogeneous. The different transportation modes offer a variety of services, each one with different attributes. For example, the Concorde airplane offers faster, noisier, and more expensive service than conventional aircraft.[6]

Economists view the demand for transportation services as a *derived* demand.[7] Transportation is not desired as an end in itself, but is used as an input in the provision of goods and services for consumers and producers. As a result, the demand for transportation is derived from, or dependent on, the demand for those goods and services. The demand for airline service, for example, depends on consumers' demand for vacations and producers' demand for business meetings. The demand for rail service depends on the demand for products, such as coal and grain, that can be hauled by the railroads. Changes in the demand for these products lead to changes in the demand for transportation services.

The exact demand for a single transportation service is determined by its price as well as the prices of services offered by competing modes. The relevant prices are not, however, simply the rates charged by the different modes. A rate is only one component of the total price of using

5. This elimination is contingent upon an evaluation of the impact of airline deregulation on domestic air service. Every two months the CAB issues a report entitled "Report on Airline Service, Fares, Traffic, Load Factors and Market Shares" (Washington, D.C.).

6. As a result, no one buys them. Of the 16 Concordes produced by French and British manufacturers, 5 are operated by British Airways, 4 by Air France, and the remaining 7 are unsold ("Output of Concordes Stopped by French, British Governments," *Wall Street Journal*, September 24, 1979, p. 18).

7. See Ann Friedlaender, *The Dilemma of Freight Transport Regulation* (Washington, D.C.: Brookings Institution, 1969), Chapter 3; and George Douglas and James Miller III, *Economic Regulation of Domestic Air Transport* (Washington, D.C.: Brookings Institution, 1974), Chapter 3.

a specific mode. A user also incurs costs due to the time element involved. For example, firms must absorb inventory costs while their goods are in transit. Passengers must forgo earnings if they cannot work while they are traveling. Freight transportation imposes additional costs when goods are damaged or stolen during the transportation process. All these factors must be considered when determining the price of using different transportation services.

As with all markets, the supply of transportation services depends on the costs of providing them. These costs can be conveniently analyzed using the standard distinction between fixed and variable costs. In transportation industries, the real world counterparts are terminal and line-haul costs. Terminal costs (fixed costs) include all the costs associated with the handling and processing of freight or passengers. Passengers must be ticketed and boarded, while freight must be sorted and loaded for delivery.[8] Line-haul costs (variable costs) are those incurred directly in transporting passengers or freight from the originating point to the final destination. They include such obvious variable costs as labor and fuel, as well as the depreciation of the transportation equipment. In general, line-haul costs vary with the length of the haul, the weight of the product, and the size of the shipment.

Of special importance to economists is how transportation costs vary in the long run. Do costs increase, decrease, or remain constant when a specific transportation mode expands its level of operations?[9] The general belief is that costs are constant in some modes (airlines, buses, barges, and trucks), and tend to decrease in others (pipelines, railroads). The difference is due to the manner in which the different modes expand their capacity. Trucking companies, for example, can increase capacity on a given route simply by adding more trucks. Each truck requires one driver and some specified amount of fuel. This is constant cost, as depicted in part (a) of Figure 12.1. The situation is different for railroads, which increase capacity by adding more cars to an existing train or, if necessary, another train. This leads to decreasing costs, because the railroad is utilizing its substantial investment in its track system more intensively. As indicated in part (b) of Figure 12.1, the long-run marginal cost of additional capacity is less than the long-run average cost.

8. Some of these terminal costs will, in fact, be variable if the transportation firm can vary some of its inputs (e.g., number of ticket agents) in response to short-run changes in demand.

9. For an example of the empirical estimation of cost curves, see T. E. Keeler, "Railroad Costs, Returns to Scale, and Excess Capacity," *Review of Economics and Statistics* 56 (May 1974): 201–8.

Figure 12.1 Long-Run Cost Curves for Different Transportation Modes

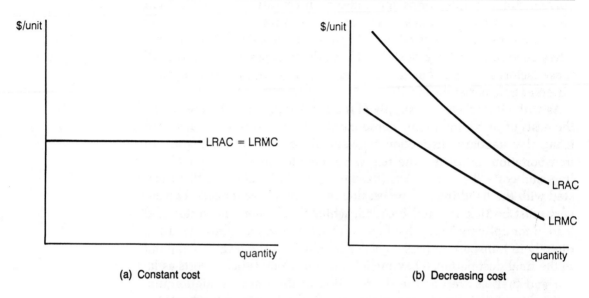

(a) Constant cost

(b) Decreasing cost

A related issue is the relative efficiency of the different transportation modes. Table 12.3 provides rough estimates of the long-run marginal costs for four modes: pipelines, barges, railroads, and trucks.[10] It is assumed that the shipment length is 500 miles and that each mode is operated at capacity. These estimates indicate that pipelines and barges have the lowest costs, although railroads are competitive for multiple-car shipments of bulk products.[11] For high-value commodities, railroads are still more efficient than trucks, the mode with the highest costs. The most efficient method of shipment for these commodities, however, is *piggybacking*, the movement of truck trailers on railroad cars. Piggybacking combines the railroads' line-haul advantage on shipments of more than 200 to 300 miles with the trucks' lower terminal costs.

The degree of intermodal competition is not based purely on costs, however. It also depends on the specific attributes of the service provided by each transportation mode.[12] Trucks, for example, offer convenient door-to-door service. They accept smaller shipments at later hours and deliver them faster and with less damage than the railroads. These ad-

10. The actual costs will also vary with other factors, such as the type of product hauled.

11. For example, the railroads haul coal on "unit" trains. These trains consist entirely of coal cars and go back and forth continually from the coal mine to the coal user.

12. See "High Trucking Costs Spur Interest in Rails For Many Companies," *Wall Street Journal*, September 19, 1979, p. 1.

Table 12.3   **Long-Run Marginal Costs for Optimal Freight Transport Operations, by Mode of Transport, 1963[a]**

Mode of Transport	Marginal Costs (mills per ton-mile)[b]
Pipeline	1.0
Water	
Manufactured commodities	4.0-5.0
Bulk commodities	1.0-2.0
Rail	
Bulk multiple-car	4.0-5.0
Bulk boxcar	7.0
Piggyback	11.4
High-value commodities	15.6
Truck	21.7

[a]Assumes shipments of 500 miles, capacity operations.

[b]One mill is equivalent to 1/10 of a cent.

Source: Ann F. Friedlaender, *The Dilemma of Freight Transport Regulation* (Washington, D.C.: Brookings Institution, 1969), Table 3.5, p. 51.

vantages can outweigh any cost disadvantages and encourage shippers to use trucks instead of the railroads. A similar situation holds for passenger transportation. A passenger traveling from Washington, D.C., to New York, for example, can choose from automobile, bus, train, or airplane transportation. Each mode offers the passenger a different combination of price, speed, and comfort. Overall, the various transportation modes supply a variety of services that are frequently substitutes, albeit imperfect substitutes, for one another.

Major Regulatory Issues

Federal regulation of transportation is currently in a state of transition. The airline and trucking industries are being "deregulated," and the same treatment is being contemplated for the railroad industry. As a result, it is difficult to predict the extent of future government regulation. Nonetheless, past policies can be compared with their current, though possibly short-lived, descendants. This is done for two major economic issues in transportation regulation: (1) number of competitors; and (2) rate-making.[13]

13. This section does not discuss the safety regulations common to all transportation modes, although they can affect efficiency. Many states, for example, place restrictions on the length and weight of truck trailers. The diversity in state restrictions makes it difficult for truckers with large rigs to make efficient cross-country hauls.

Number of Competitors

In a regulated market, the number of competitors is determined by an administrative decision. The government establishes the number of competitors in each market through its control over entry, exit, and mergers. Entry increases the number, while exit and mergers decrease it.

Before examining specific ICC and CAB policies in this area, it should be noted that not all transportation firms are the same. The most obvious distinction is between regulated and unregulated (or exempt) transportation companies. Within a given mode, some firms may not be subject to government regulation. Commuter airlines are virtually free from CAB regulation; trucks that carry agricultural products are exempt from ICC entry and rate controls.[14] Among regulated carriers, there may be further distinctions according to the specific services provided. For example, common carrier truckers have an obligation to serve the general public, while contract carriers are authorized to provide service to a limited number of customers. Even airlines have historically been classified according to whether they serve major communities (trunk lines) or small communities (local service carriers).

Entry Controls. These legal distinctions among firms resulted from the government's control over entry; more specifically, its issuance of certificates of "public convenience and necessity." These certificates were a key part of the federal legislation that established government regulation of trucking (1935) and airlines (1938). It was feared that unlimited entry would lead to "ruinous competition" in these industries. This problem could be eliminated by requiring firms to obtain a certificate before they could offer transportation services. Controlling the number of certificates issued would thus make it possible to control entry into these industries. As a procedural matter, firms offering services during some period prior to the passage of the federal laws were automatically granted certificates for those specific services.[15]

The certificates issued by the CAB and the ICC were quite detailed and hence quite restrictive. In the motor carrier industry, for example, a certificate indicated the commodities that could be hauled between two cities, as well as the exact route that must be used (including any stops

14. The CAB does, however, set limits on the maximum number of seats allowable on commuter airplanes.

15. The right of existing firms to be included in the new regulatory scheme is known as "grandfather rights." These rights minimize any adverse impacts of the new regulations on existing firms.

along the way to pick up additional business). A firm might even be authorized to haul a commodity from one city to another, but not be permitted to carry anything back on the return trip. (This is known as an empty *backhaul.*) Similarly, airline certificates granted a carrier the right to offer service between a pair of cities.

Once existing firms were "grandfathered" in, the CAB and ICC had to establish standards for awarding new certificates. Requests for operating rights came both from new firms offering initial service and from existing firms offering expanded service. The enabling legislation provided little concrete guidance, except that the awarding of new certificates should be consistent with the public interest. The general standards adopted by these agencies was that applicants must be "fit and willing" and that the service they proposed to offer must be required by the transportation needs of the country. This latter requirement generally necessitated the applicant's showing that existing service was inadequate. This placed a tremendous burden on an applicant who was strongly opposed by any existing carrier who might feel threatened by the proposed service. Not surprisingly, these proceedings quickly became dominated by the lawyers from the affected carriers. The result was that it became very difficult for a new firm to enter these industries. For example, in the first 40 years after it was established, the CAB failed to approve a single request for the creation of a new trunk line carrier.[16] Even Pan American, an international carrier, was prohibited from acquiring domestic routes.

Entry into the domestic airline industry is now less difficult and should become even easier in the future.[17] The primary reason for this change is the Airline Deregulation Act of 1978. It enabled airlines to add one route a year, beginning in 1979, without route proceedings. When proceedings are required, the burden of proof has been shifted from the applicant to the existing carrier(s) contesting the application. More important, the CAB was to lose all control over routes by 1982. In this respect, the law codifies the easier entry policy that the CAB had already adopted. For example, it had finally given Pan Am some domestic routes as well as permitting it to carry domestic passengers on the domestic segments of its international flights.[18] And it allowed the crea-

16. A major factor was the CAB's desire to improve the profitability of existing carriers instead of creating new ones (see Caves, *Air Transport*).

17. This is not necessarily true for international routes where the number of carriers is determined through bilateral agreements between the two countries involved.

18. These are known as "fill-up" rights. If Pan Am is flying from Los Angeles to London via New York, for example, it can now carry passengers for just the domestic segment—Los Angeles to New York—of that flight.

tion of new carriers such as Midway Airlines as well as the expansion of charter airlines such as World Airways. The net effect of these changes has been the virtual elimination of the once formidable barriers to entry in the domestic airline industry.[19]

Entry is also becoming easier in the trucking industry, though the changes are less dramatic than those in the airline industry. The Motor Carrier Act of 1980, for example, will make it more difficult for existing carriers to oppose the issuance of new operating certificates. Even before this act was passed, however, the ICC had made entry easier through a series of related actions. First, it expanded the urban zones within which truckers may operate without ICC regulation. This decision increases the potential business available to unregulated trucking companies. Second, the commission permitted private carriers, for the first time in 40 years, to hire out their trucks.[20] This meant that a manufacturer that delivers its products in its own trucks can carry the products of other firms on its backhauls. Finally, the ICC liberalized its policy on granting certificates to applicants, dropping the restrictive requirement that an applicant must show that existing carriers cannot provide the proposed service. This shifts the burden of proof to the existing carriers, who now must show that approval of the application would not be in the public interest. Further, only carriers that compete directly with the applicant have standing at any proceedings before the commission.

Exit Controls. Government regulators also affect the number of competitors in a market through their abandonment and merger policies. *Abandonment* occurs when a firm withdraws from a given market, terminating its transportation services. The best illustration is the railroads' decision to terminate passenger service, which they viewed as unprofitable. Intercity passenger service is no longer provided by private railroads, but by the government through Amtrak.[21] Historically, the ICC has made it difficult for railroads to abandon unprofitable lines, either passenger or freight, thereby forcing them to subsidize these operations with profits from other operations. This policy was substantially

---

19. One possible remaining barrier is the limited access to some of the more crowded airports. This problem is discussed later.

20. Toto Purchasing & Supply Co. Common Carrier Application, 128 M.C.C. 873 (1978).

21. Since the Penn Central Railroad went bankrupt, the federal government has also been involved in freight transportation. The Consolidated Rail Corporation (Conrail) has taken over the operations of the Penn Central and other bankrupt railroads with the help of federal financing.

altered by the Railroad Revitalization and Regulatory Reform Act of 1976, which made it easier for railroads to abandon unprofitable lines. Communities that would be adversely affected by abandonments can have the service continued by paying the railroad a subsidy, shared by the federal government.

Mergers have enabled transportation firms to surmount the barriers created by certificates of public convenience and necessity. A carrier can enter a new market by obtaining a certificate from the ICC or simply acquiring a firm that already has the necessary ICC certificate. Mergers have been widely used by trucking companies to expand their operations. And Pan American World Airways recently acquired National Airlines, arguing (in part) that it was the quickest way to penetrate the domestic American market. These mergers are not subject to the antitrust laws, but to the different criteria established by the ICC and the CAB. The possible impact on competition is important, but these agencies must also consider such other factors as the country's national transportation and defense requirements. The ICC in particular has generally encouraged mergers among railroads in the belief that they will yield more efficient and more profitable railroads.

Rate-making

One important function of regulatory agencies is rate-making, the establishment of prices that regulated firms can charge for their services. As noted in Chapter 11, this is not a simple task, for firms can provide a variety of services under different demand and cost conditions. It is necessary, however. Regulated firms commonly are protected from new competition, and they could easily exploit their situation if they were permitted to do so. This section briefly examines the rate-making practices employed by the ICC and the CAB.

The *rate bureau* is an important factor in the rate-making process at the ICC and the CAB. It is simply an organization of regulated carriers (rail, truck, or airline) that sets rates for the carriers' services, subject to agency approval.[22] In the trucking industry, for example, there are a dozen major regional bureaus that set rates for thousands of different services. Of particular importance are the rates for shipments that travel on two or more carriers. In these cases, it is necessary not only to set the total rate for the shipment, but also to determine how it will be divided among the participating carriers.

22. Rate bureaus were granted immunity from the antitrust laws by the Reed-Bulwinkle Act in 1948.

Within this framework, each regulatory agency must decide whether the rates proposed by the rate bureaus are legal. The enabling legislation, however, provides little guidance. The ICC, for example, will approve rates if they are "just and reasonable" and do not discriminate among individuals.[23] The ICC initially adopted a rate structure for the railroads that is known as value-of-service pricing. In general, the rates charged were proportional to the value of the product hauled; they were low for agricultural products, but high for manufactured goods. This rate structure was thought desirable because it maximized the flow of traffic between the agricultural West and the industrial East. It was supported by the railroads also because it maximized their profits.[24] In the 1920s, however, trucks began "cream-skimming," or taking the railroads' most profitable traffic—the manufactured goods. This effectively undermined the value-of-service rate structure and was instrumental in the subsequent decision to regulate the trucking industry.

After motor carriers became regulated in 1935, Congress provided more guidance to the ICC. In the Transportation acts of 1940 and 1958, it stated that rates should be set to "preserve the inherent advantages" of each mode (1940) and not to "protect" any single mode (1958). The question thus became how to determine the inherent advantage of each transportation mode. This is a very important issue, for by the rates it sets, the ICC can determine the allocation of traffic among the different modes.

The ICC's solution was to adopt a cost standard for the determination of each mode's inherent advantage. More specifically, it used *fully distributed costs* (an approximation to average total costs) to determine the least cost mode for a given service. This was illustrated in a famous decision (the "Ingot Molds" case) involving the transportation of ingot molds from Neville Island, Pennsylvania to Steelton, Kentucky.[25] The molds could be shipped by rail or by a truck-barge combination. The fully distributed (average) and out-of-pocket (marginal) costs of the truck-barge combination were both estimated to be $5.19 per ton. The same figures for rail service were $7.59 (average) and $4.69 (marginal).

---

23. Personal discrimination by the railroads (e.g., charging more for a short haul than a long haul over the same tracks) angered small shippers and was an important argument in favor of regulating the railroads.

24. Somewhat simplistically, the demand for manufactured goods was less elastic than that for food, so value-of-service pricing was a means of discriminating according to the price elasticity of demand for rail service.

25. *American Commercial Lines, Inc.* v. *Louisville & Nashville Railroad Co.*, 392 U.S. 571 (1968).

This cost situation is depicted graphically in Figure 12.2, where Q* corresponds to the shipments under discussion. Which transportation mode gets the business depends on the cost standard adopted by the ICC. Using average costs, the truck-barge combination is the least cost mode; but the situation is reversed if inherent advantage is defined using marginal costs. Because the commission adopted the average cost standard, the truck-barge combination was the least cost mode, and its price of $5.19 could undercut the railroad's $7.19. Only if the railroad were allowed to base its rates on its marginal costs would it be the more efficient mode. Note that if the shipment were less than $Q°$ or more than Q', the allocation of the traffic would not depend on the cost standard used. Rails are unambiguously more efficient for shipments greater than Q' and trucks for shipments less than $Q°$.

The CAB has also been active in the rate-making arena. Its primary concern was to establish a rate level that would maintain the financial

Figure 12.2 The Ingot Molds Case

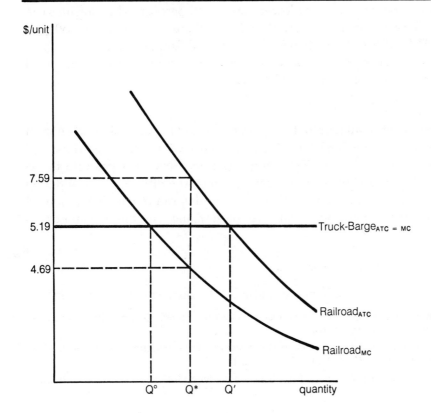

viability of the trunk airlines.[26] The specific goal was to enable the airlines to earn an after-tax return of 10.5 percent on their investment. Little attention was focused on the exact fare structures that would yield that rate of return. As a result, fares were not cost justified and there was substantial price discrimination. In an effort to reduce discrimination, the CAB adopted a fare formula consisting of a fixed terminal charge and a variable line-haul charge.[27] For example, the coach fare for a flight under 500 miles would be the sum of $12.56 plus 7.06 cents per mile. The first-class fare was based on the coach fare but could be as much as 63 percent more. In addition, the airlines could offer discount and promotional fares that would be less than the regular coach fare. All these fares had to be approved in advance by the CAB, however.

The rate-making picture has changed dramatically. The railroads, motor carriers, and airlines have all acquired some control over their rates. In general, carriers now are authorized to raise or lower their fares by some fixed percentage without having to seek approval from the CAB or ICC. The railroads, for example, can lower rates to their marginal or variable costs in every market where they do not have "dominance." Motor carriers can raise or lower rates by 10 percent, while airlines can raise fares by up to 5 percent or lower them by as much as 50 percent.[28] In effect, these changes have created "zones of reasonableness" within which regulated carriers may operate free from the traditional rate regulation of the ICC and the CAB.

Evaluation

Government regulation of transportation is not a recent phenomenon. It has existed since 1887 for railroads, since 1935 for motor carriers, and since 1938 for airlines. This long experience makes it possible to examine the impact of economic regulation on the different transportation modes. And this analysis can be used to determine whether proposed regulatory changes will improve performance in the transportation sector.

Appraisal of Current Policy

Economists have made many studies of the domestic transportation sec-

26. Local service airlines currently receive subsidies, though the trunk lines have been self-sufficient since the 1950s.

27. Civil Aeronautics Board, *Domestic Passenger-Fare Investigation, Phase 9—Fare Structure.* Docket 21866-9, Decided: March 18, 1974.

28. International fares are negotiated between the individual carriers and the CAB. Fares are no longer set collectively by the International Air Transport Association.

tor, examining the impact of regulation on the economic performance of the different modes.[29] This section briefly presents the general conclusions of those studies. Despite the seeming tendency for economists to disagree about everything, this is one area in which there has been widespread agreement among economists.

Airlines. Before the deregulation process began, both administratively and legislatively, the airline industry was subject to strict entry and rate controls. The net effect was to eliminate price competition and encourage nonprice competition. Airlines competed against one another through the scheduling of their flights and the services that they offered aboard those flights. By scheduling more and more flights, airlines offered more convenient travel times that they hoped would attract more passengers. When all carriers expanded their schedules, however, it reduced the average load factor (percentage of seats occupied) to near 50 percent—a plane's break-even point.[30] The in-service rivalry quickly expanded to include such things as free drinks, movies, piano bars, different seating arrangements, and even multicolored airplanes. The end result was that regulated carriers provided more convenient, but also more expensive, airline service. (In California, for instance, unregulated intrastate carriers consistently underpriced regulated carriers in the heavily traveled San Francisco-Los Angeles market.[31])

Although airline regulation reduced static efficiency, it is frequently credited with increasing dynamic efficiency. The CAB's fare policy allowed airlines to charge higher fares for flights using new aircraft. Airlines also viewed the adoption of the latest generation of airplanes as an important form of nonprice competition. These factors probably spurred the development of new airplanes by domestic manufacturers. At the same time, the CAB's fare policies encouraged the premature obsolescence of airplanes and discouraged the provision of low-cost service with older airplanes. The overall effect was probably a reduction in the variety of airline services offered to the traveling public.

These criticisms of airline regulation were instrumental in the pas-

29. See Friedlaender, *Dilemma of Freight Transport Regulation;* and Douglas and Miller, *Economic Regulation.* For a discussion of some other transportation services, see L. S. Keyes, "Regulatory Reform in Air Cargo Transportation" (Washington, D.C.: American Enterprise Institute, 1980) and M. E. Levine, "Regulating Airmail Transportation," *Journal of Law and Economics* 18 (October 1975): 317–59.

30. Some carriers did engage in CAB-approved capacity limitation agreements from 1971 to 1975, increasing their load factors.

31. A. M. La Mond, "An Evaluation of Intrastate Airline Regulation in California," *Bell Journal of Economics* 7 (Autumn 1976): 641–57.

sage of the Airline Deregulation Act of 1978. This act introduced fare flexibility and reduced the CAB's control over entry. These changes have increased price competition on some routes and permitted new entry as well. (The long-run implications of this act are discussed in the next section.)

Motor Carriers.   ICC regulation of the trucking industry has increased costs and, as a result, the prices paid by shippers.[32] The existence of rate bureaus inhibits independent action and thus lessens any possible price competition. More importantly, operating certificates increase the trucking companies' costs. Circuitous route restrictions prevent trucks from taking the most direct route between two cities, increasing costs without any offsetting increase in output. At the same time, commodity restrictions (empty backhauls) in combination with scheduling rivalry create excess capacity for the trucking firms. From 1940 to 1963, for example, estimates of the level of capacity utilization ranged from 43 percent to 52 percent.[33] Moreover, the costs of the administrative process should not be forgotten. Actions before the commission are rarely brief and can seldom be accomplished without the aid of lawyers familiar with transportation regulation.

In light of these obvious inefficiencies, one might expect trucking companies to be unprofitable. In fact, regulated carriers are profitable, frequently earning a higher return on their investment than does an average firm in the manufacturing sector of the economy. This is reflected by the active market in operating certificates. From 1967 to 1971, the average price of an operating certificate in 43 different transactions was $89,398.[34] This high price results from the ICC policy of restricting entry into regulated markets. If entry were not administratively restricted, the certificates would not be worth more than the administrative costs of applying for one.

The high costs of regulated carriers, in combination with their profits, has increased the prices of their services.[35]   As a result, the share of

32. Paul W. MacAvoy and John W. Snow, eds., *Regulation of Entry and Pricing in Truck Transportation* (Washington, D.C.: American Enterprise Institute, 1977).

33. Friedlaender, *Dilemma of Freight Transport Regulation*, p. 88.

34. M. Kafoglis, "A Paradox of Regulated Trucking," *Regulation* 1 (September/October 1977): 27–32. And a similar situation holds in the moving van industry. See Denis A. Breen, "The Monopoly Value of Household-Goods Carrier Operating Certificates," *Journal of Law and Economics* 20 (April 1977): 153–85.

35. For an argument that ICC regulation lowers trucking rates, see Interstate Commerce Commission, "A Cost and Benefit Evaluation of Surface Transport Regulation" (Washington, D.C.: Government Printing Office, 1976). The ICC's study is critiqued by B. Allen and E. Hymson in MacAvoy and Snow, *Regulation of Entry and Pricing*, Chapter 3.

intercity freight hauled by regulated carriers has declined constantly to its current value of approximately one-third. The remaining two-thirds are hauled by exempt carriers (primarily of agricultural products), private carriers, and illegal "gypsy" carriers who do not have operating certificates. In effect, regulated carriers have been slowly pricing themselves out of the market.

Railroads.   The railroads, like the motor carriers, are also plagued by substantial excess capacity. As shown earlier (Table 12.1), the railroads' share of intercity freight traffic declined from more than one-half in 1950 to slightly more than one-third in 1975. A major factor in their decline has been the rise of motor carriers, especially with the construction of the interstate highway system. This competitive threat has been compounded by the ICC's adoption of an average cost standard in rate-making. This penalizes the railroads, who have high fixed costs but relatively low variable costs. As in the Ingot Molds case, this deviation from marginal cost pricing shifts traffic from the low cost mode (railroads) to a less efficient mode (motor vehicles). This rate-making standard, in fact, leaves the railroads with even less freight to ship over their already underutilized track system.

Not surprisingly, the railroads' financial health is not good. They consistently earn a lower rate of return than the manufacturing sector of the economy, sometimes as little as one or two percent on their investment.[36] A major problem has been the rails' loss of high-profit business to the truckers, leaving them with the less profitable, and in some cases unprofitable, shipments. In addition, the ICC's policy toward abandonments has made it difficult to eliminate unprofitable lines. These problems were addressed in the Railroad Revitalization and Regulatory Reform Act of 1976, which made it easier to abandon unprofitable lines and to engage in more flexible pricing. The proposed rate flexibility was substantially curtailed, however, by the commission's interpretation of that act and the conditions under which rate flexibility is legal.[37]

The railroads have also been handicapped by the ICC's policy toward

36. This average figure conceals substantial variation in profitability among railroads. Railroads that have long hauls and ship bulky products, such as the Southern and the Burlington Northern, are profitable.

37. The railroads were granted rate flexibility in markets where they did not have market dominance. This required an examination of alternative supply opportunities. Through a strict interpretation of market dominance, the ICC limited the rails' flexibility to one-half their markets. For an analysis of the ICC's decision, see N. H. Jones, Jr., "The Meaning of Market Dominance," in P. W. MacAvoy and J. W. Snow, eds., *Railroad Revitalization and Regulatory Reform* (Washington, D.C.: American Enterprise Institute, 1977), pp. 203–23.

their introduction of major technological innovations. In general, the Commission has not been receptive toward rail innovations, thereby reducing the likelihood that they will be commercially successful. In the "Big John Hopper" case, for example, Southern Railway introduced a new aluminum grain car, estimating that the hopper would enable it to reduce railroad rates by 60 percent and thereby recapture some of the grain traffic from exempt motor carriers. The ICC ruled, however, that Southern could not reduce its rates by 60 percent. This jeopardized the competitiveness of the "Big John Hopper" and forced Southern to ask the Supreme Court to overturn the ICC's decision.[38] All in all, it took four years for Southern to get its rates approved by the ICC. The ICC's action threatened the success of the Hopper and created an environment that was not conducive to technological innovation.

In sum, government regulation of transportation has imposed substantial costs on society. It has led to the inefficient use of specific modes and has diverted traffic away from the most efficient mode.[39] Some dollar estimates of the economic loss from government regulation of *surface* transportation are provided in Table 12.4. These estimates, though inexact, indicate the order of magnitude involved. Thomas Moore states that "as much as one-third of the income generated in surface freight transportation could be pure waste."[40] And to these costs must be added the inefficiencies from airline regulation. It is more difficult to place a dollar value on the impact of regulation on dynamic efficiency, although it could obviously be substantial.

New Directions for Regulation

Given the extremely negative evaluation of transportation regulation, it is not surprising that most reform proposals share a common theme: deregulation. The basic belief is that performance in these markets will be improved if regulation is decreased and competition is increased. That rationale underlies the deregulation experiment with the nation's airlines. (This implies further that the major economic argument for regu-

38. *The Cincinnati, New Orleans & Texas Pacific Railway Co.* v. *United States*, 379 U.S. 642 (1965).

39. Part of the inefficiency problem is due to the government's provision of subsidies to the different transportation modes. For example, truckers benefit from the interstate highway system and barges from the inland waterway system. The subsidy issue is addressed in the overall evaluation of government intervention in Chapter 19.

40. Thomas Moore, "Deregulating Surface Freight Transportation," in *Promoting Competition in Regulated Markets*, ed. Almarin Phillips. (Washington, D.C.: Brookings Institution, 1975), p. 72.

Table 12.4 **Economic Loss from Regulation of Surface Freight, 1960s**
(Millions of dollars)

Type of Loss	Estimate of Loss		
	Low	*Medium*	*High*
Inefficient use of mode			
Common carrier trucks	1,400	1,660	1,890
Private trucks	100	200	1,000
Rails	1,700	2,000	2,400
Water carriers	200	300	300+
Pipelines	n.e.[a]	n.e.	n.e.
Subtotal	3,400	4,160	5,590+
Traffic shifted to alternate mode			
Trucks to rails	200	1,100	2,900
Water carriers to rails	n.e.	n.e.	n.e.
Pipelines to other modes	n.e.	n.e.	n.e.
Subtotal	200	1,100	2,900
Traffic not carried	175	300	400
Total estimated loss	3,775	5,560	8,890

[a] n.e.: Not estimated.
Source: Thomas Moore, "Deregulating Surface Freight Transportation," in *Promoting Competition in Regulated Markets*, ed. A. Phillips (Washington, D.C.: Brookings Institution, 1975), Table 3–2, p. 71.

lation—natural monopoly—does not apply to these transportation industries.)

Airlines. The economic evidence is very strong that the airline industry does not meet the requirements for natural monopoly. Costs do not decline with increases in output, but appear to be constant. An airline can expand or contract its operations simply by adjusting the number of planes serving specific markets. And the barriers to entry are relatively low, thereby making it unlikely that an airline could earn substantial profits without inviting entry by other carriers. One potentially major barrier—access to airport facilities—is a problem at only four airports: Kennedy and LaGuardia (New York), O'Hare (Chicago), and National (Washington, D.C.).[41] In sum, competition in the airline industry seems both feasible and desirable.

41. The Federal Aviation Administration has limited National Airport in Washington, D.C., for example, to 60 flight operations per hour. Of these 60 flights, 40 are reserved for certified carriers, 8 for commuter airlines, and 12 for general aviation, primarily corporate jets (Comptroller General of the United States, Report to the Congress, "Aircraft Delays at Major U.S. Airports Can Be Reduced," CED-79-102, September 4, 1979, p. 12).

Even though the American experience with airline deregulation is brief, it does appear to be encouraging. On the positive side, price competition has erupted on many of the major airline routes. The CAB has estimated that such price competition led to consumer savings of $2.8 billion in 1978 alone.[42] At the same time, both revenue and profits have increased as passengers flocked to the airlines. There has also been entry by small carriers and increased product variety for travelers. On the negative side, some cities have lost airline service as the airlines dropped some routes and added others. From July 1, 1978, to July 1, 1979, approximately 40 percent of city-pair markets had flight increases, 40 percent flight decreases, and 20 percent reported no change at all.[43] The total impact of regulation will not become apparent until this transitional period is over, and the airlines—both traditional carriers and new ones—have had an opportunity to buy more airplanes and determine their optimal route network.

Motor Carriers.   Of all the regulated modes, trucking offers the greatest opportunity for deregulation. Without government rate and entry controls, the industry would come as close as any industry to meeting the economist's requirements for a competitive market. Economies of scale are small, as are barriers to entry. A driver can acquire a rig and almost instantly begin to compete with established carriers. This ease of entry has been supported by the persistent efforts of the ICC to keep new companies from entering the industry. (If entry were not so easy, the ICC's entry controls would not be necessary.) At the same time, most costs are variable and place a floor to rate competition. Profit-maximizing truckers will not set rates below their variable costs. The trucking industry is thus an unlikely candidate for ruinous competition. All in all, the trucking industry and its 16,000 firms offer an ideal environment for competition.

The Motor Carrier Act of 1980 will reduce some of the inefficiencies associated with ICC regulations. Many of the route and commodity restrictions, for example, will be gradually eliminated. And carriers are granted some rate flexibility; they will be able to raise or lower rates by as much as ten percent without ICC approval. These changes should increase competition and improve market performance in this industry. At the same time, all economic regulations are not eliminated. It may

42. Civil Aeronautics Board, "Report on Airline Service, Fares, Traffic, Load Factors and Market Shares," Service Status on July 1, 1979 (see footnote 5).

43. CAB, "Report on Airline Service," p. 72.

thus be possible to obtain more cost and rate reductions through more radical, if not complete, deregulation of the trucking industry in the future.[44]

Railroads. The Carter Administration also proposed deregulating the railroad industry. Unlike deregulation in the trucking and airline industries, however, the purpose was to increase the financial viability of the railroads. This would reduce the prospect of future federal subsidies and provide railroads with the necessary funds to invest in new equipment and upgrade existing track. Deregulation proposals have focused on three main issues. First, the rails need more freedom in setting their rates. The logical solution is to permit them to adjust rates within a given percentage range without ICC approval. Second, railroads must be able to abandon unprofitable lines without undue delay. Third, mergers should be encouraged, on the grounds that mergers among railroads that are not competitors would produce more efficient service. Shipments on a single line travel more quickly and at less cost than those involving two or more railroads. The net effect of these changes would be to rationalize the existing rail system into a smaller, but more profitable and more efficient version.

Summary

Historically, the transportation sector in the United States has been subject to extensive government regulation. This regulation was rooted in the public's fear of the railroads and the drift away from the market system during the Great Depression. Economists view current regulation as unnecessary and very inefficient. Numerous proposals for deregulation have been made; the recent success in the domestic airline industry is one result. Deregulation is not just an economic issue, however. It is also a political question, as the Teamsters' and trucking companies' opposition to trucking deregulation demonstrated.[45]

44. James C. Nelson, "Implications of Evolving Entry and Licensing Policies in Road Freight Transport" (Paper given before the International Conference on Transportation Research, at the College of Europe in Bruges, Belgium, June 18-21, 1973); and James Sloss, "Regulation of Motor Freight Transportation: A Quantitative Evaluation of Policy," *Bell Journal of Economics* 1 (Autumn 1970): 327–66.

45. T. Moore, "The Beneficiaries of Trucking Regulation," *Journal of Law and Economics* 21 (October 1978): 327–43.

Suggested Readings

Douglas, George, and Miller, James, III. *Economic Regulation of Domestic Air Transport* (Washington, D.C.: Brookings Institution, 1974).

Friedlaender, Ann. *The Dilemma of Freight Transport Regulation* (Washington, D.C.: Brookings Institution, 1969).

Kolko, G. *Railroads and Regulation, 1877-1916* (Princeton, N.J.: Princeton University Press, 1965).

Moore, T. "Deregulating Surface Freight Transportation," in *Promoting Competition in Regulated Markets*, ed. A. Phillips (Washington, D.C.: Brookings Institution, 1975), pp. 55–98.

Sloss, J. "Regulation of Motor Freight Transportation: A Quantitative Evaluation of Policy," *Bell Journal of Economics* (Autumn 1970): 327–66.

Communications

Chapter
13

As people communicate with one another through the written and spoken word, they probably use communications services that are regulated or operated by the government. Interstate and foreign services such as broadcasting (radio and television) and telecommunications (telegraph and telephone) have been subject to regulation by the Federal Communications Commission since 1934.[1] During this time, both the nature and the extent of government regulation have changed as the communications sector has matured. Advances in communications technology, in particular, have threatened the traditional regulatory scheme and focused attention on the necessity for government regulation.

The Setting

A variety of communications companies provides users with an array of services—each with different characteristics and, hence, different degrees of substitutability. An important characteristic of each service is the manner in which the message (e.g., phone call, telegram, and radio or television program) is transmitted from one party to another. For instance, when American Telephone and Telegraph (AT&T) transmits long distance phone calls, it can use microwave relay towers, coaxial

---

1. Mail service provided by the U.S. Postal Service is discussed in Chapter 18.

Table 13.1　Allocation of Radio Frequencies

MHz[a]	Frequency and Allocation
.003	Very Low – Time signals
.03	Low – Air and marine navigation
.3	Medium – AM radio/amateur
3.0	High – Short-wave/amateur
30.0	Very High – FM radio; VHF television
300.0	Ultra High – UHF television; radar; land mobile
3,000.0	Super High – Satellite broadcast; microwave relay
30,000.0 } 300,000.0 }	Extra High – Sparsely used

[a]Megahertz (MHz) = one million cycles/second.
Source: "Frequency Allocation Chart," U.S. Congress, Senate Committee on Commerce, Science and Transportation, Subcommittee on Communications, *Hearings on Amendments to the Communications Act of 1934*, 96th Congress, 1st session, April 24, 25, and 26, 1979, Attachment 9.

cable, or satellite. Table 13.1 presents a simplified picture of the spectrum of radio frequencies and the government's current allocation of frequency band widths for different communications uses. It should be noted that this allocation scheme is not static and is constantly adjusted in response to changing communications requirements. For example, the unique capabilities of satellites will undoubtedly increase demand for more space for satellite transmissions.

The History of Communications Regulation

The early history of communications regulation closely parallels the rise of AT&T (or, more familiarly, "Ma Bell").[2] The Bell System began with the original telephone patent of Alexander Graham Bell. After the Bell patent was declared valid by the Supreme Court in 1876, Bell established telephone companies and integrated backward into the manufacture of telephone equipment.[3] The Bell System also aggressively acquired competing telephone companies so that it quickly became the dominant force in the telephone industry. This position was reinforced by its substantial commitment to research and development in communications technology.

2. For a brief introduction to telecommunications regulation, see M. Irwin, "The Telephone Industry," in *The Structure of American Industry*, ed. W. Adams, 5th ed. (New York: Macmillan, 1977), pp. 312–33.

3. The original patent filed by Alexander Graham Bell was central to the original control of the telephone industry and was declared valid by a four-to-three vote by the Supreme Court.

Table 13.2   The Bell System and Independent Telephone.Companies, 1976

Item	Bell	Percentage of Total	Independents	Percentage of Total	Total Industry
Telephones	126,963,000	82	28,209,000	18	155,172,000
Exhanges	6,712	38	11,040	62	17,152
Investment ($ millions)	96,340[a]	81	23,000	19	119,340
Revenues ($ millions)	33,518	84	6,300	16	39,818
Employees	778,000	83	160,000	17	938,000
Area served[b] (square miles)	1,265,310	35	1,427,035	39	3,615,211

[a] Includes AT&T's Long Lines investment and other investment used exclusively for toll.

[b] 922,866 square miles (26 percent) are unassigned; more than half of this territory is in Alaska.

Source: U.S. Congress, Senate Committee on Commerce, Science, and Transportation, Subcommittee on Communications, *Hearings on Amendments to the Communications Act of 1934*, 96th Congress, 1st session, April 24, 25, and 26, 1979, p. 480.

One key tactic employed by Bell was its refusal to interconnect its facilities with those of other telephone companies. As Bell was already the dominant firm in long distance communications, customers of its competitors could only make long distance calls if they also had a telephone provided by Bell. This weakened the competitiveness of independent companies, who, as a result, frequently sold out to Bell. It was not long, however, before regulation began at the local level and quickly spread to the federal level. In 1910, the Interstate Commerce Commission's jurisdiction was expanded to include interstate phone service.

The Bell System today is a holding company that consists of 23 separate operating companies (e.g., New Jersey Bell, Southern Bell, Illinois Bell, etc.), Western Electric, and the Bell Laboratory. Western Electric is the manufacturing arm of the Bell System, while Bell Laboratory is the research and development arm. The dominant position of the Bell System in the domestic market is illustrated in Table 13.2. In 1976 the Bell System accounted for 83 percent of the telephones, 84 percent of the revenues, and 83 percent of the employment in the American telephone industry. Even though they are individually dwarfed by the Bell System, the independent companies combined had revenues of over $6 billion and supplied 28 million telephones.

Federal regulation was subsequently extended to broadcasting with the creation of the Federal Radio Commission in 1927. Its primary function was to issue operating licenses to radio stations. Licensing made it possible to allocate the broadcasting spectrum among stations, in an attempt to minimize the interference that was so common in the 1920s. During that period, radio stations clustered around desirable wavelengths and frequently interfered with each other's transmissions. Because the broadcasting spectrum is finite, licensing was deemed necessary to insure that there would be proper spacing between stations.[4] In addition to assigning wavelengths, the FRC also determined the power and location of each station's transmitters.

In 1934, federal jurisdiction over communications was delegated to a single agency with the establishment of the Federal Communications Commission (FCC). The FCC replaced the FRC and also inherited the telecommunications responsibilities of the ICC. With the advent of television broadcasting, the FCC expanded its licensing program to cover both radio and television stations. Since that time, its jurisdiction has been extended to cable television and communications satellites. Cable television retransmits the broadcasting signals of local and distant television stations, thereby competing with local over-the-air broadcasters. Communications satellites are used in both domestic and international telecommunications and broadcasting, thereby competing with microwave radio and coaxial cable. Regulation of these innovations in communications was considered necessary for the commission to develop a coherent and rational communications system in the United States.

The Economics of Communications

Communications companies provide a means for transmitting messages from one point (the origin) to another point (the destination). Communication services are not homogeneous, however, and differ in several aspects. For example, some transmissions have two-way capability (telephones), while others are only one-way (broadcasting). Other important characteristics are unit cost, quality, and reliability. The exact array of communications services offered in the marketplace depends on the underlying demand and supply conditions.

As in the case of transportation, the demand for communications services—both broadcasting and telecommunications—is a derived demand. Users of communications services do not derive benefit from the transmission process, but from the end result of that process: the delivery of a message. The demand for telephone service, for example, depends on

4. H. Levin, "The Radio Spectrum Resource," *Journal of Law and Economics* 11 (October 1968): 443–501; and J. Minasian, "The Political Economy of Broadcasting in the 1920's," *Journal of Law and Economics* 12 (October 1969): 391–403.

the nature and frequency of the messages to be conveyed.[5] Business demand is thus different from residential demand, since a telephone is essential for communications with customers and suppliers. In the broadcasting market, the demand is generated by advertisers who want to present a message to the listening or viewing audience. Changes in a program's popularity quickly bring changes in the demand for its advertising time.

The market supply of communications services depends on the costs of providing the different services. Costs can vary because of the different technologies and factor inputs communications companies use in transmitting their messages. There are, however, similarities in the communications process that are common to all the services. First, the messages must be gathered or collected at the original point, perhaps necessitating the development of a collection network or a centralized collection point. Second, the messages must be transmitted from the original point to the final destination. As the AT&T example showed, a message can frequently be transmitted in more than one way. Finally, the message must be delivered or disseminated to the designated recipient(s). Some type of distribution system becomes necessary. Note that the same network in a single city may be able to be used for both the collection and the distribution of messages. This is the case with local telephone exchanges.

These different stages in the communications process can be illustrated for both over-the-air and cable television. The major difference between these two is the way in which the viewer receives the television signal. With over-the-air television, the viewer's television antenna picks up the broadcast signal from the air and transfers it to the TV set. With cable television, the signals are picked up by the company's antenna and transferred via a cable network to the subscriber's residence. In either case, the programming originates with ABC, CBS, or NBC, if the relevant station is affiliated with one of the major networks. The program is transmitted from the network in New York to the station via AT&T's telephone circuits. From this perspective, both over-the-air and cable television act as intermediaries between the networks and the viewing public.

As mentioned above, the television networks use the Bell System's telephone network to distribute their programming. A key element in

5. There is a substitute available for long distance calls—mail. Whether or not mail is a perfect substitute depends on such factors as time, reliability, and the desire for two-way interaction over the phone.

that network is microwave radio. It transmits messages from point to point through a system of relay stations. Each station receives a radio signal from another station, amplifies it, and then sends it to the next station.[6] The physical properties of microwave radio make it ideal for transmitting television signals as well as data. Microwave transmission is also quite economical compared to other communications systems. Not surprisingly, there is substantial variation in capacity size, installation cost, and operating costs across communications systems.[7] Moreover, making repairs is more expensive for satellite and submarine cable systems, although they are not as exposed to natural disasters as microwave and coaxial cable repeater stations are.

It should be emphasized that cost conditions in the communications area are changing constantly. Just as microwave transmissions threatened the viability of wire transmissions, new technologies threaten the competitiveness of microwave relay systems. One of the most promising developments is *optical fibers,* glass fibers smaller than a human hair. These fibers are combined into small cables with the capacity to carry 50,000 voice conversations through light pulses![8]

Another inevitable development is the expanded role of communications satellites. These satellites are positioned approximately 23,000 miles above the earth, where they can beam messages across the entire United States. They can be quite expensive, however. A major reason is the high costs of the earth stations that link a communications satellite with ground facilities. Originally, the earth stations used dish-shaped antennas that were 33 feet across and cost $100,000 each.[9] They now are 14 feet across and sell for less than $20,000. And a new communications company, Satellite Business Systems, has constructed small, two-way antennas that can be located on customers' rooftops.[10] This develop-

6. Because each station must be within sight of the next station, they usually are built approximately 20 to 40 miles apart.

7. Each channel can contain between 600 and 2,400 voice circuits. The transmittal of a television signal requires the same capacity as 500 phone conversations. See L. Waverman, "The Regulation of Intercity Telecommunications," in *Promoting Competition in Regulated Markets,* ed. A. Phillips (Washington, D.C.: Brookings Institution, 1975), pp. 201–39.

8. "Laser System to Carry D.C.—Mass. Phone Calls," *Washington Post,* January 24, 1980, p. B1.

9. "Competition Heats Up In Domestic Satellites As Technology Gains," *Wall Street Journal,* September 8, 1978. p. 1.

10. Satellite Business Systems is a joint venture of International Business Machines, Communications Satellite Corporation (Comsat), and Aetna Life and Casualty. Comsat has joined with Sears Roebuck in an effort to market and install three-foot rooftop antennas that could receive satellite communications ("Pay-TV by Comsat," *Business Week,* January 14, 1980, p. 36).

ment may finally unleash the tremendous potential of communications satellites.

The nature of communications regulation for telecommunications is different from that for broadcasting.[11] Telecommunications is subject to "traditional" regulation, with its focus on rate-making and entry controls. That is, regulators are concerned with AT&T's rates as well as the extent of its communications monopoly.[12] Broadcasting, on the other hand, was exempted by the Communications Act of 1934 from rate or profit controls. As a result, the FCC's primary responsibility is to establish standards for the issuance of new licenses and the renewal of old licenses for broadcasting companies.

Major Regulatory Issues

Telecommunications. The FCC has jurisdiction over the rates that AT&T charges for interstate and foreign communications services, while the rates for intrastate and local phone service are regulated by the appropriate state regulatory commission. An individual's phone rates are thus the result of the policies pursued by both the FCC and the state regulatory agency.

One major issue has been allocation of AT&T's investment between interstate and intrastate uses. The interstate investment is subject to FCC jurisdiction, while the intrastate portion is subject to local or state jurisdiction. There is no easy way to separate these investments, since a caller uses the same phone and its local exchange for both local and interstate calls. Initially, no local exchange costs were assigned to AT&T's interstate rate base. This allocation scheme was ruled invalid by the Supreme Court, however, four years before the Communications Act was passed.[13] The Court's decision led to substantial controversy because there is no single method for allocating fixed or overhead costs among two or more uses—in this case, local and interstate phone calls. States wanted to assign as much of the local costs as possible to the interstate rate base, thereby reducing the local rate base and local phone rates. This problem was finally resolved through a series of negotiations between the state commissions and AT&T.

AT&T's interstate rates are also negotiated, though these negotiations

11. Cable television falls between the two extremes of telecommunications and broadcasting. It retransmits the television signals of over-the-air broadcasters through its own microwave relay system.

12. The FCC also regulates Western Union's monopoly over domestic telegraph service.

13. *Smith* v. *Illinois Bell Telephone Co.*, 282 U.S. 133 (1930).

are between AT&T and the Federal Communications Commission. AT&T is permitted to charge rates that will yield it some predetermined target rate of return on its interstate rate base. Since 1976, AT&T has been permitted to earn between 9.5 and 10.0 percent on its investment.[14] The "fudge factor" of .5 percent was inserted to reward AT&T if it increased productivity. If earnings exceed the maximum allowable rate of 10 percent, its rates will be negotiated downward.

AT&T's permissible rate level can be generated by a variety of different rate structures. The exact rates reflect the compromises reached on the allocation of local exchange costs. In general, phone rates are based on the average costs of serving customers. For example, a household in a high density (but low cost) area may be charged the same monthly charge as a household in a low density (but high cost) area. There are, however, some rate adjustments for differences in cost and demand conditions. AT&T has instituted lower, off-peak rates for long distance calls, as well as charging for directory assistance requests in excess of a certain monthly "quota."[15] At the same time, local rates have a "value of service" orientation. A business pays a higher monthly fee than a household, which presumably has a more elastic demand for telephone service. In sum, there appears to be substantial cross-subsidization in AT&T's rate structure, though the direction of that subsidization is disputed. AT&T contends that it benefits residential customers, while others maintain that it benefits business customers.[16]

AT&T has used the cross-subsidization issue to support its argument that the telephone industry is a natural monopoly and should not be subjected to competitive pressures by FCC policies. The controversy centers on the exact boundary of that natural monopoly. It is generally agreed that the provision of local service through a local exchange does exhibit the cost characteristics necessary for a natural monopoly. But is this also true for providing the necessary inputs (such as telephones) as well as supplying interstate services? AT&T claims that it must control all these aspects of the telephone industry if it is to guarantee service quality. Its advertisements argue that "The system is the solution." Recently, however, the FCC has disagreed and has permitted new firms to

14. *In the Matter of American Telephone & Telegraph Co.*, 57 F.C.C. 2d (1976).

15. According to AT&T's former chairman John deButts, 20 percent of all customers were making 80 percent of all requests for directory assistance ("Tomorrow's Telephone Service," *U.S. News & World Report,* July 5, 1976, p. 85).

16. For example, a study by the New York State Public Service Commission in 1975 found that residential service was subsidizing business service.

enter and compete against AT&T.

The input issue arose in a case involving the "Carterfone Device," a piece of equipment that enables a mobile radio operator to connect into the local telephone system.[17] An individual can communicate via radio with a base station that then uses the Carterfone to plug the caller into the telephone system. AT&T viewed this device as a "foreign attachment" that could jeopardize the functioning of the Bell System. Up to that time, only equipment manufactured by Western Electric (a subsidiary of AT&T) had been used by Bell. The FCC disagreed with Bell, arguing that its prohibition of "foreign" attachments was "unreasonable, discriminatory, and unlawful." In effect, Bell's rule prohibited the installation of all devices, harmless as well as harmful, that were not produced by Western Electric. If Bell wanted to protect its system, it could simply establish standards that "foreign" attachments must meet.[18] This less restrictive solution would not damage the existing system, but would increase the variety of services available to telephone users.

The Carterfone decision was the first of several that opened up the input market to competition. Of most importance to consumers was the FCC's subsequent ruling that AT&T's rate for "protective" phone devices unnecessarily restricted consumers' rights to install their own non-Bell telephone. By requiring users of non-Bell phones to rent interconnection devices, AT&T had made it uneconomical to purchase a phone. AT&T responded to the commission's decision with a request that every household must have at least one phone—a "primary" instrument—provided by the local telephone company. The FCC rejected this request, thereby permitting users to choose whatever equipment they desired.

Just one year after the Carterfone decision, AT&T was dealt an additional setback by an FCC decision to end AT&T's monopoly over the provision of telecommunications services.[19] Microwave Communications, Inc. (MCI) wanted to provide private-line service between St. Louis and Chicago that would meet the interoffice and interplant communications needs of small businesses. MCI would thus be competing with AT&T in providing long distance microwave service for business firms. AT&T argued that MCI would be engaged in "cream skimming,"

17. *Use of the Carterfone Device in Message Toll Telephone Service*, 13 F.C.C. 420 (1968).

18. Note the similarity between this issue and the quality defense argument used to justify tying agreements (Chapter 8).

19. *Microwave Communications, Inc.*, 18 F.C.C. 953 (1969).

upsetting the cross-subsidization inherent in AT&T's rate structure. The FCC disagreed, in effect establishing a new common carrier and creating competition for AT&T. After this decision, the commission received more than 1,800 applications from firms wishing to provide similar long distance services. More recently, firms such as MCI were authorized to offer basic telephone services in competition with AT&T.[20]

Now that the FCC has permitted entry at both the input and output stages in the telecommunications industry, what is the future role of AT&T? This issue has been in the forefront of major antitrust cases filed against AT&T. Of more than 50 antitrust suits, at least two—MCI's and the Justice Department's—sought the dissolution of AT&T.[21] If AT&T were to be convicted of monopolization, it might be forced to divest itself of Western Electric and its Long Lines division that handles long distance calls. If past experience is an accurate predictor of the future, dissolution of AT&T is unlikely. In 1949, the Justice Department also sought divestiture of Western Electric. In a 1956 consent decree, however, AT&T was permitted to retain Western Electric, if it restricted its activities to only regulated communications services.

Broadcasting

In 1978, there were over 8,000 commercial broadcasters (radio and television) in the United States. In 1950, as Table 13.3 indicates, most of these stations were not in existence. This growth has placed a substantial burden on the FCC, which must license each broadcaster. Furthermore, these licenses must be renewed every three years. The FCC also issues operating licenses to cable television companies. Overall, the structure of the American broadcasting industry depends on the licensing requirements of the FCC.

The FCC must address two issues. First, how many broadcasting stations should there be? Is every city entitled to have its own radio and/or television station? Second, who will be licensed to run these stations? If two or more people want the same license, how can the commission differentiate between the competing applications?

Given the space limitations of the broadcasting spectrum, the FCC must restrict the number of stations. The maximum number possible de-

20. *MCI Telecommunications Service v. Federal Communications Commission,* 561 F.2d 365 (1977), *cert. denied,* 434 U.S. 1040 (1977).

21. *United States v. American Telephone and Telegraph Company,* U.S. District Court for the District of Columbia, Civil Action No. 74-1698 (1974). MCI prevailed over AT&T in its suit, with the jury awarding it $600 million in damages that are automatically trebled to $1.8 billion under the antitrust laws. AT&T is appealing the district court's decision.

Table 13.3   Commercial Broadcast Stations (Selected Years)

| Year | Broadcasting Stations | | | Cable Television Systems |
	AM Radio	FM Radio	Television	
1950	2,144	691	107	70[a]
1955	2,732	540	437	400
1960	3,483 (412)[b]	741 (147)	530 (161)	640
1965	4,025 (391)	1,343 (170)	588 (174)	1,325
1970	4,288 (402)	2,126 (248)	686 (191)	2,490
1975	4,488 (320)	2,847 (238)	693 (197)	3,506
1978	4,459 (319)	2,922 (252)	720 (221)	3,997

[a]Figure for 1952, not 1950.
[b]Numbers in parentheses indicate the number of stations owned by newspapers or magazines. The figures for 1960 and 1970 are for 1961 and 1971, respectively.
Sources: 1. U.S. Department of Commerce, *Historical Statistics of the United States, Colonial Times to 1970* (Washington, D.C.: Government Printing Office, 1975), p. 796, Series R 93–105.
2. U.S. Department of Commerce, *Statistical Abstract of the United States, 1979* (Washington, D.C.: Government Printing Office, 1979), pp. 585–87.

pends on the exact location and power of the transmitting stations. A major goal of the FCC has historically been to maximize the number of local stations. This is particularly evident in television, in which broadcasting interference with nearby stations is most likely. The FCC has encouraged local stations because they are viewed as outlets for local self-expression. A local station presents news and public interest features that would not be broadcast by distant, larger stations.

The second decision—whom to license—is based on a variety of factors. As might be expected, the Communications Act of 1934 granted the commission substantial discretion in determining which applicants would "serve the public interest, convenience and necessity." In a typical comparative proceeding involving two or more applicants, the Commission examines such things as the experience, local ties, and proposed programming of each applicant.[22] Given the FCC's preference

22. In proceedings involving the renewal of several of RKO General's television licenses, an important issue was the domestic and foreign payoffs made by RKO's parent, General Tire and Rubber Company. In a landmark decision, the FCC decided that RKO was unfit to be a licensee and therefore denied its application for renewal of its Boston station, WNAC (In *Re: RKO General, Inc. [WNAC-TV], Comparative Renewal Proceedings* [Dos. 18759–61], June 4, 1980.

for local diversity, an applicant's ownership of other broadcast media or newspapers can be a major factor. A single owner, for example, may have at most seven AM, seven FM, and seven television stations.[23] And the FCC will not approve any transactions that would establish commonly owned newspapers and broadcasting stations in the same town.[24]

Cable television has grown dramatically since the 1960s, as the figures in Table 13.3 show. Known as CATV (Community Antenna Television), it was originally designed to provide television service to sparsely settled areas that did not have good reception of distant television stations. CATV used a giant community antenna to pick up distant signals and then transmit them to households through a network of coaxial cables. Cable systems now receive television signals from communications satellites and have moved into more densely populated urban areas.[25] They offer "perfect" reception of local television stations as well as the importation of signals from distant stations. In addition, some systems provide a subscription service (for instance, Home Box Office) that offers feature films and sporting events without commercial interruption.

Cable television systems are regulated at both the local and federal levels.[26] At the local level, cable is a classic natural monopolist because of its extensive distribution network of cable wires attached to utility poles. Localities award the cable franchise, for which they receive from three to five percent of the system's revenue. At the federal level, the FCC has been concerned over the potential impact of cable television on local over-the-air broadcasters. In particular, cable systems may divert viewers from local stations, thereby undermining these stations' profitability and their future as outlets for local self-expression. The FCC therefore has adopted rules to protect the local broadcasters.[27] Cable systems must carry all local stations and are restricted in their ability to import distant signals. In their 1972 rule-making proceeding, the FCC permitted cable systems to offer a complement of stations. In

23. Each major broadcasting network—ABC, CBS, and NBC—is allowed to own five VHF and two UHF television stations.

24. *Federal Communications Commission* v. *National Citizens Committee for Broadcasting*, 436 U.S. 775 (1978).

25. Most cable systems remain very small, however. In 1978, only 18 percent of the cable systems had more than 5,000 subscribers (U.S. Department of Commerce, *Statistical Abstract of the United States, 1979* [Washington, D.C.: Government Printing Office, 1979], p. 585).

26. FCC jurisdiction over cable systems was affirmed by the Supreme Court in *United States* v. *Southwestern Cable Co.*, 392 U.S. 157 (1968).

27. *Cable Television Report and Order*, 24 RR 2d 1501 (1972).

television markets ranked 1 to 50, three full network stations and three independent stations were permitted. In television markets 51 to 100, three full network stations and two independent stations were permitted. And in smaller television markets (ranked below 100), three full network stations and one independent station were allowed.

Although these basic restrictions are still in effect today, the FCC has made it easier to import additional signals, if the cable company can show that these signals will not adversely affect local broadcasters. Cable systems that do not compete against a local station, or that have fewer than 1,000 subscribers, can import distant television signals without limitation.

It should be reemphasized that a primary concern of the FCC is to promote diversity in programming. Restrictions on licensing and cable television are deemed necessary to protect local stations. This indirect approach is complemented by some direct FCC controls over programming content.[28] For example, the FCC's "fairness doctrine" requires broadcasters to provide some coverage of political issues and to ensure that contrasting points of view are presented. Beginning in 1975, the FCC also required each station to provide one half-hour of its own programs before it carried the network's prime-time package from 8:00 to 11:00 P.M. Until the policy was declared unconstitutional in 1976, the FCC had also designated the 7:00 to 9:00 P.M. time slot as the "family hour."[29] Television programs shown during these two hours were supposed to be suitable for family viewing and, therefore, not to contain sex or violence. In 1979, the FCC began to consider the establishment of guidelines requiring minimum amounts of educational programming by the television networks.[30] This requirement would represent an increase in the commission's direct control over broadcasting content.

Evaluation

The communications industry is undergoing rapid changes. The development of new technologies in broadcasting and telecommunications offers the prospect of substantially improved communications services for both consumers and businesses. At the same time, these technolo-

28. There is also self-regulation through the National Association of Broadcasters (NAB). For example, the NAB has restricted prime-time commercials to six minutes per hour of a series and seven minutes per hour of a movie.

29. "TV Networks' Adoption of Family Hour Ruled in Violation of First Amendment," *Wall Street Journal*, November 5, 1976, p. 6.

30. "FCC Staff Urges Setting Minimum Time For 'Instructional' Children's Television," *Wall Street Journal*, October 30, 1979, p. 12.

gies threaten the current regulatory scheme. It is thus an ideal time to evaluate current regulatory policies and discuss proposals for their reform.

Appraisal of Current Policy

It is frequently claimed that AT&T has provided Americans with the best telephone service in the world. And most people who have traveled extensively in other countries would undoubtedly agree. This is not to say, however, that the phone service could not be better. There is also a general consensus about broadcasting, though it is not that American radio and television are the best in the world.

Telecommunications.   By any yardstick, the performance of the Bell System has been impressive.[31] In 1977, 96 percent of American households had telephones—75 phones for every 100 people. This compares with 72 per 100 in Sweden, 37 in West Germany, 8 in the Soviet Union, and 1 in Kenya. From 1967 to 1977, output per worker increased by 75.5 percent, a productivity record that can be matched by only a handful of other industries in the economy. During this same period, the price of residential phone service increased by 31.3 percent, compared with 81.5 percent for the consumer price index. And some long distance rates actually declined over time. For example, the toll rate for a three-minute phone call from New York to London was $12.00 in 1946, but only $9.60 in 1979.

Despite this enviable record, there is evidence that AT&T's performance could have been even better. Although Bell Labs made a major coup with the invention of transistors, AT&T appears to have become complacent. It took several decades to switch all customers over to dial telephones after they had been introduced. The Carterfone and MCI cases indicate that AT&T was not adequately fulfilling the new demands of its customers; it seemed content to exploit its "captive" market instead of developing new ones. Only recently, in the face of increased competition, has Bell begun to emphasize the marketing of new products and services for its customers.[32]

The entry of MCI and Carterfone also raises questions about the traditional belief that telecommunications is a natural monopoly. Few ob-

---

31. The statistics cited are from *Statistical Abstract of the United States,* 1979, pp. 414, 492, 583–84, and 910–11.

32. "The New New Telephone Industry," *Business Week,* February 13, 1978, pp. 68–78.

servers doubt the appropriateness of classifying local exchange service as a natural monopoly. The production of telephone equipment and the transmission of intercity messages are suspect, however. Western Electric's dominant position is not attributed to cost advantages, but to its unique role as input supplier to the Bell System. In fact, Western Electric's prices frequently exceed that of competitors by as much as 30 percent![33] The intercity transmission of messages apparently was a natural monopoly in the early 1940s, but not in the 1970s.[34] Increases in market demand have made it possible to have more than a single system serving a given market. For example, in the late 1960s there were approximately 79,000 interstate circuits between New York City and Philadelphia. A market of this size could support a maximum of 66 efficient-sized firms, each providing a capacity of 1,200 circuits.[35] The provision of interstate telecommunications circuits evidently has ceased to be a natural monopoly in many of the markets in the United States.

Broadcasting.   As noted earlier, the FCC has consciously pursued a policy of "localism" when awarding broadcasting licenses and establishing cable regulations. This policy has not been costless, however. It has substantially reduced the program variety available to viewers. At the same time, it has dramatically enriched those few stations that have been licensed.

Maximizing the number of local stations has reduced the total number of stations that viewers can receive. It was necessary to limit the broadcasting power of distant stations in order to accommodate more local stations in the broadcasting spectrum. Without this restriction, each city could possibly have been served by six different regional, VHF television stations.[36] The restrictive licensing policy was reinforced by the FCC's limitations on the importation of distant signals by cable television systems, which kept them from offering subscribers the full complement of programs available. At the same time, FCC policies have not been very successful at stimulating locally originated programming. The reduction in network broadcasting by one half-hour in many cases led to reruns of "I Love Lucy" and "Hogan's Heroes," not original programming. And the cable rules restricted the importation of original programming from independent stations in large metropolitan areas. All in

33. Irwin, "The Telephone Industry," p. 327.

34. Waverman, "The Regulation of Intercity Telecommunications."

35. Waverman, "The Regulation of Intercity Telecommunications," pp. 232–33.

36. R. Noll, M. Peck, and J. McGowan, *Economic Aspects of Television Regulation* (Washington, D.C.: Brookings Institution, 1973), p. 116.

all, FCC policies underestimated the substantial costs of developing local programming.

At the same time, the FCC's restrictive licensing policy has made broadcasting so profitable that receiving a broadcast license is the modern-day equivalent of inheriting a gold mine. Few industries can match the profit figures presented in Table 13.4. VHF television stations in major markets earned pretax returns of over 100 percent on their tangible investment.[37] (This is approximately four times the average for all of manufacturing; even such industrial giants as General Motors and IBM rarely have pretax returns in excess of 40 percent.) The exact value of the FCC's licensing restrictions is directly reflected in the sale price of broadcast stations. As with ICC operating certificates, there is an active market in broadcast licenses.[38] In 1978, for example, 586 radio stations were sold for a combined total of $331.6 million, and 51 television stations went for a total of $289.7 million.[39] That comes to an average price of $565,870 for a radio license, and $5,680,000 for a television license. It is hardly surprising that licensing proceedings attract so many applicants and are so fiercely contested.[40]

New Directions for Regulation

The consensus among economists is that society would benefit from deregulation of the communications industry. This could be done administratively by the FCC or legislatively by the Congress. It is not clear, however, exactly what the optimal degree of regulation, if any, should be in the communications industry. Attention has thus focused on various proposals for either completely eliminating or "fine-tuning" the current regulatory framework.

Telecommunications.   The dominant issue in the telecommunications area is the future role of AT&T. Should AT&T be dissolved as request-

37. The profitability of radio broadcasting has recently increased dramatically, although it is not as profitable as television broadcasting ("Striking it Rich In Radio," *Business Week,* February 5, 1979, pp. 58–62).

38. Technically, stations do not have property rights to their licenses, though the renewal rate is very high. From 1972 to 1974, the renewal rates for broadcast licenses exceeded 99 percent each year: 99.32 (1972), 99.19 (1973), and 99.69 (1974) (Subcommittee on Oversight and Investigations, Ninety-fourth Congress, Second Session, *Federal Regulation and Regulatory Reform* [Washington, D.C.: Government Printing Office, 1976], p. 256).

39. *Statistical Abstract of the United States, 1979,* p. 587.

40. "New Channels for TV Planned in Four Market Areas," *Wall Street Journal,* March 9, 1977, p. 4.

Table 13.4 Profitability of Commercial Television Stations, 1969

Commercial TV Stations	Number of Stations	(1) Income Before Federal Tax (thousands of dollars)	(2) Original Cost of Tangible Property Less Depreciation (thousands of dollars)	Percentage (1) of (2)
Small market (below 100)				
Network				
UHF	59	(−$900)	$ 26,584	(a)
VHF	219	33,460	127,954	26.2
Independent				
UHF	8	(−1,927)	1,847	(a)
VHF	11	(−3,330)	8,503	(a)
Total, small market	297	27,303	164,888	16.6
Large market (top 100)				
Network				
UHF	58	7,200	45,595	15.8
VHF	244	474,951	379,676	125.1
Independent				
UHF	52	(−10,345)	42,655	(a)
VHF	20	11,677	46,165	25.3
Total, large market	374	483,483	514,091	94.0
All stations				
Network				
UHF	117	6,300	72,179	8.7
VHF	463	508,411	507,630	100.2
Independent				
UHF	60	(−12,272)	44,502	(a)
VHF	31	8,347	54,668	15.3
Total, all stations	671	510,786	678,979	75.2

(a): loss.

Source: P. MacAvoy, "Memorandum on Regulatory Reform in Broadcasting," in *Deregulation of Cable Television*, ed. P. MacAvoy (Washington, D.C.: American Enterprise Institute, 1977), Table 4, p. 35.

ed in the Justice Department's antitrust suit, or should it be preserved as the core of a more competitive telecommunications market? Another option—restoring Bell's traditional position of dominance—seems less likely. AT&T's attempts to lessen competition via new legislation have so far been unsuccessful.[41]

A wholesale deregulation of interstate communications markets

41. The specific bill endorsed by AT&T was called the Consumer Communications Reform Act. Critics referred to it as the "Ma Bell Bill" or the "Monopoly Protection Act of 1976."

would have both costs and benefits. On the benefit side, increased competition might reduce costs, increase technological innovation, and guarantee marginal cost pricing of services. On the negative side, deregulation might increase contracting costs as well as end a socially beneficial cross-subsidization scheme. "Contracting costs" involve the relative costs of organizing an activity within a firm or through a system of markets. Without the Bell monopoly, local operating companies would have to negotiate contracts with more than one common carrier. Is this more or less efficient than the current system? The cross-subsidization issue arises because of Bell's practice of basing rates on average costs as well as on the value of the service provided. Regardless of the beneficiaries of this scheme, economists generally oppose cross-subsidization in rate structures, since it leads to deviations from marginal cost pricing. If subsidies are deemed worthwhile, a separate grant that does not distort service rates would be preferred. This may not be possible politically, however, so the internal cross-subsidization scheme is frequently used instead.[42]

It may be desirable to let AT&T keep Bell Labs and Western Electric in order to increase future competition. This argument is based on the common assumption that AT&T's future competition will come from IBM. In this scenario, the communications market of the future will consist of both data processing and voice processing.[43] A strong, vertically integrated AT&T would be able to provide competition against IBM, the dominant firm in the computer industry. Before this could happen, however, it would be necessary to modify AT&T's 1956 consent decree, which prohibits it from entering the unregulated data-processing market. Some firms, however, are worried that AT&T could use profits from its regulated operations to subsidize its prospective operations in unregulated markets. One alternative to dissolution is to require AT&T to establish completely separate subsidiaries for its unregulated activities. It would then be more difficult for AT&T to engage in cross-subsidization without being detected by competitors or regulators.

42. Also, consumers may not want marginal cost pricing. This was illustrated by the futile attempt of Cincinnati Bell to institute a rate structure for local calls that would charge according to their number, distance, and duration. This system was opposed by consumers, however, who preferred the current system of a single monthly charge. See "U.S. Consumer Agency Hits Phone Pricing Plan," *Washington Star*, March 13, 1979, p. E-6. For a more detailed analysis, see B. M. Mitchell, "Optimal Pricing of Local Telephone Service," *American Economic Review* 68 (September 1978): 517–37.

43. "Behind AT&T's Change at the Top—The biggest corporate reorganization in history puts Ma Bell on a collision course with IBM," *Business Week*, November 6, 1978, pp. 114–39.

Broadcasting.   The FCC has proposed to reduce substantially its control over both commercial radio stations and cable television systems. In radio broadcasting, the FCC may eliminate its restrictions on program content and the number of commercials. Currently, FCC regulations specify the minimum amount of "nonentertainment" programming (news and public affairs) that must be carried by commercial radio stations—eight percent of broadcast time for AM stations and six percent for FM stations. In addition, stations are limited to a maximum of 18 minutes of advertising per broadcast hour. The FCC is considering eliminating these rules because a staff study indicated that less than one percent of the stations sampled broadcast the maximum number of commercials, while over 60 percent broadcast more "nonentertainment" programming than required.[44] In effect, competition among radio stations for the listening audience is making these FCC regulations unnecessary.

The relaxation of cable regulations may yield similar results in the television industry. New cable systems have the capacity to offer as many as 24 different channels to subscribers. This can increase the variety of program content, for different channels appeal to different segments of the viewing audience. For example, many cable subscribers can receive 24-hour-a-day VHF stations, all-sports stations, or religious stations. There are plans for a 24-hour cable news network, a channel featuring British Broadcasting Corporation programs, and a network featuring black entertainment.[45] These programs can obviously hurt local over-the-air broadcasters by diverting viewers and reducing their advertising potential. On the other hand, unlimited cable television can provide tremendous diversity for viewers, while simultaneously reducing the need for government regulation.

Finally, many suggestions have been made for altering the present licensing process. One solution long advocated by economists is to use auctions to allocate licenses among competing individuals. In this manner, the substantial profits that currently accrue to station owners would be paid to the government as license fees. This idea has been discussed by the Congress, though it seems unlikely to be put into practice.[46] In any event, licensing will cease to be a major issue if the FCC makes it easier for cable systems to offer competing programming for over-the-air

44. "Liberating Air Time," *Regulation* 3 (July/August 1979): 6.

45. "Television's Fragmented Future," *Business Week*, December 17, 1979, pp. 60–66.

46. "House Panel's Staff Proposes Formula for Broadcast Fees," *Wall Street Journal*, July 24, 1978, p. 14.

broadcasters. Such competition should dramatically reduce the profits that result from the FCC's restrictive licensing policies.

Summary

The communications industry is currently undergoing a dramatic transformation because of changes in technology and government regulation. AT&T is encountering serious competition for the first time since the turn of the century. If predictions are correct, it will soon be competing against IBM, one of the toughest competitors in the manufacturing sector of the economy. At the same time, the broadcasting industry is going through one of its biggest upheavals since the emergence of television as a major communications medium. Deregulation in radio and cable television should benefit consumers—both listeners and viewers—as competition replaces FCC regulation and increases program variety. Some consumers and communications companies may be hurt by these changes, but that is a risk common to all markets where resources are allocated by market forces and not government regulations.

Suggested Readings

Barton, M. F. "Conditional Logit Analysis of FCC Decisionmaking," *Bell Journal of Economics* 10 (Autumn 1979): 399–411.

Bowman, G. W. "Demand and Supply of Network Television Advertising," *Bell Journal of Economics* 7 (Spring 1976): 258–67.

Irwin, M. "The Telephone Industry," in *The Structure of American Industry,* ed. W. Adams, 5th ed. (New York: Macmillan, 1977), pp. 312–33.

MacAvoy, P., ed. *Deregulation of Cable Television* (Washington, D.C.: American Enterprise Institute, 1977).

Noll, R., Peck, M., and McGowan, J. *Economic Aspects of Television Regulation* (Washington, D.C.: Brookings Institution, 1973).

Waverman, L. "The Regulation of Intercity Telecommunications," in *Promoting Competition in Regulated Markets,* ed. A. Phillips (Washington, D.C.: Brookings Institution, 1975), pp. 201–39.

Energy

Chapter 14

Before the oil embargo in 1973, energy was not a very important or controversial issue. Households and businesses annually increased their consumption of energy with little thought about its future supply or price. But after Arab oil-exporting countries temporarily stopped shipments to the United States, Americans became aware of the importance of energy in general and oil in particular. The United States' dependence on imported oil came to be viewed as a threat to economic and political independence. As a result, there have been many proposals for reducing our demand for foreign oil. Some proposals would expand the government's role in the energy sector, while others would reduce it.

The Setting

Energy is a very broad word that is used to describe a diverse sector of the economy. It includes the production of such traditional energy sources as wood, coal, oil, and natural gas, as well as the development of new sources such as solar and geothermal energy. It also includes the transportation and distribution networks that are used to deliver some of these energy sources to their ultimate consumers. For instance, natural gas is transported by pipeline from the producing well to a local gas utility and finally to households and businesses.

Table 14.1   **Primary Energy Consumption by Source, 1900–1977**
(Percentage of total Btu's)[a]

Year	Natural Gas	Oil	Coal	Hydro	Nuclear	Fuel Wood
1977[p]	28.9	45.4	18.5	3.1	3.5	.5
1970	36.5	39.9	18.9	3.9	.3	.4
1960	31.1	41.1	22.3	3.8	.01	1.8
1950	19.7	36.2	36.8	4.0		3.4
1940	11.8	30.2	49.0	3.5		5.5
1930	9.1	25.2	56.2	3.3		6.2
1920	3.7	13.8	71.4	3.7		7.4
1910	3.0	6.1	77.0	3.0		10.9
1900	3.1	2.1	70.8	3.1		20.8

[a] A Btu (British thermal unit) is the standard measure of the heat content of fuels. It is defined as the quantity of heat necessary to raise the temperature of one pound of water one degree Fahrenheit.
[p] Preliminary figures.

Sources: 1. U.S. Department of Commerce, *Historical Statistics of the United States* (Washington, D.C.: Government Printing Office, 1975), p. 588.
2. U.S. Department of Commerce, *Statistical Abstract of the United States, 1978* (Washington, D.C.: Government Printing Office, 1978), pp. 605–6, 734.

The primary energy sources used in the United States, as well as their relative importance, are presented in Table 14.1. These figures indicate the percentage of total energy consumption accounted for by each source since the turn of the century. Coal's share of the energy market declined substantially as the nation increasingly switched to two other fossil fuels—natural gas and oil. Wood has not been a major energy source since the early 1900s, while hydropower seems destined to account for a constant three to four percent of energy consumption. The use of nuclear power is a fairly recent phenomenon, and its share increased rapidly throughout the 1970s.

The History of Energy Regulation

The energy sector of the economy is subject to extensive regulation at both the state and federal levels. The differences in jurisdiction, and hence in function, generally follow from the traditional distinction between intrastate and interstate commerce. A major activity for state governments has been the regulation of local electric and natural gas utilities, while the federal government has devoted considerable time to the regulation of oil and natural gas producers.

As in the trucking industry, regulation of the oil industry was precipitated by the Great Depression. Declining demand, in combination with substantial new oil discoveries in Texas, sharply reduced the price of oil. From 1929 to 1933, the wellhead price of a barrel of oil fell from

$1.27 to $.67.[1] Producers rarely curtailed production, however, because the marginal cost of a barrel of oil from a flowing well is very small. In an effort to control excessive production, the major oil-producing states adopted "prorationing" programs. These programs established the maximum allowable production rates for all the oil wells within each state.[2] By controlling the rate of production, the states could reduce the supply of oil on the market. At the same time, controls prevented producers from withdrawing oil too rapidly and decreasing the ultimate yield from their reservoirs.[3]

State regulation was thus consistent with basic conservation principles. It was also very profitable. Through prorationing programs, the state conservation agencies—especially the Texas Railroad Commission—determined the market price of oil. The Texas commission, for example, set production rates so that the supply forthcoming would just equal the expected market demand. The federal government gave its blessing to this scheme with the passage of the Connally Hot Oil Act in 1935. This act made it illegal to ship in interstate commerce any oil that was produced in excess of a states's production rate. As a result, the domestic price of oil was increased to the point where it exceeded the world price.

As could have been expected, the higher U.S. price attracted imports of foreign oil, which threatened to undermine the prorationing system. This threat was soon eliminated, however. A voluntary import quota was established in 1957 and a mandatory one in 1959. The underlying rationale was national defense: the quota was necessary to protect domestic producers and preserve a domestic oil capability.[4] The overall impact was to create a price differential between the domestic and for-

1. U.S. Department of Commerce, *Historical Statistics of the United States: Colonial Times to 1970* (Washington, D.C.: Government Printing Office, 1975), Part 1, p. 593.

2. The states estimated the rate of production that would maximize the long-run output from a given reservoir, called the *maximum efficient rate* (MER). Producers were allowed to produce at some percentage of this rate. Some states also adopted policies that encouraged *unitization*, whereby a single reservoir would be developed jointly by its owners. Otherwise, each owner might try to increase production at the expense of the other owners, eventually reducing the total amount of oil that could be recovered from the reservoir.

3. The total amount of oil that can be recovered from a reservoir will decrease if the actual production rate exceeds the maximum efficient rate for prolonged periods of time.

4. This argument is questionable because the quotas will increase current production at the expense of future production, thereby increasing future dependence on imports. This policy has thus been called a "Drain America First Policy." For an analysis of this program, see K. W. Dam, "Implementation of Import Quotas: The Case of Oil," *Journal of Law and Economics* 14 (April 1971): 1–60.

eign prices of oil. In 1970, for example, the domestic wellhead price was $3.30 per barrel, compared with a world price of $2.00 per barrel.[5]

This situation changed dramatically just three years later with the embargo by Arab oil-exporting nations. When the embargo ended in early 1974, the world price of oil had increased beyond the American domestic price. The nature of government regulation of oil was also affected by the embargo. In November of 1973, Congress passed the Emergency Petroleum Allocation Act, establishing federal price controls and allocation regulations for crude oil and refined products. The goal of government regulation was thus shifted from maintaining a price floor for crude oil to establishing a price ceiling. These regulations are currently administered by the Department of Energy (DOE)—a new Cabinet department that was formed during the crisis from the Federal Energy Administration and the Energy Research and Development Administration.[6]

The Department of Energy also became responsible for the pricing of natural gas.[7] Federal regulation of the field or wellhead price of natural gas was mandated by a Supreme Court decision in 1954.[8] Up to that time, the Federal Power Commission (FPC) regulated only the interstate transmission and sale for resale of natural gas.[9] Regulation was instituted to prevent pipeline companies from exploiting their monopoly position in the supply of natural gas to local distribution utilities. Consuming states argued that the production of natural gas was not competitive and that the FPC should also regulate the field price of natural gas. The FPC, however, argued that the Natural Gas Act of 1938 did not empower it actually to set the field price of natural gas. The Supreme Court disagreed, thereby extending federal regulation to natural gas fields throughout the United States. Natural gas sold in intrastate markets (e.g., Texas, Louisiana), however, was not subject to FPC regulation. Nuclear power, undoubtedly the most controversial energy source, also is regulated by DOE along with the Nuclear Regulatory Commission

5. Cabinet Task Force on Oil Import Control, *The Oil Import Question* (Washington, D.C.: Government Printing Office, February 1970), p. 19.

6. The Department of Energy was established in 1977. It consolidated energy programs from the Interior Department, the Interstate Commerce Commission, and the Department of Housing and Urban Development.

7. Natural gas pricing is controlled by the Federal Energy Regulatory Commission, an independent agency within the Department of Energy. This agency has authority to over-rule the department's policies on oil pricing and allocation.

8. *Phillips Petroleum Co.* v. *Wisconsin*, 347 U.S. 672 (1954).

9. Oil pipelines have been regulated by the government since 1910, first by the Interstate Commerce Commission and more recently by the Department of Energy.

(NRC). DOE is responsible for federal funding of nuclear research projects, while NRC handles the licensing of nuclear power plants.[10]

The Economics of Energy

The "energy crisis" focused an unusual amount of public attention on the basic supply and demand conditions in energy markets. When analyzing these markets, however, it should always be remembered that the different energy sources are not homogeneous and therefore not perfect substitutes. There is substantial heterogeneity even within a given energy source. Oil, for example, can vary in heat and sulfur content as well as in the costs of drilling.

The Demand for Energy. The overall demand for energy can be analyzed conveniently as the sum of the demands of the various consuming sectors. In 1978, for example, 28 percent of primary energy consumption was attributed to the residential and commercial sector and 28 percent to the industrial sector.[11] The remaining 43 percent was divided between the transportation sector (20 percent) and electricity generation (23 percent). These figures indicate that the demand for energy in general, and for specific energy sources in particular, is a derived demand. It depends on the exact energy requirements of each consuming sector. Changes in these requirements will lead to changes in the demand for energy. This was illustrated earlier by the consumption data in Table 14.1. The dramatic decline in the use of coal and fuel wood since the turn of the century was partially attributable to the increased utilization of oil and natural gas furnaces by households and of industrial boilers by businesses. At the same time, the introduction of automobiles, airplanes, and diesel trains further increased oil's share of the total energy market. The future demand for energy thus depends on the future energy requirements of millions of American consumers and producers.

The Supply of Energy. As every economics student is aware, however, a specific energy source's share of the energy market is not based exclusively on demand considerations. Supply conditions are equally important. At the extreme, if an energy source is not available, it cannot be consumed. For example, in parts of the United States during the 1970s, local distribution utilities could not get enough natural gas from their

10. Both responsibilities had originally been vested in the Atomic Energy Commission.

11. U.S. Department of Commerce, *Statistical Abstract of the United States, 1979* (Washington, D.C.: Government Printing Office, 1979), p. 602.

suppliers.[12] As a result, they could not connect new customers and, in some cases, had to curtail supplies to existing customers.

The natural gas shortage, in combination with the Arab oil embargo, emphasized the crucial role of these two nonrenewable fossil fuels in the nation's economy. Unfortunately, America's oil and natural gas capability does not look very promising. Table 14.2 presents some data on the domestic supply of oil and natural gas since the turn of the century. Domestic production of oil peaked in 1970, while production of natural gas peaked two years later in 1972.[13] Proved reserves of these two fuels have also peaked and are likely to continue to decline.[14] This deteriorating domestic supply situation is reflected in the increased importation of foreign oil and natural gas. In 1978, for example, imports equaled 71.6 percent of domestic oil production and 4.9 percent of natural gas production. As recently as 1970, these figures were only 13.7 percent and 3.7 percent, respectively. The energy problem is thus of fairly recent origin.

The economic basis for importing foreign oil (and natural gas) is illustrated graphically in Figure 14.1, which presents the domestic supply and demand curves for oil. Without trade, the market-clearing price is P_d and output is Q_d. If the world price (P_w) is below the domestic price P_d, it will be economical for this country to import some or all of its oil.[15] In this particular case, domestic consumption will increase to Q_2, while domestic production decreases from Q_d to Q_1. The domestic price would then equal the world price and the country would import $Q_2 - Q_1$ barrels of oil. The magnitude of the oil imports depends on the difference between the domestic and world prices, as well as on the price elasticities

12. A similar situation holds for hydropower, where the constraint is the availability of suitable river sites.

13. There is some relationship between the two because natural gas is normally a joint product with oil, though natural gas is also found by itself.

14. *Proved reserves* are defined as the maximum recovery possible given current technological and economic conditions. Reserves thus vary with changes in production technology and changes in the prices of oil and natural gas. Higher prices increase proved reserves because they make it profitable to use secondary recovery techniques. It should be noted that these estimates are not very exact. As one oil expert noted:

> Estimating oil reserves is like guessing the number of beans in a jar—only the jars are buried deep underground and you aren't even sure exactly where they are hidden (*Time*, May 9, 1977, p. 76).

In sum, even though the world's supply of fossil fuels is finite, it is very difficult to estimate the total amount that may be ultimately recovered.

15. It is implicitly assumed that the supply of oil is perfectly elastic, so that the country can import all the oil that it wants at P_w. This assumption is appropriate for small countries, but not for large ones such as the United States.

Table 14.2 Domestic Supply of Oil and Natural Gas, 1900–1978

Year	Oil (billions of barrels[a])			Natural Gas (trillions of cubic feet)		
	Production	Imports	Proved Reserves	Production	Imports	Proved Reserves
1978[p]	3.178	2.275	27.804	19.661	.965	200.000
1970	3.517	.483	39.001	21.921	.821	290.746
1960	2.575	.372	31.613	12.771	.156	262.326
1950	1.974	.178	25.268	6.282		184.585
1940	1.353	.043	19.023	2.734		85.000
1930	.898	.062	13.600	1.979		46.000
1920	.443	.106	7.200	.812		
1910	.210		4.500	.509		
1900	.063		2.900	.128		

[a] A barrel contains 42 gallons.
[p] Preliminary figures.
Sources: 1. U.S. Department of Commerce, *Historical Statistics of the United States* (Washington, D.C.: Government Printing Office, 1975), pp. 593–95.
2. U.S. Department of Commerce, *Statistical Abstract of the United States, 1979* (Washington, D.C.: Government Printing Office, 1979), pp. 759, 763.

Figure 14.1 The Supply and Demand for Oil

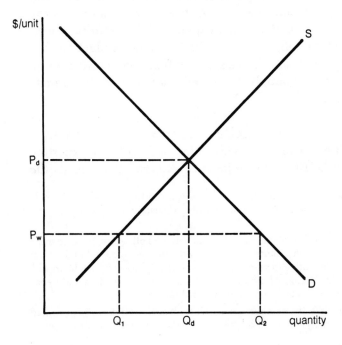

of demand and supply. Other things being equal, oil imports will be larger, the more elastic the demand and supply as price decreases from P_d to P_w.

The shape and position of the domestic supply curve depends on several different factors. First is the number and type of producing wells. Oil wells are classified according to the means used to bring oil to the surface. In "natural drive" wells, natural gas pressure within the oil reservoir forces the oil to the surface. When the gas pressure weakens over time, it can be increased by the reinjection of natural gas, water, or chemicals. These "secondary recovery" techniques increase total oil production, but also increase drilling costs. Whether or not firms adopt these techniques will depend on the price of oil. Second, the position of the supply curve over time depends on the rate of production from existing oil fields as well as the discovery of new ones. If current oil production exceeds the discovery of new reserves, proved reserves will decrease, thereby decreasing the maximum future rate of production. (Conversely, if production is less than new reserves, proved reserves will increase and future production can be greater.) Finally, the position of the supply curve is also affected by the time preferences of oil producers. Quite simply, if a barrel of oil is produced today, it cannot be produced tomorrow.[16] A high rate of current production can also reduce the total amount of oil that can ultimately be obtained from a reservoir. For example, if two producers share an oil reservoir, each one has an incentive to maximize production at the expense of the other producer. If one doesn't take out the oil, the other will. The total production over the reservoir's lifetime will thus be less than if there were a single producer.[17] In sum, the market supply curve of oil depends on the interaction of these three factors.

The Role of OPEC. The decline of the American oil industry is in marked contrast to the rise of the Organization of Petroleum Exporting Countries (OPEC).[18] OPEC is the infamous oil cartel that adjusts the

16. This is a major concern for OPEC countries such as Kuwait and Saudi Arabia, which do not want to bankrupt future generations by prematurely exhausting their most important natural resource.

17. As noted in footnote 2, this was the rationale for unitization of oil reservoirs. Under the "rule of capture" enunciated by the courts, producers were entitled to the oil under their own land. This created the incentive to pump the reservoir dry before your neighbors did. A similar problem exists in fishing, where overfishing may reduce breeding and hence future yields. Independent action is thus restricted by fishing permits.

18. OPEC was formed in 1960. Its members are Saudi Arabia, Kuwait, Iran, Iraq, United Arab Emirates, Libya, Nigeria, Venezuela, Indonesia, Algeria, Ecuador, Qatar, and Gabon.

world price of oil at its semiannual meetings. OPEC can control the price of oil because of its dominant position in the world petroleum market. As Table 14.3 indicates, one member alone, Saudi Arabia, controls approximately one-fourth of the world's proved reserves of oil. OPEC was not always a successful cartel; it was only during the Yom Kippur war in 1973 that it truly became united and flexed its oil muscles.[19] From January 1, 1973 to January 1, 1974, it raised the official price of oil from $2.59 to $10.95 per barrel—an increase of 323 percent![20] In 1979 alone, the price nearly doubled—from $13.34 on January 1, 1979, to $26 on January 1, 1980.[21]

The rapid and substantial increases in the price of oil have focused worldwide attention on non-OPEC energy sources. Figure 14.2 illustrates the relative costs of different energy options as of March 1979. Middle Eastern countries were clearly the low-cost producers of oil, with unit costs of less than $1 per barrel. North Sea and Alaskan oil were economical only at substantially higher prices. But alternative energy sources such as coal gasification and solar hot water were far less efficient. The attractiveness of these options, however, obviously depends on the price of oil. As the price increases, it increases the desirability of less productive oil fields and less efficient energy sources. (Even by the end of 1979, the doubling of oil prices has already made these comparisons outdated!)

The Risk Factor.   One final, but controversial aspect of the supply of energy concerns the risk element—the threat that the utilization of different energy sources poses to human lives. The most obvious examples are liquefied natural gas (LNG) and nuclear power. Natural gas as a liquid is transported on special ships. In this form, natural gas is extremely explosive and could cause considerable damage as it is unloaded near population centers. The risk posed by nuclear power has received more attention, especially after the accident at Three Mile Island, Pennsylvania, in 1979. The main fear is not a nuclear explosion (which is impossible) but a "meltdown." If the primary and emergency cooling systems were to malfunction, the nuclear reactor's uranium core would overheat and eventually discharge radioactive gases into the surround-

19. A major turning point was the oil embargo initiated by the Arab members of OPEC—Saudi Arabia, Kuwait, Iraq, United Arab Emirates, Libya, Algeria, and Qatar.

20. The OPEC price is for the "benchmark" or light oil sold by Saudi Arabia. This oil is low in sulfur and more easily refined than other oil, which sells for a lower price.

21. There currently is no single OPEC price. Different producers have been charging different prices since they have been unable to reach agreement on a single price.

Table 14.3   Proved Reserves of Oil and Natural Gas, 1979

Area and Country	Crude Oil[a]	Natural Gas[b]
Western Hemisphere	96	426
United States	39	219
Canada	8	71
Mexico	30	46
Venezuela*	14	43
Other	5	47
Middle East	384	845
Saudi Arabia*	150	106
Kuwait*	71	35
Iran*	60	600
Iraq*	36	35
United Arab Emirates*	34	35
Other	33	34
Africa	59	211
Libya*	25	25
Nigeria*	19	46
Algeria*	7	127
Other	8	13
Western Europe	31	177
United Kingdom	20	46
Norway	8	25
Other	3	106
Asia-Pacific	22	105
Indonesia*	14	21
Other	8	84
Communist countries	65	862
USSR	40	812
China	20	25
Other	5	25
World	657	2,626

[a] Billions of barrels.
[b] Trillions of cubic feet.
*OPEC member.
Source: Central Intelligence Agency, "International Energy Statistical Review," February 7, 1979, p. 4.

ing atmosphere, causing almost unlimited damage to neighboring areas. A new dimension was added to this debate over risk by the publication in 1979 of a study examining the relative risks of different energy sources.[22] Inhaber concluded that nuclear power was less risky than most other energy sources, reasoning that conventional energy sources such as coal impose high costs on society because of pollution damage

22. Herbert Inhaber, "Risk with Energy from Conventional and Nonconventional Sources," *Science* 203 (February 23, 1979): 718–23.

Figure 14.2   **The Great Energy Dilemma**

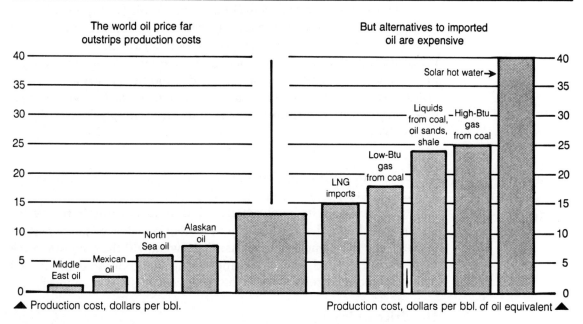

Data: Shell Briefing Service, BW
Reprinted from the March 12, 1979 issue of *Business Week* by
special permission, © 1979 by McGraw-Hill, Inc. All rights reserved.

and occupational injuries. Regardless of the outcome of this controversial debate, it is clear that no source of energy is riskless.

The Marketing of Energy.   The discussion so far has focused exclusively on the production of oil and natural gas, ignoring their transportation and ultimate distribution to consumers. Both these fuels are transported and distributed through an extensive network of interstate and intrastate pipelines. In 1978, for example, there were 1,013,000 miles of natural gas pipelines.[23] Of this total, 75,000 miles of pipeline were used to gather gas from different producing wells, and 261,000 miles were used to send it to consuming centers where it was distributed through 678,000 miles of pipelines. These distribution systems served approximately 46 million customers, most of them residential consumers in the midwestern and northeastern sections of the country.

Natural gas, like oil, can also provide energy indirectly through the generation of electricity. It is not the leading fuel for electric utilities, although it is an important source of energy. In 1978, utilities' consump-

23. U.S. Department of Commerce, *Statistical Abstract, 1979*, p. 614.

tion of energy was divided among the following sources: coal (44.4 percent), hydro (12.7 percent), gas (13.8 percent), oil (16.5 percent), and nuclear (12.5 percent).[24] Once the electricity is generated, it is sent by transmission lines to one or more distribution networks. A local electric utility may perform all three of these functions, or it may simply purchase the electricity from another utility and then distribute it to its customers. This latter system is more common in small towns than in large cities, where privately owned utilities supply most of the electricity.

Major Regulatory Issues

Throughout the 1970s, the government became increasingly involved in the energy sector of the economy. Unless recently passed laws are subsequently modified, its involvement will diminish greatly in the 1980s. For the time being, however, the government remains an active participant in three basic energy decisions: First, what will the domestic price of energy be? Second, how will available energy supplies be distributed among competing users? Third, who will provide these resources?

The Price of Energy

The government is involved in the rate-making process at all three stages of the energy supply function: production, transportation, and distribution. It determines the field or wellhead price of oil and natural gas. It sets the pipeline rates for the interstate shipment of those fuels. Finally, it establishes the rate levels and rate structures of local distribution utilities.

Production. The government has regulated the field price of natural gas since 1954 and that of oil since 1971.[25] There are many similarities between natural gas and oil; they are substitutes for some consumption purposes and are frequently produced jointly.[26] Emphasis will be

24. U.S. Department of Commerce, *Statistical Abstract, 1979*, p. 608.

25. As noted earlier, the field price of natural gas sold in interstate commerce became regulated because of the Supreme Court's decision in *Phillips Petroleum* v. *Wisconsin*, 347 U.S. 672 (1954). Federal regulation was subsequently extended to intrastate natural gas markets by the Natural Gas Policy Act of 1978. Federal regulation of oil prices was initiated with the establishment of President Richard Nixon's price stabilization program in 1971.

26. Natural gas and oil compete in the home heating market, where owners of a new house may install a gas or oil furnace. Once this decision is made, however, it is not easy or cheap to switch between the two fuels. The greatest substitution possibilities occur in industries, especially electricity generation, where natural gas and oil are used as boiler fuels.

placed on the government's longer experience with the regulation of natural gas.

Federal regulation of the price of natural gas was mandated by the Supreme Court in 1954.[27] This ruling posed a major problem for the Federal Power Commission, for there were thousands of natural gas producers scattered throughout the United States. As traditional public utility regulation was administratively impossible, the FPC adopted a system of area-wide pricing.[28] On the basis of production cost similarities, the FPC divided the United States into 23 natural gas-producing regions and then established a separate two-tier price structure for each region. There was one price ceiling for gas currently being produced ("old" gas) and a separate, higher price ceiling for gas from new wells ("new" gas). For example, in 1961 the FPC set a price of 14.5 cents per 1,000 cubic feet (Mcf) of old gas and 16.5 cents per Mcf of new gas for the Permian Basin—one of the largest American natural gas fields, covering nearly 100,000 square miles in Texas and New Mexico. The rationale behind this two-tier price system was both to prevent owners of existing wells from receiving "windfall" profits, and to provide an incentive for the discovery and exploitation of new gas fields.[29] The two-tier system was retained when a single national price structure replaced the different area structures in 1974.[30]

The simple two-tier price structure was short-lived, however. The Natural Gas Policy Act of 1978 created more than two dozen different categories of natural gas for pricing purposes. More important, it also ordered the decontrol of the price of new natural gas on January 1, 1985.[31]

The government's price regulations for oil are similar to those for natural gas. They also differentiate between "old" and "new" production. In addition, there is an exemption for oil from "stripper" wells—wells with a daily output of 10 barrels or less. The decontrol program for oil is

27. *Phillips Petroleum Co. v. Wisconsin*, 347 U.S. 672 (1954).

28. *Permian Basin Area Rate Cases*, 390 U.S. 747 (1968). The FPC has since been replaced by the Federal Energy Regulatory Commission (FERC), part of the Department of Energy.

29. The basic assumption is that the price elasticity of supply for old gas is less than that for new gas.

30. *Opinion and Order Prescribing Uniform National Rate*, Federal Power Commission Opinion No. 699, issued June 21, 1974.

31. After price controls have been removed for a six-month period, either the Congress or the President can reimpose controls if they feel that prices are rising too rapidly. These controls would last for 18 months. By December 31, 1988, all controls on new gas will be removed unless Congress passes a law reestablishing price controls.

somewhat different from that for natural gas, however. First, decontrol is set for an earlier date. New oil (oil from wells that began production after June 1, 1979) is already free to sell at the world price, while all oil will be decontrolled by October 1, 1981.[32] Second, President Carter sought, and Congress passed, a tax on "windfall" profits to complement the decontrol program. The tax was designed both to prevent the oil companies from benefiting too much from deregulation and to provide funds for government energy programs.

Transportation.   Oil and natural gas pipelines have long been subject to regulation by the Interstate Commerce Commission (1906) and the Federal Power Commission (1938), respectively. Federal authority was subsequently delegated to the Federal Energy Regulatory Commission (FERC), a part of the recently formed Department of Energy. The central feature of pipeline regulation is traditional public utility rate-making. The government determines a pipeline's rate base, rate level, and rate structure. The ICC, for example, allowed crude pipelines an 8 percent return and product pipelines a 10 percent return on the "fair value" of their investment, where "fair value" is historical cost adjusted for inflation. These proceedings were normally quite bland and attracted little attention. That atmosphere changed with the construction of the Alaskan oil pipeline and the submission of several requests for natural gas pipelines in Alaska. These pipelines necessitate the expenditure of billions of dollars and are subject to more risk than pipelines in the continental United States. The attractiveness of these investments to private firms will depend greatly on the rate-making principles adopted by the FERC.[33]

Distribution.   Government regulations currently determine the retail price of both natural gas and gasoline, a refined oil product. The retail price of natural gas, as well as electricity, has traditionally been set by state public service commissions. Users are divided into customer categories (such as residential, commercial, industrial) and then charged according to the rate schedule for that class. Recently, however, the federal government has become more actively involved in local rate-

32. Approximately two-thirds of the oil consumed in the United States is already sold at the world price, leaving one-third to be decontrolled by 1981 ("House Kills Bid For Price Reins On Domestic Oil," *Wall Street Journal*, October 12, 1979, p. 4).

33. FERC recently established its rate-making principles in *Trans-Alaska Pipeline System*, Docket No. OR78-1, issued February 1, 1980.

making. First, the natural gas deregulation law has shifted most of the burden of higher prices to industrial users. Utilities must establish "incremental" pricing systems that increase industrial natural gas prices until fuel oil becomes competitive. At that point, further price increases are spread among all users—residential, commercial, and industrial. The purpose of this price structure is to soften the impact of deregulation on residential consumers. Second, local utilities are required by federal law to examine rate structures that would encourage energy conservation. The most obvious rate structure is peak load pricing. The New England Electric System, for example, charges residential consumers 60 percent less for electricity used during the off-peak period of 9:00 P.M. to 8:00 A.M.[34] This pricing system can reduce the demand for new power plants, while increasing the utilization of existing plants.

The federal government is most actively involved in determining gasoline price ceilings for the nation's 200,000-plus gasoline stations. It has devised a complex formula based on the gas station price in May 1973 (before the oil embargo) plus subsequent cost increases. A station can, for example, increase its gasoline price to reflect increases in both its operating expenses and the wholesale price of gasoline. In 1979 the Energy Department increased a dealer's maximum markup to 15.4 cents per gallon.[35] At the same time, it discontinued the controversial policy of permitting dealers to "bank" allowed price increases and use them in future years. Under that policy, if a dealer did not charge the maximum price allowed, it could "bank" the price difference and add it to the ceiling price later. This system led to substantial price increases during the 1979 gas shortage, producing tremendous variations in prices among local dealers.

The Demand for Energy

In addition to affecting energy demand indirectly through the price mechanism, the government also directly affects the demand for energy in general and specific energy sources in particular. In mid-1979, for example, President Carter ordered thermostats in most nonresidential

34. "New England Electric System: 'Embracing the Conservation Ethic'," *Business Week*, December 10, 1979, pp. 119-20. Also, see J.T. Wenders and L.D. Taylor, "Experiments in Seasonal-Time-of-Day Pricing of Electricity to Residential Users," *Bell Journal of Economics* 7 (Autumn 1976): 531-52.

35. "U.S. Agency Allowing Gasoline Dealers A 15.4-Cent-a-Gallon Maximum Markup," *Wall Street Journal*, July 17, 1979, p.3.

buildings to be set at 78° in the summer and 65° in the winter.[36] The Energy Department also banned the installation of new outdoor gaslights and required the elimination of gas supplies for existing lights.[37] DOE also has the authority, under the Industrial Fuel Use Act of 1978, to require new plants to use coal and existing plants to convert to coal. Finally, the government has forced private industry, notably the automobile manufacturers, to increase the energy efficiency of many products. For example, by 1985, each auto company's new car fleet must average 27 miles per gallon.

The Supply of Energy

The federal government has a major hand in determining the domestic supply of energy and its allocation among users. Supply is partially determined by pricing regulations for oil and natural gas and by import policies for these two fuels. For instance, President Carter imposed quotas on the importation of oil; in 1979, imports could not exceed a daily average of 8.2 million barrels. Also in 1979, the government negotiated an agreement to import gas from Mexico at $3.63 per Mcf. This agreement concluded two years of negotiations that had become deadlocked over the contract price of natural gas.

In the event of a national emergency, the government can augment the oil supply of private companies with its Strategic Petroleum Reserve. Under the Energy Policy and Conservation Act of 1975, the government was authorized to store a three-months supply of oil, which could be used to partially offset the effects of any future embargo by oil producers. The reserve—since doubled from the original 500 million barrels to one billion barrels—was to be stored underground in salt caverns along the Gulf Coast. The project was subject to substantial cost overruns, however, and fell behind schedule. As of October 1979, the reserve consisted of 92 million barrels—slightly more than *one week's* imports.[38]

Government regulations determine how the nation's supply of crude and refined petroleum products is allocated among users. These regula-

36. "Carter Imposes Mandatory Curbs on Thermostats," *Wall Street Journal*, July 11, 1979, p.5.

37. "Energy Department Adopts Rule Banning Gas in Outdoor Lights," *Wall Street Journal*, May 10, 1979, p.4.

38. Comptroller General of the United States, "U.S. Strategic Petroleum Reserve at a Turning Point," EMD-80-19, January 2, 1980, p.2.

tions were required by the Emergency Petroleum Allocation Act of 1973. Two regulations of particular importance are the supplier/purchaser freeze and the "entitlements" program. The supplier/purchaser freeze required suppliers to offer buyers the same volume of products as they had in 1972, the base year for the allocation program. Buyers were not required to purchase the same volume, however. The Department of Energy currently allocates gasoline using a base period of November 1977–October 1978.

The "entitlements" program was designed to equalize the average cost of crude oil supplies across refiners. With the divergence between world and domestic prices of crude oil, a refiner's costs depended on its input mix of domestic and foreign crude oil. The entitlements program tries to spread the low-cost domestic oil among refiners, giving each refiner a guarantee of its share of controlled domestic oil. Small refiners are granted additional entitlements to improve their competitive position vis-à-vis the major refiners.

Finally, government regulations determine what firms are allowed to supply energy. More specifically, the issue is the extent to which oil companies are allowed to diversify into non-oil energy sources. Table 14.4 presents data on the diversification of the major oil companies among oil, coal, and uranium. As of 1979, eleven oil companies owned 25 percent of the total coal reserves in the United States.[39] Although there have been many proposals to restrict the entry of oil companies into other energy sources, such expansion is currently legal unless it violates the antitrust laws. The Justice Department generally views the diversification process as being procompetitive, not anticompetitive.[40]

Evaluation

In the mid-1970s, there were severe shortages of natural gas in many sections of the country. In the spring of 1979, gasoline shortages became common from California to New York. And from 1973 to 1978, American annual imports of oil approximately doubled, from 1.18 to 2.27 billion barrels.[41] The "energy crisis" is obviously not over. As a result, strong criticisms have been directed toward existing policies and almost unlimited suggestions made for their modification.

39. "The Oil Majors Bet On Coal," *Business Week*, September 24, 1979, p. 106.

40. "Justice Unit Says Oil, Nuclear Firms Should Be Allowed to Be in Coal Business," *Wall Street Journal*, May 16, 1978, p. 8.

41. U.S. Department of Commerce, *Statistical Abstract, 1979*, p. 605.

Table 14.4   Btu Reserves by Firm, 1975[a]

Firm	Total Btu Reserves (trillions of Btu's)	Percentage of Total Reserves Oil	Coal	Uranium
Exxon	253,430	18.4	78.6	3.0
Texaco	79,676	40.4	59.6	0
Shell	138,653	43.0	57.0	0
Standard of Indiana	23,939	100.0	0	0
Gulf	110,259	12.8	56.0	31.2
Standard of California	18,880	93.2	0	6.8
Atlantic Richfield	78,192	33.2	66.8	0
Mobil	72,907	18.6	81.4	0
Getty	21,538	60.1	0	39.9
Sun	63,205	14.7	85.3	0
Union	10,898	100.0	0	0
Phillips	62,273	15.2	76.1	8.6
Continental	333,768	1.9	94.9	3.2
Cities Service	9,043	100.0	0	0
Marathon	6,979	100.0	0	0
Amerada Hess	4,668	100.0	0	0
Tenneco	45,443	11.2	88.8	0
La. Land & Exploration	2,348	100.0	0	0
Pennzoil	2,776	100.0	0	0
Superior	4,642	100.0	0	0
Union Pacific	240,943	0.6	98.5	0.9
Sante Fe	9,627	8.8	91.2	0
International Paper	943	100.0	0	0
Kerr McGee	129,977	0.9	51.1	48.0
Standard of Ohio	53,892	60.8	35.2	4.0
General American	1,217	100.0	0	0
Ashland	22,733	6.1	93.9	0
American Petrofina	517	100.0	0	0
Diamond Shamrock	1,840	100.0	0	0

[a] A Btu (British thermal unit) is a measure of the energy content of different fuels. It is defined as the quantity of heat required to raise the temperature of one pound of water one degree Fahrenheit.
Source: Mark Frederiksen, "Patterns of Inter-Fuel Diversification by Petroleum Firms" (Paper presented at the Eastern Economics Conference, Spring 1977), p. 14, Table VI.

Appraisal of Current Policy

The main criticism of current energy policies is that they have worsened the energy crisis by interfering with the market process, adversely af-

Figure 14.3 Government Regulation of Natural Gas

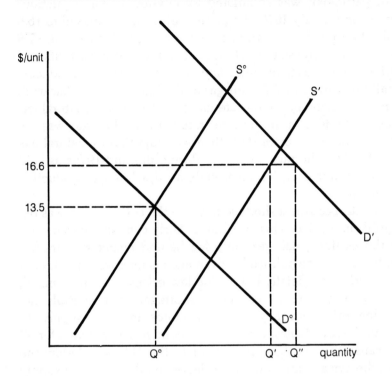

fecting the normal market forces of supply and demand. A brief discussion of this argument follows.[42]

The Price of Energy. Economists rarely advocate price controls, whether they are for agriculture, apartments, or energy. The reason is clearly illustrated by the American experience with the regulation of the price of natural gas.[43] Federal regulation began in 1954, although area-wide price ceilings were not adopted until 1960. At that time, the average price of natural gas was 13.5 cents per thousand cubic feet (Mcf) and, as Figure 14.3 illustrates, the market was in equilibrium. Through-

42. For more detailed analysis of energy policies, see Edward Erickson and Leonard Waverman, eds., *The Energy Question: An International Failure of Policy* (Toronto: University of Toronto Press, 1974), vols. 1 & 2.

43. P. MacAvoy, "The Regulation-Induced Shortage of Natural Gas," *Journal of Law and Economics* 14 (April 1971): 167–200.

out the 1960s, both demand (D′) and supply (S′) shifted to the right. Demand, in particular, was stimulated by environmental regulations and the price controls. By 1970, the price ceiling had increased to 16.6 cents, an absolute increase of 23.0 percent but a real decrease of −7.6 percent.[44] The real decrease in price began to affect drilling activity and the dedication of new gas to the interstate market. Natural gas producers quite logically preferred to sell their gas at the higher prices that were available in the unregulated intrastate markets. As a result, natural gas shortages began to develop in the interstate market. More gas was demanded at the controlled price (Q″) than was supplied by natural gas companies (Q′). The shortage worsened during the mid-1970s as cold weather and economic growth increased demand, while gas production had peaked in 1972.

The price control caused a shortage because the ceiling price was below the equilibrium price. This situation is fairly common, because increases in the ceiling price generally lag behind changes in market conditions. It may also be politically advantageous for government regulators to keep prices artificially low.[45] The low prices increase demand, but decrease supply, thereby causing a shortage. Price controls can guarantee a low price, but they cannot guarantee an ample supply. In the case of oil, the low domestic price actually increased demand for oil imports. Because the average price of oil in the U.S. was below the world price, the price controls in effect decreased the domestic supply of oil, and so increased the demand for foreign oil! This is not the way to solve the energy crisis.

Decontrol of oil (1981) and new gas (1985) has been a very controversial issue.[46] While everyone agrees that decontrol will make oil and gas production more profitable, many disagree about the expected impact of the higher, deregulated prices on consumption and production. In economic terms, what are the price elasticities of demand and supply? The

44. U.S. Department of Commerce, *Statistical Abstract, 1979*, p. 604.

45. In many states, government regulators are elected officials who are more responsive to political pressure from consumers than from utilities. Officials may thus jeopardize the financial health of local utilities in order to be reelected to the state public service commission.

46. For an analysis of natural gas deregulation, see W. Mead, "The Natural Gas Policy Act of 1978: An Economic Evaluation," in *Contemporary Economic Problems, 1979*, ed. W. Fellner (Washington, D.C.: American Enterprise Institute, 1979), pp. 325-55; and for oil deregulation, see K. Arrow and J. Kalt, *Petroleum Price Regulation—Should We Decontrol?* (Washington, D.C.: American Enterprise Institute, 1979).

demand for energy is undoubtedly very inelastic.[47] Consumption has responded to the higher prices, however. The nation's annual increase in demand for electricity has been approximately halved from its pre-1973 rate of 7 percent. And, from 1973 to 1976, industrial consumption of energy per unit of output decreased by 13 percent.[48] The question now is how much more industry and consumers can reduce their consumption in response to higher prices. The elasticity of supply is surely positive. Beyond that, it is impossible to predict the supply response, given the uncertain nature of the oil and gas industries. Since the discovery in 1968 of the Prudhoe Bay oil field in Alaska, there have been no new commercial discoveries, even though approximately 200 wells have been drilled.[49] And in the Baltimore Canyon off the East Coast, oil companies have paid the federal government over one billion dollars for the right to drill, but the results to date have been very discouraging. Overall, the higher price will increase drilling activity, but it is not certain how much new oil and gas will be found.[50] Deregulation will not increase domestic oil and gas production to their old levels, but it will slow down the rate of decline. And this will, in turn, reduce America's demand for foreign oil and natural gas.

The Demand for Energy.   Direct government controls on energy demand illustrate the equity issues raised by energy policies. The obvious goal of these controls is to reduce energy consumption. A given reduction can be obtained by imposing a tax or mandatory restrictions on use. The difference is that the tax approach preserves the right to consume energy, whereas the direct control prohibits it. The tax is thus consistent with consumer sovereignty, even though not all consumers will have sufficient income to participate in the marketplace. This issue was ad-

47. There have been many studies of the price elasticity of demand for energy. See, for example, L. D. Taylor, "The Demand for Electricity: A Survey," *Bell Journal of Economics* 6, (Spring 1975): 74–110; R. Halvorsen, "Energy Substitution in U.S. Manufacturing," *Review of Economics and Statistics* 59 (November 1977): 381–88; and J. Ramsey, R. Rasche, and B. Allen, "An Analysis of the Private and Commercial Demand for Gasoline," *Review of Economics and Statistics* 57 (November 1975): 502–7.

48. "Energy-Saving Efforts By Industry Diminish Effect of Oil-Price Rise," *Wall Street Journal,* January 17, 1979, p. 1.

49. "After 200 Dry Holes, Oil Companies Turn Cool Toward Alaska." *Wall Street Journal,* November 26, 1979, p. 1.

50. "Escalating Energy Prices Spur Oilmen to Try Exotic Oil-Recovery Techniques," *Wall Street Journal,* March 4, 1980, p. 20; and "Price Decontrol for Natural Gas Found at 15,000 Feet or More Spurs Exploration," *Wall Street Journal,* March 27, 1980, p. 46.

dressed when Congress considered taxing or banning "gas guzzlers." A total ban would have spread the sacrifice among all car buyers, while a tax still permits people to drive large cars, if they are willing to pay for them. Given Americans' traditional general preference for large cars, it is not surprising that Congress imposed a tax instead of a total ban on large cars.

The Supply of Energy.   Most of the government's policies toward supply have been strongly criticized. First, it is generally agreed that the import quotas will not be binding for several years, giving the administration time to determine how the quota program will be administered. It should be noted, however, that quotas play a limited role in the energy crisis. They will definitely reduce demand for foreign oil, but at what cost?[51] If there are still price controls on oil and natural gas, the quotas will lead to a domestic shortage. If oil and gas are decontrolled, the quotas will put upward pressure on domestic prices, thereby increasing the price of energy to consumers. In short, do the benefits of quotas exceed their costs?

Second, the Department of Energy's allocation rules are credited with causing the gasoline shortages in 1979. Since the rules are always based on some prior base year, they can quickly become outdated. Fast-growing areas have gas shortages, while slow-growing areas have a glut of gasoline. Government regulators simply cannot allocate resources as efficiently as an unregulated market.

Finally, the government has been criticized for allowing oil companies to diversify into non-oil energy sources. It is feared that this will lessen competition in the energy industry.[52] It is argued that the oil companies will retard the development of alternative fuels in order to maximize their profits from oil and natural gas. This does not seem likely. As Table 14.5 indicates, the energy industry is relatively unconcentrated, no matter what definition is used. If anything, the diversification of oil companies into other energy sources should be procompetitive, not anticompetitive. The managerial and technological skills of the oil industry are highly regarded and should be encouraged to enter related fields. The oil companies also have the profits to commit to expensive and risky research in alternative energy sources.

51. Edward J. Mitchell, "Oil Import Quotas Won't Work," *Wall Street Journal,* August 27, 1979, p. 14.

52. Another competition issue is the ownership of oil pipelines by the major oil companies. For an excellent discussion of the issues involved, see E. Mitchell, ed., *Oil Pipelines and Public Policy* (Washington, D.C.: American Enterprise Institute, 1979).

Table 14.5   Concentration Ratios of the Energy Industry, 1974
(Percentage of total Btu's)

Concentra-tion Ratio	Oil	Oil and Gas	Oil, Gas, and Coal	Oil, Gas, Coal, and Uranium	Oil, Gas, Coal, Uranium, and Geothermal
4-firm	26.0	25.1	19.1	18.4	18.4
8-firm	41.7	39.2	31.5	29.7	29.7
20-firm	61.4	59.0	49.6	47.8	47.8

Source: Jesse Markham, "Market Structure and Horizontal Divestiture of the Energy Companies," in *Horizontal Divestiture in the Oil Industry*, ed. Edward Mitchell (Washington, D.C.: American Enterprise Institute, 1977), p. 25.

New Directions for Regulation

The most promising direction for energy regulation is less of it. And, regulation will be reduced in the pricing area unless Congress reimposes price controls on oil and natural gas. On the other hand, the Carter administration has proposed that the government assume a major role in the development of synthetic fuels.

The Price of Energy.   Increasing the price of gasoline by increasing the federal tax on gasoline has been much discussed. It is frequently argued that other nations use less gasoline because their gasoline taxes are higher. As Table 14.6 indicates, they are indeed substantially higher

Table 14.6   Gasoline Taxes for Different Countries, 1978

Country	Tax per Gallon	Increase 1973–1978 (percentage)
Belgium	$1.18	22
France	1.10	62
Germany	1.02	6
Italy	1.54	161
Netherlands	1.12	19
Spain	.35	30
Sweden	.69	−4
United Kingdom	.75	108
United States	.12	0

Source: U.S. Department of Commerce, *Statistical Abstract of the United States, 1978* (Washington, D.C.: Government Printing Office, 1978), p. 655.

than American taxes. An increase of perhaps 50 cents per gallon in the gasoline tax would undoubtedly decrease consumption of gasoline. It also undoubtedly would increase inflation, be inappropriate until better mass transportation facilities are available, and end the political career of any politician who approved it.[53]

The Demand for Energy. One popular alternative to an increase in the gasoline tax is rationing. This approach is popular with politicians because it does not require an increase in the price of gasoline. It is also deemed desirable on equity grounds, for the burden of a gasoline shortage would be spread among all users. The problem with rationing is to devise a system that is considered "fair" to all of the parties involved. If gasoline coupons are awarded to all registered car owners, for example, rich people who own many cars will benefit. Others might buy useless "clunkers" in order to receive more coupons. If coupons are given to licensed drivers instead, rationing may benefit people with large families and few cars; there is not necessarily a direct relationship between the number of drivers and the number of cars. Finally, no rationing program can take into account differences in commuting patterns. A coal miner in West Virginia may drive 100 miles a day, while the author drives only 10 miles a day in Washington, D.C. In sum, there is no easy way to compromise the conflicts inherent in any rationing system.

The Supply of Energy. Next to the development of nuclear power, the most controversial energy policy issue is undoubtedly the appropriate role of the government in developing synthetic fuels.[54] President Carter proposed a massive program of subsidies and price supports for synthetic fuels. Billions of dollars would be used to extract oil from shale rock and gas from coal. The rationale for government intervention is that the great risk and substantial investments of these projects make it unlikely that the private sector will pursue them without government subsidies. Joskow and Pindyck provide a strong counterargument to government intervention in synthetic fuels.[55] They question the risk argument, noting that private oil firms frequently spend billions of dollars on oil

53. For an analysis of the problems of mass transit, see J. R. Meyer, J. F. Kain, and M. Wohl, *The Urban Transportation Problem* (Cambridge, Mass.: Harvard University Press, 1965).

54. For a discussion of the economic issues surrounding nuclear power, see P. L. Joskow and M. L. Baughman, "The Future of the U.S. Nuclear Energy Industry," *Bell Journal of Economics* 7 (Spring 1976): 3-32.

55. P. Joskow and R. Pindyck, "Should Synfuels Be Subsidized?" *Regulation* 3 (September/October 1979): 18-24.

leases without any guarantee that they will find oil; these companies also financed the multibillion dollar Alaskan oil pipeline without government subsidies. Joskow and Pindyck claim that a major obstacle to private development of synthetic fuels is, instead, government regulation. The uncertainties surrounding possible environmental and price restrictions make firms reluctant to commit resources in this area. This argument should be examined more carefully before the government commits itself and the American people to a multibillion dollar subsidy scheme.

Summary

Since 1950, oil and natural gas have accounted for more than one-half the United States' energy requirements. Recently, however, the nation has been increasingly unable to satisfy its demand by domestic production of these two fuels. This became self-evident with the oil embargo in 1973 and the natural gas shortage in 1975. Throughout this period, these two industries operated in a market environment that was heavily regulated by the government. Indeed, it has been argued that these regulations caused the natural gas shortage and actually increased domestic demand for imports after the embargo was over. Many proposals have since been made for improving performance in the domestic energy industries. The most common proposal by economists—and one reluctantly adopted by politicians—has been deregulation of the wellhead prices of crude oil and natural gas. These industries have been regulated for so long that it is not clear what the short-run impact of deregulation will be. In the long run, however, it should increase domestic supplies of energy while reducing domestic demand.

Suggested Readings

Adelman, M. *The World Petroleum Market* (Baltimore: Resources for the Future, 1972).

Joskow, P. and Pindyck, R. "Should Synfuels Be Subsidized?", *Regulation* 3 (September/October 1979): 18-24.

MacAvoy, P. "The Regulation-Induced Shortage of Natural Gas," *Journal of Law and Economics* 14 (April 1971): 167-200.

Measday, W. "The Petroleum Industry," in *The Structure of American Industry*, ed. W. Adams (New York: Macmillan, 1977), pp. 130-64.

Mitchell, E., ed., *Horizontal Divestiture in the Oil Industry* (Washington, D.C.: American Enterprise Institute, 1978).

Pindyck, R. S. "The Optimal Exploration and Production of Nonrenewable Resources," *Journal of Political Economy* 86 (October 1978): 841-61.

Evaluation of Economic Regulation

Chapter
15

Economic regulation is a severe type of government intervention in a market economy. It represents a substantial departure from the traditional reliance on private market forces to allocate resources throughout the nation's economy. The regulatory process supplants the market process as the mechanism for making the basic economic decisions on price, profits, and entry. As such, it deserves careful scrutiny. This chapter evaluates the overall American experience with economic regulation, emphasizing its implementation, operation, and possible modification.

Appraisal of Current Economic Regulation

Any assessment of current economic regulation should address three important questions. First, is economic regulation of specific economic activities necessary? Second, is economic regulation of these activities effective? Third, what is the cost of this type of government intervention?

The Necessity of Economic Regulation

As discussed in Chapters 11 through 14, substantial segments of the transportation, communications, and energy sectors of the economy are subject to varying degrees of economic regulation. Is this regulation necessary? The standard economic rationale for economic regulation is the natural monopoly argument: A natural monopoly exists when a single firm can supply a particular product or service more efficiently than two or more firms. Economic regulation is necessary in this situation to ensure that consumers are not exploited by the natural monopolist.

Does the natural monopoly argument explain the historical pattern of economic regulation in the United States? The answer is both yes and no. On the affirmative side, some regulated activities are considered to be classic natural monopolies, such as the supplying of electricity, natural gas, water, telephone service, and cable television at the local level. On the negative side, many regulated activities do not experience the cost conditions necessary for a natural monopoly. The most obvious examples are trucking, airlines, and oil and natural gas production. In sum, the natural monopoly argument applies in some cases, but not in others.

Two reasons are commonly put forth to explain the regulation of firms that cannot be characterized as natural monopolies. First, demand and cost conditions can change over time, eliminating the need for economic regulation, though not the regulation itself. For example, increases in demand can permit the existence of additional suppliers in a previously monopolistic market. This is the case with long distance telecommunications, where increases in demand have made it feasible to have two or more suppliers in most major markets.[1] Yesterday's natural monopoly can become today's oligopoly. Or, changes in technology can create substitute goods, thereby eliminating the monopoly power that originally led to regulation. The introduction of trucks, in combination with the extensive interstate highway system, has drastically reduced the market power of the railroads.[2] In sum, economic conditions frequently change, but economic regulation remains.

Second, economic regulation may be instituted not for the benefit of society, but for the benefit of the regulated firms. Firms may actively seek regulation as a means of suppressing "ruinous" or "destructive" competition. In effect, the firms are trading the uncertainty and competitiveness of the free market for the certainty and hoped-for financial security of the regulatory environment. The "capture" theory thus

1. Leonard Waverman, "The Regulation of Intercity Telecommunications," in *Promoting Competition in Regulated Markets*, ed. A. Phillips (Washington, D.C.: Brookings Institution, 1975), pp. 201–39.

2. Norman H. Jones, Jr., "The Meaning of Market Dominance," in *Railroad Revitalization and Regulatory Reform*, ed. Paul MacAvoy and John Snow (Washington, D.C.: American Enterprise Institute, 1977), 203–23.

provides an alternative explanation to the traditional public interest theory of economic regulation. Federal regulation of television broadcasters and state regulation of occupations support this explanation.[3] Perhaps the best example, however, has been the Interstate Commerce Commission's regulation of railroads and trucking companies. It has been argued that in the 19th century, the railroads sought regulation to eliminate periodic price wars on major routes.[4] Regulation was later extended to trucking to protect the railroads from this new competitive threat. This "creeping" regulation is definitely consistent with the capture theory of economic regulation.

The Effectiveness of Economic Regulation

Once economic regulation is implemented in a market, is it effective?[5] More specifically, does it reduce the market power of natural monopolies? To answer this question, it is necessary to examine the impact of regulation on three different dimensions of firm performance: price level, price discrimination, and rate of return. If regulation is effective, it should lead to lower prices, less price discrimination, and lower profit rates. A different outcome can be expected if the regulated firms are not natural monopolies, however. The capture theory would suggest that in these cases, regulation may lead to higher prices, more price discrimination, and higher profit rates. In sum, the impact of regulation may vary with the structure of the regulated market.

Price Level.   The primary economic argument against monopoly is that it leads to high prices. An obvious test of the effectiveness of regulation is to examine its impact on the price level of regulated firms. Is its effect on prices positive, negative, or zero?

Several studies have attempted to estimate the effect of regulation on electric utility rates.[6] In their pioneering study of this issue, Stigler and Friedland compared electric rates in states with regulation with rates in

3. See Chapters 13 and 8, respectively.

4. G. Kolko, *Railroads and Regulation, 1877–1916* (Princeton, N.J.: Princeton University Press, 1965).

5. The discussion following is based on William Jordan, "Producer Protection, Prior Market Structure and the Effects of Government Regulation," *Journal of Law and Economics* 15 (April 1972): 151–76.

6. G. Stigler and C. Friedland, "What Can Regulators Regulate? The Case of Electricity," *Journal of Law and Economics* 5 (October 1962): 1–16; and T. Moore, "The Effectiveness of Regulation of Electric Utility Prices," *Southern Economic Journal* 13 (April 1970): 365–75.

states without it.[7] After controlling for other factors that could affect rates, they found that regulation did not have any significant impact on average electric rates in 1912, 1922, 1932, and 1937. Using a different technique, Moore concluded that regulation reduced rates from 1952 to 1962, but by a maximum of only five percent.[8]

Regulation has had a more substantial impact on the prices of oil and natural gas. Natural gas has been controlled since 1954 and crude oil since 1971. In that time, the imposition of price ceilings kept oil and natural gas prices significantly below their equilibrium values.[9] This is a fairly common result of price ceilings, especially during inflationary periods. Regulators respond to changes in market supply and demand with a lag, making it likely that the price ceiling will be below the equilibrium price.

Finally, economic regulation has actually increased prices in two industries frequently cited as examples of the capture theory—trucking and airlines. Trucking rates for regulated commodities are significantly higher than those for unregulated commodities, where rates are set by competition. This was dramatically illustrated in the mid-1950s when the carriage of frozen foods became exempt from ICC rate regulation. Deregulation led to an average rate reduction of 19 percent.[10] In the airlines industry, unregulated intrastate carriers in California have consistently underpriced their regulated interstate rivals. It has been estimated that in 1965 unregulated coach fares were 32 to 47 percent lower than if they had been set by the CAB.[11]

Price Discrimination.   Price discrimination occurs when prices do not accurately reflect cost differences for separate transactions.[12] This was a major concern of farmers in their effort to regulate the railroads in the late 1800s. Indeed, a major objective of federal regulation of railroads was to end the extensive personal discrimination they practiced. Eco-

7. Stigler and Friedland, "What Can Regulators Regulate?"

8. Moore, "The Effectiveness of Regulation."

9. P. MacAvoy, "The Regulation-Induced Shortage of Natural Gas," *Journal of Law and Economics* 14 (April 1971): 167–200.

10. G. Hilton, "The Transportation Act of 1958" (1969), reporting findings from *Interstate Trucking of Frozen Fruits and Vegetables Under Agricultural Exemption, Marketing Research Report No. 316* (U.S. Department of Agriculture, Marketing Division, Agricultural Marketing Service, 1959).

11. William Jordan, *Airline Regulation in America: Effects and Imperfections* (Baltimore: Johns Hopkins, 1970); see pp. 73–104.

12. For a more detailed discussion of price discrimination, see Chapter 8.

nomic regulation has not ended price discrimination by the railroads, however. Railroads continue to charge different markups for different groups of commodities. For example, in 1966 the ratio of rail revenue to out-of-pocket costs varied from 0.90 to 3.65 for different product groups.[13] It seems unlikely that there would be more rate discrimination in the absence of government regulation.

Price discrimination is not, of course, confined to the railroad industry. Consumers are probably most familiar with the discrimination engaged in by the airlines. Airline fare structures are loaded with special discounts depending on the passenger's length of stay, number of children, and so on. A major purpose is to differentiate between business travelers (inelastic demand) and vacationers (elastic demand). Local telephone and electric utilities have also engaged in price discrimination, tending to discriminate in their rate structures against residential consumers and in favor of commercial and industrial users.[14] It should be noted, however, that some price discrimination is necessary if a natural monopolist is to cover its costs. In fact, price discrimination will be consistent with efficient pricing if, for example, it is based on the inverse elasticity rule.[15]

Rate of Return. Through their rate-making powers, regulatory agencies can control the rate of return that a regulated firm receives on its assets. If the realized return is too high (or low), the regulators can lower (or raise) rates in an effort to achieve the desired rate of return. Given this authority to control rates, what has been the actual impact of regulation on the rates of return of regulated firms? The empirical evidence is mixed. Stigler and Friedland did not find any impact of regulation on utility stock prices, suggesting little, if any, effect on rates of return.[16] On the other hand, regulation has apparently had both positive and negative impacts in other regulated industries.

Table 15.1 presents the rates of return on the book value of assets for selected regulated industries.[17] These rates are compared with the average rate for 10 unregulated service industries. Several things should be noted about these rate figures. First, rates for the regulated industries

13. T. Moore, "Deregulating Surface Freight Transportation," in *Promoting Competition in Regulated Markets*, ed. A. Phillips (Washington, D.C.: Brookings Institution, 1975), pp. 84–85.

14. See Jordan, "Producer Protection," pp.160–61.

15. This optimal pricing rule is discussed in Chapter 11.

16. Stigler and Friedland, "What Can Regulators Regulate?"

17. For a more detailed discussion, see the original source for this data: Paul MacAvoy, *The Regulated Industries and the Economy* (New York: Norton, 1979), Chapter 2.

Table 15.1   **Rates of Return on Book Value of Assets
in the Regulated Industries[a]**
(Average annual rate in percent)

Regulated Industry	1959–61	1962–65	1966–69	1970–73	1974–77
Electricity	4.6	4.9	5.0	5.3	5.8
Gas transportation	4.8	4.9	4.7	5.2	5.7
Gas utilities	4.7	5.0	5.1	5.2	6.1
Telephone	5.1	5.2	5.2	5.4	5.8
Railroad transportation	5.4	3.3	3.3	3.4	4.2
Airline transportation	2.3	4.0	4.6	2.8	3.7
Motor freight transportation	3.4	5.5	5.8	5.9	6.1
Unregulated service industries	6.4	5.9	6.2	6.0	6.6

[a] Book value weighted average of retained earnings plus dividends plus interest payments divided by the book value of assets.
Source: Paul MacAvoy, *The Regulated Industries and the Economy* (New York: Norton, 1979), App. C, p. 151.

are consistently less than those for the unregulated industries. This result is expected, for regulated industries are considered to be less risky and therefore more desirable to investors. The question is, how much should returns be lowered to compensate for the reduction in risk? Unfortunately, there is no easy answer to this question.[18] Second, these figures do not reveal the return that the firms received on their actual investment or equity—the relevant profit rate for the firm. This rate varies considerably by industry; in 1971, for example, the return on equity was 9.2 for all manufacturing, 0.0 for railroads, 9.6 for barges, and 16.2 for trucking.[19] While trucking was substantially more profitable than the average manufacturing industry, railroads did not receive any return on their equity.

Like trucking, both television broadcasting and oil and natural gas production are very profitable. Over-the-air broadcasters have benefited from the FCC's restrictive licensing policies, which effectively blockaded entry into most markets. Profits are likely to decline in the future,

18. MacAvoy attempts to control for risk in *The Regulated Industries.*

19. U.S. Department of Transportation, "The Northeast Problem," in *Railroad Revitalization and Regulatory Reform,* ed. P. MacAvoy and J. Snow (Washington, D.C.: American Enterprise Institute, 1977), p. 18.

however, as cable television and pay television compete more with over-the-air broadcasters. The profits of oil and natural gas companies have been reduced by the government's imposition of price controls, but have begun to increase as some controls are removed (see Chapter 14). Oil is currently very profitable, though its future profitability will be reduced by the windfall profits tax passed by Congress.[20]

The Cost of Economic Regulation

Regardless of whether economic regulation is necessary or effective, one thing is certain—it is not costless. Both direct and indirect costs are associated with economic regulation.[21] Direct costs arise from the implementation and operation of the regulatory process. These costs, such as salaries of regulators and employees who interact with them, are common to all types of government intervention and are therefore discussed in Chapter 19. The indirect costs of economic regulation are due to the incentives and disincentives regulation creates for regulated firms. In particular, is economic regulation compatible with both static and dynamic efficiency?

Static Efficiency.   As discussed earlier (Chapter 3), there are two requirements for static efficiency. First, each firm must minimize the costs of producing its output. This requires both the adoption of the most efficient production technology available and the utilization of the minimum resources necessary. Second, society's resources must be optimally allocated across the different markets. This condition is satisfied when competitive markets are in long-run equilibrium. Economic regulation can thus affect the degree of static efficiency through its impact on the utilization of resources within regulated markets.

Economic regulation frequently is criticized for not forcing regulated firms to minimize their costs. This is a major problem in regulated markets because there is no price competition among regulated firms. It is difficult for regulation to mandate efficient behavior; in fact, it seems in many cases to encourage inefficient behavior instead. For example, economic regulation frequently uses cost-plus pricing. That is, prices are set to cover the regulated firm's total costs, including a normal rate of

20. Congress established a lower tax for new oil (30 percent) than for old oil (70 percent), thereby establishing an incentive for exploration and development of new oil fields. (See the Crude Oil Windfall Project Tax Act of 1980, PL 96–223, April 2, 1980.)

21. For an excellent discussion of the overall costs of economic regulation, see U.S. Senate Committee on Governmental Affairs, *Study on Federal Regulation*, vol. 6, "Framework for Regulation" (Washington, D.C.: Government Printing Office, December 1978), Chapter 3.

return on its investment.[22] The result is to reduce management's incentive to seek the lowest input prices and to negotiate lower wage agreements with unions. And it is impossible for regulators to determine whether a firm is minimizing the quantity and price of its inputs.

A regulated firm can also increase its costs by not selecting the least-cost combination of factor inputs. For example, a firm might adopt a capital-intensive technology when it would be cheaper to use a labor-intensive one. Averch and Johnson have shown that, theoretically, a regulated firm is too capital-intensive if its allowed rate of return exceeds its cost of capital.[23] This result, known as the "A-J effect," follows from the firm's goal of profit maximization. Because the allowed return exceeds the cost of capital, the firm can increase its profits simply by adding more and more capital to its rate base. An electric utility might, for example, underprice electricity to peak users in order to increase demand and thereby justify the construction of new plants. Or it might increase its rate base by maintaining more standby capacity than necessary. All in all, the A-J effect is very interesting because it means that economic regulation creates distortions whenever the allowed return does not equal the cost of capital.[24] Unfortunately, empirical evidence for the A-J effect is mixed, making it impossible to determine its importance in the regulated sector of the economy.[25]

Regulation does, however, provide one major incentive for firms to minimize their costs—*regulatory lag.* This is the delay inherent in the regulatory rate-making process; it is defined as the time lag between the filing for a rate increase and its subsequent enactment by the regulatory commission. Regulatory lag creates an incentive for firms to minimize their costs, because they will not be compensated immediately for any cost increases. They must wait until the commission acts. In the interim, they will minimize their losses by minimizing their costs. The impact of regulatory lag has recently diminished as more and more regulatory commissions have adopted some type of fuel adjustment clause to com-

22. An exception to this traditional public utility approach is provided by regulation of natural gas. For a discussion of the pricing standards employed, see *Permian Basin Area Rate Cases*, 390 U.S. 747 (1968).

23. H. Averch and L. Johnson, "Behavior of the Firm under Regulatory Constraint," *American Economic Review* 52 (December 1962): 1052-69.

24. If the allowed rate of return is less than the cost of capital, the regulated firm will use too little capital.

25. See, for example, P. Joskow, "Inflation and Environmental Concern: Structural Change in the Process of Public Utility Price Regulation," *Journal of Law and Economics* 17 (October 1974): 291–327; and H. Peterson, "An Empirical Test of Regulatory Effects," *Bell Journal of Economics* 6 (Spring 1975): 111–26.

pensate firms for the sudden and dramatic increases in fuel prices. These clauses, though necessary during periods of substantial inflation, reduce firms' incentives to procure low-cost fuel supplies; their increased prices are passed directly through to consumers.[26]

Finally, economic regulation can also lead to a misallocation of resources *across* markets, as when regulation leads to too many or too few resources being committed to a regulated market. For example, economic regulation by the CAB and the ICC resulted in excess capacity in the airline and trucking industries, respectively. By prohibiting price competition, regulation intensified nonprice competition such as rivalry in scheduling. Airplanes made more flights, though often they were only half full. Regulation also led to excess capacity in the oil industry. There, producers tried to evade prorationing limits by adding more and more oil wells to their fields. In 1975, the United States produced 20.2 percent of the non-Communist oil in the world, although we have 88.7 percent of the oil wells.[27] As a final example, ICC regulation of the railroads severely restricted their ability to abandon unprofitable lines. This abandonment policy impaired the ability of the railroads to transfer their resources into their most highly valued uses.

Dynamic Efficiency.   Whereas static efficiency concerns the utilization of society's resources at a given time, dynamic efficiency focuses on their utilization over time. More specifically, it examines the rate of technological progress—the invention and innovation of new products and new production processes. Economic regulation can affect the rate of technological progress by influencing the rate of inventive and innovative activity in regulated markets. Any possible impact would be due to the regulators' control over the key economic decisions of price, profits, and entry. Their rate-making and entry decisions determine the profitability, and hence the likelihood, of innovative activity by the firms that they regulate.

So far, the empirical evidence is mixed, although apparently economic regulation does tend to impede technological progress.[28] On the positive side, CAB regulation is credited with stimulating the development

26. F. Gollop and S. Karlson, "The Impact of the Fuel Adjustment Mechanism on Economic Efficiency," *Review of Economics and Statistics* 60 (November 1978): 574-84.

27. Senate Committee on Governmental Affairs, *Study on Federal Regulation*, vol. 6, p. 44

28. W. Capron, ed., *Technological Change in Regulated Industries* (Washington, D.C.: Brookings Institution, 1971).

of new commercial aircraft.[29] The CAB established a fare structure that encouraged airlines to adopt new aircraft, and the airlines also used the introduction of new aircraft as a major means of nonprice competition. On the negative side, the ICC and FCC have impeded the rate of technological progress in the transportation and communications industries. ICC regulations delayed the introduction of such important transportation innovations as unit trains, piggybacking, and the Big John Hopper.[30] Until recently, FCC policies hindered the expansion of cable and pay television, while restricting the ability of independent firms to compete against AT&T and Western Electric as common carriers and equipment manufacturers. In general, it seems that regulators tend to regard technological change as a disruptive influence on the regulatory status quo. As a result, they are not likely to pursue regulatory policies that will increase the rate of technological progress in their markets.

As the previous section indicated, economic regulation is not without its faults. These are both numerous and substantial. As a result, many proposals have been made to alter the current regulatory environment. This section examines three possible avenues of change for economic regulation: reduction, improvement, and replacement.

New Directions for Economic Regulation

Less Economic Regulation

Economic regulation is deemed necessary to prevent natural monopolists from exploiting their market power. When the regulated firms are not natural monopolists, however, economic regulation is not necessary. It is then possible to reduce regulation and rely on competition to determine market performance.

Deregulation requires a substantial lessening of regulatory control over rate-making and entry. If market performance is to be improved, it is essential to restore price competition. This can be accomplished by preventing firms from colluding on prices and by granting firms some control over their prices. Trucking companies, for example, will now be allowed to raise or lower prices within a "zone of reasonableness" without ICC approval. At the same time, new firms must be able to enter the

29. R. Caves, *Air Transport and Its Regulators: An Industry Study* (Cambridge, Mass.: Harvard University Press, 1962).

30. P. MacAvoy and J. Sloss, *Regulation of Transport Innovation* (New York: Random House, 1967).

regulated market more easily. Actual entry by new firms, as well as the threat of future entry by other firms, increases price competition and forces firms to be efficient. This is undoubtedly the reason why existing trucking companies have so strenuously opposed the relaxation of entry controls by the ICC and by the Congress.

It seems feasible to have partial or complete deregulation in most regulated industries. This belief has been supported by legislation to deregulate the airlines, phase out domestic price controls on oil and natural gas, and increase the pricing flexibility of railroads and trucking companies. The FCC has permitted firms to compete against AT&T in supplying both products and common carrier services to telecommunications users.[31] In addition, it is considering a substantial relaxation of controls over both radio stations and cable television companies. It may even be possible to increase competition in the electric power industry. Weiss argues that it may be possible to have competitive generating companies in large metropolitan areas.[32] These companies would compete against one another for the right to supply electricity to the local electric distribution company. This proposal recognizes that the distribution of electricity remains a natural monopoly, but its generation can be competitive in many places.

Although deregulation is desirable on economic grounds, it may not be practical on political grounds. If the regulated firms benefit from the current regulatory scheme, they will strenuously oppose deregulation, and it will occur only if their opposition can be overcome. This may be unlikely, for the benefits of regulation commonly accrue to a few groups, while its costs are borne by many groups.[33] Trucking regulation, for example, has made operating rights extremely valuable and raised the wages of the drivers (Teamsters).[34] All consumers pay the resulting higher prices for transportation, although they are probably not aware of it. In this situation, consumers perceive little gain from deregulation,

31. Two AT&T economists have argued that it may be necessary to regulate entry into markets characterized as natural monopolies. See J. Panzar and R. Willig, "Free Entry and the Sustainability of Natural Monopoly," *Bell Journal of Economics* 8 (Spring 1977): 1–22.

32. L. Weiss, "Antitrust in the Electric Power Industry," in *Promoting Competition in Regulated Markets,* ed. A. Phillips (Washington, D.C.: Brookings Institution, 1975), pp. 135–73.

33. Theoretically, it should be possible in this situation for those who would benefit from deregulation to offset any losses from regulated firms. See Gordon Tullock, "Achieving Deregulation—A Public Choice Perspective," *Regulation* 2 (November/December 1978): 50–54.

34. T. Moore, "The Beneficiaries of Trucking Regulation," *Journal of Law and Economics* 21 (October 1978): 327–43.

while the trucking companies and the Teamsters Union have a strong financial stake in retaining regulation.[35] One possible compromise is to reduce regulation over a period of time. This transition period would provide time for regulation firms to adapt to the new market environment and would moderate any losses imposed on the companies and their workers.[36]

Better Economic Regulation

Several suggestions have been made for improving economic regulation in those areas where deregulation is not politically possible or economically justified. The most common proposal is to increase the quality of regulators. Undeniably, regulators, at both federal and state levels, have not distinguished themselves by their competency or integrity.[37] Regulatory positions have all too often been viewed as a source of patronage or, in some states, as a minor elected office. The quality of regulators appears to be improving, however, and more and more federal and state commissioners have some expertise in areas related to economic regulation.[38]

A second major area of concern is rate-making. First, the delay inherent in the rate-making process threatens the financial viability of regulated firms during inflationary periods.[39] Cost increases rapidly erode profits while firms are petitioning the regulatory commissions for rate relief. One possible solution is to expand the use of "escalator" or adjustment clauses. Cost increases would then be quickly and directly passed on to consumers via higher rates. An increased use of escalator clauses, however, would require reexamination of the incentives for regulated firms to be efficient. This incentive could be reinforced by tying management compensation to the firm's performance. Or, as Kendrick suggests, rate changes might be linked to changes in labor productivity.[40] Finally, rate-making must be depoliticized. A firm's rate level

35. A similar situation holds in the broadcasting industry where radio and television licenses may be worth millions of dollars.

36. Alfred Kahn, however, argues that a shorter transition period is more efficient ("Applying Economics to an Imperfect World," *Regulation* 2 [November/December 1978]: 17–27).

37. L. Kohlmeier, Jr., *The Regulators* (New York: Harper & Row, 1969).

38. L. Smith, "State Utility Commissioners—1978," *Public Utilities Fortnightly*, February 16, 1978, pp. 9-15.

39. "A Dark Future For Utilities," *Business Week*, May 28, 1979, pp. 108–24.

40. J. Kendrick, "Efficiency Incentives and Cost Factors in Public Utility Automatic Revenue Adjustment Clauses," *Bell Journal of Economics* 6 (Spring 1975): 299–313.

and rate structure should not be determined by purely political considerations. An efficient rate structure requires rates that are based on the costs of providing service to customers.

Alternatives to Economic Regulation

One final solution to the problems raised by economic regulation is simply to replace regulation with an alternative economic institution. The most obvious institution is public enterprise. Instead of regulating a firm in the public interest, the government can serve the public interest by supplying the service itself. For example, a small town may decide to distribute electricity itself instead of paying a private electric company to perform this service. The advantages and disadvantages of this option are discussed in Chapter 18.

A second, and very unusual proposal has been advanced by Demsetz, who would replace economic regulation with franchise bidding.[41] Demsetz's main point is that the focus in the natural monopoly debate is misdirected: a monopoly in production does not necessarily imply monopoly prices. If there is competition among firms for the franchise, the winning bid can lead to competitive pricing. The winning firm would be a monopolist, but would be setting price equal to average total cost. Economic regulation would then not be necessary. Williamson has criticized this argument for ignoring the transaction costs associated with the franchise bidding process.[42] More specifically, it is frequently difficult to determine consumer preferences, compare competing bids, and write an adaptable franchise contract. As demand and cost conditions change over time, it may be necessary to renegotiate the franchise contract. The franchise approach thus still requires some degree of economic regulation by the government. Nonetheless, Demsetz's approach is useful for focusing attention on alternative institutional arrangements for dealing with natural monopolies.

Summary

A substantial portion of America's industrial infrastructure—transportation, communications, and energy—is subject to economic regulation by local, state, or federal government. Economic regulation has, however, been very controversial. According to many of the studies in this area,

41. H. Demsetz, "Why Regulate Utilities?" *Journal of Law and Economics* 11 (April 1968): 55–65.
42. O. Williamson, "Franchise Bidding for Natural Monopolies," *Bell Journal of Economics* 7 (Spring 1976): 73–104.

economic regulation is not justified in many markets and is not very effective even when it is justified. At the same time, it weakens incentives for firms to minimize costs and to adopt new technology. In sum, economic regulation is not always in the public interest and may, in fact, promote private interests instead. The most obvious remedy is to increase competition in regulated markets whenever it is feasible. Where regulation is still necessary, market performance may be improved by hiring more qualified regulators and by providing more incentives for efficiency.

Suggested Readings

Capron, W., ed. *Technological Change in Regulated Industries* (Washington, D.C.: Brookings Institution, 1971).

Jordan, W. "Producer Protection, Prior Market Structure and the Effects of Government Regulation," *Journal of Law and Economics* 15 (April 1972): 151–76.

Kohlmeier, L. *The Regulators* (New York: Harper & Row, 1969).

MacAvoy, P. *The Regulated Industries and the Economy* (New York: Norton, 1979).

Stigler, G., and Friedland, C. "What Can Regulators Regulate? The Case of Electricity," *Journal of Law and Economics* 5 (October 1962): 1–16.

Phillips, A., ed. *Promoting Competition in Regulated Markets* (Washington, D.C.: Brookings Institution, 1975).

Part Four

Social Regulation

Environmental Protection

Chapter 16

Since its founding, the United States has been viewed as a country of almost unlimited natural resources. As a result, people have used these resources with little regard for their depletion and possible exhaustion. The air and water have become polluted, and some species of wildlife are threatened with extinction. The extent of environmental degradation was vividly illustrated when the floating pollutants in Cleveland's infamous Cuyahoga River actually caught fire spontaneously. In response to the deteriorating situation, the federal government embarked on an ambitious—and controversial—program of environmental regulation. This chapter examines the rationale for, and effectiveness of, this type of government intervention.

The Setting

The environment can be broadly defined as humans' surrounding habitat. At a minimum, this would include those basic resources necessary for human survival: food, water, and oxygen. In addition, the environment includes any other resources that are consumed by humans throughout their life cycle. From this perspective, humans are not distinguishable from other living organisms in the world. What differentiates humans is their tremendous ability to alter the environment. Swamps have been drained to eliminate the breeding grounds of mosquitoes, the carrier of dreaded malaria. Desert lands have been irrigated and transformed into oases. The list of improvements is almost endless.

Unfortunately, humans can worsen the environment as well as improve it. This is readily apparent to citizens of large cities who must endure a seemingly endless series of "smog alerts" on hot, humid, summer days. And little relief can be provided by local rivers and lakes, which now are commonly unfit for swimming or boating. Even trips to the country can be unsatisfying as litter mars the natural landscape, and parks and beaches become overcrowded. In sum, humans are unique in their ability to control their environment, for better or worse.

The History of Environmental Regulation

Environmental problems are not new, although they are probably more widespread and more widely publicized than in earlier times. Efficient sewage systems are a relatively recent development, for example. Citizens of Amsterdam and Venice have long used their famous canals for both transportation and sewage disposal. And before automobiles and trucks began to pollute the air, London was preoccupied over the pollution problem caused by another type of transportation—horse manure!

Environmental pollution arises because of a conflict between two constraints. The first constraint results from one of the immutable laws of physics: matter can neither be created nor destroyed. Industrial processes that create consumer goods also generate solid, liquid, and gaseous waste products. The subsequent consumption of consumer products yields still more waste material—garbage and sewage—that also must be disposed of. The second constraint is imposed by the environment itself. Environmental resources have a finite capacity to absorb society's various waste products. For example, the atmosphere can disperse limited quantities of hydrocarbons and particulate matter without any adverse impact. A river can accommodate some sewage without damage to marine life. Pollution occurs when the quantity of emissions discharged into the air or water exceeds the natural assimilative capacities of those resources.

Pollution has not been considered a major problem in the United States until recently. Its belated arrival has been attributed to the post-World War II acceleration of two processes: urbanization and industrialization.[1] Urbanization intensifies the waste disposal problems of house-

1. For a good discussion of the causes of pollution, see B. Commoner, "The Environmental Costs of Economic Growth," in *Economics of the Environment*, ed. R. Dorfman and N. Dorfman (New York: Norton, 1977), pp. 331–53.

holds because it concentrates more and more people in a finite geographic area. Each new person adds more garbage and sewage to the existing total. The problem is compounded by the increasingly heavy demands placed on the surrounding environment by industry. Increased production means increased discharge of industrial waste products. These two forces have combined to place excessive demands on the environment's finite capacity to absorb waste products.

The major sources of air pollution emissions are presented in Table 16.1, for 1977. Not surprisingly, the transportation sector is a major polluter. Motor vehicles—automobiles, buses, and trucks—discharge carbon monoxide, nitrogen oxide, and hydrocarbons produced by the combustion of fuel. In the presence of sunlight, nitrogen oxide combines with hydrocarbons to form smog. The two major sources of sulfur oxides and particulates are industrial production processes and the combustion of fuel by households and industry. Sulfur trioxide can be especially dangerous because it can convert to sulfuric acid in the atmosphere! *Particulates* is a broad term that refers to the various solids and liquids that are discharged into the air. Common examples are lead from automobiles and ash from smokestacks. Clearly, a substantial part of the air pollution problem is due to the combustion of fossil fuels, especially coal and oil.[2]

Table 16.1　**Sources of Air Pollutant Emissions, 1977**
(Percentage of total emissions)

Pollutant	Transportation	Fuel Combustion	Industrial Processes	Solid Waste Disposal	Miscellaneous	Total[a]
Carbon monoxide	83.5	1.1	8.0	2.6	4.8	100.0
Sulfur oxides	3.0	81.8	15.2	0.0	0.0	100.0
Hydrocarbons	40.7	5.4	35.6	2.6	16.0	100.0
Particulates	8.8	38.7	43.8	2.9	5.8	100.0
Nitrogen oxides	39.6	56.1	3.1	0.4	0.4	100.0

[a] Totals may not add up to 100% because of rounding off.
Source: U.S. Department of Commerce, *Statistical Abstract of the United States, 1979* (Washington, D.C.: Government Printing Office, 1979), p. 212.

2. Natural gas is a cleaner fuel than either coal or oil, although it also emits carbon dioxide when it is burned. These carbon dioxide emissions from fossil fuels may be increasing the amount of carbon dioxide in the atmosphere and thereby increasing the earth's temperature ("Carbon Dioxide Rise in the Atmosphere is Reported by U.S.," *Wall Street Journal,* May 29, 1979, p. 12).

Water pollution results from the direct discharge of organic and inorganic wastes into lakes, rivers, and oceans. Consumers pollute water by dumping their raw and treated sewage into it. The main problem is that the decomposition of these wastes uses up scarce oxygen in the water, thereby making it more difficult for fish and other marine life to survive. This problem is compounded by the runoff of nitrogen fertilizer from farmland, which stimulates the growth of algae, another cause of oxygen starvation. The end results are fish kills and water that both looks and smells bad. Inorganic wastes pose different problems. They can be both poisonous and long-lasting. Kepone, for example, continued to be found in fish long after it was discharged into the James River in Virginia. Similar stories can be told for DDT and mercury, which accumulate in tissues. Once these chemicals enter the food chain, it is difficult for them to be removed from it. Inorganic pollutants thus complicate an already complex situation in the nation's waters.

Public concern over the deteriorating environment led in the 1960s to federal legislation on water and air quality. The Environmental Protection Agency (EPA) was established in 1970 to spearhead the federal effort to preserve and enhance the nation's environmental resources. The EPA's mandate was broadened by new legislation throughout the 1970s. Some of the major legislation enforced by the EPA is:
— Clean Air Act of 1970 and Amendments of 1977
— Federal Insecticide, Fungicide and Rodenticide Act of 1972
— Federal Water Pollution Control Act of 1972
— Noise Control Act of 1972
— Energy Supply and Environmental Coordination Act of 1974
— Safe Water Drinking Act of 1974
— Toxic Substances Control Act of 1976
The EPA's primary responsibility is to regulate the discharge of pollutants into the nation's air, land, and water. To achieve this objective, the EPA coordinates its policies with state and local governments.

The Economics of the Environment

The environment provides essential services to both consumers and producers. Air, land, and water satisfy basic human needs, while simultaneously providing a convenient means for the disposal of human and industrial wastes. As a result, there is both a demand for and a supply of environmental services. From this perspective, the environment is not distinguishable from any other good or service in the economy. The pol-

Figure 16.1   **Supply and Demand for Environmental Services**

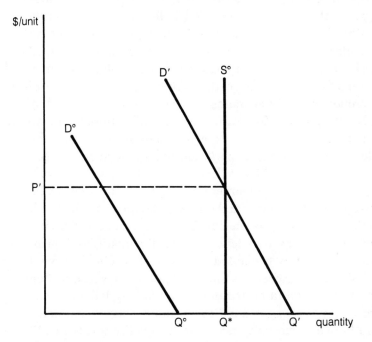

lution problem, as well as policies for its curtailment, can thus be conveniently analyzed in a market framework.[3]

Figure 16.1 graphically depicts the supply of and demand for environmental services. The market demand curve ($D°$) is downward-sloping, indicating that users will demand more services as the price is lowered. In effect, environmental services are no different than labor or capital services to a firm. They are all inputs in the firm's production process. The market supply of services ($S°$) is fixed at Q^*. Supply is thus unresponsive to price and depends solely on the assimilative capacity of the particular environmental resource.[4]

Since no one owns the environment, there is no charge for using its

3. For an excellent survey of the relevant economic issues, see A. Fisher and F. Peterson, "The Environment in Economics: A Survey," *Journal of Economic Literature* 14 (March 1976): 1–33.

4. The assimilative capacity of a river, for example, depends on the river's depth, temperature, and flow.

resources.[5] They are free goods. At a price of zero, consumers and producers demand Q° units of environmental resources. There is no pollution, however, since the quantity demanded is less than the quantity supplied. This situation prevailed prior to World War II. The postwar increases in urbanization and industrialization shifted market demand to D', while market supply remained unchanged at S°. Pollution is now inevitable since market demand exceeds market supply at a price of zero. The environment's ability to assimilate wastes is overwhelmed by the demands placed upon it. Moreover, the onset of pollution can reduce the environment's assimilative capacity, thereby worsening the pollution problem.[6] For example, as pollution reduces a river's oxygen supply, it reduces the river's ability to decompose organic wastes. Only at the nonzero price of P' will the market for environmental services be in equilibrium—the quantity demanded equal to the quantity supplied.

Even though the price of environmental services is zero, this does not mean that pollution is costless to society. It lowers the quality and quantity of environmental services available to all users, households as well as factories. Probably the most serious impact of pollution is its effect on people's health. Though pollution is rarely immediately lethal, it may shorten life spans over time. Lave and Seskin found a significant negative relationship between mortality rates and air-quality levels in 117 metropolitan areas throughout the 1960s.[7] A more common problem is the hospitalization of people with respiratory problems during the smog season in urban areas. In Los Angeles, the smog problem is so severe that many factories must curtail production during especially bad periods. Kaiser Steel Corporation claims that these curtailments cost it $250,000 a day in lost production.[8] Water pollution can also impose costs on society. Polluted water is unsightly, smelly, and unfit for human consumption or recreation. It can also reduce fish catches for both commercial and recreational fishermen. Overall, the discharge of pollutants, though free to the polluter, is not free to society.[9]

5. In other words, there are no property rights to environmental resources. If there were, users would have to pay for them as they do for any other resources.

6. In the case of wildlife, overfishing or hunting also can lead to the extinction of a particular species.

7. L. Lave and E. Seskin, *Air Pollution and Human Health* (Baltimore: Johns Hopkins, 1977). Air pollution can also lower property values. See J. Anderson, Jr., and T. Crocker, "Air Pollution and Residential Property Values," *Urban Studies* 8 (1971): 171–80.

8. "The Billowing Cost of Los Angeles Smog," *Business Week*, August 7, 1978, pp. 32–34.

9. Technically, pollution is not free to the user either, since the user also suffers from it. The individual polluter's contribution to total pollution may be small, however, and presumably less than the benefits received from it.

Table 16.2   **Comparison of National Pollution Damage Estimates**

Medium: Study	Base Year	Cost Estimates ($ billion)	
		Base Year Dollars	1975 Dollars
Air: Ridker (1966)	1970	7.3–8.9	10.1–12.3
Air: Gerhardt (1969)	1968	6–15.2	9.2–23.3
Air: Barret and Waddell (1973)	1968	16.1	24.6
Air: Babcock and Nagda (1973)	1968	20.2	30.9
Air: Justice, Williams and Clement (1973)	1970	2–8.7	2.8–12
Air: Waddell (1974)	1970	6.1–18.5	8.4–25.6
Air: National Academy of Sciences (1974)	1973	15–30	17.9–35.8
Air: Heintz and Hershaft (1975)	1973	9.5–35.4	11.3–42.2
Water: Abel, Tihansky, and Walsh (1975)	1970	5.5–15.5	7.6–21.4
Water: Horak and Heintz (1975)	1973	4.5–18.6	5.4–22.2

Source: Reproduced from United States Senate, Committee on Governmental Affairs, *Study on Federal Regulation*, vol. 6 (December 1978), Table 3-3, p. 40.

There have been many attempts to estimate the total cost to society from pollution. Some of those estimates are presented in Table 16.2. For comparison purposes, the different estimates are also expressed in terms of 1975 dollars. These estimates range from a low of $2.8 billion to a high of $42.2 billion for air pollution, and from $5.4 to $22.2 billion for water pollution. This variation is not surprising, given the difficulty of quantifying such pollution damages as loss of human lives and deterioration of scenic views.[10] Nonetheless, these figures do indicate that pollution imposes substantial costs on society.

Pollution costs will not, however, affect the decision-making processes of polluting producers and consumers. A firm bases its production decisions purely on the costs of its purchased inputs, thereby ignoring any impact its discharges may have on surrounding firms and households. And consumers do not think of society, but only of themselves, when they drive a car and throw litter on the highway. In short, consumers and producers do not consider all the costs of their actions. They

10. See, for example, M. Bailey, *Reducing Risks to Life—Measurement of the Benefits* (Washington, D.C.: American Enterprise Institute, 1980); and G. Brown, Jr. and H. Pollakowski, "Economic Valuation of Shoreline," *Review of Economics and Statistics* 59 (August 1977): 272–78.

Figure 16.2   Externalities and Market Equilibrium

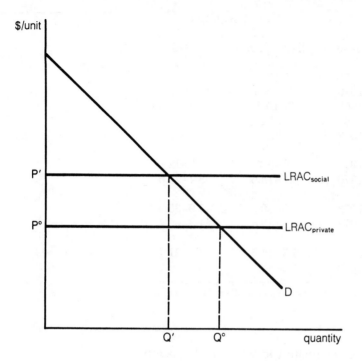

focus only on their private costs, which are less than the social costs. Economists refer to this difference between social and private costs as an *externality*.[11]

The impact of an externality, such as pollution, on market performance is illustrated in Figure 16.2. In long-run equilibrium, market price will be $P°$ and output $Q°$, because the firms' output decisions are based purely on their private costs. Social costs exceed private costs, however, because of the pollution externality. If the firms had to take *all* the social costs of their production into consideration, the long-run equilibrium solution would be P' and Q'. A competitive market will lead to a market failure—overproduction of goods that pollute the environment.[12] Since the environment is a "free" good, there is little incentive for a firm (or consumer) to voluntarily restrict its emission of pollutants. Even if a firm chose to do so, it would increase its costs and be at a disadvantage

11. An externality can also result from a divergence between private and social benefits from some action. This situation is discussed in Chapter 18.

12. There may not be an overproduction of the good, if the producing market is monopolistic instead of competitive. See J. M. Buchanan, "External Diseconomies, Corrective Taxes and Market Structure," *American Economic Review* 59 (March 1969): 174–77.

compared with competitors who were not so civic minded. Government intervention becomes necessary to counter the market failures created by consumption and production externalities.

Most federal environmental regulations are issued by the Environmental Protection Agency.[13] The EPA has a broad mandate to control the discharge of emissions into the nation's air, land, and water.[14] It must thus establish policies to regulate these discharges. As noted in Chapter 1, social regulation is different from economic regulation. The regulators do not have control over key economic variables such as price and entry. Instead, they can establish policies that modify a firm's behavior and, hence, its performance. A major issue for the EPA is the extent to which environmental policies should rely on market incentives to regulate household and industrial discharges of pollutants.

Major Regulatory Issues

Air Pollution

The main objective of the Clean Air Act is "to protect and enhance the quality of the Nation's air resources so as to promote the public health and welfare and the productive capacity of its population."[15] To achieve this objective, the EPA established national air quality standards for major pollutants. Each state must submit a compliance plan indicating how it will meet the national standards. If a state's plans are not acceptable, the EPA can prevent new industrial growth in that state, as well as withhold federal funds for highways and sewage treatment plants. At the same time, the EPA is empowered to directly regulate emissions from mobile and stationary pollution sources. This provision gives it authority to regulate the major sources of air pollution—the combustion of fuel in the transportation (mobile) and industrial (stationary) sectors of the economy.

Mobile Sources. The number one mobile source of pollution is obviously the automobile. It is a major source of hydrocarbons, nitrogen ox-

13. The EPA was established in 1970. It combined 15 separate environmental programs that had previously been operated by five different departments and agencies.

14. The EPA also enforces the Noise Control Act of 1972. It has reduced the noise allowed from heavy trucks and is currently examining the noise created by home appliances. Airplane noise is handled by the Federal Aviation Administration. See W. F. Baxter and L. R. Altree, "Legal Aspects of Airport Noise," *Journal of Law and Economics* 15 (April 1972): 1–113.

15. 42 U.S.C.A. Sect. 1857(b)(1) (1974).

Table 16.3   **Automobile Pollutant Emissions, 1957–1967,
and Federal Emission Standards, 1970–1981**
(In grams per mile)

| Period | Automobile Pollutant Emissions | | |
	Hydro-carbons	Carbon monoxide	Nitrogen oxides
Average Emissions			
1957-1967	8.7	87	(NA)
Federal Standards			
1970-1971	4.1	34	a
1972-1974	3.0	29	3[b]
1975-1979	1.5	15	2[c]
1980	.41	7	2
1981	.41	3.4	1

NA=Not available.

[a] No standard.

[b] Effective for 1973 model cars.

[c] Effective for 1977 model cars.

Source: U.S. Department of Commerce, *Statistical Abstract of the United States, 1979* (Washington, D.C.: Government Printing Office, 1979), p. 213.

ides, and carbon monoxide. In 1970, the EPA began to set emission standards for automobile pollutants. As Table 16.3 indicates, these standards have become increasingly stringent over time. By 1981, for example, a car will be allowed to emit only 10 percent of the hydrocarbons and carbon monoxide it was allowed to emit in 1970–1971. Automobile manufacturers have responded to these emission standards by installing exhaust and crankcase controls as well as catalytic converters. The exhaust and crankcase controls return gases to the combustion chamber, while the catalytic converter reduces the emissions of hydrocarbons and carbon monoxide by promoting their oxidation in the exhaust system.

While emission controls systems can bring about a substantial reduction in automobile pollution, they will not be effective if they malfunction over time. The Clean Air Act also requires auto manufacturers to warrant emission control systems for 50,000 miles or five years, whichever comes first. The systems also will not operate effectively if the driver uses leaded gasoline or deliberately sabotages the system.[16] This is why the EPA required new cars to use only unleaded gasoline begin-

16. A study conducted for the EPA found that approximately 20 percent of the sample cars had been tampered with, and tampering was suspected for 50 percent of the cars ("Antipollution Gear of Many U.S. Cars Disabled on Purpose," *Wall Street Journal*, December 18, 1978, p. 7).

ning with the 1975 model year. It is also encouraging states to adopt inspection and maintenance programs for emission control systems.[17]

Stationary Sources. The major problem in emissions from stationary sources, such as smokestacks, is the discharge of sulfur oxides. These result when coal and oil are burned by industrial firms, especially electric utilities. Electric utilities use the fuel to heat boilers, thereby creating the steam necessary to drive their turbine generators. A firm can reduce its sulfur emissions by burning low-sulfur coal or oil, which are available, though at a higher price. An alternative approach is to install smokestack "scrubbers"—chemical-mechanical devices that use limestone to wash sulfur dioxide out of the gases escaping up smokestacks. Which approach is more efficient depends on the firm's access to low-sulfur fuels and the cost of installing scrubbers. Each firm will choose that approach that minimizes its costs of complying with the sulfur emission standards.

In some cases, EPA has even established the permissible level of emissions for individual smokestacks.[18] In Ohio, for example, EPA allows Cleveland Electric's Avon Lake plant to emit 6.2 pounds of sulfur dioxide per million Btus of heat generated, while its East Lake plant is restricted to 6.7–6.8 pounds per million Btus.[19] Such thorough, source-by-source regulation is not only very time consuming, but can also be too restrictive, especially when it mandates the specific pollution-control technology that a firm must install.

In an effort to improve its regulations, EPA announced two new policies:"offsets" and "bubbles." The "offset" policy enables firms to build new plants in areas where the EPA's emission standards would be exceeded. A firm must simply offset the emissions from its new plant by reducing emissions from existing sources. It can install pollution equipment on its own facilities and/or those of other local firms. The offset policy thus makes it possible for new plants to be built in dirty areas without worsening pollution. In fact, it may even improve air quality, since the EPA normally requires the reduction in existing emissions to be slightly larger than the expected increase in new emissions.

The "bubble" policy is a step away from source-by-source regula-

17. "Sharper Teeth for Air Monitors," *Business Week*, October 30, 1978, pp.131–34.

18. The EPA is empowered to set emission standards for all new plants constructed in the United States. In addition, it can set emission levels for existing plants in states that do not have acceptable pollution control programs.

19. "EPA May Ease Emission Rules for 2 Ohio Plants," *Wall Street Journal*, June 7, 1979, p. 14.

tion.[20] Instead of focusing on an individual vent or smokestack, the policy considers the emissions from a complete plant—in effect, viewing the plant as being covered by a giant bubble. The EPA monitors the total emissions from that bubble, not from each smokestack inside it. The policy's objective is to give firms more discretion in complying with emissions standards. If it is cheaper to reduce emissions from one source than from another one, a profit-maximizing firm will do so. The same overall level of emissions reduction can thus be achieved at less cost to the firm and, hence, to society.

Water Pollution

The nation's policy toward water pollution is enunciated in the Federal Water Pollution Control Act of 1972, as amended in 1977. It has two main objectives. First, the nation's water should be of sufficient quality to support fishing and swimming by 1983. Second, all discharges of pollutants into navigable waters should be terminated by 1985. These objectives are to be accomplished by reducing industrial and household pollution.

Water pollution by households will be decreased through the construction of municipal sewage treatment plants. In 1973, for example, 22 percent of the population was not served by a sewer system.[21] The 1972 act created a strong incentive for municipalities to construct sewage treatment systems, for it increased the federal government's share of construction costs from 55 to 75 percent.

A different approach was adopted toward industrial polluters. Industry must attain the targeted level of "no pollutants" in a two-step sequence. By mid-1977, industry was expected to have adopted the "best practicable control technology." The EPA was to judge this step in light of such factors as the firm's production technology, expected reductions in emissions, etc. By mid-1983, however, each firm is expected to have adopted the "best available technology" regardless of cost. The 1977 amendment to the act extended these deadlines to April 1, 1979, and mid-1984, respectively.[22] These requirements are enforced through the EPA's awarding of discharge permits to major polluters.

20. "Air Pollution Control; Recommendation for Alternative Emission Reduction Options Within State Implementation Plans," *Federal Register* 44, no. 239 (December 11, 1979): 717–80.

21. U.S. Department of Commerce, *Statistical Abstract of the United States, 1979* (Washington, D.C.: Government Printing Office, 1979), p. 213.

22. The 1977 amendment actually divides pollutants into three categories and establishes a separate timetable for each category. The control of toxic chemicals, for example, is given a higher priority than that of human wastes.

Land Pollution

The most visible type of land pollution is litter, trash thrown on the ground or highway instead of into a garbage can. State and local governments first responded to this problem by fining litterers, and posting signs along highways notifying drivers that they will be fined some amount (perhaps $100) for littering. Some states have further reduced the financial incentive to litter by placing a deposit on beverage containers, a major source of litter.[23] A standard deposit, say five cents, is collected on each beverage container when it is sold. For example, a six-pack of beer would increase in price by 30 cents regardless of the type of container—steel, aluminum, or glass. The consumer receives the deposit back when the containers are returned to a retail outlet. The deposit is designed to encourage consumers to recycle their own containers and possibly even the discarded containers of others. The apparent success of these deposits in some states has led to demands for federal legislation mandating a nationwide container deposit.[24]

Another, more serious, type of land pollution is the dumping of hazardous wastes into the ground. For years, industrial firms have simply disposed of their by-products by burying them at special dump sites. This practice was unnoticed and unregulated until the case of the Love Canal in Niagara Falls, New York, where many families had to be moved from the polluted land.[25] The canal had been used as a storage site by Hooker Chemicals and Plastic Corporation in the 1940s. Over time, the chemicals seeped out of the storage site and into surrounding homes. This is apparently the reason why local residents have higher-than-average rates of miscarriages, birth defects, and liver ailments. Unfortunately, the Love Canal experience may be repeated elsewhere, as there are an estimated 51,000 storage sites for hazardous chemicals throughout the United States.[26] The EPA in 1979 announced rules to initiate regulation in this extremely important area.[27]

---

23. "A Key Battle in Ohio on Container Deposits," *Business Week*, November 5, 1979, pp. 59–62.

24. "The Threat of a Federal Ban on Throwaways," *Business Week*, January 29, 1979, pp. 36–37.

25. "U.S. Sues Chemical Dumpers," *Washington Post*, December 21, 1979, p. A8.

26. "Major Risks Are Posed By Years of Dumping of Industrial Wastes," *Wall Street Journal*, May 22, 1979, p. 1.

27. The proposed rules would require producers to keep track of their wastes and to store them in facilities that comply with EPA standards.

Endangered Species

The existence of wildlife is threatened by people's pollution and elimination of their natural habitats. In 1979, there were 260 mammals, 211 birds, 58 reptiles, 14 amphibians, 39 fishes, 3 snails, 25 clams, 1 crustacean, 6 insects, and 20 plants listed as endangered species—species that are in danger of becoming extinct.[28] In an effort to prevent the extinction of endangered species, Congress passed the Endangered Species Act of 1973. This act directs federal agencies to ensure that their activities do not jeopardize the continued survival of endangered species.

The inevitable conflict between economic development and endangered species was not long in coming. The endangered species was the snail darter *(Percina tanasi)*, a three-inch-long member of the perch family. Its only known habitat was threatened by the construction of the Tellico Dam on the Little Tennessee River. When completed, the Tellico Dam was expected to generate electricity for 20,000 homes, encourage regional economic development, expand recreational opportunities, and control flooding. Congress had spent $100 million on the dam when the Supreme Court ruled that it could not be completed because it violated the Endangered Species Act that Congress had just passed.[29] The snail darter's victory was short-lived, however. Congress exempted the Tellico Dam from the act, thereby enabling it to be completed. (The snail darter was transplanted to the nearby Hiwassee River and is reportedly doing fine.)

Evaluation

Environmental regulations have been extremely controversial. Industry argues that they are too strict; environmentalists claim that they are too weak. Most people seem to be caught in the middle. They want a cleaner environment, but they are not sure that they can afford it. This section examines our limited experience with environmental regulation and then discusses some of the proposals for its reform.

Appraisal of Current Policy

Environmental regulation raises two specific related issues. First, what is the desired level of emission reduction? Should emissions of a specific pollutant be reduced by 50, 80, or 100 percent? Second, what is the best policy of achieving the desired reduction in emissions? Should the

28. U.S. Department of Commerce, *Statistical Abstract, 1979,* p. 214.

29. *Tennessee Valley Authority* v. *Hill,* 437 U.S. 153 (1978).

Figure 16.3   **Marginal Costs and Benefits of Emission Reductions**

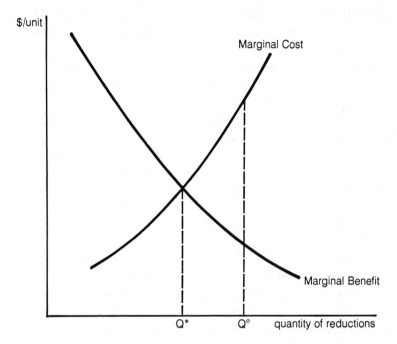

government specify the appropriate pollution control technology, or should it leave that decision up to an individual firm? Most of the controversy surrounding current environmental regulations has centered on the issues of emission levels and emission policies.

Emission Levels.   Theoretically, the discharge of a particular pollutant into the atmosphere can be halted completely. For example, a given gas could be bottled and stored underground instead of allowed to escape up a smokestack. This solution is not costless, however. It would require the utilization of some of society's scarce resources and would substitute a land pollution problem for air pollution. This suggests that there should be some type of balancing of the costs and benefits of emission reductions.

   Figure 16.3 presents an economic perspective on the costs and benefits of emission reductions. The focus is not on the total cost and total benefit of emission reduction, but rather on the marginal cost and marginal benefit of an incremental reduction in emissions. For example, what is the benefit and cost to society of a one percent reduction in the emission of hydrocarbons by automobiles? The figure indicates that the marginal benefit of additional reductions in emissions declines continuously, while the marginal cost of obtaining those reductions increases continuously. If society wants to maximize its welfare, it should reduce emissions until the marginal cost incurred is just equal to the marginal benefit received. There is thus an optimal level of emissions, Q^*. If emissions are reduced beyond this point to $Q°$, society will be worse off, because the marginal cost of the reductions is greater than their marginal benefit.

Before evaluating current emission standards, it is worthwhile to examine the shapes of the marginal cost and benefit curves in more detail. The downward-sloping marginal benefit curve indicates that the first percentage reduction in emissions is more valuable to society than the last percentage reduction. This relationship is due to the nature of the primary benefits that emission reductions bring—health and scenic value. The initial reduction in emissions may save human lives, while succeeding reductions decrease respiratory problems continually until all health complications are finally eliminated. A major problem, then, is how to place a dollar value on these benefits so that they can be compared with costs. It is relatively easy to assign a dollar value to medical care (e.g., a day in a hospital or medications administered), but what is the value of a human life?[30] Economists approximate it by an individual's earning capacity, although this is clearly a lower bound on any individual's value to society.[31]

The upward-sloping marginal cost curve indicates that it becomes increasingly more expensive to achieve a given percentage reduction in emissions. This indicates that there are diminishing returns to pollution control. The steel industry, for example, has estimated that the final *2 percent* reduction in their water discharges accounted for *40 percent* of total treatment costs![32] And in the automobile industry, executives have long claimed that it is becoming increasingly costly to eliminate addi-

---

30. For a discussion of the problems involved in measuring the value of recreational services, see J. Knetsch and R. Davis, "Comparisons of Methods for Recreation Evaluation," in *Economics of the Environment*, ed. Dorfman and Dorfman, pp. 450–68.

31. This approach must be used with caution, however, for it would suggest that the life of a poor or elderly person is worth very little, while the life of the town banker is almost of unlimited value to society. One way around this problem is to simply use an average figure whenever estimating the benefits of lowering mortality rates. This issue is also important in the area of consumer and worker protection (Chapter 17).

32. T. Alexander, "It's Time for New Approaches to Pollution Control," *Fortune*, November 1976, pp. 227–32.

tional emissions from cars.[33] It is far easier to quantify the costs of pollution control than the benefits. A firm incurs these costs when it pays a premium for low-sulfur oil or when it builds taller smokestacks and installs scrubbers inside them. The situation becomes more complicated, however, if environmental regulations lead to plant closings and increase the inflation rate.[34]

It is not possible, however, to quantify all the benefits and costs to determine whether current regulations are too strict or too lenient. The EPA has compared the quantitative data available on both the costs and the benefits of pollution control due to federal regulations. As would be expected, the costs substantially exceed the benefits. EPA estimated that the cumulative cost of complying with the Clean Air and Clean Water Acts from 1970 to 1977 was $84.8 billion.[35] In addition, it is expected that pollution costs would total $360 billion for the period 1977–1986. With regard to macroeconomic impacts, a study prepared for the EPA suggests that environmental regulations have had a relatively minor impact on the consumer price index—perhaps .2 to .3 percent per year. From January 1971 on, environmental regulations were a significant factor in the closing of 132 plants that employed 24,500 people. On the benefit side, attention has focused on the damages resulting from air and water pollution as figures that would indicate the potential benefits from cleaning up the environment. The estimates of pollution damages have been very crude and vary considerably. As illustrated earlier in Table 16.2, the estimates for air pollution range from $2.8 to $42.2 billion, while those for water pollution range from $5.4 to $27.2 billion in 1975 dollars.

Overall, it would seem that the total costs of pollution control vastly outweigh its potential benefits. As noted earlier, however, it is not possible to quantify accurately the value of a human life, of air that is easy to breathe, of a wildlife species, or of a scenic view. There is thus a systematic bias toward the understatement of potential benefits, and it becomes impossible to determine whether the United States is discharging the "optimal" amount of pollutants into its environment. It can

33. L. Iacocca, "Making Automobile Rules Work Better," *Enviromental Science & Technology*, January 1977, pp. 32–35.

34. See, for example, R. Hartman, K. Bozdogan, and R. Nadkarni, "The Economic Impacts of Environmental Regulations on the U.S. Copper Industry," *Bell Journal of Economics* 10 (Autumn 1979): 589–618.

35. All of the figures presented on the costs and benefits of environmental regulation are from the EPA's *The Cost of Clean Air and Water—Report to Congress, August, 1979.*

be concluded, however, that any policy to eliminate all discharges (such as the Clean Water Act) is clearly not in the best interest of society.

Emission Policies. Given that society wants to reduce emissions by some amount, do current government policies achieve that desired reduction as efficiently as possible? The general answer would have to be no, though the future does appear to be more promising. The general problem is that environmental regulations have removed a firm's natural incentive to minimize costs. The Federal Water Pollution Control Act, for example, requires most cities to build waste treatment plants regardless of the nature of their wastes or their impact on the environment. Many small towns on the West Coast, for example, were required to build these plants even though it was more efficient and environmentally sounder to dump their wastes directly into the ocean.[36] The government's heavy subsidy for these plants has encouraged many towns to build plants that they cannot afford to operate and maintain properly over time. A common complaint about air pollution control is that the EPA tends to specify the pollution control technology (e.g., scrubbers) that a firm must use. To specify the technique instead of the performance standard reduces a firm's incentives to develop new, more efficient, pollution control technology. Finally, by regulating the discharge from each source of pollution, the EPA prevented firms from reducing pollution where it was easiest to do so. The EPA's new bubble policy was designed to meet this problem, though it is too soon to tell how effective it will be in practice.[37] Overall, environmental regulations have consistently paid insufficient attention to the economic costs and benefits of compliance with government regulations.

New Directions for Environmental Regulation

Given the above criticisms, it is not surprising that most proposals for reforming environmental regulations would place more emphasis on market forces. Their general objective is to increase the incentives for

36. "EPA Push for National Sewage Policy is Meeting Criticism on the West Coast," *Wall Street Journal*, August 20, 1979, p. 7.

37. Initial comments from industry were encouraging. DuPont, for instance, estimated that under the bubble policy it would be able to cut its air pollution treatment costs from $136 million to $55 million a year ("EPA Hopes to Achieve Cleaner Air at Less Cost," *Washington Post*, December 3, 1979, p. A2). For a good discussion of the new policy's limitations, see "Blowing Bubbles at EPA," *Regulation* 3 (March/April 1979): 5–6.

firms efficiently to reduce their discharge of pollutants into the environment. This section examines two solutions frequently proposed: bargaining and taxes.

Bargaining.   The bargaining solution tries to correct the pollution market failure by assigning property rights to the environment.[38] For example, environmental property rights could be assigned to the local factory or to the local government. The factory and the government would then negotiate an agreement to limit the factory's emission of pollutants. If the town owned the property rights, the firm would pay for the right to pollute. Alternatively, if the firm held those rights, the town would pay the firm not to pollute. In both cases, the pollution externality is internalized by the factory and the amount of emissions is reduced.[39]

The bargaining solution has two major drawbacks, however. First, one side may have a substantially stronger bargaining position, leading to a one-sided solution. For example, if the factory is the only employer in town, it may threaten to relocate to another, more "hospitable" area.[40] The town then faces the unenviable choice between a clean environment and an employed citizenry. Second, the bargaining unit, say, the town, may not be sufficiently large to contain all of the factory's externalities.[41] Air and water discharges may affect more than a single town, and so all the affected localities would have to be on the "bargaining team." This solution may not work, however, because of a "free rider" problem. One town may intentionally understate its own willingness to pay the factory, because it will automatically benefit from any reductions negotiated by the other towns.

Taxes.   The tax solution is straightforward—simply place a tax on the emissions that polluters discharge. For example, the EPA considered

38. The assignment of property rights has proved successful in correcting market failures in the natural resource area. See R. Agnello and L. Donnelley, "Property Rights and Efficiency in the Oyster Industry," *Journal of Law and Economics* 18 (October 1975): 521–33.

39. R. Coase, "The Problem of Social Cost," *Journal of Law and Economics* 1 (October 1960): 1–44.

40. The imbalance in bargaining strengths is illustrated every time states compete aggressively against one another for new manufacturing plants ("States Offer Wine, Song and Other Lures in Effort to Attract Foreign Investments," *Wall Street Journal*, March 11, 1980, p. 10).

41. "U.S. Conversion to Coal Would Add to 'Acid Rain' in Canada," *The Washington Post*, February 7, 1980, p. A12.

establishing a tax on sulfur emissions by industrial firms.[42] An electric utility could pollute, but it would incur a cost every time it did so. The pollution externality is thus internalized by the polluter. In an effort to minimize its total production costs (factor inputs plus the pollution tax), the firm will reduce its emissions whenever it is profitable to do so; that is, when the marginal cost of reducing emissions is less than the tax. On the other hand, if the tax is less than the marginal costs of pollution control, the firm will pay the tax. This still increases the firm's costs and so creates an incentive to develop production technologies that minimize pollution costs. In sum, pollution taxes are considered desirable because they create an incentive for all polluters to reduce their emissions when it is efficient to do so.

The tax approach is commonly criticized on two grounds. First, it may not be possible to monitor a firm's emissions accurately in order to assess the taxes. A firm might, for example, locate any monitoring device upwind from the smokestack, thereby giving an inaccurate picture of its level of emissions. This is one reason why some regulators like to control a firm's emissions directly by having them install a specified device such as a scrubber. Second, there is no prior guidance as to what the appropriate tax should be. The regulators would have to engage in a trial-and-error process that could be very time consuming and, hence, costly to society.

Summary

Pollution occurs when society's discharge of solid, liquid, and gaseous wastes exceeds the environment's capacity to absorb those wastes. Consumers and producers pollute because the price of doing so is zero, while the benefits are greater than zero. Pollution is not costless to society, however. It imposes costs on both consumers and producers. The presence of these externalities creates market failures, thereby necessitating government intervention. EPA regulations can require firms to reduce emissions and may even specify the technique to be employed. This approach has been strongly criticized for not being efficient. As a result, the EPA has begun to adopt policies that rely more heavily on a firm's natural incentives to minimize costs. It is too soon to tell whether this new approach will lead to a more efficient reduction of emissions.

42. J. M. Griffin, "An Econometric Evaluation of Sulfur Taxes," *Journal of Political Economy* 82 (July/August 1974): 669–88; and A. Schlottmann and L. Abrams, "Sulfur Emissions Taxes and Coal Resources," *Review of Economics and Statistics* 59 (February 1977): 50–55.

Agnello, R., and Donnelley, L. "Property Rights and Efficiency in the Oyster Industry," *Journal of Law and Economics* 18 (October 1975): 521–33.

Coase, R. "The Problems of Social Cost," *Journal of Law and Economics* 1 (October 1960): 1–44.

Gordon, H. S. "The Economic Theory of a Common-Property Resource: The Fishery," *Journal of Political Economy* 62 (April 1954): 124–42.

Lave, L., and Seskin, E. *Air Pollution and Human Health* (Baltimore: Johns Hopkins, 1977).

Ruff, L. "The Economic Common Sense of Pollution," *The Public Interest* 19 (Spring 1970): 69–85.

Suggested Readings

Consumer and Worker Protection

Chapter 17

People perform two related economic functions—production and consumption. As workers, people produce the goods that are supplied throughout the economy. As consumers, people purchase some of those goods for their own use. In both situations, people evaluate their options and then choose those that best promote their self-interests. Situations may arise in the marketplace, however, when people cannot accurately evaluate their options. As a result, they may make decisions that are not in their best interests. Government intervention may then be necessary to protect society's consumers and workers.

The Setting

Citizens of a society can require many types of protection. It may, for example, be necessary to protect them from dangers of which they are unaware. A newly developed drug may be unsafe or a particular workplace may be unhealthy. At the same time, it may also be necessary to protect people from dangers of which they *are* aware. Indeed, it often seems that people need more protection from themselves than from anything else.[1] Motorcyclists may thus be required to wear helmets, and

1. In 1977, for example, there were more accidental deaths (103,202) and suicides (28,681) than homicides (19,968) (U.S. Department of Commerce, *Statistical Abstract of the United States, 1979* [Washington, D.C.: Government Printing Office, 1979], pp. 80, 181).

cigarette manufacturers must place a warning on cigarette packages. All in all, there are clearly many situations—at home, at work, and in between—that can be dangerous and may require government intervention.

The History of Consumer and Worker Regulation

At the heart of a market economy is the economic principle of consumer sovereignty. Consumers determine the allocation of society's resources through their expenditure decisions. Each consumer selects that combination of goods that will maximize his or her utility. Throughout this market process, however, consumers must safeguard their own interests. They must be on guard against deceptive and untruthful sales practices. The consumer's responsibility in this regard was long recognized by the legal principle of *caveat emptor:* "let the buyer beware." Any risk associated with a market transaction traditionally resides with the purchaser.

Purchasers did have the right to sue a seller if they were actually injured by the consumption of the product. This private legal right, however, did not adequately protect consumers against unsafe products. Individual consumers might not know their legal rights or might not have adequate financial resources to enforce them. Even if they won in court, they could recover only the actual damages inflicted on them. They could not prevent the product from being sold to others, who might be similarly harmed. Finally, an unknowing consumer cannot always determine the cause of an injury. For instance, it is not easy to isolate the damage inflicted by a particular food or drug, especially if the damage occurs over an extended period of time.

Dissatisfaction with the recourses available to consumers led to federal regulation of consumer products. In quick succession, Congress passed the Food and Drug Act of 1906 and the Meat Inspection Act of 1907.[2] These two acts addressed growing public concern over the adulteration of essential consumer products. The Department of Agriculture enforces the provisions of the Meat Inspection Act, while the Food and Drug Administration (FDA) is responsible for the regulation of food, drugs, and cosmetics.

Additional consumer protection legislation was passed in the years after World War II, culminating in the creation of the National Highway Traffic Safety Administration (NHTSA) in 1970 and the Consumer Product Safety Commission (CPSC) in 1972. The NHTSA was established in

2. These acts were amended in 1938 by the Food, Drug and Cosmetic Act.

an attempt to reduce the number and seriousness of motor vehicle accidents. To achieve these objectives, the NHTSA is empowered to issue safety standards for automobiles. The CPSC was authorized to implement several existing laws: the Flammable Fabrics Act of 1953, the Refrigerator Safety Act of 1956, the Federal Hazardous Substances Act of 1960, and the Poison Prevention Packaging Act of 1970. It can establish safety standards for consumer products, as well as provide consumers with information about the comparative safety of different products.

The Federal Trade Commission (FTC) is also active in the area of consumer protection. Its concern is not product safety, but "unfair or deceptive acts or practices."[3] Of particular importance is the truthfulness of information provided by manufacturers through their advertisements. The FTC also administers the Lanham Trademark, Truth-in-Lending, and Fair Packaging and Labeling acts.

The history of worker protection parallels that of consumer protection.[4] Following the industrial revolution, more and more workers were employed in factories, where they commonly performed repetitive, though potentially dangerous, tasks. If a worker was injured on the job, he or she could sue the employer for compensation for those injuries. Private lawsuits were generally not successful, however. Employers argued that the worker was negligent and therefore not entitled to compensation. More importantly, any worker who initiated a suit might be fired by the factory owner, along with the supporting witnesses. In an era without unemployment or welfare benefits, this threat constituted a strong deterrent to private legal action.

The workers' plight was initially addressed around the turn of the century by the passage of workmen's compensation laws, which provide a worker with compensation for job-related injuries. Although provisions vary from state to state, this compensation normally covers a worker's medical expenses as well as some percentage of lost wages. It does not, however, provide compensation for any pain or suffering associated with the disabling injury.

Though workers' compensation laws were better than nothing, they did not aim at preventing injuries, but simply provided some compensation once injuries had occurred. In an effort to reduce job-related injuries, Congress passed the Occupational Safety and Health Act of 1970.

3. The original Section 5 of the FTC Act prohibited only unfair methods of competition. It was amended by the Wheeler-Lea Act in 1938 to prohibit deceptive acts and practices also.

4. This discussion closely follows that of T. Harron, *Law for Business Managers—The Regulatory Environment* (Boston: Holbrook Press, 1977), Chapter 14.

This act established the Occupational Safety and Health Administration (OSHA), an agency within the Department of Labor that is empowered to set and enforce health and safety standards in the nation's workplaces.

The Economics of Consumer and Worker Regulation

In a market economy, people's consumption and production decisions are voluntary and, therefore, presumably beneficial. Whether or not these decisions are indeed beneficial depends on the amount of information available throughout the decision-making process. The model of perfect competition presented in Chapter 2 explicitly assumes that both producers and consumers have *perfect* information. That is, consumers are aware of the numerous goods available in the marketplace, as well as their prices and relevant characteristics. Workers are similarly aware of the employment opportunities available in the marketplace, as well as their wages and working conditions. As a result, in this perfect situation, consumers and workers always make the market decisions that maximize their welfare.

In fact, it is extremely unlikely that consumers and workers do have perfect information about their market opportunities. They will thus make "incorrect" decisions—decisions that they would not make if they had more information. The primary focus in this chapter is on how risk can affect people's decisions as consumers and producers.

Information and Risk-taking.   Figure 17.1 presents a simplified picture of the role of risk in consumption and production decisions. Part (a) depicts the supply and demand for cigarettes, a consumption decision. Initially, the cigarette market is in equilibrium at a price of $P°$ and quantity of $Q°$. Assume that the government now provides some information that was not previously available to the public: cigarettes can cause cancer. How will this new information affect the cigarette market? The initial demand curve for cigarettes was constructed on the assumption that smoking was not harmful. This assumption is no longer valid, and cigarette smokers are presented with a trade-off between smoking and good health. Some smokers will be unaffected, while others will reduce their consumption or even quit altogether. The net effect will be a decrease in market demand from $D°$ to D'. This will lower the equilibrium price to P' and quantity to Q'.

The role of risk in production decisions is illustrated in part (b) of Figure 17.1, which presents the supply and demand for coal miners.

Figure 17.1 The Risk Element in Consumption and Production

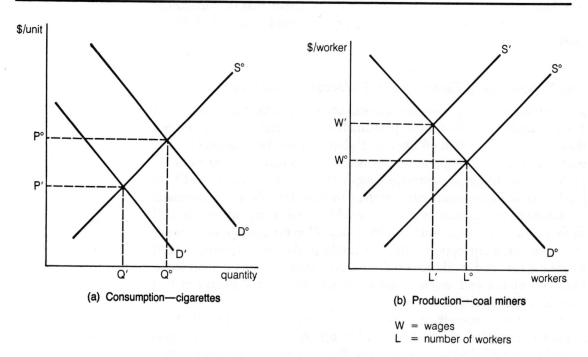

(a) Consumption—cigarettes

(b) Production—coal miners

W = wages
L = number of workers

The labor market is initially in equilibrium at a wage of W° and an employment level of L°. Assume that miners now learn that working in the coal mines can lead to "black lung" disease.[5] Coal miners must now determine whether they are willing to continue working in light of this new information. If this health hazard discourages some miners from continuing in their current employment, market supply will shift to the left. This shift will be reinforced by any risk premium that the remaining miners require. The end result will be a higher equilibrium wage (W') but a lower equilibrium employment (L') in the market for coal miners.

These examples indicate that, for consumers or workers, *known* risks will lead to adjustments in both price and output levels in affected markets. More specifically, the price of a hazardous product will decrease, while the wage for a hazardous occupation will increase.[6] If risks are not

5. Black lung disease (pneumoconiosis) results from the continual inhalation by miners of coal dust in the coal mines. The Federal Coal Mine and Safety Act of 1969 provides benefits to miners who are disabled by this disease.

6. W. K. Viscusi, "Wealth Effects and Earnings Premiums for Job Hazards," *Review of Economics and Statistics* 60 (August 1978): 408–16.

known, however, market failures will result. Consumers and workers will make riskier decisions than if they were fully informed.

The Market for Information.   The critical issue is whether a private market provides sufficient information for consumers and workers. Information is a commodity—resources must be utilized to acquire it and disseminate it, and it has economic value to decision-makers. A good (and successful) example is the magazine *Consumer Reports,* which provides information about the quality and safety of various consumer products. This information enables readers to make more intelligent decisions in the marketplace. Unfortunately, private information sources such as *Consumer Reports,* though obviously beneficial, provide less information than is socially desirable. This is illustrated in Figure 17.2 with some hypothetical cost and demand curves for *Consumer Reports.* In this situation, profits will be maximized by selling Q° magazines at a price of P°. This is not the socially desirable price and output, however, because the magazine's price exceeds its marginal cost of production and dissemination. From society's perspective, the optimal price and quantity would be P' and Q'. At this price, *Consumer Reports* could not

Figure 17.2   **A Hypothetical Market for *Consumer Reports***

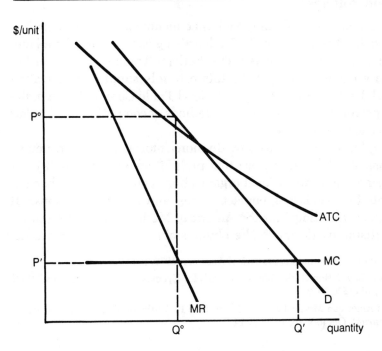

cover its costs, however. In this case, *Consumer Reports* will be market-ed, but not in sufficient quantities and not at the correct price.

In sum, the private market can supply some information, but not enough from society's perspective. The problem is that the marginal cost of simply disseminating information can be very small. For exam-ple, a business newsletter can be quickly and cheaply reproduced on a copying machine. A price set equal to marginal cost would not enable a private firm to cover the costs incurred in acquiring the information in the first place. As a result, private markets will not supply enough of the information that is necessary for consumers and workers to make correct decisions in the marketplace. Government intervention becomes necessary.

Major Regulatory Issues

The government has two broad policy options when formulating its pol-icies to protect consumers and workers. First, it can provide and dissem-inate information to consumers and workers. Second, it can establish safety standards for workplaces and consumer products. This section ex-amines some of the major policies adopted by the different federal agen-cies that are responsible for protecting the nation's consumers and workers.

Information Policies

The most important marketing tool that manufacturers of consumer products use is advertising. In 1978, advertising expenditures for all me-dia totaled $43.7 billion dollars.[7] The Federal Trade Commission has undertaken a major effort to make this privately supplied information more useful. Under Section 5 of the Federal Trade Commission Act, the FTC is empowered to prohibit unfair methods of competition and unfair or deceptive acts or practices.

For example, in an effort to provide more information to consumers, the FTC has attacked regulations that prohibit advertising. In 1978, it ruled that states and professional organizations could no longer ban ad-vertisements for eyeglasses, contact lenses, and eye examinations.[8] It also ruled that it is illegal for the American Medical Association to re-strict advertising by doctors.[9] The obvious objective is to increase the

7. U.S. Department of Commerce, *Statistical Abstract, 1979*, p. 595.

8. "FTC Adopts Regulation Outlawing Ban on Ads for Eyeglasses or Examinations," *Wall Street Journal*, May 25, 1978.

9. "FTC Tells American Medical Association to End Its Curbs on Doctors' Advertising," *Wall Street Journal*, October 25, 1979, p. 14.

information supplied to potential customers, who currently have little information about the prices charged for different medical services. It is one of the few areas where a consumer receives a service and then discovers the price.

Increasing the amount of advertising available to consumers is not a panacea for the information problem. Advertising can be deceptive or misleading as well as informative. The FTC has adopted numerous policies to reduce deceptive advertising and increase the informational value of advertisements. First, advertisers must be able to substantiate any claims made in their advertisements. For example, the FTC ordered Warner-Lambert to stop making claims that its oral antiseptic Listerine could prevent or cure colds. In addition, Warner-Lambert was required to run corrective advertising stating that "contrary to prior advertising, Listerine will not help prevent colds or sore throats or lessen their severity."[10] Second, firms must state in their advertising that sale items actually are available at their stores. This prevents firms from attracting customers with ads for one product and then encouraging them to switch to more expensive products, a sales tactic known as "bait-and-switch." Third, people who endorse products must actually use those products, if the ads depict them doing so. Consumers must also be able to expect comparable performance from the endorsed product. Finally, the FTC has tried to increase the informational value of advertising by stimulating comparative advertising. In these ads, one manufacturer openly compares its product with a competitor's brand. The intention is that direct comparisons of competing products will inform consumers better and enable them to make more intelligent market choices.

Product Safety Policies

Three major federal agencies have responsibility for the safety of consumer products: the Consumer Product Safety Commission, the Food and Drug Administration, and the National Highway Transportation Safety Administration. This section discusses briefly some of the major policies that have been adopted by these three agencies.

Consumer Product Safety Commission (CPSC). The CPSC, established in 1972, has broad jurisdiction over the approximately 10,000 products that Americans purchase for home or recreational use. It has begun, for example, to establish safety standards for different products.

10. *Warner-Lambert Co.* v. *Federal Trade Commission,* 562 F.2d 749 (1977), *cert. denied,* 435 U.S. 950 (1978).

One early move was to require aspirin producers to market their product with child-resistant tops, to reduce accidental ingestion of aspirin by young children. This packaging standard was subsequently expanded to numerous products, including prescription drugs. In addition, the CPSC has promulgated safety standards for matchbooks, lawn mowers, and swimming pool slides. It is currently examining the fire hazards posed by upholstered furniture, with the objective of specifying flame-resistant material and thereby reducing the incidence of fires caused by burning cigarettes.

Food and Drug Administration (FDA). The primary purpose of the FDA is to protect consumers from unsafe food, drugs, and cosmetics. Under the Delaney Act, the FDA must ban any food additives that have been found to cause cancer in humans or animals. This strict requirement has focused attention on the tests that are conducted to determine whether a specific product is carcinogenic. The FDA has created considerable controversy with its proposal to ban saccharin, an artificial sweetener widely used in diet soft drinks. If saccharin is banned, it would join a list that includes cyclamate (another sugar substitute), Red No. 2 (food coloring), and acrylonitrile bottles (plastic soft drink containers).[11]

The saccharin controversy was ignited by a Canadian study that found that saccharin caused cancer in rats. These results were ridiculed by the public because of the heavy dosages to which the test rats were subjected; it was estimated that the equivalent dosage for a human would be 1,250 12-ounce diet sodas or 4,000 packets of saccharin a day for an entire lifetime.[12] The purpose of the dosage used in testing, however, is not to re-create the human experience, but to see whether the material might be carcinogenic. Contrary to popular belief, all substances do not cause cancer in rats. In fact, of the approximately 7,000 substances that have been tested, 6,500 were considered to be safe.[13] Table 17.1 lists 18 food components that have been found to be carcinogenic agents in test

11. The FDA is also considering a ban on the use of antibiotics in animal feed. Cattle farmers use them because they act as a powerful growth stimulant. There is concern, however, that this may lead to the development of antibiotic-resistant bacteria that could be transferred to the intestines of humans ("A Drive to Limit the Antibiotics in Animal Feed," *Business Week*, January 16, 1978, pp. 55–56).

12. "Fight Starts to Beat the Ban on Saccharin," *U.S. News & World Report*, March 28, 1977, p. 49.

13. J. Randal, "This Rat Died In a Cancer Lab to Save Lives," *Washington Post*, July 22, 1979, p. D1.

Table 17.1 Common Carcinogenic Food Components[a]

Benzene in root beer, sarsaparilla
Bracken fern in greens or salads
Cadmium in food, water
Caffeine in coffee, tea, cocoa
Chloroform in water
Cycasin in cycad nut
Cyclochlorotine in rice
Egg yolk and egg white
Ergot in rye
Isopropyl oils in water and fruit oils
Lactose and maltose
Luteoskyrin in rice
Oil of calamus as a flavoring agent in food
Peanuts, corn products, and milk containing aflatoxins
Pyrrolizidine alkaloids in cereals
Safrole in spices
Tannic acid in coffee, tea, cocoa
Vitamin D_2

[a]Have been found to be carcinogenic in laboratory animals.
Source: U.S. Senate Committee on Agriculture, Nutrition, and Forestry, *Food Safety: Where Are We?* (Washington, D.C.: Government Printing Office, July 1979), pp. 293–94.

animals. This list will undoubtedly grow as more and more substances are subjected to detailed tests.[14]

The Canadian study was supported by findings from a National Cancer Institute study, which found that users of saccharin were more likely to have bladder cancer than nonusers.[15] This effect was magnified for heavy cigarette smokers. It is not clear how this information will affect the future of saccharin. Congress placed a moratorium on the FDA's proposed ban of saccharin while it considered amendments to the Delaney Act.

The FDA has regulated drugs since 1906. Beginning in 1938, pharmaceutical manufacturers of a new drug were required to file an application with the FDA. In this application, the manufacturer had to provide evidence that the new drug was safe. Unless the FDA rejected the ap-

14. This is a very slow and expensive process. It has been estimated that a test may cost up to $750,000 and take three and a half years ("New Laboratory Tests for Chemicals' Safety Stir Scientific Dispute," *Wall Street Journal*, May 16, 1977, p. 1).

15. "Estimate of Saccharin Risk Scaled Back," *Washington Post*, December 21, 1979, p. A6.

plication within 60 days, the application was approved and the manufacturer could market the new drug.

The regulatory process was substantially altered in 1962 with the passage of the Kefauver-Harris amendments, which were designed to strengthen the premarketing requirements for new drugs. The increased concern about drug safety was partially attributable to the well-publicized side effects of the European drug thalidomide. When this sedative was used by pregnant women, their babies were seriously malformed. The objective of the amendments was to lessen the chance of this type of disaster occurring in the United States. Pharmaceutical firms are now required to conduct clinical tests on both animals and humans before receiving FDA approval. In addition, drugs are approved only if they are both *safe* and *effective*.[16] The FDA later initiated a program of postmarketing surveillance, where pharmaceutical firms must monitor the usage and side effects of drugs after they are marketed.

National Highway Transportation Safety Administration (NHTSA). The NHTSA has the authority to establish safety standards for automobiles. Throughout the 1960s and 1970s, it promulgated a variety of regulations regarding the interior and exterior design of cars. Cars must be equipped with seat and shoulder belts, head restraints, windshield wipers and washers, padded dashboards, improved side door strength, and theft protection systems, among other things. Beginning in 1982, large car models must be equipped with a "passive restraint system," while mid-sized and small cars must have such systems by 1983 and 1984, respectively. Passive restraint systems are designed to protect passengers in accidents by restricting their movement inside the car. Unlike seat belts and shoulder harnesses, passive systems do not require any positive actions by passengers to be effective. These systems are considered necessary because of the public's unwillingness to use the seat belts that NHTSA has required manufacturers to install since the 1960s. A recent study by the Department of Transportation indicates that as few as *14 percent* of drivers use their seat belts.[17] NHTSA's initial attempt to require mandatory seat belt usage—the interlock system—was a failure. With the interlock system, a car could not be started unless all front-seat passengers had their seat belts fastened. This system so irritated drivers (for instance, a bag of groceries in the front seat had to be buckled in or

16. The effectiveness criterion is illustrated by the recent experience with laetrile, a possible anticancer drug (*United States* v. *Rutherford*, 61 L. Ed. 2d 68 [1979]).

17. "14% of Drivers Use Seat Belts," *Washington Post*, December 18, 1978, p. D9.

the car wouldn't start!) that many of them disconnected the systems. Congress ended up banning the interlock system in the same year that it was installed in automobiles!

Automobile manufacturers have taken two different approaches to this problem. Volkswagen has installed automatic-belt systems that are attached to the car door. When the door is closed, passengers are automatically strapped in. American manufacturers have pursued a different route, airbags. The basic idea is simple. On contact with another car or a stationary object, an airbag will inflate in a split second, thereby preventing passengers from hitting the car's dashboard. The bag then quickly deflates and passengers can exit from the car unharmed.

Occupational Safety Policies

The Occupational Safety and Health Administration (OSHA) was established in an effort to reduce job-related injuries and was authorized to establish safety standards that would reduce job hazards in workplaces. On construction sites, for example, it requires that the sides of trenches be secured in order to prevent collapses. Inside factories, it can determine the location of machinery as well as its proper operation. OSHA has the right to inspect workplaces to ensure that firms are complying with safety standards.[18] For each willful violation of a standard, an employer can be fined $10,000 and/or imprisoned up to six months if the violation resulted in the death of an employee.

A different problem is posed by workers' exposure to hazardous substances. Some industrial processes are suspected of causing cancer. Definite evidence of this relationship, however, may not appear until after prolonged exposure over a period of years. A 1978 study by the National Cancer Institute and the Center for Disease Control, for example, found that Georgia residents who worked in shipyards during World War II had a significantly higher risk of lung cancer.[19] This relationship was believed to be due to the workers' exposure to asbestos at the shipyards. Moreover, the risk of lung cancer was greatest for those workers who also smoked cigarettes.

Exposure of workers to hazardous substances is a major regulatory problem for OSHA. It must set standards for exposure limits when the exact relationship between exposure and suspected illnesses is not

18. OSHA inspectors do, however, need a search warrant to inspect an employer's workplace (*Marshall* v. *Barlow's Inc.*, 436 U.S. 307 [1978]).

19. "Georgians Working in Shipyards in '40s Found to Have Higher Lung Cancer Risk," *Wall Street Journal*, September 21, 1978, p. 12.

known with certainty.[20] The problems inherent in this type of regulation are illustrated by OSHA's experience with benzene, which is used
in the manufacture of tires, detergents, paints, and pesticides, among
other products. It is also suspected of being carcinogenic; in particular,
it may cause leukemia. As a result, workers' exposure to it has been regulated. Since 1946, the number of airborne benzene particles allowable
has been progressively reduced from 100 parts per million (100 ppm) to
10 ppm. In 1977, OSHA adopted a more stringent standard of 1 ppm.
Industry fought this new standard, claiming that it would prevent only a
few leukemia cases while imposing substantial costs on industry. The
estimates of these costs range from $500 million to as much as $5 billion.
The Supreme Court ruled that OSHA's standard was invalid.[21] Although it is difficult to generalize from this decision (five of the nine
Justices wrote opinions), it seems that OSHA failed to show that its standard was "reasonably necessary and appropriate" to protect workers.

Evaluation

There is widespread dissatisfaction with regulations to protect consumers and workers. While consumers and workers regularly denounce the
regulations as being too lenient, industry counters that they are too
strict. A major issue in this debate is the appropriate role for economics,
especially the economist's tool of benefit-cost analysis. This section analyzes current regulatory policies and then discusses the major proposals
for their reform.

Appraisal of Current Policy

The major criticism of current policy is that regulators do not assess the
economic impact of their regulations adequately, if at all. Regulations
are promulgated with minimal regard for their cost.[22] The government,

20. This issue is complicated by the rights of workers to refuse work that they perceive to
be dangerous ("High Court Considers Workers' Right to Refuse Duties They See as Unsafe," *Wall Street Journal*, January 10, 1980). Another issue concerns the right of women
to work in areas that may be unsafe for a fetus ("Faceoff on Hazardous Jobs: Women's
Rights, Fetus Safety," *Washington Post*, November 3, 1979).

21. *Industrial Union Dept., AFL-CIO v. American Petroleum Institute*, No. 78–911, slip
opinion, July 2, 1980.

22. R. David Pittle, a member of the CPSC, has stated: "When it involves a product that
is unsafe, I don't care how much it costs the company to correct the problem"
(M. Weidenbaum, *Government-Mandated Price Increases* [Washington, D.C.: American
Enterprise Institute, 1975], p. 31). OSHA did not have a single economist on its staff until
the summer of 1979 ("That Explains It," *Wall Street Journal*, October 17, 1979, p. 26).

like any consumer or worker, will not make efficient decisions if it focuses only on the benefit side of the equation.

Information Policies. The FTC has been vigorous in attacking deceptive advertisements and bans on advertising. Its policies provide consumers with more information on which to base their market decisions. The need to run corrective advertising creates a strong incentive for firms not to engage in deceptive advertising in the first place. And allowing professionals to advertise their services and products should increase competition and benefit consumers. Indeed, Benham has estimated that advertising restrictions raised the retail price of eyeglasses from 20 to 100 percent.[23] In a similar vein, Maurizi and Kelly found that the posting of retail gasoline prices by service stations led to lower prices.[24]

All the government's policies toward advertising have not been successful, however. In 1977, the FTC initiated a case against Kroger Company, the nation's second largest food chain.[25] It claimed that Kroger was engaging in deceptive advertising with its "price patrol," an advertising campaign that compared Kroger's prices with those of its competitors for 150 brand-name products. The administrative law judge ruled that this comparison did not give Kroger a "reasonable basis" for stating that it was the low-price leader in a given market. As a result, Kroger stopped the advertising campaign, thereby reducing the amount of information available to consumers. This FTC action was obviously not in the public's interest.

Product Safety Policies. The major accomplishment of the CPSC has been the adoption of child-resistant packaging by aspirin manufacturers. This regulation is credited with reducing young children's accidental ingestions of aspirin by as much as 41 percent.[26] Although this figure is disputed, this packaging regulation clearly has been beneficial at little additional cost to consumers. The CPSC has been criticized, however, for not extending the regulation rapidly enough to other substances that

23. L. Benham, "The Effect of Advertising on the Price of Eyeglasses," *Journal of Law and Economics* 15 (October 1972): 337–51.

24. A. Maurizi and T. Kelly, *Prices and Consumer Information* (Washington, D.C.: American Enterprise Institute, 1978).

25. *In the Matter of the Kroger Company*, Docket No. 9102, Decision Issued June 11, 1979.

26. "'Child-Resistant' Drug Packaging Is Praised, But Critics Say Many Poisons Aren't Included," *Wall Street Journal*, May 11, 1978, p. 42.

children accidentally ingest. Aside from safety packaging, the commission's achievements have been minor. Indeed, one of its few mandatory safety standards was voided by a federal appeals court.[27] The court ruled that the Commission did not show that the standard was reasonably necessary to reduce the risk of injuries. In general, the CPSC does not use economic analysis to establish its priorities or to evaluate its proposed standards.[28]

One of the most controversial areas of product safety regulation is the FDA's control of carcinogenic substances. As noted earlier, the Delaney Amendment to the Food, Drug and Cosmetic Act requires the FDA to ban any food additive that is carcinogenic in man or animals. This approach is clearly inappropriate. A total ban of a particular product prevents the use of that product in situations where it may be beneficial. In the case of saccharin, a total ban would deny this artificial sweetener to diabetics who cannot consume sugar.[29] At the same time, it adversely affects the millions of Americans who use diet products to control their weight. In short, a total ban on a suspected carcinogen ignores any possible benefits associated with its use.

The sharpest criticism of the FDA, however, has arisen over its regulation of drugs. More specifically, it is claimed that FDA regulation has created a "drug lag," whereby new drugs are introduced into the United States long after they have been used successfully in foreign countries. The lag has been blamed on restrictive FDA licensing following the passage of the Kefauver-Harris Amendments in 1962. These amendments increased the amount of testing necessary for FDA approval of new drugs and have been said to double the cost and time of obtaining that approval. In a pioneering study of drug regulation, Peltzman showed that there was a decline in the introduction of new drugs after 1962.[30] His results have been supported by a more sophisticated study by Grabowski, Vernon, and Thomas, indicating that the productivity of pharmaceutical research in the United States is less than that in Great

27. *Aqua Slide "N" Dive Corp.* v. *Consumer Product Safety Commission,* 569 F.2d 831 (1978).

28. H. G. Grabowski and J. M. Vernon, "Consumer Product Safety Regulation," *American Economic Review* 68 (May 1978): 284–89.

29. For a good discussion of these issues, see W. Havender, "Ruminations on a Rat: Saccharin and Human Risk," *Regulation* 3 (March/April 1979): 17–24.

30. S. Peltzman, "An Evaluation of Consumer Protection Legislation: The 1962 Drug Amendments," *Journal of Political Economy* 81 (September/October 1973): 1049–91. For an analysis of the drug industry prior to 1962, see P. Temin, "Technology, Regulation, and Market Structure in the Modern Pharmaceutical Industry," *Bell Journal of Economics* 10 (Autumn 1979): 429–46.

Britain.[31] The end result is that American consumers are deprived of the benefits of new drugs while they are being evaluated by the FDA.

Since 1966, the NHTSA has issued over 50 safety standards for automobiles in an effort to reduce fatalities and injuries. Have these standards been effective? Somewhat surprisingly, the empirical evidence on this important issue is mixed. Peltzman argues that safety regulations did not significantly decrease highway fatalities over the period 1966–1972.[32] His conclusion is disputed by a study conducted by the General Accounting Office, analyzing the deaths and injuries associated with different car models.[33] The GAO study concluded that the 1966–1968 safety regulations reduced fatalities and serious injuries by 15 to 25 percent. Peltzman, on the other hand, believes safety regulations may increase the probability of having an accident by making drivers more secure and, hence, more willing to take risks. This may lead to more accidents involving property and pedestrians. In any event, there is no doubt that cars are safer now than they were in the early 1960s. One thing that should be noted is the importance of automobile speed in fatal accidents. In 1974, the year that the mandatory speed limit was reduced to 55 mph, there were 46,400 motor vehicle deaths.[34] This represented a decline of 16 percent from the 1973 total of 55,500.

Occupational Safety Policies.   OSHA was established in response to congressional concern about rising workplace injuries in the 1960s. After its inception in 1970, on-the-job fatalities declined from 13,800 to 12,900 in 1977.[35] This small decrease has embarrassed OSHA, especially since fatalities have been increasing since 1976. Although these figures depend on many factors, they have focused attention on OSHA's shortcomings. A major problem is the agency's priorities. It has focused on the establishment and enforcement of extremely trivial safety standards; for example, the exact height for wall-mounted fire extinguishers and the appropriate design for toilet seats. Not only do such standards use OSHA's resources inefficiently, they also needlessly antagonize the

31. H. Grabowski, J. Vernon, and L. Thomas, "Estimating the Effects of Regulation on Innovation: An International Comparative Analysis of the Pharmaceutical Industry," *Journal of Law and Economics* 21 (April 1978): 133–63.

32. S. Peltzman, "The Effects of Auto Safety Regulation," *Journal of Political Economy* 83 (August 1975): 677–726.

33. Comptroller General of the United States, "Effectiveness, Benefits and Cost of Federal Safety Standards for Protection of Passenger Car Occupants," Report to the Committee on Commerce of United States Senate, CED-76-121, July 7, 1976.

34. U.S. Department of Commerce, *Statistical Abstract, 1979,* p. 643.

35. U.S. Department of Commerce, *Statistical Abstract, 1979,* p. 431.

firms that they regulate. In addition, OSHA tends to establish design standards instead of performance standards. This distinction is illustrated by OSHA's policy toward cotton dust in textile plants. OSHA ruled that firms must adopt specific engineering controls to clean the air rather than requiring workers to wear respirators, even though the respirator solution was substantially cheaper. Design standards thus prevent firms from adopting more efficient solutions to safety problems.

The most difficult issue for OSHA is establishing standards on workers' exposure to suspected carcinogens. This issue is extremely important because scientists believe that as much as 90 percent of human cancer cases can be attributable to factors outside the human body.[36] The problem, as illustrated in the benzene case, is to determine the appropriate or acceptable level of exposure. On the one hand, should a worker be exposed at all to a suspected carcinogen? Shouldn't the workplace be completely free of the substance? If this solution were technically feasible, it might not be economically feasible. On the other hand, the world is not riskless, so does it make sense to make the workplace riskless? If consumers are willing to pay any price to eliminate the risks surrounding them, they should never travel in automobiles, cross busy intersections, or smoke cigarettes. From this perspective, the exposure issue is but one part of society's total effort to protect its citizens.

New Directions for Consumer and Worker Regulation

Along with the widespread criticism of current regulations, there is a plethora of reform proposals. Some would increase the scope of regulatory agencies, while others would reduce it and, instead, rely on economic incentives for efficient behavior. This section discusses the major proposals for reforming consumer and worker regulations.

Imperfect Information. The government requires many manufacturers to provide consumers with information about their products. Some food companies, for example, must list the ingredients and nutritional value of their products. The FTC requires cigarette companies to list a brand's tar and nicotine content in all advertisements. And the Department of Agriculture establishes standards for meat and poultry products. As Table 17.2 indicates, these standards can be quite detailed. The government is currently considering plans to increase the amount of

36. E. Wynder and G. Gori, "Contribution of the Environment to Cancer Incidence: An Epidemiologic Exercise," *Journal of the National Cancer Institute* 58 (April 1977): 825–32.

Table 17.2   Federal Standards for Poultry Products

Item	Minimum Percentage of Poultry Meat Required
Poultry almondine	50
Poultry barbecue	40
Poultry paella	35[a]
Poultry hash	30
Poultry chili	28
Poultry croquettes	25
Poultry cacciatore	20[b]
Poultry casserole	18
Poultry chili with beans	17
Poultry tetrazzini	15
Poultry pies	14
Poultry brunswick stew	12[c]
Cabbage stuffed with poultry	8
Cannelloni with poultry	7
Poultry tamales	6
Poultry chop suey	4
Chop suey with poultry	2

[a] Or 35 percent poultry meat and other meat (cooked basis); no more than 35 percent cooked rice; must contain seafood.

[b] Or 40 percent with bone.

[c] Must contain corn.

Source: M. Weidenbaum, *Government-Mandated Price Increases* (Washington, D.C.: American Enterprise Institute, 1975), p. 39.

information provided on food packages.[37] For example, food companies may be required to list the vitamins and spices in a product as well as its cholesterol content, and the requirement to list nutritional information may be extended to meat and poultry products. Such information will enable consumers, especially those on restricted diets, to eat more well-balanced meals.

The FTC has begun to consider a proposal that would substantially increase the government's influence on information supplied to consumers. The proposal would ban all advertising directed at children under eight years of age, on the ground that any such advertising is inherently deceptive because children do not understand that advertising

37. "Plans to Require More Explicit Labeling on Many Foods are Proposed by the U.S.," *Wall Street Journal*, December 20, 1979, p. 17. For an analysis of the government's experience with the labeling of whiskey, see R. Urban and R. Mancke, "Federal Regulation of Whiskey Labeling: From the Repeal of Prohibition to the Present," *Journal of Law and Economics* 15 (October 1972): 411–26.

is designed to sell products. A major problem with this proposal is that it would establish the FTC as the nation's arbiter of advertising campaigns. An FTC staffer has commented, for example, that electric hair dryer ads are "unfair" because "there is not an opportunity for someone to say that if you wait 15 minutes, your hair gets dry anyway."[38] In any event, it is unlikely that the FTC will open this regulatory Pandora's box. Such a rule would probably violate firms' freedom of speech rights under the First Amendment. It also should be noted that advertising bans may not always achieve their stated purpose. Doron has shown that the banning of cigarette advertising from the nation's broadcast media in 1971 has had the perverse effect of increasing smoking.[39] One problem was that the banning of cigarette advertisements also led to the elimination of highly effective antismoking ads! The requirement to list tar and nicotine content may, however, have spurred the development of new, safer cigarettes.

Product Safety. A major issue in the product safety area is the consumer's freedom of choice. Should the government simply ban products that it deems to be unsafe, or should it allow their continued consumption by an informed citizenry? The saccharin incident led to many proposals to follow the latter path. The FDA would be given authority to evaluate both the costs and benefits of food additives when formulating regulatory policy and could then adopt a policy tailored to the specific circumstances at hand. In the saccharin case, for example, the National Academy of Sciences has recommended that saccharin should not be banned, though users should be informed of the potential risks.[40] Consumers who highly value saccharin could continue using it. Those who did not could decrease or even eliminate their usage. This is the policy that has already been adopted toward cigarettes, where the risks are well recognized by both smokers and nonsmokers. This approach has not been used in the area of automobile safety, where standards mandate the specific safety equipment that each car must have. It is interesting to note that 70 percent of General Motors car owners have stated that they would voluntarily purchase airbags, even if they cost as much

38. "The FTC Broadens Its Attack on Ads," *Business Week*, June 20, 1977, p. 27.

39. G. Doron, "Smoking and the Advertising Ban," *Regulation* 3 (March/April 1979), 49–52.

40. Committee for a Study on Saccharin and Food Safety Policy, *Food Safety Policy: Scientific and Social Considerations* (Washington, D.C.: National Academy of Sciences, March 1, 1979).

as $360.[41] The other 30 percent opted for less expensive safety systems. If people are willing to use seat belts, it would be inefficient to require them to also purchase airbags.[42]

Several bills before Congress would substantially alter the government's regulation of drugs. Their major purpose is to reduce the time it takes for the FDA to approve a new drug. It is estimated that it now takes approximately seven years for a new drug to receive FDA approval.[43] If the FDA's regulatory process were streamlined, pharmaceutical manufacturers would be able to receive a quicker return on their considerable investments in new drugs. At the same time, other proposals would require pharmacists to dispense generic equivalents for brand-name drugs unless the prescribing doctor specified otherwise. This could save consumers money, for brand-name drugs sell at significantly higher prices than their generic equivalents. While consumers will benefit from low-priced generics, however, this policy will reduce the profits that pharmaceutical manufacturers claim are necessary to develop new drugs.[44]

Occupational Safety.   The main proposals for reforming OSHA are designed to increase its efficiency. There are several areas of concern. First, OSHA should concentrate its efforts where occupational injuries are most common. Inspections of plants with good safety records would be reduced, while inspections of plants with poor records would be increased. The prospect of this inspection exemption would provide an incentive for firms to reduce injuries. Second, OSHA should adopt performance standards instead of design standards, providing an incentive for firms to adopt innovative safety technology in their workplaces. Each firm can adopt that approach that will yield the desired end result at least cost. Third, it might be desirable to experiment with financial

---

41. "GM Buyers Want Airbags, Studies Show," *Washington Post,* December 7, 1979, p. E1. For an analysis of the effectiveness of airbags, see J. Tomerlin, "Billion Dollar Trial Balloon: The Facts Behind the Airbag Mandate," *Road & Track,* May 1979.

42. In addition, people could be required to use their seat belts. In countries that have such laws, the compliance rate is approximately 70 percent. If the same rate occurred in the U.S., it would reduce fatalities by 5,200 per year ("Belts, Buckles, and Bags," *Regulation* 1 [September/October 1977], 6–7).

43. "A Drug Bill Congress May Buy," *Business Week,* August 13, 1979, p. 29.

44. The profitability of brand name drugs will be further eroded by the end of 1980 when patents for 83 of the 100 top-selling drugs will have expired ("The Drugmakers' Rx for Living with Generics," *Business Week,* November 6, 1978, pp. 205–8).

incentives for workplace safety.[45] One common proposal is to tax a firm for each occupational injury. The tax could vary with the seriousness of the disabling injury. Firms would have an incentive to reduce these injury taxes, and by adjusting the tax, OSHA could affect the level of on-the-job accidents. Overall, these proposals will yield a more rational allocation of resources, and improve the level of occupational safety.

Summary

The world is not risk-free. People injure themselves at home, at work, and while commuting to and from work. Some injuries occur because consumers and workers do not have adequate information about the risks surrounding them at work and at home. This information will not, however, be produced in sufficient quantity by a private market. As a result, the government intervenes in the marketplace in order to protect consumers and workers. Regulatory agencies adopt safety regulations for workplaces and consumer products. Such standards are inefficient if they do not achieve the desired reduction in injuries at the least cost to society. In this case, it is possible to devise new safety strategies that will yield more safety for the same cost or the same safety at less cost. One possibility is to adopt policies that create economic incentives for safer behavior.

Suggested Readings

Baily, M. J. Reducing Risks to Life—Measurement of the Benefits (Washington, D.C.: American Enterprise Institute, 1980).

Cornell, N., Noll, R., and Weingast, B. "Safety Regulation," in Setting National Priorities, The Next Ten Years, ed. H. Owen and C. Schultze (Washington, D.C.: Brookings Institution, 1976), pp. 457–504.

Grabowski, J., Vernon, J., and Thomas, L. "Estimating the Effects of Regulation on Innovation: An International Comparative Analysis of the Pharmaceutical Industry," Journal of Law and Economics 21 (April 1978): 133–63.

MacAvoy, P. W., ed. OSHA Safety Regulation (Washington, D.C.: American Enterprise Institute, 1977).

Peltzman, S. "The Effects of Auto Safety Regulation," Journal of Political Economy 83 (August 1975): 677–726.

Seidman, D. "The Politics of Policy Analysis: Protection or Overprotection in Drug Regulation?" Regulation 1 (July/August 1977): 22–37.

45. Firms have always had financial incentives to reduce job-related accidents—any compensation that must be provided as well as the temporary loss of a trained worker. The belief is, however, that these incentives have been too low to achieve the optimal degree of accident reduction. For an analysis of different financial incentives, see W. K. Viscusi, "The Impact of Occupational Safety and Health Regulation," Bell Journal of Economics 10 (Spring 1979): 117–40.

Part Five

Direct Participation

Government Consumption and Production

Chapter 18

The preceding chapters have examined three different types of government intervention: antitrust enforcement, economic regulation, and social regulation. These three policies have one thing in common: they all involve government control of *private* firms. The fourth option possessed by the government—and one of generally last resort in a market economy—is to participate directly in the market as a consumer and/or producer of goods and services. Instead of regulating a monopolist, for example, the government can produce the good itself. This chapter examines the government's role as a producer and consumer in the American economy.

As noted in Chapter 1, the government sector purchases approximately 20 percent of the nation's total output of goods and services. Even though the government is a substantial consumer, it is not a very large producer. The federal government operates the post office, Veterans Administration hospitals, and passenger railroad service; state and local governments may own local utilities, hospitals, and, in 17 states, liquor

The Setting

Table 18.1   **Government Capital Outlays, 1977**
(Millions of dollars)

Function	Level of Government			
	Local	State	Federal	Total[a]
National defense	——	——	21,541	21,541
Space research	——	——	185	185
Education	6,321	2,914	2	9,237
Highways	3,035	9,462	68	12,565
Natural resources	301	953	5,276	6,529
Health and hospitals	985	1,086	596	2,667
Sewerage	4,208	——	——	4,208
Local parks, recreation	1,109	——	——	1,109
Housing, urban renewal	1,247	93	605	1,944
Air transportation	481	106	318	905
Water transport	247	118	283	648
Local utilities	6,107	——	——	6,107
All other	3,970	2,154	1,122	7,246

[a] Totals may not add up exactly because of rounding off.

Source: U.S. Department of Commerce, *Statistical Abstract of the United States, 1979* (Washington, D.C.: Government Printing Office, 1979), p. 288.

stores.[1] A more detailed picture of the government sector's economic functions is presented in Table 18.1. This table examines the investment pattern for federal, state, and local governments in 1977. Not surprisingly, most of the federal government's funds were allocated to national defense, while state and local governments invested in their traditional areas of responsibility—education, highways, and public utilities.

The History of Government Consumption and Production

The existence of a government obviously requires the consumption of resources, but the exact amount of resources required depends on the services that government must provide. As society demands more (or less) services, the size of the government sector will generally increase

1. In 1977, liquor stores accounted for less than one percent of state and local governments' revenue (U.S. Department of Commerce, *Statistical Abstract of the United States, 1979* [Washington, D.C.: Government Printing Office, 1979], p. 289). For an analysis of this type of public enterprise, see Julian L. Simon, "State Liquor Monopolies," *Journal of Political Economy* 74 (1966): 188–94.

(or decrease).[2] In the United States, the government sector has increased substantially since the Great Depression in the 1930s.[3]

At the state and local levels, the major components of government expenditures are education, health, highways, and police protection. The state and local government sector has increased continuously since the end of World War II as fundamental changes occurred in American society. The "baby boom" required large expenditures for public education, while urbanization of the population necessitated more public services. At the same time, Americans demanded more and more new highways for automobile travel. All these factors combined to increase the public's demand for those services traditionally provided by their state and local governments.

At the federal level, the major expenditure item historically has been national defense. Therefore, the federal government's share of gross national product usually increases during wartime and decreases during peacetime. In earlier times, the United States maintained a skeleton defense force in peacetime because the probability of a foreign invasion was remote. The Atlantic and Pacific Oceans isolated America from the numerous and periodic foreign wars. Once war broke out, however, America could mobilize its forces and subsequently enter the conflict. When the conflict was over, the armed forces could once again be reduced to the normal peacetime contingent.

This cyclical pattern was interrupted after World War II. The United States reduced defense expenditures, but not to prewar levels. This change was due to two new military factors. First, America's two oceans no longer protected it from surprise attacks. The introduction of missiles into the military arsenal raised the constant threat of military aggression and made it necessary to maintain a higher level of military preparedness than before. Second, the United States and the Soviet Union became involved in an arms race. Each country accelerated its development of nuclear missile technology in an effort to stay ahead of the other country. This race increased defense expenditures and expanded the military's share of each country's gross national product.

The arms race problem can be conveniently analyzed as a variant of the classic "prisoner's dilemma." This classic situation is depicted in

2. For an excellent discussion of the nonmarket decision-making process, see Dennis C. Mueller, "Public Choice: A Survey," *Journal of Economic Literature* 14 (June 1976): 395–433.

3. G. Warren Nutter, *Growth of Government in the West* (Washington, D.C.: American Enterprise Institute, 1978).

part (a) of Figure 18.1. Two people—Smith and Jones—have committed a crime and are currently being interrogated by the local district attorney. The district attorney does not, however, have sufficient evidence to convict Smith or Jones unless one of them confesses. The "prisoner's dilemma" arises because Smith and Jones are interrogated separately, without knowledge of the other's statements. In this situation, each prisoner has two options: to confess or to "stonewall." If only one of them confesses, the DA will make a deal and let that person off with a one-year sentence, while the person who holds out receives 10 years (1,10). If both Smith and Jones confess, both lose their bargaining power and each will receive a five-year sentence (5,5). If neither confesses, however, the DA cannot convict them and they will both go free (0,0). The dilemma arises because the prisoners are separated and cannot coordinate their strategies. Since they cannot communicate, they do not know what the other person is doing. The obvious solution is for both to refuse to confess and so go free. But, if the other person has confessed, the one who has not will go to prison for 10 years. In this situation, it is likely that both prisoners will confess in order to reduce their *maximum* prison sentence to five years.[4] Smith and Jones are both worse off than if they could coordinate their actions and reduce their mutual distrust of each other.

A similar situation holds for the arms race between America and the Soviet Union,[5] as seen in part (b) of Figure 18.1. In this case, each country's options concern its level of defense expenditures (high or low), which in turn determines the relative military position of each country (inferior, superior, or parity). The United States and the Soviet Union will achieve military parity if they *both* choose the same option—low or high military expenditures. If one country has high expenditures while the other one has low expenditures, however, it will achieve a position of military superiority. As a result, neither country is likely to gamble and unilaterally reduce its expenditures to the low level.[6] The penalty for guessing wrong—military defeat—is too great. Both countries thus achieve parity at a high level of expenditures instead of the more desirable low level. Each country continues to spend billions and billions of

4. The underlying assumption is that each person will adopt that strategy leading to the shortest possible maximum prison sentence.

5. For a detailed economic analysis of the arms race, see M. D. Intriligator, "Strategic Considerations in the Richardson Model of Arms Races," *Journal of Political Economy* 83 (April 1975): 339–53; and M. McGuire, "A Quantitative Study of the Strategic Arms Race in the Missile Age," *Review of Economics and Statistics* 59 (August 1977): 328–39.

6. This is especially true now since there is a long lead time for the development of advanced weapons systems.

Figure 18.1   The Prisoner's Dilemma and the Arms Race

Jones's options

	confess	stonewall
confess	5, 5	1, 10
stonewall	10, 1	0, 0

Smith's options

(a) Prisoner's dilemma

America's options

	low	high
low	P, P	I, S
high	S, I	P, P

Soviet Union's options

(b) Arms Race

P = parity
I   = inferiority
S = superiority

dollars trying to protect itself against any unforeseen advance in military technology by its adversary. In this climate of mutual suspicion, it is unlikely that defense expenditures will be contained. Indeed, the United States increased its defense spending following the Soviet invasion of Afghanistan.

The government also produces goods, though not on the same order of magnitude as it consumes them. In the United States, government production is generally called "public enterprise," which is a more acceptable term than "socialism." Regardless of the name chosen, the government or "public" owns some productive resources and uses them to provide goods for the public.

There is little public enterprise at the national level in the United States. The federal government has operated the nation's postal system since the Continental Congress established a government postal monopoly in 1775.[7] Aside from the U.S. Postal Service, major federal enterprises include Veterans Administration hospitals (medical services), the Tennessee Valley Authority (electricity generation), Amtrak (passenger railroad service), and the Army Corps of Engineers (construction projects). At the state and local levels, governments own transit companies, airports, water and sewage systems, electricity and natural gas distribution systems, and the aforementioned liquor stores. Overall, there is a significant public enterprise sector in the American economy, though it is, on the whole, smaller than that in other industrialized countries. Table 18.2 presents some figures on estimated public sectors for five countries in the early 1960s. In the United States, the total share is 15 percent, which is less than that for Austria, Sweden, and the United Kingdom, but greater than that for Japan. In all these countries, public enterprise is more common in the transportation, communication, and utilities sectors than in the economy as a whole.

The Economics of Government Consumption and Production

At the risk of oversimplifying the situation, the government can be considered a major consumer and a minor producer in the American economy. Still another issue, however, is why it is necessary for the government to be both a consumer and a producer in a market economy. What factors determine the existence and magnitude of the government's direct participation?

7. See G. Priest, "The History of the Postal Monopoly in the United States," *Journal of Law and Economics* 18 (April 1975): 33–80.

Table 18.2   **Public Ownership Shares in Major Sectors**
(Percentage of labor force)

Country	Total	Total Material Sectors[a]	Utilities[b]	Transportation and Communication
United States, 1960	15	5	28	18
Japan, 1960	10	5	20	42
Sweden, 1960	20	6	71	53
United Kingdom, 1962	25	17	70[c]	70[c]
Austria, 1966[d]	31	27	100	78

[a] Includes utilities; transportation and communication; construction; manufacturing and mining; and agriculture, forestry, and fishing.

[b] Gas, electricity, water, and sanitation.

[c] Data for transportation and communication and utilities are combined.

[d] Based on gross national product data.

Adapted from F. Pryor, "Public Ownership: Some Quantitative Dimensions," in *Public Enterprise*, ed. W. G. Shepherd (Lexington, Mass.: D.C. Heath, 1976), p. 11.

Government Consumption.   In Chapter 16, the economic concept of *externalities* was introduced. Externalities, both positive and negative, occur whenever there is a divergence between private and social costs or benefits. In this situation, one person's consumption and/or production decisions are not completely independent from those of other people. A homeowner who kills off crabgrass, for example, gives benefits to neighbors as well as receives benefits. At the same time, if a homeowner mows a weedless lawn at six o'clock on Saturday mornings, this will surely impose costs on those same neighbors. In both of these cases, the presence of externalities will not lead to the socially desirable level of the activities in question.[8] The problem is that the homeowner does not receive all of the benefits or incur all of the costs associated with spraying and mowing operations.

This section is concerned with a special class of goods that generate *positive* externalities. In particular, these goods are characterized by there being no rivalry in their consumption. That is, one person's consumption of this good does not preclude its simultaneous use by someone else. Both individuals can benefit from their concurrent use of this

8. Because the homeowner does not take these externalities into account in the decision-making process, he or she may spray too infrequently and mow too frequently.

good, and so it is called a *public* good.[9] The classic example is a light-house: one ship's use of the lighthouse does not prevent other nearby ships from benefiting from it. A public good thus contrasts with a *private* good, where one person's consumption does preclude simultaneous consumption by others: if I eat the last piece of cake, it cannot be eaten by any other member of the household. In practice, it is not always easy to classify a good as public or private. There are many shades of gray. A large ship may block small ships' view of the lighthouse. The cake may make me fat and disagreeable to look at (a public "bad").

The important thing to note is that public goods will be under-produced in a market economy. This market failure is illustrated in Figure 18.2. For simplicity, it is assumed that there are only two consumers, A and B. Their demand curves indicate that B is willing to pay $2 for one unit of the public good, while A will pay half of that, or $1. In this case, neither consumer will purchase the public good because the minimum supply price for the first unit is $3. Note, however, that the "true" market demand for the public good is greater than that perceived in the marketplace. Since consumers A and B can benefit simultaneously from the public good, the market demand is the *vertical* summation of their individual demand curves.[10] As they are willing to pay a total of $3 ($1 plus $2) for the first unit of the public good, one unit of the public good should be produced by society. But it will not be produced unless the government intervenes. Government consumption is thus a necessary response to the market failure associated with public goods.[11]

One final issue is the method of financing the provision of public goods. In many cases, it is not possible to prevent people from using a public good. User fees are not practical because of the "free rider" problem: why should people pay when they can receive the service for free? This would be the case with national defense, for instance. Even if I didn't pay a monthly "defense" fee, I would still be protected by the nation's armed forces. There are some public goods, however, from which people can be excluded and user fees can be instituted. Pay television is a good example. Over-the-air broadcasting is a public good

9. For a more detailed discussion, see N. Singer, *Public Microeconomics*, 2nd ed. (Boston: Little, Brown, 1976), Chapter 6.

10. Note the contrast with a private good, where the market demand curve is the *horizontal* summation of the individual consumer's demand curves.

11. Government intervention may not always be necessary, however. See H. Demsetz, "The Private Production of Public Goods," *Journal of Law and Economics* 13 (October 1970): 293–306; E. A. Thompson, "The Private Production of Public Goods: A Comment," *Journal of Law and Economics* 16 (October 1973): 407–12; and J. M. Buchanan, "An Economic Theory of Clubs," *Economica* 40 (February 1965): 1–14.

Figure 18.2 The Supply and Demand for Public Goods

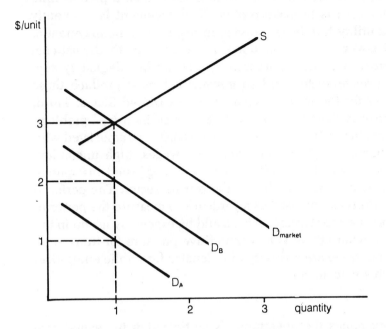

from which no television set owner can be excluded, but pay television scrambles its broadcasting signals so that a special attachment is required to unscramble them. Users are charged a monthly fee for this attachment, and so there are no free riders. If it is possible to exclude consumers from the public good, a user fee can be charged to pay for it. Otherwise, the good will be financed from a general revenue source such as income taxes.

Government Production. Given the apparent need for public goods, should these goods be produced by the government sector or the private sector? Although this issue commonly arises in the context of public goods, it is actually a broad policy option that the government can use for many different market failures. Government can, for example, regulate a monopoly or it can be the monopoly. It can require employers to maintain safe workplaces, or it can operate those workplaces itself.

Aside from the fact that it is one possible policy option, what is the rationale for public enterprise? Several reasons are commonly put forth to justify government production. First, the provision of basic human necessities should be in public, not private, hands. In many cities, for example, it is argued that the local electric company should be owned by the public instead of private investors. It is claimed that the government would be more responsive to human needs than a private firm, whose main concern is to make profits. (This argument is frequently raised when a utility terminates service in response to nonpayment of bills.) Second, government production may be necessary for the national defense. A critical material or weapon would not be adequately supplied by the private sector, and so government must produce those goods necessary for the military security of the United States. Third, public enterprise is the best solution to the "sick industry" problem. Government nationalization can minimize the hardships associated with declining industries, such as low prices and wages, high unemployment, and excess capacity. Finally, it has been suggested that public enterprise can be used as a model for the private sector. The performance of public firms can be used as a yardstick to measure the performance of their private counterparts. This could be especially useful in the regulated sector where there is no competitive pressure for firms to be efficient. In sum, there are a variety of rationales for public enterprise, not all of which are economic.

Major Government Activities

This section examines the government's participation in several economic activities. On the consumption side, the government's involvement in education and national defense is discussed. On the production side, two federal enterprises are analyzed: the Tennessee Valley Authority and the U.S. Postal Service. These examples of consumption and production, though limited, illustrate the economic issues raised by this specific type of government intervention.

Government Consumption

Like any other consumer, the government must determine how it will allocate its limited resources among alternative uses. National defense and education have consistently been two of the government's biggest expenditure items. In 1978, for example, the government sector spent $105.2 billion on national defense and $141.2 billion on education.[12]

Education. The public education system in the United States consists of elementary, secondary, and higher education schools. It was ostensibly designed to provide educational opportunities to all children regard-

12. U.S. Department of Commerce, *Statistical Abstract, 1979*, pp. 137, 364.

less of their parents' incomes. All states require some compulsory education, generally until the child becomes 16. Further secondary education, as well as higher education, is optional. Two issues in higher education have received considerable attention. First, why is it necessary for the government sector to subsidize higher education? Second, who is providing this subsidy?

At first, it may not be apparent why higher education is considered a public good. Why did states build large public universities to complement the existing private institutions of higher learning? Undoubtedly, a major reason is society's belief that there is a divergence between private and social benefits from a college education. The private benefits accrue to the student—an increase in knowledge and access to a white-collar job—and are certainly taken into account in the student's decision to attend college. There are also benefits to society, which the student will not take into consideration in making a decision about college. Two are frequently mentioned. First, an educated citizenry is essential for the maintenance of the democratic political process. (Voter participation rates, for example, increase with education.[13]) Second, educated people commit fewer violent crimes, thereby lowering society's crime rate. (They will, however, create more white-collar crime, such as embezzlement and income tax evasion.) Overall, the total social benefits of a college education exceed a student's private benefits. There will thus be a market failure—too few college-educated people—unless the government intervenes.

The government has responded to this market failure by heavily subsidizing higher education. State-supported universities, for example, have much lower tuition rates than private schools. The objective is to increase student enrollments by reducing the price of attending college. From a student's perspective, the subsidy reduces the total investment necessary for college, thereby increasing the expected rate of return from a college education. This will increase enrollments in colleges and universities. From society's perspective, the subsidy is a social investment on which it earns a social rate of return. This return includes the positive externalities from education.

Subsidies for education are not free to society, however. Government investments have opportunity costs just as private investments do. Government taxes could be used for other purposes or, at the extreme, be

13. In 1978, for example, 57.3 percent of college-educated people voted in national elections compared with 45.3 percent for high school graduates and 34.9 percent for people with less than a high school education (U.S. Department of Commerce, *Statistical Abstract, 1979*, p. 514).

returned to the taxpayer. The source of government funds varies with the level of government. Local governments are heavily dependent on property taxes, while state governments derive substantial revenue from sales and income taxes. The federal government receives most of its revenue from personal and corporate income taxes. There is thus an income transfer from all of these various taxpayers to college students every time the government sector subsidizes college education.[14] State residents are normally willing to subsidize their state university because it will benefit local children (possibly even their own) who are likely to remain in the state. This will allow the state to benefit from their education, which is not the case with out-of-state students, who are more likely to return home after graduation. As a result, tuition rates for out-of-state students are substantially higher and may even equal the true social cost of providing the education. The higher tuition for nonresidents also prevents one state from educating all its students at the expense of a neighboring state. This cross-subsidy issue is less of a problem with federal funds that are collected throughout the country. If these funds are allocated equally across universities, students will receive the same federal subsidy regardless of which school they attend.

National Defense.   The defense budget is always controversial. Each year, "hawks" complain that the budget is too small, while "doves" argue that it is too large. Along with the issue of the level of defense spending, the question arises as to how those resources are going to be allocated among different defense projects. Once these issues are resolved, the government must still determine which civilian contractors will be awarded specific defense contracts.

It is not easy to determine the overall level of defense spending. Traditional benefit-cost analysis cannot be employed, for it is virtually impossible to place a dollar value on preserving the nation's security. It is possible, however, to establish a particular defense objective and then attain that objective at the least cost to society. This, in effect, is what the United States has done. The primary objective of the Defense Department is to maintain a second-strike capability in the event of a surprise nuclear attack by the Soviet Union.[15] It is this threat of retaliation with the second-strike capability that is supposed to provide a de-

14. More generally, of course, this happens every time the government establishes a subsidy program, whether it is for students, shipbuilders, or farmers.

15. Other important defense objectives are the ability to wage a major conventional war and the ability to establish a worldwide presence.

terrent to aggression: presumably neither side will initiate a nuclear war without being able to win it.

The United States has tried to achieve its primary objective (a second-strike capability) through the trilateral force concept. In this concept, the U.S. has a triad of nuclear delivery systems: Trident submarines, B-52 bombers, and Minuteman intercontinental ballistic missiles (ICBMs). In the event of a war, the U.S. could either launch missiles from land or sea, or it could drop bombs from the B-52s. For any Soviet first strike to be completely successful, it would have to neuturalize all three delivery systems in the triad. This would not be an easy task because the U.S. would place these weapons on alert as soon as any Russian missiles were launched.

In 1972, the United States and the Soviet Union signed the first Strategic Arms Limitation Treaty (SALT I). This treaty placed a limit on the number of strategic launchers that each country could have. The U.S. was limited to a maximum of 1,054 ICBMs, 656 submarine-launched missiles, and 387 long-range bombers, or a total of 2,097 strategic launchers.[16] The Soviets were limited to a total of 2,507 strategic launchers: 1,527 ICBMs, 845 submarine-launched missiles, and 135 bombers. In a further step to limit the arms race, a second agreement, SALT II, was negotiated in 1979. This agreement would, among other things, limit both countries to 2,250 strategic launchers through 1985.[17] Its ratification by the U.S. Senate was jeopardized, however, when the Soviets invaded Afghanistan.

Regardless of the level of defense expenditures, the Defense Department still must award contracts to competing civilian contractors. Prior to World War II, this was not a major problem because the government produced most of its own weaponry at government arsenals and shipyards.[18] What changed this situation was the airplane. The government lagged behind the private sector in developing airplanes, so it turned to private contractors.[19] At the same time, the private sector has always had

16. "What the Deadlock in Arms Talks is All About," *U.S. News & World Report,* April 11, 1977, pp. 24–25.

17. "Carter Says SALT Pact Will Make World A Safer Place and Bolster U.S. Security," *Wall Street Journal,* June 19, 1979, p. 2.

18. Even after World War II, Werhner von Braun, the German rocket expert, did much of his initial research at the U.S. Army Ordinance Corps test facility, White Sands, NM.

19. The private production of weapons systems also created a civilian lobby (defense contractors, labor unions, and home-state politicians) that actively supported their funding by the Congress. For an excellent background discussion of the contracting process, see M.J. Peck and F.M. Scherer, *The Weapons Acquisition Process* (Boston: Harvard University School of Business, 1962).

the advantage of being able to pay its employees larger salaries than the government could offer. In any event, new weapons systems are now supplied by private contractors.

When the government decides that it wants a new project, it must decide which firm will supply it. At first glance, the obvious solution would simply be to have firms submit sealed bids and then accept the lowest bid. This is not realistic, however, in the case of advanced weapons systems for which there are no fixed specifications. Instead, the government has relied on prototype, design, and management competition among competing contractors. Once it has selected a contractor, the government faces the traditional regulatory problem of encouraging the contractor to minimize costs. It can choose among three different types of contracts: (1) fixed price; (2) cost plus fixed fee; and (3) cost plus incentives. With a fixed price, all of the uncertainty is placed on the contracting firm, who must supply the good at the agreed-upon price. With a cost plus fixed fee contract, however, the government absorbs the burden of any cost overruns. The contractor is guaranteed that costs will always be covered. These overruns may be substantial because of the uncertainty associated with advanced weapons systems.[20] One possible compromise solution is the incentive contract, whereby the government and the contractor divide any cost overruns between them.[21] In all cases, the government contracting process for major weapons systems is an expensive, time-consuming process.

Government Production

As a producer, the government faces the same problems as any other firm in the economy. It must decide which production technology to use and which factors of production to employ. Once it has produced a good, it must set its price. This section examines two of the most well-known federal enterprises: the U.S. Postal Service and the Tennessee Valley Authority.

United States Postal Service (USPS).   The United States Postal Service is one of the most prominent, if not most controversial, public enterprises in the United States. By almost any measure of size, it is large. In

20. For example, the initial cost estimate for developing the F-111 airplane was $700 million, while its actual development costs exceeded $2 billion. See F.M. Scherer, "The Problem of Cost Overruns," in *The Military Budget and National Economic Priorities*, Part 1, Hearings of the Joint Economic Committee, U.S. Congress, June 1969.

21. J.M. Cummins, "Incentive Contracting for National Defense: A Problem of Optimal Risk Sharing," *Bell Journal of Economics* 8 (Spring 1977): 168-85.

1978, for example, the USPS operated 30,518 post offices, handled 96.9 billion pieces of mail, employed 656,000 people, earned total revenue of $15.8 billion, and incurred a loss of $379 million.[22] The Postal Service is also very new. It was created by the Postal Reorganization Act of 1970 to replace the existing U.S. Post Office Department. The primary motive behind this change was to reduce postal deficits by creating a more efficient, less political, public corporation.

The USPS is controlled by a board of governors who are appointed by the president of the United States with the approval of the Senate. The board oversees postal operations, appoints the postmaster general, and passes judgment on the postal rate decisions of an independent Postal Rate Commission. (This commission was designed to be a partial check on the independence of the USPS.) In another phase of reorganization, postal employees were removed from the federal civil service system and allowed to engage in collective bargaining with the USPS. All these changes were designed to increase the incentives for efficient operations by modeling the Postal Service more along the lines of a private corporation.

Since its creation, the Postal Service has taken several steps to become more efficient. First, it has reduced the number of employees— from 741,000 in 1970 to 656,000 in 1978, a decrease of 85,000 or 11.5 percent of its original work force.[23] (This reduction was accomplished through natural attrition of its employees.) Second, over this same period, the Postal Service closed 1,484 of the original 32,002 post offices that it had inherited.[24] These post offices were located in small towns and were not considered to be economical. Finally, the Postal Service has adopted more capital-intensive technologies in an effort to increase productivity. This is most apparent in the parcel post area, where USPS constructed 23 highly automated, regional bulk-mail sorting centers. These centers are part of an effort to regain market share from the USPS's primary competitor, United Parcel Service (UPS).

Tennessee Valley Authority (TVA).   The TVA was established in 1933, during President Franklin D. Roosevelt's New Deal era,[25] with the goal of developing the Tennessee River into a major source of hydroelectric power. The Tennessee was well suited for this purpose, for the sur-

22. U.S. Department of Commerce, *Statistical Abstract, 1979,* pp. 578, 580.

23. U.S. Department of Commerce, *Statistical Abstract, 1979, p. 580.*

24. U.S. Department of Commerce, *Statistical Abstract, 1979, p. 578.*

25. The following discussion is based on L. Weiss, *Case Studies in American Industry,* 3rd ed. (New York: Wiley, 1980), pp. 148-54.

rounding area was hilly and received substantial rainfall. As is often the case, such a hydroelectric project could serve more than one purpose simultaneously. The dam system necessary to generate electricity also serves to control flooding. Hydroelectric power also provides cheap electricity that can be used to attract industry to poor areas of the country. All these factors were clearly in the minds of congressmen when they elected to add one more public enterprise to the government sector in the United States.

The TVA, though a government-owned corporation, has private management and its employees do not belong to the civil service system. It is required to charge rates that cover its costs, though these rates are not regulated by federal or state commissions. As a government corporation, it also benefits from the good credit rating of the federal government, receiving low interest rates on its loans. And it is exempt from corporate income taxes, though it does follow the government's practice of making contributions to local governments in lieu of property taxes. Overall, the TVA is a mix between the public and private sectors and was undoubtedly the model for the reorganized Postal Service.

Evaluation

Whenever the government spends money, it is in fact spending its citizens' money for them. This fact guarantees that there will be some public criticism of the government's expenditure decisions. The same thing happens when government elects to produce for itself what it would otherwise purchase from someone else. The government's role as a consumer and producer can be analyzed more objectively from an economic perspective. In particular, are the government's activities consistent with the economic performance criteria of efficiency and equity? This economic perspective is also helpful for suggesting ways to modify current government activities in consumption and production.

Appraisal of Current Policy

Current government policies have frequently been criticized for being inefficient. This is particularly true of national defense and the Postal Service. Education presents a mixed picture, while the Tennessee Valley Authority is generally regarded as a model public enterprise.

Government Consumption. Current government policies toward higher education have raised issues of both efficiency and equity. With respect to efficiency, there is considerable discussion as to whether

America is "overinvesting" in higher education. Two factors have influenced this discussion: the prospect of declining enrollments throughout the 1980s and the worsening job market for college graduates.[26] The rationale for continued subsidies is weakest at the graduate level, where there is a glut of graduates in many fields and the externality argument is not as strong. Presumably, any citizenship benefits from higher education are achieved with a bachelor's degree. In addition, graduate students are more likely ultimately to leave the state providing the subsidy. On the equity side, it appears that many state universities are financed by the poor for the benefit of the rich.[27] The state taxes that finance higher education tend to be regressive, while poor people are less likely to attend college and benefit from their tax dollars.

Expenditures on national defense are frequently claimed to be inefficient for two reasons. First, "too much" money is spent on defense. The primary culprit is the arms race. The SALT agreements with the Soviet Union are designed to reduce the mutual suspicion that fuels this race, but even if SALT II were ratified by the U.S. Senate, it has been estimated that it will still increase defense expenditures as the U.S. modernizes its weapons systems.[28] Second, the defense contracting process tends to produce cost overruns. These are mainly attributable to the high degree of uncertainty surrounding advanced weapons systems. In these cases, the Defense Department is negotiating for weapons systems that are at the frontier of technology. Unexpected difficulties or modifications initiated by the government can increase costs and lead to overruns. On the other hand, there have been overruns on projects that were not technologically advanced. Contractors may "buy in" on projects by submitting unrealistic bids in the belief that they will subsequently be bailed out by the government. In general, defense contracting has the same problem as economic regulation — how to provide incentives for firms to be efficient.

Government Production.   In 1979, the U.S. Postal Service set a record. For the first time in 34 years, the nation's postal service generated a surplus—$469.9 million, to be exact.[29] Despite this notable achieve-

26. Freeman argues that there was a decline in the rate of return to college education of two to four percentage points in the early 1970s (R. Freeman, "The Decline in the Economic Rewards to College Education," *Review of Economics and Statistics* 59 [February 1977]: 18-29).

27. W. Adams, "Financing Public Higher Education," *American Economic Review, Papers and Proceedings* 67 (February 1977): 86–89.

28. "Salt II's Paradox: Higher Defense Costs," *Business Week*, May 28, 1979, p. 47.

29. "A Postal 'Achievement'," *Business Week*, December 10, 1979, p. 44.

ment, the future of the USPS does not look promising. First, the growth in first class mail has been sluggish. This is important to the Postal Service because first class mail subsidizes the other mail classes.[30] This trend will undoubtedly continue as Americans continue to use long distance phone calls instead of writing letters, and banks introduce electronic funds transfers that reduce the need to use the mail for business transactions. Second, the Postal Service's bulk-mail centers have not operated as planned. Several of the centers have had tendencies to mangle and even lose boxes. As a result, its share of the parcel post market has declined from approximately 56 percent to 24 percent.[31]

The TVA, in contrast with the USPS, has earned a reputation as an efficient, well-run corporation. Its rates are consistently among the lowest in the nation, though it does benefit from low interest rates and access to some hydroelectric power. Nonetheless, its performance in the Tennessee Valley has been impressive. When it is criticized, it is for moving away from its original purpose of developing the river by building nuclear and fossil fuel power plants. TVA does, however, provide some additional evidence in the debate over the relative efficiency of public versus private firms.[32] All public enterprises need not be as inefficient as the Postal Service.

New Directions for Direct Participation

Numerous proposals to reform the government's consumption and production activities have been made. A theme common to many of them is to interject competition in the government sector. This is a standard policy prescription of economists whenever there is a misallocation of resources and competition is feasible.

Government Consumption. It is doubtful that additional competition is needed in education. As excess capacity increases throughout the

30. G. M. Wattles, "The Rates and Costs of the United States Postal Service," *Journal of Law and Economics* 16 (April 1973): 89–117.

31. "Postal Service Legislative Proposals" (Washington, D.C.: American Enterprise Institute, October 6, 1977), p. 5.

32. There have been many empirical studies of the relative efficiency of private versus public firms. See, for example, L. Neuberg, "Two Issues in the Municipal Ownership of Electric Power Distribution Systems," *Bell Journal of Economics* 8 (Spring 1977): 303–23; D. G. Davies, "The Efficiency of Public versus Private Firms, The Case of Australia's Two Airlines," *Journal of Law and Economics* 14 (April 1971): 149–65; and C. M. Lindsay, "A Theory of Government Enterprise," *Journal of Political Economy* 84 (October 1976): 1061–77.

1980s, there should be an increase in attrition, especially among small liberal arts colleges. Competition among graduate programs should also intensify in areas where the labor market is glutted. This "shake-out" process should reduce the overinvestment in higher education.[33] At the Defense Department, policy-makers are experimenting with ways of increasing competition among contractors.[34] Prototype competition will become more common for products that will have long production runs. Another source of competition will be provided by foreign countries; western European countries, in particular, are producing more and more sophisticated weapons systems. The potential drawback is that the United States is unlikely to rely on foreign countries for its weapons. Nonetheless, there should be increased competition for weapon sales to third parties, and this may lead to superior products and more efficient production.

Government Production. One suggestion made for the Postal Service is to restrict its operations to those areas that are clearly natural monopolies. Presumably the USPS would continue with the local distribution and collection of mail, but sorting and intercity transportation could be contracted out to private firms. Although this proposal would decrease some of the inefficiency in the present system, it seems more likely that the Postal Service will become more politicized and less efficient. By an overwhelming vote of 350 to 14, the House of Representatives voted in 1979 to increase the Postal Service's annual subsidy from $920 million to $1.3 billion and simultaneously to abolish its political independence.[35]

The presence of public goods mandates a role for the government as a consumer of goods. The government may elect to produce public goods itself. On the consumption side, the government sector commits substantial funds to the protection of the country and the education of its

Summary

33. If more competition is deemed desirable, governments could cease giving subsidies directly to schools and instead give them to students in the form of vouchers. Students could then choose among different schools and use their vouchers to attend the school that offers them the best educational services. This would intensify competition among schools for students and could even eliminate the need for public universities. See M. Friedman, *Capitalism and Freedom* (Chicago: Phoenix Books, 1963).

34. "Pentagon to Try Awarding Contracts for Same Weapon to 2 Manufacturers," *Wall Street Journal,* November 21, 1977, p. 14.

35. "House Votes Rise in U.S. Subsidy to Postal Service," *Wall Street Journal,* September 10, 1979, p. 10.

people. There is evidence, however, that the government may be over-investing in these two public goods. On the production side, the government is a small, though not insignificant, producer. There is no economic rationale for government production instead of private production, though several social factors may be decisive. In general, there is no pronounced overall tendency for public enterprise to be less efficient than its private counterpart. In some cases, it may be more efficient (Tennessee Valley Authority) and in other cases less so (U.S. Postal Service).

Suggested Readings

Coase, R. H. "The Lighthouse in Economics," *Journal of Law and Economics* 17 (October 1974): 357–76.

Freeman, R. "The Decline in the Economic Rewards to College Education," *Review of Economics and Statistics* 59 (February 1977): 18–29.

Myer, R. "Publicly Owned Versus Privately Owned Utilities: A Policy Choice," *Review of Economics and Statistics* 57 (November 1975): 391–99.

Nutter, W. *Growth of Government in the West* (Washington, D.C.: American Enterprise Institute, 1978).

Priest, G. "The History of the Postal Monopoly in the United States," *Journal of Law and Economics* 18 (April 1975): 33–80.

Shepherd, W. G. *Public Enterprise: Economic Analysis of Theory and Practice* (Lexington, Mass.: Lexington Books, 1976).

Part Six

Conclusion

Overall Evaluation of Government Intervention

Chapter 19

The government currently intervenes in the American economy in a variety of ways. This book has examined four major types of government intervention: antitrust enforcement, economic regulation, social regulation, and direct participation. Emphasis was placed on explaining the rationale for, and the effectiveness of, these different government policies. This concluding chapter is an overall assessment of America's experience with government intervention and its possible modification in the future.

As the United States entered the 1980s, government intervention became increasingly controversial. Consumers as well as producers have continually questioned the government's extensive control of private economic activity. This section addresses three interrelated questions raised by government intervention. First, is government intervention necessary? Second, is it effective? Third, what is its cost?

Appraisal of Government Intervention

The Necessity for Government Intervention

Government intervention in the American economy is traditionally viewed as a necessary response to the failures that can arise in a market system. The occurrence of market failures, such as monopoly and imperfect information, mandates an active role for the government. From this perspective, government intervention promotes the public interest by improving market performance. An alternative theory maintains that government intervention is not a response to market failures, but to certain groups' wishes to be regulated. From this perspective, government intervention promotes private interests and so may conflict with the public interest.

A substantial amount of government intervention is consistent with the public interest theory. Most antitrust enforcement, for example, addresses the market failure caused by monopoly power. This is illustrated by the strict policy toward horizontal mergers as well as the per se prohibitions against price-fixing and market-sharing agreements. Monopolization suits are a direct attack on the possession of monopoly power in a given market. Where competition is not feasible, economic regulation is appropriate. This is the case with such traditional natural monopolies as local telephone service and the retail distribution of electricity and natural gas. Finally, government protection of the environment, consumers, and workers can be justified by imperfect information and by externalities in consumption and production. Social regulation is thus also consistent with the public interest theory of government intervention.

At the same time, some government policies are not consistent with the public interest. In the antitrust area, the Robinson-Patman Act is more concerned with the protection of small competitors than with the promotion of market competition. Economic regulation has not been restricted to natural monopolies. For instance, intercity telecommunications and the provision of equipment to the Bell System cannot be considered natural monopolies, nor can the railroads in most markets. The "destructive competition" argument is particularly ill suited for the trucking industry. These examples of government intervention are more consistent with the protection of private interests than the promotion of the public interest.

Overall, government intervention is warranted in some areas, but not in others. This "unnecessary" intervention may never have been meant to promote the public interest. Or it may have been necessary originally, but became unnecessary as market conditions changed over time. Regardless of the reason, the scope of government intervention is greater than market failure considerations alone can justify.

The Effectiveness of Government Intervention

Government intervention is ostensibly designed to promote the public interest—to correct the market failures that can result from the competitive market process. Has government intervention achieved this economic objective? Has it improved market performance in those markets where government policies have been implemented?

There are instances in which government intervention has unambiguously improved market performance. Antitrust enforcement, for example, has undoubtedly prevented the industrial cartelization that became so common in Europe. It has also prevented a repetition of the "merger for monopoly" wave that created monopolies in many industries around the turn of the century. Economic regulation is beneficial when it prevents regulated firms from exploiting any monopoly power they possess. The evidence on this score is mixed, however, and no firm conclusion seems warranted. With regard to social regulations, environmental rules that require consumers and producers to internalize externalities should improve market performance; the provision of information enables consumers to make more well-informed decisions in the marketplace.

Government intervention has not always been beneficial, however. It can worsen market performance as well as improve it. A particular problem area is economic regulation. In the surface freight transportation industry, the Interstate Commerce Commission's policies have historically operated to worsen both static and dynamic efficiency. Government regulation of energy has led to widespread shortages of natural gas and gasoline, and has provided an incentive for the construction of inefficient oil refineries. Even antitrust enforcement is not immune. The Robinson-Patman Act is frequently cited for reducing price competition and slowing the demise of inefficient small businesses.

The overall picture, then, is mixed: Government intervention has improved market performance in some cases, but worsened it in others. Any attempt or effort to evaluate the total picture is further complicated by the federal government's subsidy program. The magnitude and nature of this subsidy program is depicted in Table 19.1. In 1975, the total federal subsidy amounted to $95.1 billion dollars, approximately six percent of the gross national product. It consisted of direct cash subsidies (12.9 percent), tax subsidies (62.8 percent), credit subsidies (3.0 percent), and benefit-in-kind subsidies (21.2 percent). Such subsidies redistribute income and alter the allocation of resources across markets.

Table 19.1   **Summary of Federal Subsidy Costs, 1975**
(Billions of dollars)

Economic Activity	Direct Cash Subsidies	Tax Subsidies	Credit Subsidies	Benefit-in-Kind Subsidies	Total
Agriculture	0.6	1.1	0.7	–	2.5
Food	–	–	–	5.9	5.9
Health	.6	5.8	–	10.2	16.6
Manpower	3.3	.7	–	.1	4.1
Education	5.0	1.0	.1	.4	6.5
International	–	1.5	.9	–	2.4
Housing	1.7	12.9	1.1	–	15.7
Natural resources	.1	4.1	–	.1	4.4
Transportation	.6	.1	–	1.7	2.3
Commerce	.3	19.3	–	1.9	21.5
Other	–	9.4	.1	–	13.2
Total[a]	12.3	59.7	2.9	20.2	95.1

[a] Individual items may not add to totals because of rounding.

Source: Subcommittee on Priorities and Economy in Government, Joint Economic Committee, *Federal Subsidy Programs* (October 18, 1974), p. 6.

Agricultural subsidies, for example, can lead to too many resources in farming, while tax subsidies for municipal bonds can encourage too many cities to build their own electric generating plants and/or distribution networks. All in all, subsidies support levels of economic activity that could not exist in an unregulated market environment.

The Cost of Government Intervention

Regardless of the exact impact of government intervention, one thing is certain—it is not free. As noted throughout the book, government intervention can affect, both directly and indirectly, the allocation of resources throughout the economy. There have been several attempts to estimate costs associated with government intervention.[1] A recent effort by the Office of Management and Budget (OMB) is presented in Table 19.2. OMB collected estimates of the costs of many of the government activities discussed in this book (e.g., transportation regulation) as well as some programs not addressed here (e.g., minimum wage laws). *Gross*

1. See Murray L. Weidenbaum and Robert DeFina, "The Cost of Federal Regulation of Economic Activity," Reprint No. 88 (Washington, D.C.: American Enterprise Institute, May 1978); Arthur Anderson & Co., *Cost of Government Regulation Study,* March 1979; and Ralph Nader and Mark Green, "Economic Regulation vs. Competition: Uncle Sam the Monopoly Man," *Yale Law Journal* 82 (April 1973): 871–89.

Table 19.2   **Office of Management and Budget's Estimates**
of the Cost of Regulation, 1975
(Billions of dollars)

Item	*Estimated Cost* Gross	Net
Economic Regulation		
Trade Restrictions		
Foreign		15.0
Domestic		
Fair trade laws		2.0
Robinson-Patman Act		NA[a]
Regulated Industries		
Transportation		
Surface		4.0–9.0
Air		2.0–4.0
Maritime		NA
Communications (television)		8.0
Energy (gas, electric, nuclear)		NA
Financial institutions		NA
Agricultural marketing orders		NA
Labor		
Minimum wage		7.0–9.0
Davis-Bacon Act		1.0
State and Local Regulation		
Insurance, banking and transportation		NA
Price fixing (milk, real estate settlement fees)		NA
Professional and occupational licensure		NA
Building codes and zoning requirements		2.0–4.0
Environmental, Health, and Safety Standards		
Environment		
Automobile emissions		6.0
Other clean air	40.0–60.0	
Safety		
Automobile	.5	NA
OSHA	3.5	NA
Food and Drug Quality		.3–.4
Direct Cost		
Public Sector		
Federal	2.0	NA
State and local	NA	NA
Private Sector		
Paperwork	1.0	NA
Other (Washington lawyers, etc.)	4.0–5.0	NA

[a] NA = not available.

Source: Committee on Governmental Affairs, United States Senate, *Study on Federal Regulation*, vol. 6, *Framework for Regulation* (December 1978), Table 3–5, pp. 64–65.

costs are the total estimated cost of a specific regulation, while *net costs* are the difference between gross costs and any benefits associated with the regulation. Assuming that gross costs are at least equal to net costs where no estimates are available, the total gross cost of government regulation would range between $98.3 and $130.4 billion; that is, from 6.4 to 8.5 percent of gross national product in 1975.

It should be stressed, however, that these figures are only estimates. The General Accounting Office, for example, evaluated OMB's study and concluded that the costs of regulation are substantially less—between $33.8 and $38.8 billion.[2] On the other hand, OMB was not able to quantify all the costs associated with government regulations. There are no estimates for the regulation of financial institutions or professional and occupational licensing, for example. And it may not be possible to place a dollar value on the delay and uncertainty inherent in the regulatory process. These by-products of government regulation have become particularly burdensome in the increasingly important energy sector of the economy.[3] In sum, the cost of government regulation, though not always quantifiable, is not of a minor order of magnitude.

New Directions for Government Intervention

It should be obvious by now that government intervention, like the world, is not perfect. The question then becomes—What is the appropriate future role of this imperfect institution in an imperfect world? Given the widespread dissatisfaction with current government intervention, some change seems necessary. This section examines two broad policy options. First, where government intervention is deemed both necessary and beneficial, the regulatory process should be improved. Second, where government intervention is not so justified, it should be reduced, if not completely eliminated.

Improving Government Intervention

There is no shortage of proposals to reform government intervention in the American economy. Their primary objective is to increase the quality of the decisions made by regulatory agencies, either indirectly, by

2. General Accounting Office, "An Economic Evaluation of the OMB Paper on 'The Cost of Regulation and Restrictive Practice'," staff paper published by the Subcommittee on Oversight and Investigations, House Committee on Interstate and Foreign Commerce, September 1975.

3. "Planners End 4 Nuclear Projects in Ohio, Citing Political, Regulatory Uncertainty," *Wall Street Journal*, January 23, 1980, p. 8; and "Local Opposition Halts Oil-Refinery Projects Along the East Coast," *Wall Street Journal*, June 27, 1979, p. 1.

improving the agency decision-making process, or directly, by exercising final control over agency decisions.

Decision-making in Regulatory Agencies. One important criticism of regulatory agencies—perhaps the major one—is that they give insufficient attention to the administrative and compliance costs of their actions and emphasize only the benefits. Many proposals, therefore, have suggested that regulators be required to introduce economic analysis into their decision-making process. The most common proposal is that agencies should undertake benefit-cost analyses of proposed regulations. As part of this analysis, agencies may even be required to evaluate the competitive impact of proposed regulations. This would reduce complaints that regulations are inadvertently eliminating small businesses throughout the economy.[4] It should be stressed that the introduction of economic analysis does not have to hamstring regulators and kill beneficial regulations, but should allow regulators to consider alternative solutions to a problem and adopt the most efficient one. At the same time, economic analysis is not a panacea for all regulatory ills. It will not lead to more efficient decision-making unless it is performed competently and accepted willingly by regulators.

This last point emphasizes the human aspect of the regulatory problem. The administrative process is plagued constantly by personnel problems. Practitioners before regulatory agencies, for example, often complain that many administrative law judges are not qualified for their important positions. Proposals have been made for a more thorough selection process for new administrative law judges and an evaluation process for existing ones. Many regulatory agencies also have high turnover among their personnel. This problem appears to be particularly acute in such agencies as the Federal Trade Commission and Justice Department, where young lawyers serve a brief apprenticeship before leaving for more lucrative careers in the private sector.[5] Staff turnover deprives

4. See "Study Says U.S. Policies Imperiling Small Business," *Washington Post*, January 13, 1980, p. A5; and "Now Small Business Can Pay Its Pollution Tab," *Business Week*, November 21, 1977, p. 90. Government regulations may also have an adverse impact on large corporations. See Kenneth W. Clarkson, Charles W. Kadlec, and Arthur B. Laffer, "Regulating Chrysler out of Business?" *Regulation* (September/October 1979): 44–49.

5. During the fiscal years 1974–1976, for example, 18 percent of the FTC's career service personnel (GS-13 through GS-18) left the commission. The FTC had the highest turnover of nine major regulatory agencies (Subcommittee on Oversight and Investigations, House Committee on Interstate and Foreign Commerce, *Federal Regulation and Regulatory Reform* [Washington, D.C.: Government Printing Office, October 1976], Appendix A-12, p. 590).

the agencies of seasoned personnel and prevents continuity in the development of major cases.

The government must address this turnover issue if it wants to be able to attract and retain capable employees.

External Controls on Agencies. Dissatisfaction with the regulations issued by federal agencies has led to demands for stronger outside control over their activities. A common proposal is to give one branch of government—either the legislative or executive—the right to veto agency regulations.[6] This veto power would be in addition to Congress's current oversight authority for federal agencies. While the ostensible purpose of such veto power is to improve the quality of regulations, it is not clear how this would be accomplished by a politically conscious legislature or president.[7] Indeed, this proposal goes against a major reason for having agencies: to obtain expert and impartial judgment.

There does, however, appear to be a need for a way to resolve conflicts among different government programs. Such conflicts can arise between two regulatory programs (environment vs. energy) or between a regulatory program and a macroeconomic policy (occupational safety vs. inflation). Currently, the Council on Wage and Price Stability intervenes at agency proceedings with regard to the inflationary impact of different regulations, and President Carter established a Regulatory Analysis Review Group to review major regulatory decisions.[8] There also have been proposals to establish a regulatory budget that would limit the total costs that different regulations could impose on the economy in a given time period.[9]

President Carter, as part of his energy program, also advocated the creation of an Energy Mobilization Board that would be empowered to resolve any conflicts between energy policies and government regulations. Overall, it is essential that there be some means of resolving conflicts among different government programs. It is not obvious, however,

6. "President Should Get Power to Overrule Regulatory Agencies, Law Group Urges," *Wall Street Journal,* August 15, 1979, p. 7; and Antonin Scalia, "The Legislative Veto: A False Remedy for System Overload," *Regulation* (November/December 1979): 19–26.

7. See, for example, "Two Senators Clash on Kind of Bumpers to Be Used on Autos—Byrd is for Steel, Magnuson, Aluminum as Others Are Likely to Join the Fray," *Wall Street Journal,* March 27, 1979, p. 17.

8. Christopher C. DeMuth, "Constraining Regulatory Costs—Part I: The White House Review Programs," *Regulation* (January/February 1980): 13–26.

9. Christopher C. Demuth, "Constraining Regulatory Costs—Part II: The Regulatory Budget," *Regulation* (March/April 1980): 29–44.

whether these conflicts would best be resolved by the president, Congress, or a "superagency."

Reducing Government Intervention

Government intervention is not always necessary. It is possible to reduce government intervention—to deregulate an industry—and in the process improve the welfare of society. There are other instances, however, where intervention is justified, but society does not choose the most efficient type of government intervention. The analysis of the relative advantages and disadvantages of different types of government intervention is called *institutional choice*.

Deregulation.   If a particular type of government intervention is not justified, the obvious solution is to eliminate it. Unfortunately, deregulation is not always possible. The firms subject to regulation may prefer to remain regulated instead of being exposed to the uncertainty and competitiveness of the unregulated marketplace. And it may not be politically advantageous for Congress and/or the president to support deregulation. In short, a unique combination of factors is needed before deregulation can be a viable policy option. One suggested solution has been the adoption of *"sunset laws."* Under the sunset law concept, specific government programs expire automatically after a specified period of time unless they are renewed by Congress. This theoretically makes it less likely that unnecessary government programs will persist for very long. The major drawback is the additional burden that sunset laws would place on an already overburdened Congress. In such a climate, proposals to renew specific programs would probably not receive the scrutiny that they deserve.

Institutional Choice.   Once the government decides to intervene in a particular market, which type of intervention should it use: antitrust enforcement, economic regulation, social regulation, or direct participation? For example, what is the government's optimal response to a monopoly? Should the government dissolve it, regulate it, or operate it? The actual decision should take into account the apparent advantages and disadvantages of each type of government intervention. Economic regulation, for example, requires the establishment of a regulatory commission and reduces incentives for the monopolist to minimize costs.[10]

10. Indeed, a firm may actually incur costs in order to obtain the monopoly position (Richard Posner, "The Social Costs of Monopoly and Regulation," *Journal of Political Economy* 83 [August 1975]: 807–27).

It also does not seem to promote dynamic efficiency. Direct participation is not necessarily more efficient than private production, and it may be less efficient. It probably is more likely to maintain unprofitable uneconomic services and to receive government subsidies. If competition is feasible, antitrust enforcement becomes an appealing alternative. It can create a more competitive market through the dissolution of the existing monopoly. Antitrust enforcement is not without problems, however. Monopolization suits are lengthy and dissolution is unlikely. At the same time, the threat of a suit may provide an incentive for dominant firms to "pull their punches" and not compete aggressively against smaller, less efficient competitors. In sum, the government, if it chooses to intervene, must choose among imperfect institutions.[11]

The most efficient solution is to choose the type of government intervention that will yield the desired improvement in market performance at the least cost to society. Based on our previous experiences, this suggests more reliance on antitrust enforcement and less on economic regulation and direct participation. In the health care area, for example, it might be possible to control medical costs more effectively by increasing competition among hospitals rather than by regulating them or having the government operate them. Any health care policy adopted should not ignore the relative advantages and disadvantages of the different types of government intervention.

Summary

The government intervenes extensively throughout the American economy. Sometimes the intervention is justified, and sometimes it is not. Sometimes the intervention improves market performance, and sometimes it worsens it. Government intervention is obviously an imperfect institution in an imperfect world. As a result, more attention should be focused on the rationale for, and the effectiveness of, government intervention. Policies should be adopted only if they will clearly promote society's interest. Once adopted, they must be carried out more efficiently than at present. Only in this manner will it be possible to reduce the widespread criticism of government intervention.

---

11. Given the known weakness of each type of government intervention, society may be better off if the government does not intervene in a market. As Friedman has stated: "If tolerable, private monopoly may be the least of the evils"(Milton Friedman, *Capitalism and Freedom* [Chicago: Phoenix Books, 1963], p. 28).

Breyer, Stephen. "Analyzing Regulatory Failure: Mismatches, Less Restrictive Alternatives, and Reform," *Harvard Law Review* 92 (January 1979): 547–609.

Caves, Richard. "Direct Regulation and Market Performance in the American Economy," *American Economic Review* 54 (May 1964): 172–81.

Friedman, Milton. *Capitalism and Freedom* (Chicago: Phoenix Books, 1963).

Jacoby, Neil H., ed. *The Business-Government Relationship—A Reassessment* (Pacific Palisades, Cal.: Goodyear Publishing, 1975).

Weidenbaum, Murray. *Government-Mandated Price Increases* (Washington, D.C.: American Enterprise Institute, 1975).

Suggested Readings

Credits

Index

United Shoe Machinery, 104n
Uranium cartel, 117-18
U.S. Steel Corp., 135n, 137; monopoly case, 94, 102
Utah Pie Co., 165
Utilities, 373-74; capital-output ratio, *table* 215; energy sources, 287-88; mergers, 137-38; government spending for, *table* 366, *table* 371; pollution by, 329-30; price discrimination, 306; rate of return, *table* 307; regulation, *table* 213, 214, *table* 214, 290-91, 304-05

Vanderbilt, William, 3
Von's Grocery Co., U.S. v., 144, 149

Water Pollution Control Act (1972), 8, 322, 330, 336
Waterways, 235-36, *tables* 235, *table* 241
Webb-Pomerene Act (1918), 81
Weidenbaum, Murray L., 10
Weiss, L., 206-07, 312
Western Electric Co., market share, *table* 103; profit rate, *table* 91; *see also* AT&T
Westinghouse Corp., 118, 119; light bulb patent, 186
Williamson O., 153-54, 314
Worker protection, 342-43, 388; economic assumptions, 343-46; hazardous substances, 351-52; injuries, 351, 359, 360; Occupational Health and Safety Administration, 8, 342-43, 351-52, 359-60; role of risk in decisions, 343-45, *fig* 344

Xerox Corp., 37, 87, 99, 181; licensing agreements, 191, 194; profit rate, *table* 91